PRAISE FOR *GOD AN*

'At a time when, as Pattison concludes, accelerating impacts of technology across the whole of human life mean that the nature of human being (let alone God as being) is put into question, it is ultimately reassuring to see the Lady Margaret Professor of Divinity at Oxford urging us to our knees in praise of God as Being, whose gift is being-itself.'

John Saxbee, *Church Times*

'Here are imaginative and often elegant reflections which will strike chords, jog memories, and provoke reciprocal reflection.'

G. M. Newlands, *Journal of Theological Studies*

For Jane
with best wishes

God and Being

An Enquiry

" Look ! "

GEORGE PATTISON

George Pattison

Lichfield 2013

OXFORD
UNIVERSITY PRESS

OXFORD

UNIVERSITY PRESS

Great Clarendon Street, Oxford, OX2 6DP,
United Kingdom

Oxford University Press is a department of the University of Oxford.
It furthers the University's objective of excellence in research, scholarship,
and education by publishing worldwide. Oxford is a registered trade mark of
Oxford University Press in the UK and in certain other countries

© George Pattison 2011

The moral rights of the author have been asserted

First published 2011
First published in paperback 2013

British Library Cataloguing in Publication Data
Data available

Library of Congress Cataloging in Publication Data
Library of Congress Control Number: 2010940323

ISBN 978–0–19–958868–8 (Hbk)
978–0–19–967397–1 (Pbk)

It is not any thing,
And yet all being is;
Being, being, being,
Its burden and its bliss.
How can I ever prove
What it is I love?
(From 'All We' by Edwin Muir)

Preface

This book has been a long time in preparation. Many conversations, formal and informal, have contributed to its formation. Administrative obligations delayed work on it by a couple of years, but it is probably better for that. In any case I am grateful to the Faculty of Theology at Oxford and to Christ Church for the two terms' leave that enabled me to bring it to near-completion. Sections of various chapters first saw the light of day in seminar and conference presentations, especially in connection with the Oxford Centre for Theology and Modern European Thought, the Research Seminar of the Systematic Theology Department of the Faculty of Theology in the University of Aarhus, and at the Centre for Subjectivity Research in the University of Copenhagen. Much of Chapter 1 took shape in the context of teaching for the Final Honours School in the Faculty of Theology in Oxford and the outline originally evolved in connection with the same teaching (although the final shape is very different from that of the course in question). I am grateful to those individuals with whom I have discussed the book in whole or in part and especially those who have commented on early drafts and loaned or directed me towards important materials. It would be invidious to single out individuals, but Hilary Pattison has not only provided important bibliographical assistance but has also lived with this book for several years: thank you.

I have generally avoided abbreviations. Where I have cited English-language translations from Heidegger or from German works not in his collected works I have given the volume number of the *Gesamtausagabe* together with other publication details. Similarly, when citing English translations of Kierkegaard I have given a volume reference to *Søren Kierkegaards Skrifter*, the definitive Danish edition of his works.

I am grateful to Faber Ltd. for permission to reproduce selections from T. S. Eliot, *Four Quartets* and from Edwin Muir, *Collected Poems*, and to Harcourt for US permission for the rights to the T. S. Eliot material.

Contents

Introduction   1

1. Being, Salvation, and the Knowledge of God   17

2. Presence and Distance   56

3. Time and Space   103

4. Language   149

5. Selves and Others   200

6. Embodiment   238

7. Possibility, Nothingness, and the Gift of Being   277

Bibliography   325
Index   341

Introduction

We live in a time when the existence of God has once again become a matter of intense public debate. In some ways this makes it the worst of times to write a book that is not primarily concerned to 'set out a stall', to 'answer the critics', or to pick a quarrel, but seeks only to invite readers to a more reflective and open meditation on some basic questions concerning what we mean by God. I began to write this book in a year in which the debate about God reached the point at which rival camps were sponsoring advertisements on London buses—one side suggesting that God probably doesn't exist, the other that he probably does. Whether one finds such episodes entertaining or depressing, they make it hard to imagine that there will be much of an audience for a book that is not interested in reducing the question of God to a slogan. At least, it would make it hard to imagine if I did not have many contrary experiences of university, school, church, and further education environments—not to mention conversations with friends—in which I have been privileged to learn that many people are hungry for something more than the kind of debate that ends in posturing and sloganizing.

I have to admit at once that this is not a book—or not 'the' book—that some of them are perhaps waiting for. By selecting what looks at first glance like the most formidably abstract of all abstract concepts as my focus I will have immediately put off many potentially interested readers. Nor is there any doubt that many of the pages that follow will demand a certain aptitude for a particular kind of what, for want of a better word, might be called philosophical reflection. Even the names of some of my main interlocutors—Hegel, Kierkegaard, Sartre, Heidegger, and Derrida—will doubtless be off-putting to a number of my fellow English speakers.

However, before they stop reading, I would like sceptical readers to consider that, abstract as it may seem, the question of God and Being is not entirely remote from even quite popular ways of talking about God. After all, the key question addressed in much contemporary debate is simply whether or not God exists. But in talking about the existence of God we are already talking about God and Being, for how could God exist if God didn't have or wasn't some kind of Being? In fact, the way in which the standard arguments for the existence of God found in every introductory textbook on the philosophy of religion are developed shows that they usually do rely on a certain understanding of God's Being. This even makes it possible to read them not so much as 'proofs' but as reflections on the kind of Being that is proper to God. The most striking example is, of course, the ontological argument associated with Augustine, Anselm, and Descartes, amongst others. Here the whole movement of the argument depends on a certain definition of God's way of Being, as 'that than which nothing greater can be thought' and as a being that 'exists so truly that it cannot even be thought not to exist' (Anselm's formulations). But the same is true of other familiar arguments. When, for example, the existence of God is inferred from the need to have a First Cause that is not itself caused by anything else (so avoiding the possibility that all explanation vanishes in an infinite regress), then this too contains an implicit understanding of the kind of Being that it is appropriate to ascribe to God, namely, that it is not a Being that stands within the chain of finite causes, that God's Being is a Being not caused by anything outside of or prior to itself or, to put it in more positive terms, God's way of being is to be the cause of his own Being, to have a way of being unique to and definitive of God.

If this is so, then reflecting on the kind of Being that we think of as proper to God and asking what it is for God *to be* as God or how God *is* God would seem to have a certain priority over the question as to the existence of God. Nor is this an especially esoteric point. Even a 6-year-old can understand that if God exists then God doesn't exist in exactly the same way as other entities, such as the tree in the garden, the bird in the sky, or other human beings. Perhaps—and I have heard 6-year-olds discussing this—God exists in the same way as thoughts or feelings, as some invisible presence spread throughout the universe, or perhaps outside the universe altogether. In considering the existence of God we don't normally proceed as if we were dealing with the existence of empirical objects, and it is open to question whether the model of intellectual or emotional events is appropriate either. Probably, we are dealing with something unique. When Paul Tillich said that God didn't *exist*, he was simply spelling out that if God exists, he doesn't exist in the same way as anything else and that our standard concepts of existence are inapplicable to God. God's unique way of being is part of what it is for God to be God. Arguments for the existence of God may therefore seem an appropriate place to begin a theology or a philosophy of religion, but perhaps they already assume too much. The more basic question is surely the kind of Being that is at stake in a question such as 'does God exist' or 'is there a God'?

I hope, then, that some who might have been immediately repelled by the word 'Being' will stay with me a little longer. However, I am aware that there will be others, especially those who have followed the development of the philosophy of religion over the last thirty or so years, who will be surprised that I regard writing about 'God and Being' as still worth doing. Surely, they will say, this is yesterday's news: God and Being went their separate ways quite some time ago. Every second-year student now knows that 'Being' is the mere residue of a busted metaphysics and that believers have long since learned to speak of God without letting themselves be trapped in the empty categories of Greek philosophy before which one can neither dance nor sing nor bow down in worship.

This objection relates especially to the currency that Martin Heidegger's critique of what he called 'the onto-theological constitution of metaphysics' has gained in some circles, a critique reinforced by the subsequent rise and dissemination of deconstruction and other so-called postmodern philosophies. I shall shortly turn to look at what Heidegger did, in fact, say and to the question as to what this means for our contemporary task of thinking, but one thing needs to be said straightaway. Philosophy, not least philosophy that has learned anything from Heidegger, is not a science that delivers results that subsequent generations can build on. As Hannah Arendt, one of Heidegger's own more distinguished pupils, especially emphasized in her lectures on *The Life of the Mind*, the first move in philosophy is simply just stopping to think.[1] Philosophy is learning to see what is questionable in what is most taken for granted. Or, to paraphrase Heidegger himself, it is learning to attend to what calls for thinking. It follows that anyone who imagines that either Heidegger or Derrida overcame metaphysics, or that overcoming metaphysics is some sort of project that a group of sufficiently dedicated researchers might accomplish in the near future, just isn't taking this kind of philosophical thinking seriously. Metaphysical ideas don't go away just because someone gave a lecture criticizing them. On the contrary, the more metaphysical ideas are in decline, the more their extraordinary power and impact comes into view and the more questions they provoke. Nietzsche spoke of a cave where one could supposedly still see the shadow of the Buddha thousands of years after his death and so too we might expect ideas such as Being to continue to haunt us and to shape our thinking for a long time to come.[2] Moreover, if the metaphysics of Being lives on in contemporary technology and in an academic culture shaped, even in the humanities, by technological thinking (as Heidegger himself believed[3]), no

---

[1] Hannah Arendt, *The Life of the Mind*, 1-volume edn. (San Diego: Harcourt, 1977, 1978), 175—but see the whole section on 'The Answer of Socrates' for the full force of this image.

[2] See F. Nietzsche, *Die fröhliche Wissenschaft*, aphorism 108 in K. Schlechta (ed.), *Werke*, ii (Frankfurt am Main: Ullstein, 1969), 389.

[3] See the essay 'Die Zeit des Weltbildes' in M. Heidegger, *Holzwege* (*Gesamtausgabe*, vol. v) (Frankfurt am Main: Klostermann, 1950), 73–110.

one who speaks of their 'research' or their 'project' can safely assume that they are thinking 'after metaphysics'. Of course, theologians will have their own reasons for seeing the 'overcoming of metaphysics' as a deed for which theology itself is pre-eminently suited, but here too there is scope to stop and think from time to time. Whatever the legitimate tasks of doctrinal theology may be, they do not include the task of turning philosophical questions into articles of belief.

As far as this present work is concerned, I am certainly not ignorant of the Heideggerian critique of the metaphysics of Being. However, I do not regard this critique as a historical event comparable to the splitting of the atom or the Iranian Revolution, i.e., something that happened at a particular time and place, nor is it straightforwardly comparable to the solving of a problem in natural science, which, once solved, can become the secure basis for future research. As a critique and not a doctrine Heidegger's work chiefly engages us as a call to think, to question, and to take time to ponder all that might be involved in the matter at issue, in this case, the question of God and Being. For if God is not Being or is to be somehow dissociated from Being, as a simple reading of the Heideggerian critique might suggest, this really does throw wide open the further question as to what and how we are thinking when we think about God. Once thinking has cut itself loose from a certain understanding of Being, its task and its possibilities are neither obvious nor readily definable. There is something vertiginous merely in asking how, in such a situation, we might best think about God, and the mere possibility that we might be able to engage in such thinking is almost miraculous ('miraculous' in thinking's own quiet way)—something to be thankful for, perhaps.

But for those for whom the critique of onto-theology has not yet become a matter of intellectual habit, I should briefly recap some of the key points of Heidegger's discussion and some of the ways in which philosophers and theologians have responded to it.

The key lecture 'The Onto-theo-logical Constitution of Metaphysics' begins as a reflection on Hegel. However, it soon widens out to the point at which it makes some extremely general remarks about the history of Western philosophy from ancient Greece down to the present. A key issue is that of Being and the question as to how Being can be thought. Heidegger's answer—and it should be emphasized that this summary does scant justice to the subtlety of his presentation—is that Being is thought of by Hegel and by the tradition of philosophy in which he stands as the 'ground', basis, *ratio*, or *logos* of beings. To think of something with regard to its Being is to think of what makes it really what it is. Metaphysics, however, doesn't just think of something but of all things, 'beings as such, as a whole', as Heidegger puts it.[4] As he adds, 'Metaphysics thinks of the Being of beings both in the ground-giving unity of what is most general, what is indifferently valid everywhere, and also in the unity of the all that accounts for the ground, that is, of the All-Highest.'[5] In other words, metaphysical thinking is thinking that offers an account of all that is and does so by tracing this 'all' back to its most basic ground, to what makes it be what and as it is, its first cause, or ultimate reason or *ratio*. This means that it can be described as onto- (from the Greek *ontos*, being) because it views the world with regard to its being, theo- (from the Greek *theos*, God) because it deals with the ultimate cause of the world, and 'logical' because it offers an account or discourse (from the Greek *logos*, word or discourse) of its subject matter. At different historical epochs, this 'Being of beings' has been conceived in fundamentally distinct ways. Later in the lecture Heidegger will list *physis* (nature), *logos*, the One, Idea, *energeia*, Substantiality, Objectivity, Subjectivity, the Will, and Will to Power as amongst the historically significant examples of how the Being of beings has in fact been conceived.[6] In all its varied forms, however, metaphysics has figured the world (or beings in general) as derivable from or explicable in terms of some more basic principle that is fundamentally different from them, a first cause as opposed to the chain of secondary causes, or a necessary Being as opposed to the merely contingent beings that make up the world of our experience. Since beings do not explain themselves, whatever we take as explaining them has to be somehow different from them. Yet, at the same time, this ground, first cause, or ultimate *ratio* of things is thought of by metaphysics solely with regard to its relation to beings. The first cause is defined precisely by reference to the chain of secondary causes of which it is the first; necessary Being is defined exclusively with regard to its relation to contingent beings. In this connection, Heidegger suggests that what the entire history of metaphysics has failed to pay sufficient attention to is precisely the difference: what it is that makes the world and its ground distinct and how, given this distinction, the two can nevertheless be understood as belonging together. Because metaphysics always presupposes this difference, its 'key terms' (including 'Being' itself) are no longer adequate to express it. Thinking today must step outside (or, as Heidegger puts it, step *back*) from its customary concepts and categories

---

[4] M. Heidegger, *Identity and Difference*, trans. J. Stambaugh (New York: Harper and Row, 1969), 58/125 (this is a dual language edition: 58 refers to the English text, 125 to the German (*Gesamtausgabe*, vol. xi)). 'Identity and Difference' is the title of another lecture included in the same volume, but the following references are to the book, not the lecture.

[5] Ibid. 58/125.

[6] Ibid. 66/134.

and seek to begin again, to find a 'new beginning' of thinking at the end of a history that has stretched from the pre-Socratics down to the present.

This proposal has immediate consequences for thinking about God. If metaphysics has determined the way in which we think about God (and Heidegger is mindful that Catholic theology at least explicitly affirmed metaphysics as an element of theology), then moving beyond metaphysics would seem also to involve moving away from God. Is his critique of metaphysics therefore also a critique of theology? Certainly it is a critique of any theology that construes itself as metaphysics. However, if that means identifying God with the first cause who is *causa sui* (cause of himself), this is a god to whom 'man can neither pray or sacrifice ... Before the *causa sui*, man can neither fall to his knees in awe nor can he play music and dance before this God.' To which Heidegger adds that 'The god-less thinking which must abandon the god of philosophy, god as *causa sui*, is thus perhaps closer to the divine God.'[7] From early in his career, Heidegger had been attentive to Luther's desire to place theology exclusively on the ground of faith, not on the ground provided by the Aristotelian natural theology of the Middle Ages.[8] However, the kind of thinking about God that his later critique of the onto-theo-logical constitution of metaphysics opens up also impacts on Lutheran and other notions of faith that claim to have dispensed with metaphysics. Thus, Heidegger suggests, Luther did not notice the power of 'The little word "is," which speaks everywhere in our language and tells of Being even where It does not appear expressly',[9] and therefore he could still speak confidently about God being gracious, merciful, etc. But this little word already 'contains the whole destiny of Being'.[10] For what would a theology be like in which we could not say 'God is ...' this or that? Surely, being able to predicate one or more attributes of God or to be able to say in an absolute sense 'that God is' must be fundamental to any meaningful theology? Theologians cannot therefore smugly sidestep the issue and look condescendingly at those who persist in defending or explaining the metaphysical God: Heidegger's critique, I suggest, poses a

---

[7] M. Heidegger, *Identity and Difference*, trans. J. Stambaugh (New York: Harper and Row, 1969), 72/140–1.

[8] See, e.g., M. Heidegger, *Being and Time*, trans. J. Macquarrie and E. Robinson (Oxford: Blackwell, 1962), 30/10 (here and in subsequent references to *Being and Time*, the first number refers to the pagination of the original German edition, preserved in later editions). Heidegger's earlier writings, however, tend to take a more positive attitude towards medieval philosophy. This shift is noted and discussed in John D. Caputo, *Heidegger and Aquinas: An Essay in Overcoming Metaphysics* (New York: Fordham University Press, 1982). Despite the fact that not all the relevant texts had at that time been published this remains a good and nuanced discussion.

[9] *Identity and Difference*, 73/142.

[10] Ibid.

fundamental challenge to the very possibility of speaking about God in a meaningful way.

But how might—how has—theology responded to this challenge?

One strategy has been to contest its basic terms. This is unsurprisingly a common move in the English-speaking world, in which German philosophy has had a rather bad name for at least two hundred years. John Marenbon, having given a very concise statement of Heidegger's critique of the onto-theological constitution of metaphysics, and having allowed himself to 'suppose—what is open to question—that Heidegger's ideas about onto-theology are a valuable piece of philosophy within the context of Heidegger's work', nevertheless concludes that 'Few examples of an apparently historical statement made by a philosopher are so poorly supported, if taken as history, as Heidegger's claim that all Western metaphysics has an onto-theological constitution.'[11]

But even before we begin to talk about 'onto-theology', the word Being itself is already more than enough for many philosophers in the Anglo-American tradition. In his essay 'The Quest for Being' Sidney Hook voiced a widespread misgiving regarding 'Being' when he wrote that 'despite the enormous literature which has been written about Being, it is very difficult to find anything clear or intelligible in writings that contain that expression'. To which he adds that 'The reasons are obvious. In ordinary discourse every significant word has an intelligible opposite. Being, however, as an all-inclusive category does not seem to possess an intelligible opposite.'[12] Hook includes Thomas Aquinas amongst those whose philosophies of Being he dismisses, and it is striking that many contemporary Anglo-American philosophers who approach Thomas in an analytic perspective significantly downplay 'Being' as a major focus of their interpretations.[13]

I do not wish to spend long considering these basic objections, although they probably merit more attention than I shall give them. Being committed to the view that a philosophical text, like any other, needs both to be read in context and to be read as extensively as possible before being dismissed, I think that there is a task of reading that must precede any simple endorsement or dismissal. It is only on the basis of what will often be difficult interpretative work that we will know what we are doing when we say Yes

---

[11] J. Marenbon, 'Aquinas, Radical Orthodoxy and Truth', in W. J. Hankey and D. Hedley (eds.), *Deconstructing Radical Orthodoxy: Postmodern Theology, Rhetoric and Truth* (Aldershot: Ashgate, 2005), 57–8.

[12] Sidney Hook, *The Quest for Being and Other Studies in Naturalism and Humanism* (New York: Delta, 1963), 147. I'm not sure that I entirely understand this objection: what, for example, is the 'intelligible opposite' of the 'significant word' 'flower'?

[13] See Ch. 1 n. 62.

or No to Heidegger's thesis—by which point a simple Yes or No may no longer be the most interesting thing to say.

However, another, opposite strategy of non-reading is perhaps more influential in recent theology. This does not so much involve dismissing Heidegger as outbidding him. Just as the nineteenth century witnessed a sequence of young philosophers who claimed to have 'gone beyond' Hegel (and were lampooned by Kierkegaard for doing so), so too the last fifty years have seen a sequence of philosophies and theologies that have sought to 'go beyond' Heidegger and to reveal how even Heidegger himself failed to 'overcome metaphysics' but remained trapped within essentially metaphysical presuppositions. That is, for example, one way of reading Jacques Derrida's introduction of the term *différance*, i.e. as a way of performing what Heidegger's still too theoretical concept of 'difference' was unable to achieve. The assumption seems to be that there are traces of Being everywhere in our thinking and the critical task of each new philosophical generation is to root them out and expose them to all round derision. In this spirit, the hallmark of intellectual credibility is the thoroughness with which beings are emptied of Being.

An interesting twist in this tale is the claim made by John Milbank that 'only theology overcomes metaphysics'. Milbank claims that whilst Heidegger's critique may be valid in relation to all philosophical concepts of Being that do not rest on the Christian premises of Thomist thought, Thomism's understanding of Being is something quite different from what Heidegger is attacking. Heidegger, having limited himself to considering Being from the point of view of its phenomenal appearances in the world, was unable to see the very different meaning of Being which is derived analogically from 'a doctrine of mystical return to God as unknown source' and which finds its full and rich expression via Thomas in Catholic doctrine.[14]

Perhaps also in the spirit of this response, there are those who avowedly embrace a theo-ontological approach, according to which 'God' is not construed in terms of some pre-existent philosophical theory of Being but Being is construed in the perspective of divine revelation. This is, for example, the gloss put on the work of the great Thomist thinker Étienne Gilson by Y. Floucat.[15] A vigorous defence of a Trinitarian theo-ontology is also found

---

[14] John Milbank, 'Only Theology Overcomes Metaphysics', in idem, *The Word Made Strange* (Oxford: Blackwell, 1997), 42. As noted above (see n. 8) the possibility of a positive reading of Thomas in a Heideggerian perspective is considered by Caputo in *Heidegger and Aquinas* and he too connects this with the lived experience of mystical vision. However, Caputo rejects the claim that this can become the basis for a presumed knowledge of God and does not regard Thomas's own thought as adequately reflecting the meaning of such mystical states.

[15] See Y. Floucat, 'Étienne Gilson et la métaphysique de l'acte de l'être', *Revue Thomiste*, 102/3 (July–September 1994), 365. We shall spend more time on Gilson himself in Chapter 1.

in Stanley J. Grenz's formidably entitled *The Named God and the Philosophy of Being: A Trinitarian Theo-Ontology.*[16]

Related, but somewhat different, is the appeal to religious practice. Noting Heidegger's comment that 'man can neither fall to his knees in awe nor can he play music and dance' before the God of onto-theology, Merold Westphal has suggested that in an experience of singing the chorus 'Oh Mary, don't you weep', 'It seemed that as we joined the slaves in their song we had overcome onto-theology without even trying.'[17]

Yet Heidegger himself never called on anyone to 'overcome' onto-theology and coined a rather untranslatable term, which, though akin to 'overcome', means something more like 'recover' or 'recuperate'.[18] Onto-theology is not an enemy to be defeated, but a trait of thinking from which we need—as the original lecture on 'The Onto-theo-logical Constitution of Metaphysics' put it—to 'step back' so as to come into a free and thoughtful relation to it. Maybe it can never be overcome. Maybe language itself, or, at least, Indo-European languages, will always trick us into it. Maybe the best we can do in relation to it is to learn to think what we are saying. Paradoxically enough, then, this might mean stepping back several paces and, before picking up the baton of secular or Christian anti-metaphysicians, thinking some more about Being itself and, especially, about the conjuncture of God and Being.

For, notwithstanding Marenbon's comment as to the historical flaws in Heidegger's argument, it is undoubtedly the case that the Western Christian tradition has invested heavily in the essential congruence of God and Being.

---

[16] Stanley J. Grenz, *The Named God and the Philosophy of Being: A Trinitarian Theo-Ontology* (Louisville, Ky.: Westminster John Knox Press, 2005).

[17] M. Westphal, 'Overcoming Onto-theology', in John D. Caputo and Michael J. Scanlon (eds.), *God, the Gift and Postmodernism* (Bloomington, Ind.: Indiana University Press, 1999). See also idem, *Overcoming Onto-theology: Toward a Postmodern Christian Faith* (New York: Fordham University Press, 2001). There are a number of places where Heidegger seems to hint—and more than hint—that theology or authentic religious thought has no intrinsic interest in defining itself in terms of ontology and that the death of the God of onto-theology is by no means identical with the death of the living God. See, for example, the passage in the introduction to the lecture on 'What is Metaphysics?', where he distinguishes a theology based on 'the experience of Christianity' from onto-theology, noting that the former had from the beginning been willing to accept that its truths would be in contradiction with the wisdom of the world (see M. Heidegger, *Was ist Metaphysik?* (*Gesamtausgabe*, vol. ix) (Frankfurt am Main: Klostermann, 2003), 19–20); see also the lecture on 'Nietzsche's Saying "God is Dead"', where Heidegger points out how the madman who announces the death of God is portrayed precisely as one who arrives in the marketplace crying out 'I seek God! I seek God!' and is mocked by the bystanders who no longer believe in God—as if seeking and crying out for God is the condition of being able to know what the death of God could mean: see Heidegger, *Holzwege*, 262–3.

[18] See M. Heidegger, 'Die Überwindung der Metaphysik', in idem, *Metaphysik und Nihilismus* (*Gesamtausgabe*, vol. lxvii) (Frankfurt am Main: Klostermann, 1999).

Whether this is how we should continue to think of God, and whether we might escape from doing so by a theological version of deconstruction or simply by singing choruses are matters that we could only really decide once we knew more about what it meant to construe God in terms of Being and, as preliminary to that, what it might mean to think of beings with regard to their Being.

At a purely practical level, one motivation in attempting the present work—apart from the intrinsic interest of the subject—is the repeated observation made over many years of teaching modern theology that many younger scholars who are attracted by the kind of post-metaphysical thinking associated directly or indirectly with Heidegger's critique tend to assume that a certain watershed has been crossed, a certain result attained. However, in a purely pedagogical perspective, it seems to me that it is virtually impossible to understand Heidegger's critique of metaphysics (or Derrida's or Lévinas's critiques of Heidegger) without some greater sense for the depth, length, height, and breadth of the metaphysical tradition itself and even of its pre-Heideggerian modern critics than many students actually have. In a throwaway remark in his lectures *What is Called Thinking?* Heidegger commented that one should not read Nietzsche until one has studied Aristotle for twenty-five years, and the evidence is that Heidegger himself only came to his critique of metaphysics through an extensive and deep engagement with the great texts of the tradition, including Aristotle, to whose work he devoted several lecture courses in the 1920s and 1930s.[19] This enquiry does not presume to even remotely match Heidegger's engagement with the ancient sources of philosophy, but I do follow Heidegger's lead in suggesting that fully to understand where we are now involves digging back, in some measure, into the time before the present and its all too demanding voices.

The aim, then, is to 'step back' into the question of God and Being as that has been bequeathed to us by the tradition and taken up and transformed in modern philosophy and theology. In the first instance, this will mean turning to normative sources in the Christian tradition itself, to Augustine and Aquinas, and especially to how they were interpreted by some of their twentieth-century heirs. I shall say again later, but wish to emphasize now, that I am a scholar neither of medieval nor of classical thought, and must therefore essentially limit myself to the reception of the medieval and classical heritage in the modern world. But although I do not regard myself as competent to adjudicate on how little or how far one or other contemporary

---

[19] See, e.g., Heidegger's use of Aristotle discussed in Chapter 4 below. For a good general survey of his engagement with Aristotle in this period see T. Kisiel, *The Genesis of Heidegger's Being and Time* (Berkeley and Los Angeles: University of California Press, 1993), 221–308. At least eight volumes of the *Gesamtausgabe* are largely or entirely devoted to lectures on Aristotle.

'Thomism' authentically witnesses to the original meaning of Thomas in his own time and place, the after-life or reception of a text—what has been called its 'effective history'—is also, in the end, part of its meaning in such a way that discussion of Thomism need not be limited to those who are historical specialists in Thomas. In fact, 'Thomas' mostly exists for us only as one or other interpretation of Thomas, whether the interpretation in question is that of Suarez, Gilson, Maritain, Rahner, or Lonergan. Conversely, it is ultimately arbitrary to discuss the Christian metaphysics of the Middle Ages without consideration of the patristic and classical sources on which the medieval thinkers drew. In such an extension of the enquiry not only Plato and Aristotle but also Plotinus and the Pre-Socratics (together with their commentators) would need to be given their full due. It is also increasingly clear that future work in this area will need to take fuller account of the contribution of Jewish and Islamic ways of understanding and applying Greek philosophy and there are already signs that these traditions may offer significant resources for deepening or reframing the Heideggerian critique of onto-theology.[20] However, in lieu of an appropriate expertise in all such sources, one can at least be conscious of and acknowledge the limits of one's own approach and refrain from claims one cannot substantiate.

In the first instance I shall be turning to the work of Étienne Gilson, one of the most scholarly and influential exponents of modern Thomism. From there I shall take up the critique of Christian doctrines of Being by Sartre but, refusing the seductive nihilism of his sweeping verbal gestures, I shall explore what Sartre takes to be the 'impossibility' of Being, a point he argues in terms of how the modern experience of subjectivity establishes a 'distance' between the self and its being. I examine this distance in terms of some of its defining dimensions: time, space, language, the relations of selves and others, embodiment, and possibility. These will, in turn, lead us to a considerable number of subordinate topics and questions. The risk of digression is constant, but the aim is in each case to keep the discussion focused, as far as possible, on the implications of, e.g., time or language, for thinking of Being and, therewith, for thinking of God as Being.

But what kind of study is this?

The two key words of the title indicate the disciplines that we are accustomed to call 'theology' and 'philosophy'. However, we have already had sufficient warning that the kinds of issues to which we shall be led will call into question the basic assumptions of those fields themselves. The enquiry concerns God—thus it is theological: but whether any given theology is adequate to the task of thinking about God is a question that cannot be

---

[20] See, e.g., Nader El-Bizri, *The Phenomenological Quest between Avicenna and Heidegger* (Binghamton, NY: State University of New York Press, 2000).

decided in advance of attempting that task (and whether or not 'theology' designates an approach that is in principle closed to non-believers is similarly undecidable a priori). The enquiry concerns Being—thus it is philosophical: but whether it signals an error to be dispelled by a more critical philosophizing or the very basis of any philosophy worthy of the name is itself disputed by philosophers (and who, in this context, decides what is or isn't authentically 'philosophical' seems to be an open question: no one, as far as I know, owns the copyright on the word 'philosophy').

It was perhaps characteristic of the twentieth century's sense of great traditions being in crisis that new methods emerged to address, dissolve, overcome, or redefine the key questions of faith and philosophy. Whatever their other differences (and they are considerable) this is as true of the dialectical theology of Karl Barth as it is of logical positivism, of Husserlian phenomenology, and of Derridean deconstruction. Today, neither theology nor philosophy offers anything like a general consensus, either with regard to which questions are most worth asking or as to how they should be tackled. Heidegger is a particularly acute focus of controversy in this conflict of the schools. For some his name indicates a point of fundamental orientation in modern philosophy: for others he is one of the modern world's great impostors.[21] In this situation, it is both tempting but perhaps also unwise to inscribe oneself too exclusively in one or other of the great schools. To do so offers the benefits of a certain discipline and focus, but also the risk of becoming constitutionally inattentive to what (perhaps) most needs to be noticed. One might also note the warning implicit in Paul Feyerabend's comment that 'the history of science will be as complex, chaotic, full of mistakes, and entertaining as the ideas it contains, and these ideas in turn will be as complex, chaotic, full of mistakes and entertaining as are the minds of those who invented them'.[22]

In what follows, I have therefore chosen to be guided by those whom I judge to offer the most interesting and important contributions to the different permutations of the question that occur in the course of the enquiry. Heidegger is a primary interlocutor, but so too are Gilson, Hegel, Kierkegaard, Dostoevsky, Sartre, Jankélévitch, Lévinas, Merleau-Ponty, Marion, and Derrida —some of whom might predictably be grouped together, others not. Loosely speaking, my 'method' is critically hermeneutical, in that the work takes shape as a series of interpretations of the works of others, guided by but also critically questioning those who, at any given point, have become my main conversation partners. However, precisely because of the diversity of these same discussants and of the perspectives they open up (one cannot read

---

[21] See, e.g., Paul Edwards, *Heidegger's Confusions* (New York: Prometheus Books, 2004).
[22] Paul Feyerabend, *Against Method* (London: Verso, 1988), 11.

Dostoevsky in the same way that one reads Hegel or even Kierkegaard), I do not commit myself to any particular hermeneutical method, but seek only to respond in an appropriate manner to what is most relevant in the text at issue.

A number of those I spend a lot of time with are often regarded—and in some cases regarded themselves—as practising phenomenology. This is obviously true of Heidegger himself, but also of Sartre, Lévinas, Merleau-Ponty, Marion, and, in a different sense, Hegel (and not a few readers of Kierkegaard read him too as a proto-phenomenologist). However, despite Husserl's hopes for phenomenology as a 'rigorous science', the fact that his own work inspired very diverse kinds of phenomenological research somewhat falsifies those hopes. Heideggerian phenomenology is already a very different kind of enquiry from that of Husserl and that of Lévinas is quite different again, despite both Husserl and Heidegger being decisive in Lévinas's own intellectual development.[23] Furthermore, there are significant questions about the applicability of phenomenology to fundamental issues in theology, not only with regard to the question of God (for how might phenomenology guide us to a God who genuinely transcends human experience?) but also vis-à-vis the religious life, if this is assumed to be inseparable from human beings' relation to the (as yet) unknown God who is its ground and goal. In this respect I share the reservations of D. Janicaud concerning the possibility of a 'theological turn' in phenomenology, albeit for rather opposed reasons.[24] Yet to spurn the wealth of rich descriptions of bodily, mental and spiritual life offered by modern phenomenology would be a gratuitous act of self-denial—even if there are open questions about the ultimate status of phenomenological enquiry itself. As in the choice of texts, the extent to which I am prepared to be a fellow traveller with phenomenological research is always open to review, but whether with regard to texts or to phenomenology, the decisive factor is and must be the spirit of Husserl's injunction to look to 'die Sache selbst' ('the matter at issue') and to take our bearings from that and that alone. In the case of such incalculable matters as God and Being, that is not such an easy injunction to follow, but it is nevertheless the aim.

---

[23] Apart from the 'canonical' statements of phenomenological method to be found in Husserl's main works, helpful reflections on the range and scope of phenomenological approaches can be found in, e.g., E. Lévinas, 'Reflections on Phenomenological "Technique"', in idem, *Discovering Existence with Husserl*, trans. Richard A. Cohen and Michael B. Smith (Evanston, Ill.: Northwestern University Press, 1998) and M. Merleau-Ponty, 'Phenomenology and the Sciences of Man', in idem, *The Primacy of Perception*, trans. J. M. Edie (Evanston, Ill.: Northwestern University Press, 1964).

[24] See D. Janicaud, *Le Tournant théologique de la phénoménologie française* (Combas: Éditions de l'Éclat, 1991). A driving force in Janicaud's study is to expose what he sees as the inappropriate intrusion of theological agendas into the disinterested work of philosophy.

Even without the work being committed a priori to any particular philosophical school, theologians may for their part fear that it is too philosophical in its general orientation to serve the interests of theology. Influenced by Karl Barth's insistence on the exclusivity of God's self-revelation as the source and criterion of theological work, many twentieth-century and contemporary theologians have repeatedly insisted on the need for what has been called a 'properly theological theology', that is, a theology that is not dependent on any other academic discipline for its contents or methods. Especially it has been argued that the doctrines of Christ and of the Trinity provide the sole authentic starting point or point of reference for such a theological theology. Anything else is likely to end up being what Barth himself called a case of 'the anthropological tail wagging the theological dog'.[25] To those who adopt this kind of rhetoric, the present work will doubtless look like a mere 'tail' and a rather scrappy one at that. Nevertheless, Barthian treatments of the relationship between act and being and the nature of revelatory communication show such remarkable and extensive analogies with such of Barth's contemporaries as Martin Buber and even Heidegger as to invite reflection as to whether even the most theological theology can ever entirely purge itself of the intellectual horizons of its time and place. The same is true of recent theologies that use the tropes of post-metaphysical philosophy to position claims for the independence of theological enquiry.[26] In any case, it would seem that some kind of understanding of Being is implied in any theological statement. To say that 'Jesus Christ *is* the Word of God' does not of itself decide what force or what ontological understanding is being borne by the word 'is'. To insist further that Jesus Christ alone is the measure of reality, i.e., that Jesus Christ alone determines what it is for anything truly to be what and as it is, does not of itself demonstrate that an entirely original sense of reality is in play, least of all if this is said in the context of a conversation with those who do not share the kind of cognitive access to reality that some theologians regard as exclusive to believers. If believing theologians are happy to talk only to each other, perhaps they can get away with such claims—but if they wish to be taken halfway seriously by anyone else this simply won't do. To be sure, it is equally true that reflection on the meaning of Being will not of itself decide to what or to whom we must make our own moral and religious commitments—even if those commitments may be implicit in the mode or manner in which that

---

[25] I am unable to trace the precise source of this quotation, although I believe it fairly represents his view of what he saw happening in, e.g., the theology of Rudolf Bultmann.

[26] For a sensible discussion of some of the issues here see Gavin Hyman, *The Predicament of Postmodern Theology: Radical Orthodoxy or Nihilist Textualism?* (Louisville, Ky.: Westminster John Knox Press, 2001).

reflection is conducted. To be quite clear at the outset: this enquiry does not constitute an argument for Christianity nor do I intend to claim that Christianity has to adopt a particular ontological understanding.[27] Perhaps many unnecessary misunderstandings could be avoided if we were simply to think of an enquiry such as this as 'para-' rather than 'pre'-theological, since it by no means presumes to establish a basis, foundation, or starting point for theology, but merely to clarify in a thoughtful manner what is actually being said in theology itself. In this spirit, I do not believe that the position arrived at precludes preaching or prayer or the practice of faith or hope or love in a manner consistent with historical Christianity. If these reflections have any positive outcome for theology as such, it is therefore not in terms of revising any particular point of doctrine but more in the way of making theology— and not just the theologian—freer, more humble, and therefore more joyful in offering theology's 'reasonable sacrifice'. In the same spirit, I would hope that it might serve an analogous end also for those who are content to ponder existence, and do not feel compelled to name the source and goal of their existence as 'God'.[28]

I have given some time to thinking about the genre of this work. In what follows I shall most frequently refer to it as *an enquiry*. This is because it is first and foremost an attempt to pursue a question and even if it doesn't issue in a clear-cut result or even proceed in a definite and uniform direction I hope that the constancy with which the guiding question is kept in view will give it sufficient consistency and purpose to sustain the readers' attention. However, I should point out that whilst the style of writing may often have a strongly linear form, the topics of time, space, language, selves and others, embodiment, and possibility do not follow on from each other like links in a chain nor do I argue for one as grounding the others. Rather, they are more like 'dimensions', i.e., different aspects or modes of one and the same basic phenomenon, the distancing of the self and Being. What is said about embodiment does not depend on what is said about language, but in each case what is said co-implicates the other, and both (I hope) offer a certain mutual illumination.[29]

---

[27] In this respect—and despite some convergence in theological interest—it differs fundamentally from, e.g., Oliver Davies's *A Theology of Compassion: Metaphysics of Difference and the Renewal of Tradition* (London: SCM Press, 2001). There, as the title suggests, Davies argues for there being an intrinsic connection between a particular ontology (the ontology of compassion) and theological reflection.

[28] The issue of the relationship between the perspectives of believers and non-believers is revisited in the final chapter.

[29] It might seem that, in the end, I do give a certain priority to embodiment. But whilst I do argue that the body provides a unique measure for ontological claims, I am not supposing the body to be some kind of 'base' or 'substructure' such that the other dimensions of consciousness are mere epiphenomena. When embodiment is understood not in terms of some set of

One seemingly trivial matter (that could, nevertheless, be of crucial importance for everything that is to be said) concerns the word Being itself. Does one write it with a lower-case 'b' (as in 'being') or with an upper-case 'B' (as in 'Being')? In the event, I have decided against simple consistency. When I am quoting English-language sources, I have, of course, kept the form that appears in the text being quoted. Where that text then guides my own discussion I have retained the relevant form for the relevant part of the discussion. Where I am not guided by cited material I have tried to reserve 'Being' for Being in an absolute sense, understood apart from or transcending the phenomena in which it or by means of which it is made known (or, conversely, concealed). On the other hand I have used 'being' when referring to particular entities or groups of beings. For reasons that will become ever clearer, this is not a stable or clear-cut distinction, and I cannot claim to have achieved absolute consistency. There is much to be said against 'Being' with a capital 'B', since it could be read as implying that Being is some kind of metaphysical entity (and maybe already load the dice in favour of interpreting Being as God as meaning Being=God), and we do well always to bear in mind the motives that led Heidegger to sometimes write Being under erasure (B̶e̶i̶n̶g̶). Despite such reservations, I am nevertheless crediting those who read beyond this introduction with qualities of intellectual caution, attention to context, and a sense for the larger direction of the argument that will enable them to recognize where what is being said about both Being and God is not intended to be more than provisional, hypothetical, and partially and intentionally equivocal. It is in the spirit of such trust in the mental agility of my readers that I therefore allow myself the indulgence of often using 'Being', which also has the merit of keeping it distinct from 'beings' (i.e., entities), which, after all, are not—or which we cannot assume to be—the same. But that, of course, is a question that, if not identical with the question of God and Being, is of decisive importance for how we approach this latter. Is Heidegger correct in seeing the dominant tradition of Western metaphysics as only having been able to construe Being and therewith God in terms of beings? If he is not correct, does what Western theology has said about God and Being point us to possibilities unthought in a more narrowly philosophical metaphysics? Or, if he is correct, and if Western theology has itself been circumscribed by the metaphysical paradigm, what can we now retrieve for our own thinking about God from the metaphysical resources of theology's own past?

---

physiological processes but as the lived body of human experience, it should be clear that there is equally no 'body' without time, space, language, or relations to others.

1

Being, Salvation, and the Knowledge of God

'I AM WHO I AM'

To say that God is properly spoken of as Being or Being-Itself may seem a startling claim. Yet it is a claim that has been central to the mainstream of Western Christian theology. Apart from any philosophical qualms about the intrinsic coherence of that kind of metaphysical language, it is an assertion that seems curiously remote from the spontaneous language of religious belief and practice—whoever named God in prayer as 'Being'? Don't prayer and worship turn more readily to such expressive divine names as Father, Lord, Maker, and Redeemer? Before turning to issues as to just what this way of speaking of God means in a philosophical perspective and to the force of such technical terms as essence, substance, nature, and existence I shall therefore begin by looking at the specifically *religious* meaning of Being in Western Christian theology.

It is natural to suppose that when theologians identified God with Being or Being-Itself they had some religious motivation for doing so. Theology is not solely a school of metaphysical speculation (although it has often engaged, for good or ill, in metaphysical thinking), and if it is a systematic reflection on the faith of the Christian community (as it is often said to be) it should not fail to reflect the religious interests of that faith—nor, in fact, has it done so. Yet nothing could seem more abstract, more remote from the passions of penitent and worshipping hearts or from the practical demands of living the religious life, than to speak of God in terms of Being or Being-Itself. Nevertheless, even this most abstract formulation expresses a very recognizable human and religious interest. Above all, I shall suggest, this has to do with human beings' experienced need of or longing for salvation and the conviction that, for God to be truly God, 'He' must be known as capable of effecting saving us.[1]

---

[1] This connection between soteriology (the doctrine of salvation) and theology proper (the doctrine of God) is concisely stated than in Luther's assertion that the subject matter of theology

For Christian theology it is inevitable that any claim about God will involve an appeal to biblical testimony—but it is precisely this that seems to be most problematic in this instance. In a renowned fragment, the mathematician and Christian apologist Blaise Pascal contrasted the God of the philosophers with the God who was the God of Abraham, of Isaac, and of Jacob.[2] But what God could be more of a philosopher's God than a God who is called 'Being-Itself'? What could have less to do with the living God of biblical witness—the God who dined with Abraham at Mamre or wrestled with Jacob at the brook? And where in the Bible do we find any mention of God as Being or Being-Itself?

Yet—and here we encounter another startling claim—those committed to understanding God in terms of Being (and they include all the main representatives of Latin Christianity) have no doubt that the Bible does speak of God in this way and does so at a decisive moment in the story of salvation. This is the moment when God calls to Moses from the burning bush, a moment that marks the beginning of a new chapter in God's dealings with Israel as he reveals his power to save his people from slavery in Egypt. As such it is therefore paradigmatic of God's action as Saviour and Redeemer: it is not just a story about how God commissioned Moses, it is a new self-revelation on the part of God, who now makes known the name by which he wishes to be called from henceforth. Let us briefly recap what happens: Moses has had his attention drawn by the burning bush and, as he turns aside to investigate, God calls him by name, warning him not to draw near but to take off his shoes because the ground on which he is standing is holy. Then God introduces himself by announcing that he is 'the God of your father, the God of Abraham, the God of Isaac, and the God of Jacob' (Exod. 3: 6) before proceeding to give Moses his commission. In response, Moses asks God to tell him *his* name, so that he can tell the Israelites who it is who has sent him. Here are vv. 14 and 15 in the King James Version, a translation that, in this respect, stands in the broad mainstream of Christian translations, closely reflecting (for example) the Latin Vulgate.

And God said unto Moses, I AM THAT I AM: and he said, Thus shalt thou say unto the children of Israel, I AM hath sent me unto you. And God said moreover unto Moses, Thus shalt thou say unto the children of Israel, The LORD God of your fathers, the God of Abraham, the God of Isaac, and the God of Jacob, hath sent me unto you: this is my name for ever, and this is my memorial unto all generations.'[3]

---

is 'guilty and lost man and the justifying and saving God'. See G. Ebeling, *Introduction to a Theological Theory of Language*, trans. R. A. Wilson (London: Collins, 1973), 47–8.

[2] See Blaise Pascal, *Pensées*, trans. A. J. Krailsheimer (Harmondsworth: Penguin, 1966), 309.

[3] Compare the Vulgate rendering: 'Dixit Deus ad Moysen: EGO SUM QUI SUM, Ait: Sic dices filiis Israel QUI EST, misit me ad vos.'

It is on the authority of this text and God's self-naming as 'I AM' or 'He Who is'[4] that Christian tradition has forged a link between the God of Abraham, of Isaac, and of Jacob and the God who is Being or Being-Itself. At the beginning of Book V of *The Trinity* Augustine states, 'There is at least no doubt that God is substance, or perhaps a better word would be being [*essentia*]; at any rate what the Greeks call *ousia*'[5]—a statement which he immediately 'proves' by quoting Exodus 3: 14. Similarly, and at an equally crucial juncture, Thomas Aquinas responds to the assertion that there is no God by citing the same text.[6] Even in this most rarefied formulation, the dependence on the biblical text means that we have at least the possibility of interpreting it out of the resources and testimony of Judaeo-Christian faith rather than on the basis of Greek and Latin philosophy and therefore seeing the view of God that the text underwrites as 'metaphysics of exodus' and not merely a 'metaphysics'.[7] But what exactly does this seemingly tautological name mean?

Until the twentieth century the translation tradition reflected in the King James Version of the Bible was rarely questioned. More recent translators and commentators, however, have argued that this is not the self-evident rendering of the Hebrew text that the tradition had presupposed. Not only the internal logic of the story of Moses' call but also its relation to the preceding and subsequent narrative as well as to analogies in other ancient Near Eastern sources have been ransacked to throw more and new light on the passage and on the self-naming of God at its centre.[8] A new interpretative paradigm emerged in Martin Buber's and Franz Rosenzweig's collaborative translation of the Scriptures. In his essay 'The Eternal', Rosenzweig takes his starting point from the translation 'The Eternal' used by Calvin and Mendelssohn[9] or the more conventional Christian 'Dominus' ('the Lord') and explains why he cannot accept either. Even if Mendelssohn was also aware of and attempted to convey the Midrashic interpretation of 'the eternal' in the sense of God being

---

[4] See preceding footnote.

[5] Augustine, *The Trinity*, trans. E. Hill (Brooklyn, NY: New City Press, 1991), 189.

[6] Thomas Aquinas, *Summa theologiae*, trans. T. McDermott OP (London: Eyre and Spottiswode, 1964), 2–3, Q. 1a.2.3.

[7] 'Metaphysics of exodus' is an expression associated with Étienne Gilson. See E. Gilson, *The Spirit of Mediaeval Philosophy*, trans. A. H. C. Downes (London: Sheed and Ward, 1936), 133. See also Y. Floucat, 'Étienne Gilson et la metaphysique de l'acte de l'être', *Revue Thomiste*, 3 (1994), 361.

[8] For full discussion of textual and interpretative issues see, e.g., B. S. Childs, *Book of Exodus: A Critical Theological Commentary* (Louisville, Ky.: Westminster John Knox Press, 2004), 47–89. Good general discussions can also be found in André LaCocque and Paul Ricœur, *Thinking Biblically: Exegetical and Hermeneutical Studies* (Chicago: Chicago University Press, 2003), ch. 5 'The Revelation of Revelations'; many of the key theological points are already noted in Ronald Gregor Smith, *The Doctrine of God* (London: Collins, 1970), ch. 3 'God as Being', 78–109.

[9] And familiar to readers of the Moffatt translation of the Bible.

the one who was and is and will be constant in his being with his people, his translation assimilates the Name too much to the eternally necessary Being of Aristotle, which is not only characteristic of Christian theology but can be traced back already to Philo of Alexandria. 'The Lord' is in a certain sense better, Rosenzweig says, precisely because it is less specific. However, he adds, in its Latin usage the connotation of 'domination' swamps the idea of 'helping' that is intrinsic to the biblical-Judaic notion of Lordship. Yet each of these occludes the indissolubility of the connection between the Name and the presentness of the moment of revelation, a presentness in which the speaker, the word of address, and the listener are all co-present. It is this that Rosenzweig hopes to indicate by the insertion of 'there' (*Da*) into the divine Name:

> But God said to Moses,
> I will be there as the one I will be.
> And said:
> You should speak thus to the sons of Israel,
> I am there sends me to you.[10]

As Rosenzweig sums up his argument, God's self-naming says 'I-am-who-I-am-and-will-be', that is, he will be who He is by being *there* with and for his people. Furthermore, when this name is, in turn, spoken by the human being, it can only be truly spoken in the mode of 'vocativity', as address, appeal, invocation. The Name is not a 'designation' (*Beiname*) that can be separated from the moment of revelation, even if, grammatically, it can function that way. It is precisely here, Rosenzweig asserts, that the Christian tradition of interpretation goes astray: 'The Jewish Bible calls out "Eli! Eli! My God, my God!" and the Old Testament scholars shake their heads and explain, "He is calling for Elias".'[11] So much more, we might think, when God names himself as I-am-who-I-am-and-will-be by being there for my people and Christian theology understands this as Being-Itself![12]

Questions of translation cannot be sidestepped. However, since the present enquiry is being guided in the first instance by the 'classical' versions of Christian faith found in the defining theologians of the Latin Church they

---

[10] The German reads, 'Gott aber sprach zu Mosche: Ich werde dasein, als der ich dasein werde. Und sprach: So sollst du zu den Söhne Jissraels sprechen: ICH BIN DA schickt mich zu euch.' See F. Rosenzweig, 'Der Ewige', in *Kleinere Schriften* (Berlin: Schocken/Jüdischer Buchverlag, 1937), 185.

[11] Ibid. 195.

[12] Rosenzweig's innovatory translation has proved fruitful also for Christian theologies of political liberation, linking as it does the themes of promise, hope, and liberation. See also Richard Kearney, *The God who May Be: A Hermeneutics of Religion* (Bloomington, Ind.: Indiana University Press, 2001).

are not absolutely decisive. At a much later point, we shall explore some of the implications opened up by the newer tradition of translation regarding the futurity and possibility of God.[13] But in both older and newer traditions, whatever the undeniable differences, it is equally essential that the utterance of this name identifies God as a God who has power to save. But how, more particularly, does it do so?

BEING AND SALVATION: AUGUSTINE TO AQUINAS

Many commentators have drawn attention to the salient differences of both style and substance between Augustine and Thomas Aquinas and their respective disciples. Nevertheless, there are also—arguably more important—continuities and commonalities.[14] Axiomatic for both is the connection between God's self-naming as 'I am who I am' and 'his' power to save. In connection with this, it is similarly axiomatic that human beings' need of or longing for God is also a longing for a fuller, firmer, and better relation to their own being and that this longing finds its goal in the contemplation of God.[15] In both cases, this nexus of ideas means being able to pass almost effortlessly from apparently abstract philosophical propositions or arguments to directly religious applications. Take the passage from Augustine's writing on the Trinity to which we have already referred. Augustine begins by making what looks like a purely philosophical definition of God:

Now other things that we call essences or substances admit of accidents, by which they are modified and changed to a great or small extent. But God cannot be modified in any way, and therefore the substance or essence which is God is alone unchangeable, and therefore it pertains to it most truly and supremely to be [*ipsum esse*], from which comes the name essence.

The implications of such abstract definitions for human salvation start to emerge in the contrast that Augustine then goes on to draw between the divine Being and all other beings: 'Anything that changes does not keep its being, and anything that can change even though it does not, is able not to be

---

[13] See Ch. 7 below.

[14] For discussion of various aspects of such commonalities see Michael Dauphinais, Barry David, and Matthew Levering (eds.), *Aquinas the Augustinian* (Washington, DC: Catholic Universities of America Press, 2007).

[15] This scarcely seems to need arguing in the case of Augustine. With regard to Thomas, I follow the view argued by Henri de Lubac in his *The Mystery of the Supernatural*, trans. R. Sheed (London: Geoffrey Chapman, 1967).

what it was; and thus only that which not only does not but also absolutely cannot change deserves without qualification to be said really and truly to be.'[16] It follows that the God who is Being-Itself (*ipsum esse*) is a God who can save because, in contrast to everything that undergoes change and which by being transformed in one way or another can become other than it is, true Being, the Being of God and the kind of being unique to God, is what it is in constant and eternal selfsameness.

This statement implies that there is something unsatisfying about experiencing change and with becoming other than one is and this is indeed Augustine's view. In fact, it is scarcely an exaggeration to say that it is a central pillar of his whole religious world-view. It is precisely the selfsameness of the immutable divine Being that makes it appropriate for it to be the pre-eminent object of desire on the part of creatures—human beings—who have become conscious of their inconstancy and mutability. The point is succinctly spelt out in the following passage from *The Confessions*:

> Wherever man's soul may turn, it only encounters suffering if it settles anywhere but in you [i.e. God], even if it is to attach itself to beautiful things outside of you and of itself; for there would be nothing if they were not by you; they appear and disappear; their advent is like a beginning of being, they grow to perfect it and once this perfection is attained, they come apart in old age and in death and all of them do not reach old age, but all go towards death. For when they appear and lead to being, the faster they grow to get there, the faster also they rush into nothingness.[17]

This is arguably a tendentious translation, but it epitomizes a pervasive theme of Augustine's thought: that life in time is unavoidably subject to mutability and life subject to mutability is no less unavoidably subject to suffering and death; it is life 'rushing into nothingness'. It is from such a life that Christianity offers deliverance, so that we too, albeit in a subordinate way, may participate in an appropriate measure in the divine Being qua immutable selfsameness.[18] For Augustinian theology, therefore, thinking of God as Being is inseparable from thinking of God as the ground, guarantor, and goal of salvation. Only such a God can save: only a Being capable of saving from the ills of change and decay can be God. To put it in technical terms, the idea of God as Being or Being-Itself is soteriologically determined.[19]

---

[16] *The Trinity*, 190 (translation adapted).

[17] Augustine, *Confessions* IV, 10, trans. Emilie zum Brunn, in idem, *St Augustine: Being and Nothingness* (New York: Paragon House, 1986), 2–3.

[18] In a Thomist perspective, note Gilson's statement that 'To the *Ego sum qui sum* of Exodus, there exactly corresponds this other word of Malachi (iii. 6): *Ego dominus et non mutor* [I am God and I do not change].' See Gilson, *The Spirit of Mediaeval Philosophy*, 65.

[19] See n. 1.

Two further points may be mentioned briefly here, although both merit a far more extensive commentary. The first is that Augustine and his heirs see God's power to save as inseparable from his identity as creator of all that is. God is able to save because he is the one who has made all things out of nothing—a claim that frequently leads Augustine back, from another angle, to the relationship between time and eternity.[20] In this connection too we might add that we can only seek a fuller being for ourselves because, in some degree or manner, we already *are* and therefore are able to experience the goodness and delight of being. The second is that Augustine's anxiety about mutability is not only anxiety about biological decay and death but also, and perhaps more importantly, about the moral, intellectual, and spiritual mutability of the human mind when it is not focused on its proper object—God himself.

We shall return in a subsequent chapter to further aspects of Augustine's teaching on time and the contrast between the mutability of human experiences of time and the immutability of the divine eternity, but I should like at this point briefly to illustrate the point further with reference to Augustine's sermon on Psalm 42. The key image of this psalm is of a wounded deer, longing for water, which the psalmist takes as a figure for his longing to worship in God's Temple.[21] In Augustine's interpretation, we ourselves are the deer, 'if we be but willing', only our longing is directed towards a better knowledge of God: 'Come, my brethren, catch my eagerness; share with me in this my longing: let us both love, let us both be inflamed with this thirst, let us both hasten to the well of understanding', he calls out—an exhortation that reflects his introductory comments that, since it is about longing, the psalm can only really be understood when the preacher himself speaks longingly and in such a way as to correspond with the longing of his auditors. So what is it that we seek in thus seeking a better understanding of God? It is 'a Truth not subject to change, a substance not capable of failing. The mind itself is not of this nature: it is capable of progress and of decay; of knowledge, and of ignorance; of remembering or forgetting; at one moment it wishes for this thing, at another it does not wish for it.' By way of contrast, 'That mutability is not incident to God.' Therefore, in finding God one enters into a joy that is intrinsically 'without end'. 'In the "house of God" there is a never-ending

---

[20] See also the section 'Being, Salvation and Creation' below.

[21] Perhaps the psalm is best known in the English-speaking world in the metrical version, of which verse 1 runs: 'As pants the hart for cooling stream, | When heated in the chase, | So longs my soul for thee, Oh God | And thy refreshing grace.' The quotations that follow are taken from St Augustine's *Expositions on the Book of Psalms*, vol. ii (Oxford: Parker, 1848), 178 ff.

festival: for there it is not an occasion celebrated once, and then to pass away. The angelic choir makes an eternal "holiday:" the presence of God's face, joy that never fails. This is a "holiday" of such a kind as never to be opened by any dawn, nor terminated by any evening.' This theme is taken up and repeated many times in subsequent Latin theology.[22]

It has now become almost customary to note that the famous chapters of Anselm's *Proslogion*, in which he sets out his so-called ontological argument, are in fact preceded and introduced by a passage that depicts a scenario with which we are now becoming familiar. As is so often the case in Augustine's writings, Anselm's account of the human predicament is voiced in the form of a prayer:

But, alas, pitiable me, one of the miserable sons of Eve far removed from God—what did I set out to do; what have I achieved? Where was I heading; where have I arrived? To what was I aspiring; for what do I sigh? I sought after good things and, behold, here is turmoil. I was reaching out for God, but tripped over myself. I was seeking rest in solitude, but I found tribulation and grief in my inmost self. I wanted to laugh with joy of mind, but am constrained to cry out in lamentation of heart. I hoped for joy, but, lo, my sighs increase! O Lord, how long? How long will You forget us? How long will You turn your face away from us? When will you look upon us and hear us? When will you enlighten our eyes and show us Your face? When will You restore Yourself to us? Look upon us, O Lord, hear us, enlighten us, reveal yourself unto us.[23]

In giving voice to its search for God the soul shows itself to be conscious both of its separation from God and of its internal divisions, exiled 'from the delight of immortality into the bitterness and horror of death'. This is the soul that now seeks to expound its faith that redemption is nevertheless possible and does so by demonstrating the indubitability of a God who exists 'so truly that [he] cannot be thought not to exist'.[24] The ontological definition of God as necessary Being or as the Being who cannot not be corresponds to the specific religious need of divided and estranged self of the preceding chapter of Anselm's work.

---

[22] As well as in the Reformation transformation of Latin theology. See, e.g., the Book of Common Prayer's service for the Burial of the Dead: 'Man that is born of a woman hath but a short time to live, and is full of misery. He cometh up, and is cut down, like a flower; he fleeth as it were a shadow, and never continueth in one stay. In the midst of life we are in death . . .' or the still popular nineteenth-century hymn 'Abide with me' which is premised on the thought that 'change and decay in all around I see, | O Thou who changest not, abide with me'.

[23] J. Hopkins and H. Richardson (ed. and trans.), *Anselm of Canterbury*, vol. i (London: SCM Press, 1974), 92. We should not perhaps presume that we are dealing with a simple outpouring of Anselm's soul. Recent scholarship has suggested that this prayer marks a definite rhetorical strategy vis-à-vis Anselm's auditors who may have been alarmed by the apparent rationalism of the *Monologion*.

[24] Ibid. 94.

As the Being who is Being-Itself, the Being who cannot not be and who is always and everywhere present in constant selfsameness, God shows himself to be the only possible agent and object of human salvation. But this is not simply a matter of God helping human beings out of the whirlwind of change, decay, and death—saving them from the shipwreck of existence, like a kind of cosmic lifeguard. Instead, being saved by such a God means acquiring something of the constant selfsameness that is integral to the divine blessedness. In being saved, we too may hope not only to be blessed, not only to have joy, but to be joyfully blessed with that same constant selfsameness as we now see only in God, to keep the 'eternal holiday' of which the commentary on Psalm 42 spoke. To be saved is to come to participate in the divine way of Being—albeit in a manner and a degree appropriate to our status as created beings.

In the Augustinian tradition, this participation was primarily or ultimately achieved through contemplation: through a simple beholding of the divine Being in which and by which the seer would become conformed to the seen, the contemplator to the contemplated, the human (and mutable) to the divine (and immutable). To be saved is to see God's substance, to contemplate his Being as it is.

There were, naturally, various views as to how far this was possible or could be anticipated in this present life. It was sometimes thought possible that holy souls could achieve some degree of contemplation in this world, but, on the whole, it was deemed that as long as the soul was involved with a world of change and chance by virtue of its embodiment it could not by definition be in that final and constant state of immutable joy and blessedness which it was seeking. Yet those such as Thomas Aquinas who took a stern view on the possibility of contemplation in this life were generally in no doubt that the intrinsic intellectual character of the soul nevertheless made it capable of the vision of God and, in and through that vision, capable of partaking of eternal life.[25] As opposed to the kind of seeing we are able to enjoy in this life ('in a glass darkly', as he writes, quoting St Paul), Thomas asserts that 'then, shall we see God face to face, in the sense that we shall see Him without a medium, as is true when we see a man face to face'.[26] This is a vision of the

---

[25] De Lubac notes dissenting voices to this claim in the Middle Ages, but sees them as answered by the majority of authoritative opinions. See *Mystery of the Supernatural*, 56 ff.

[26] Thomas Aquinas, *On the Truth of the Catholic Faith (Summa Contra Gentiles)*, trans. V. J. Bourke (New York: Image Books, 1956), Book 3, part 1, 205 (ch. 51, 6). Further references will be to SCG, followed by book, chapter, and section numbers. Compare Augustine, in virtually the closing words of *The City of God*: 'There we shall be still and see; we shall see and we shall love; we shall love and we shall praise. Behold what will be, in the end, without end! For what is our end but to reach that kingdom which has no end?' (Augustine, *Concerning the City of God*

divine essence, of God in his selfsame immutable Being, and it is the means by which the soul too comes to acquire something of that same immutability and thus be redeemed from the dangers of time and chance. 'In this vision', Thomas adds, 'we become most like unto God, and we are partakers in His happiness.'[27] And, spelling out what this means, he explains:

... eternity differs from time in this way: time has its being in a sort of succession, whereas the being of eternity is entirely simultaneous. But we have shown that there is no succession in the aforesaid vision; instead, all things that are seen through it are seen at once, and in one view. So, this vision is perfected in a sort of participation in eternity. Moreover, this vision is a kind of life, for the action of the intellect is a kind of life. Therefore the created intellect becomes a partaker in eternal life through this vision.[28]

The logic of eternity and immutability and of like being known by like thus means that once this vision has been granted, it will be forever: 'the nearer a thing is to God, Who is entirely immutable, the less mutable it is and the more lasting... But no creature can come closer to God, than the one who sees His substance. So, the intellectual creature that sees God's substance attains the highest immutability. Therefore it is not possible for it ever to lapse from this vision.'[29]

For Thomas, as for his Augustinian predecessors and contemporaries, this vision is perfectible only in a realm separate from that of bodily life in the world as we know it. In this regard, we should not forget the distance of the medieval world from our modern assumptions about biology and human identity nor should we underestimate the strangeness (to us) of the medieval vision. For even if both Thomists and Augustinians acknowledged that the immortal soul is not without some kind of body (the resurrected and glorified body of which the New Testament speaks), this is a body radically changed from anything that modern physiology or medical science might regard as a 'body'. Every moment and every aspect of life this side of the grave is therefore

---

against the Pagans, trans. II. Bettenson (Harmondsworth: Penguin, 1972), 1091). For a further account of contemplation of God as contemplation of the divine Being see also, e.g., *Works of St Bonaventure: Itinerarium Mentis in Deum* (The progress of the mind towards God), ed. P. Boehner and Z. Hayes (Saint Bonaventure, NY: Saint Bonaventure University Press, 2002), ch. 5, 'Speculation on the Divine Unity through God's Primary name, which is Being'.

[27] SCG III.I, 51, 6.
[28] SCG III.I 61, 2.
[29] SCG III.I 62, 11. This also offers a kind of retrospective argument as to the impossibility of enjoying such a vision in this life, since even the most eminent mystics claim only an occasional or momentary access to the highest states of contemplation and therefore their visions cannot be a direct, participative beholding of the immutable God but, at most, a kind of secondary vision of God as reflected in some creaturely and therefore also mutable form.

by definition only problematically or inadequately capable of knowing the Being of God—although, equally, unless its own being was in some measure informed or sustained by the divine Being it would fall away into utter nothingness and cease to be. Despite the common-sense materialism that some commentators ascribe to Thomas, he, like Augustine, shares a view of human life on earth as being ultimately incapable of fulfilling our most fundamental needs. Being saved by the God who is Being-Itself means being saved from this life, for another. But is this eschatological dualism what is really decisive in the texts we have been considering? Is their power dependent on our being able to share their eschatological commitments? Is this kind of distinction between the earthly and the heavenly realms in which they work out the meaning of 'Being saves' truly central or basic to that meaning? Or can we perhaps understand the link between salvation and Being to which they testify in such a way as to circumvent the issue of their other-worldliness? Can we, for example, understand the formal dualism of this position as a kind of internal dualism, in the sense that it points towards a view of human existence as never being without some relation to its supernatural end, as saying something important about who we are, here and now, as well as what we might become in another life?[30]

BEING AND SALVATION: A MODERN VERSION

Without claiming that human beings today no longer believe in a life after, outside, or in some other way 'beyond' the life of the biological individual of the human species, the view that this life is all there is seems to have become culturally prevalent—in whatever way 'this life' is more nearly defined. But even where such a more this-worldly view of human existence has taken root it has not invariably led to an abandonment of the idea of God as Being or Being-Itself as answering to an experienced need of salvation. A particularly striking example of how this idea might be reworked within the horizons of a thorough-going acceptance of this-worldliness is to be found in the work of the Lutheran-Evangelical theologian Paul Tillich, a decisive influence on much, especially North American, theology in the mid-twentieth century.[31]

---

[30] As in de Lubac's concept of the 'supernatural' as always both natural and supernatural—although de Lubac himself insists upon the non-negotiability of faith in an eternal life.

[31] A similar focus, although more directly dependent on the Thomist tradition, is found in the work of the Anglican theologian John Macquarrie. See J. Macquarrie, *Principles of Christian Theology* (London: SCM Press, 1997), especially ch. 5, 'Being and God'.

Tillich did not look for salvation in another world or in a heavenly realm that we can only access on the condition of the death of the body. Rather, he described salvation as a way of being in the world.

Yet if Tillich let go of the mutable body/immutable soul distinction shared by Augustine and Aquinas, he nevertheless maintained a kind of dualism— and could one imagine any kind of understanding salvation or hope of salvation that was not in some way or other 'dualistic'? Tillich's dualism, however, is not between this life and the next but between the self that has become estranged from its essential being and the self that has been renewed in its 'courage to be'. If this distinguishes him from the ancient and medieval tradition, there is nevertheless a significant continuity, since although the earlier view culminated in the unchanging bliss of the heavenly vision of God it was also a matter of immediate and urgent relevance to the divided and anxious soul struggling to find or to hold on to faith in the midst of life's fearful changes and chances. Fulfilment was for the future, but believing in the possibility of such fulfilment meant the transformation of life here and now. Apart from and prior to the issue of body/soul dualism, there is already a dualism of understanding and decision. Or, still more primitively, there is a dualism—or, since we are not here talking about a theoretical position, i.e., an -ism, let us say a duality, a twofoldness—that is experienced in the restlessness, turbulence, and longing that grips the soul as the ground and possibility of its religious awakening. For Augustine, this restlessness was a basic feature of the soul's life in earth,[32] but whether we regard it as a universal feature of human existence or, more limitedly, as a feature of the lives of those experiencing religious awakening (perhaps as the effect of a special divine grace), it is readily articulated as a sensed need of salvation. The more urgently this need is experienced and the more it comes to define the very existence of the self and to encompass the self's whole life in the world, so much the more appropriate will it seem to understand it in terms of two modes or kinds of Being. And that is as true of a theology like Tillich's that is born out of the modern experience and that has internalized the discoveries of Darwin and Einstein as it is of those earlier theologies that inhabited a geocentric universe and what has been called a two-decker universe.

Tillich states that 'God is Being-Itself' is the one non-symbolic statement we can make concerning God. This means that we cannot speak of the existence of God in a way that would imply that God was 'a' being. As he puts it in his *Systematic Theology*: 'If God is *a* being, he is subject to the categories of finitude,

---

[32] As articulated in the celebrated profession of faith in ch. 1 of *The Confessions* that 'you have made us for yourself and our hearts are restless [*inquietum*] until they rest [*requiescat*] in you'.

especially to space and substance. Even if he is called the "highest being" in the sense of the "most perfect" and the "most powerful" being, this situation is not changed.'[33] He can therefore state that 'it is as atheistic to affirm the existence of God as it is to deny it'.[34] For similar reasons he speaks elsewhere of the real God as a 'God above God' and of 'theism transcended', where 'The God of theological theism is a being beside others . . . He is seen as a self which has a world . . . He is a being, not being-itself'.[35] As did Augustine and Aquinas, Tillich affirms that God 'is' in a unique way, quite distinct from any of the ways in which anything else 'is'. He further understands this as meaning that God is also beyond the contrast between what he calls essential and existential being, i.e., the contrast between Being that is unchanging, infinite, and eternal on the one hand and being that is changeable, finite, and mortal on the other. God is beyond the duality of essence and existence.[36] This leads Tillich rather swiftly into an almost impenetrable thicket of qualifications, since, as the finite human beings that we are, we are simply not equipped to think 'beyond' such a duality and we find it difficult to hold on to the simplicity of what is intended by designating God as Being-Itself. It is much easier for us if we can think of God as a being, and even the challenge of a sophisticated metaphysical concept of God is really rather less strenuous than the paradox of Being-Itself, utterly simple, utterly beyond, yet utterly present to all that is. Perhaps it is in an attempt to avert 'Being-Itself' being turned a 'concept' or 'idea' of Being, that Tillich likes to speak of God also as the 'power' or the 'ground' or the 'abyss' of Being, all ways of reminding us that Being-Itself is somehow prior to and more fundamental than any given idea or concept of Being.

In all of this, Tillich's thought is shaped by a certain understanding of how thinking of God as Being-Itself answers to a human need, a certain turbulence in the self that can be understood in religious terms as a longing for salvation. Tillich himself is entirely straightforward about this. 'The question of being', he states, 'is produced by the "shock of non-being",'[37] an expression which, as he also says, 'points to a state of mind in which the mind is thrown out of its normal balance, shaken in its structure'.[38] Just as the earlier Augustinian tradition saw life in time as ineluctably prone to experience change as one or other form of suffering and therefore driven to look for an immutable happiness beyond the world of time, so Tillich, as a

[33] Paul Tillich, *Systematic Theology*, 3 vols. in 1 (Welwyn Garden City: Nisbet, 1968), i. 261.

[34] Ibid. i. 263.

[35] Paul Tillich, *The Courage to Be* (London: Fontana, 1962), 178.

[36] Again, this is not of itself opposed to the view of the Catholic tradition, as we shall shortly see.

[37] *Systematic Theology*, i. 207.

[38] Ibid. i. 126.

modern Augustinian,[39] sees human existence as constitutionally prone to experience this shock and therefore forced to confront the question of Being.

Our capacity to experience the shock of non-being is rooted in the situation that, apart from God, every other form or manifestation of Being is in some way or other influenced by or subjected to the power of non-being. Again, this seems to be a fairly standard Augustinian argument,[40] although Tillich expounds it in a very distinctive way. For, as he sees it, the very act of existing involves that which exists as being in some way separated from its pure essential being. To exist, as he sometimes puts it, is to stand out into nothingness. No actual tree is a tree as such, no human being is humanity as such. To exist is to express what one essentially is only partially or in a fragmentary way and is therefore to be subject to the categories of finitude in which the wholeness of Being-Itself is refracted through a series of polar structures such as freedom and destiny, dynamics and form, individualization and participation. In an unfallen or paradisal world, these polarities would remain harmoniously integrated into the whole of Being-Itself, but in the world as we know it, the fallen world (and Tillich seems not to concede that any actual world could be other than 'fallen'[41]), they are broken and divided. Whereas the basic structure of Being is such that we cannot be free without a context or world in which to exercise our freedom (the polarity of freedom and destiny), in the world as we know it we typically experience our freedom as being blocked or crushed by our human or natural environment and the dimension of destiny appears to us as an alien and inhibiting fate. In place of a creative dialectic of freedom and destiny, we find ourselves in a situation of having to choose between rebellion and slavery. In this and similar ways the structures of Being are degraded into 'structures of destruction' and the very order of the world in which we live comes to be experienced as antithetical to human flourishing. The ground of our being seems to fall from under our feet, and we experience the shock of non-Being, threatening us in our very core. It is this shock that, in turn, first raises the question as to what it would be for us to be otherwise, for us really *to be*, that is, *to be* in such a way that our being was not constantly under threat of diminishment or even destruction. Because—as for Augustine, Anselm, and Aquinas—the epitome of the shock of non-being is the realization of mortality, the confrontation with the ineluctable

---

[39] For Tillich's view of Augustine, whom he explicitly hails as the primary source for a contemporary philosophy of religion 'which is based on the immediacy of truth in every human being', see Tillich, *A History of Christian Thought* (London: SCM Press, 1968), 103–33.

[40] And, of course, a view that pre-dates Christianity, as we shall touch on briefly below.

[41] From the standpoint of orthodox Christian belief, this may seem a worrying concession although, arguably, it is an inevitable result of Tillich's refusal of all other-worldliness. As at other points of his system, one can see here the influence of Schelling's late philosophy.

fact that we shall one day cease to be. At an individual level this is a human constant—'The face of every man shows the trace of the presence of death in his life, of his fear of death, of his courage towards death, and of his resignation to death . . . [This is] the real and ultimate object of fear from which all other fears derive their power, the fear that overwhelmed even Christ in Gethsemane.'[42] But it is also a shock and a fear that ebbs and flows within the course of individual lives and the lives of societies. Tillich could therefore interpret the story of his generation as a story of a particularly acute and shattering revelation of death.

Born in 1886, Tillich came to adulthood in the relative stability of the Wilhelmine era, the German counterpart of the long, golden sunset of Britain's Edwardian period, a world that believed in an inevitable and continuous progress that would both gradually extend the span of human life and reduce death to a managed and remote event. 'And suddenly,' Tillich writes, in 1914

the lid was torn off. The picture of Death appeared, unveiled, in a thousand forms. As in the late Middle Ages the figure of Death appeared in pictures and poetry, and the Dance of Death with every living being was painted and sung, so our generation—the generation of world wars, revolutions, and mass migrations—rediscovered the reality of death. We have seen millions die in war, hundreds of thousands in revolutions, tens of thousands in persecutions and systematic purges of minorities.[43]

As he goes on to add, all those driven by such events into becoming refugees and migrants, 'carry in their souls, and often in their bodies, the traces of death, and they will never completely lose them'.[44] Nor are these merely rhetorical lines: Tillich himself served as an army padre on the Western Front in the First World War and became amongst the first political refugees from Hitler's Germany. The 'shock of non-being', then, is not simply a kind of metaphysical puzzlement: it is a concrete human experience, shattering but also marking and shaping how we are in the specifics of our existence.

Tillich's response, however, is not to seek escape from a world in which each of us is condemned to die and millions of us are condemned to die horrifically. As for Augustine, the 'answer' to this predicament is the renewal of the relation to Being-Itself. This does not lead to immortality or to deliverance from the change and chance of existence, however. Instead, it occurs as the advent of a 'new being' in which the severed and conflicting structures of Being are experienced as reintegrated into and supportive of a life-enhancing

---

[42] Tillich, *The Shaking of the Foundations* (London: SCM Press, 1949), 170.
[43] Tillich, *The New Being* (New York: Scribner, 1955), 171.
[44] Ibid.

whole. Salvation in Christ is precisely the revelation of this new being, of 'essential being under the conditions of existence, conquering the gap between essence and existence'.[45] Or, as he puts it in a sermon entitled 'The New Being': 'The message of Christianity is . . . a New Reality. A New state of things has appeared, it still appears; it is hidden and visible, it is there and it is here. Accept it, enter into it, let it grasp you.'[46] This is not a call to 'flee the world' but to be in the world otherwise than we are when we succumb to the shock of non-being. To be saved is to find the 'courage to be' in the face of and despite the horror and the shock of non-being.[47]

For all the differences from the classical Augustinian account, Tillich's understanding of the meaning of Being is shaped from start to finish by the exigencies of the self that experiences the need of salvation. Yet, on his view, this awakening need not take a self-conscious or even a specifically religious form. In Tillich's vocabulary it is primarily existential and, as such, may be the fear of death, a dumb sense that 'there must be more to life than this', a nagging feeling of incompleteness in which I experience life as passing me by (or experience my own life as slipping away from me). All of which are nicely epitomized in Iago's comment that 'I am not what I am'.[48] And when a self experiences itself in that way, what could be more fitting than that it should turn to one, to a God, who can say of himself, 'I am that I am', to a God whose emphatically selfsame way of Being is the prescribed antidote to a loss of being that has split the very centre of the 'I'.

BEING, SALVATION, AND CREATION[49]

The focus of this chapter has so far been on the soteriological imperatives effective in the construal of God as Being or Being-Itself. However, these are not

---

[45] *Systematic Theology*, ii. 136.

[46] *The New Being*, 24.

[47] The possibility of finding such courage, as Tillich repeatedly emphasizes, is first and foremost to be found in the experience of love, as in the sermon 'Love is Stronger than Death', previously quoted.

[48] W. Shakespeare, *Othello*, Act 1, Scene 1. By way of contrast, note what Iago says of Othello: 'He's that he is' (Act 4, Scene 1).

[49] When I follow Augustine and other Christian thinkers in speaking of creation as a past event or of the original goodness of creation it does not mean that I am endorsing creationism in the sense it has recently acquired, i.e., as a kind of anti-scientific world-view. Even in Augustine the connection of his reflections on creation with experiences of alienation and exile should alert us to the fact that what is going on here is not primarily an exercise in cosmology but a meditation on the possibility of human fulfilment in a world such as that in which we find

the only religious or theological factors that are relevant to this way of thinking about God. As it has been developed in the tradition, thinking about God as Being has also been associated in a fundamental way with the doctrine of creation.[50] For if Christian theology teaches that creation occurs as God calling all that is into being out of nothing, who might be capable of such a 'Fiat!' other than one who was in 'himself' the plenitude of Being? Thus, for Augustine, creation is based on nothing other than 'God's good purpose to create good'[51] and, since the 'one sole good'[52] is God himself in his simple and unchangeable Being, the existence of creation is possible only as the donation of a measure of being to everything that might possibly be capable of coming into existence. Everything that exists is good in the degree and in the way that it exists:

And so all nature's substances are good, because they exist and therefore have their own mode and kind of being, and, in their fashion, a peace and harmony amongst themselves...Now God supremely exists, and therefore he is the author of every existence which does not exist in this supreme degree...nothing could exist in any way, if it had not been created by him.[53]

If, for such reasons, the identification of God with Being or Being-Itself is seen as fundamental to the doctrine of creation, this doctrine might seem to merit a certain priority over considerations deriving from the experienced need of salvation. Isn't creation more basic than salvation? Isn't the story of creation appropriately the subject of the very opening chapter of the Bible? Where else should the Bible begin but 'in the beginning'? And isn't faith in God as creator of heaven and earth equally appropriately the first item in the Church's creed? How could there even be talk of creatures needing salvation if they hadn't been created first?

---

ourselves and in which we can only deny the kind of experiences that Tillich described as 'the shock of non-being' by self-deception or wilful ignorance.

[50] Thus Gilson notes the inevitability of certain adaptations to Aristotelianism, once this was incorporated into the theologies of Islam and Christianity: 'Inasmuch as it is an abstractly objective interpretation of reality, philosophy is not interested in actual existence; on the contrary, inasmuch as it is primarily concerned with human individuals and the concrete problems of their personal salvation, religion cannot afford to ignore existence.' And: 'In the twelfth century after Christ, two religions, both stemming from the Old Testament, agreed in teaching that there is a supreme God, Who truly is and Who is the Maker of the world...Now, if we believe that the world has been created, what is the very first thing that happened to it at the very time when it was created, if not *to be*? The sovereign importance of existence and its factual primacy cannot possibly be overlooked by men who believe that things have been created out of nothing' (E. Gilson, *Being and Some Philosophers* (Toronto: Pontifical Institute of Mediaeval Studies, 1952), 51–2).

[51] *City of God*, 455 (XI, 23).

[52] Ibid. 440 (XI, 10).

[53] *City of God*, 476–7 (XII, 5).

Whatever the final answers to such questions, the fact is that doctrines of salvation and creation are intimately interwoven in actual theological exposition. Continuing to bear in mind the chapters on creation in Augustine's *City of God*, we can see how his account of creation is constantly criss-crossed by reflections on our actual experience of the world as marked by evil, i.e., by a recognition of the difference between the world that we know and the original creation. The account of the bliss of the holy angels in the beginning of creation is thus followed by reflections on the fallen angels and the origin of the Devil (XI, 13–15); the praise of the great chain of being (XI, 16) is followed by considering how this is enhanced and not diminished by the phenomenon of evil (XI, 17–18); the affirmation of the goodness of God as the sole basis of creation (XI, 21) is followed by reflections on the apparent evil in the universe (X, 22). Starting from where we start, 'midway this way of life we're bound upon', we can reflect on the original goodness of creation only in relation to our actual experience of a fallen world. This is not to say that the creation was somehow fallen in its very first moment or tending towards its fall, and Augustine for one is insistent on the unqualified goodness of its original state as well as emphasizing that, despite the Fall, the world we inhabit is nevertheless continuous with that first creation.[54] Yet our interest in the question as to whether we can trust in the original goodness of the world, whether we can believe in a goodness 'deep down things', cannot but be conditioned by our awareness of the constant threat to that goodness in the world that we know and our own constant exposure to the possibility of falling out of existence into nothingness. And even in that good original creation as described by Augustine, the very fact of its being created 'out of nothing' already allows for the possibility of its somehow failing to become or to remain all that it could be when sustained and held in being by the unchangingly good will of God. Evil is caused by a falling away from good, but the possibility of that falling 'is due to its creation out of nothing'.[55] Theologically, then, the affirmation of the original goodness of creation can never be separated from the larger context of the whole dramatic sequence of creation, fall, and redemption. It is not a question of prioritizing one doctrinal topic over another but of seeing the interconnection of the whole and following the movement of thought that connects the whole sequence into a meaningful religious view. In contemplating creation, the human creature—the living, actual human beings that we are—is also implicitly taking account

---

[54] Tillich, however, does seem to accept that the separation of existence from essence that is intrinsic in any form of coming into being means that nothing can exist except in some degree of estrangement from its true nature or Being.

[55] *City of God*, 572 (XIV, 13).

of its own situation as banished from the garden and far from heaven. The affirmation of the goodness of creation as grounded in the one true Being of God is thus also at the same time dependent on being able to affirm the possibility of salvation, a way back from exile, and a way forward to redemption. It is also to ground the possibility that our longing for salvation is not only driven by a kind of lack or desperate need, but is still more fundamentally rooted in love, in the recognition that God and the soul are, as it were, 'made for each other'. What draws us to God is not merely our subjective emptiness, but what Dante called 'the love that moves the sun and other stars'.[56] To say 'God is good' is not simply to assure ourselves of the goodness of the world God has created, but also to affirm something that is integral to any hope that the world as we know it is a world open to the fullest possibilities of human flourishing—whether in its own terms or as a staircase to heaven. Both doctrines of creation and salvation may therefore, in effect, be merely diverse ways of explicating the core affirmation that God is Being or Being-Itself.[57]

All of the foregoing has been presented as a reflection on some of the religious motivations invested in understanding God as Being or Being-Itself. However, this is not to say that this idea does not also have a certain origin in philosophy. Whilst we began by asking how this apparently abstract way of thinking about God might express genuine religious concerns, the formulations used by Augustine, Aquinas, and Tillich are undeniably formulations that have a certain background in philosophy, as each of them was well aware and fully acknowledged. But we would misconceive the relationship between theology and philosophy at this point if we thought of theology as expressing the living religious passions of the restless heart and philosophy as some kind of detached theoretical enquiry. As a number of recent commentators have noted, the philosophy of the ancient world—to which Augustine had a direct and personal relation—was not what we tend to think of as a purely academic or 'scientific' business. Rather, it had a distinct existential character directed towards the improvement of the philosopher's own life, in some cases broach-

---

[56] This is the final line of Dante's *Divine Comedy*. The thought here lies at the root of what many medieval authors described as a passage from the self-centred love (*amor*) to a love that forgets itself in the contemplation of God's goodness (*caritas*): the point being that the first nevertheless contains the possibility for human beings to experience and be transformed by charity. See, e.g. William of Saint-Thierry, *The Nature and Dignity of Love* (*Amor*). The tradition is continued in, e.g., François de Sales, *Traitté de l'amour de Dieu*, in *Œuvres de St François de Sales*, vol. iv (Annecy: Niérat, 1894).

[57] A striking contrast to such a Christian ontology of creation is the teaching of Schopenhauer, for whom the world cannot be called 'good' since it is simply the product of a blind and purposeless will in relation to which human flourishing and human suffering are matters of complete indifference.

ing on questions of salvation.[58] Many in the ancient world saw Christianity itself as a kind of philosophy—Jesus himself being depicted in many early works of Christian art robed in the philosopher's pallium and instructing his disciples in the manner of a philosophical master. That, prior to and in the commencement of Christian theology, philosophy had already turned to understanding the world in terms of a dialectic of Being and non-being and to pondering the more precise nature and depth of true Being may therefore be taken as indicative of a certain soteriological interest at work in philosophy itself. Although we may not be convinced by the claims of Augustine and other religious apologists that such continuities were to be explained by Plato or other Greek philosophers having read or indirectly learned from God's self-naming to Moses or from the treatment of Being and goodness in Genesis 1,[59] we might pause before rejecting their intuition that the motivations behind the philosophers' attempts to reflect on the meaning of Being were not entirely different in kind from those of the believers, even if (in the eyes of the believers) their answers ultimately fell short. Thinking about what it could mean for humans and other beings really to be what they had the possibility of being was from the beginning, and even from before the beginning of either philosophy or theology as we know them, a challenge that neither philosophers nor theologians could evade. And once the turbulence and anxiety that the early thinkers experienced in themselves became articulated as a restlessness in the very Being of human beings, how could they do otherwise than speak in the language of ontology, of Being, Being-Itself, and non-being? However, when the question of Being is transposed into the mode of philosophy it receives a new and distinctive accent. For what the philosopher is characteristically preoccupied with is not simply the desire to experience the fullness of Being but to know what it is that is being given or that is occurring in this experience. The longing for salvation may be undiminished, but it acquires a new form in the desire for knowledge.

CHRISTIAN ARISTOTELIANISM

No Christian philosopher has, to my knowledge, claimed that we can simply 'know' God in a direct and unproblematic way. Yet the claim is made that, nevertheless, we do know God in some way and know him not just in the

---

[58] See, e.g., P. Hadot, *Exercices spirituels et philosophie antique* (Paris: Albin Michel, 2002 [1993]).

[59] *City of God*, 453 (XI, 21).

manner of an ineffable moment of intuition but in such a way that our knowledge has a definite and well-grounded content, is demonstrably reliable in itself, and indispensable not only for theology but for the whole system of knowledge.

Such claims are especially clearly represented in the systems of Christian metaphysics that developed in the Middle Ages and that, for the Roman Catholic Church, are normatively articulated in the particular system known as Thomism. This, in turn, rests upon a certain understanding of the metaphysics of the ancient world, especially Aristotle—but it is not my aim here to consider whether the understanding of Aristotle developed by Thomas and his successors is historically well justified. In the twentieth century Heidegger famously depicted the translation of Greek philosophy into Latin as bringing about the eclipse of what was most important in that philosophy itself. Many non-Heideggerians would also have reason to question one or other aspect of Thomas's understanding of Aristotle on purely historical or textual grounds. Such questions have their own legitimacy and interest, but I am not attempting to engage with them here. Likewise, I shall not attempt to test the extent to which modern versions of Thomism have correctly interpreted their master.[60] Insofar as our enquiry is about what it means to understand God in terms of Being or Being-Itself in the specific context of modern theology and philosophy the fact that one or other version of Thomism was historically inaccurate in presenting its classical sources would not of itself make it not worth studying—provided that it offered a significant and coherent statement of the issue in its own terms.[61] And this,

---

[60] One question, of course, is whether Thomas does actually give a coherent and consistent account of Being, and, if so, whether it is philosophically persuasive. See Anthony Kenny, *Aquinas on Being* (Oxford: Oxford University Press, 2002). Kenny concludes by implying that 'Aquinas' theory of God as subsistent being is nothing but sophistry and illusion' (p. 194). This is clearly damaging to the claims that there is a distinctive Thom*ist* doctrine and that that doctrine should play a normative role in our own reflection on the question.

[61] Of course, if such a Thomism also claimed attention and even authority on the basis of a specific historical affiliation and that historical affiliation were to be undermined, then that would have a significant impact on those specific claims. However, we might still be left with an intrinsically interesting theological and philosophical construct. As a matter of fact, those versions of Thomism that will be considered here do present themselves as authentic interpretations of Thomas. Maritain said of himself that 'I am not a neo-Thomist. All in all I would rather be a paleo-Thomist than a neo-Thomist. I am, or at least I hope I am, a Thomist.' See J. Maritain, *Existence and the Existent* (New York: Image Books, 1948), 11. A further question would, of course, be whether the various versions of the so-called 'transcendental Thomism' continue the earlier Thomist concern for the question of Being. It might seem that the transcendental Thomists' starting point in the subjective conditions of knowledge involved—as for Kant—a significant abandonment of this question. However, even if 'being' only emerges as the outcome of a subjective act of judgement, judgements of being are typically said to be the proper goal of the subjective quest for knowledge—as, for example, in Lonergan's lapidary

I suggest, is what we do in fact encounter in the Thomism of the mid-twentieth century.[62] That being said, the way in which modern Thomism has typically claimed not only to be expounding Thomas but also that Thomas himself is an exemplary reader of Aristotle, makes it appropriate and even necessary to begin with some reference back to the basic Aristotelian sources that come to play a defining role in Christian metaphysics.

Given the foundational role of Aristotle in Western thought, it is scarcely surprising that his texts have been scrutinized in minute detail over many centuries and are interpreted in widely diverse ways. Here we are pursuing only one interpretation of Aristotle, an interpretation that specifically focuses on the theological understanding of Being.[63] And if there is anything uncontentious that can be said about Aristotle's metaphysics, it would seem to be that it is centrally concerned with the question of Being. That being said, questions immediately start to multiply in many directions, not least as regards the translation of the most basic terms in which Aristotle addresses the question. A case—and a crucial case—in point is the translation of the pivotal term *ousia*. In his guide to *The Greek Philosophical Vocabulary*, J. O. Urmson notes that 'philosophically' *ousia* means 'nature, essence, substance, being',[64] which,

assertion that 'knowing is knowing being' (in Bernard J. F. Lonergan, *Insight* (New York: Philosophical Library, 1970), 357). This is striking in that Lonergan is perhaps furthest from approaching the central questions of philosophy in terms of objective Being. A useful exchange of views between Lonergan and E. Coreth can be followed in B. Lonergan, 'Metaphysics as Horizon', in idem, *A Lonergan Collection*, ed. F. Crowe (Montreal: Palm, 1967), 188 ff. and E. Coreth, 'Immediacy and the Mediation of Being: An Attempt to Answer Bernard Lonergan', in P. McShane, *Language, Truth and Meaning: Papers from the International Lonergan Conference 1970* (Dublin: Gill and Macmillan, 1971), 34 ff.

[62] And one that is still relevant. It is, for example, striking that several of the key elements of Gilson's Thomism, including his view as to the flattening out of Christian metaphysics after Thomas and the perils of ontologism and essentialism, clearly anticipate the theses of Radical Orthodoxy. See also n. 69 below. However, it is striking that recent interpretations of Thomas by more analytically inclined interpreters significantly underplay the theme of Being that plays such a key role in both Gilson and Maritain. See, e.g., Brian Davies, *The Thought of Thomas Aquinas* (Oxford: Oxford University Press, 1992). The word 'Being' does not appear in Davies's index and even in the text there are rather few passages where he discusses the ontological themes that are so central to Gilson. See also E. Stump, *Aquinas* (London: Routledge, 2003). Although there is some discussion of God being his own being, this is chiefly as a sub-theme in the treatment of divine goodness.

[63] Perhaps the most compendious study of Aristotle's account of Being in the twentieth century was that of J. Owens, *The Doctrine of Being in the Aristotelian 'Metaphysics': A Study in the Greek Background of Mediaeval Thought* (2nd edn. Toronto: Pontifical institute of Mediaeval Studies, 1963). Owens's neo-scholastic context is reflected in the way he speaks of Aristotle's 'doctrine of Being', in contradiction to Heidegger's insistence on the *question* of Being.

[64] J. O. Urmson, *The Greek Philosophical Vocabulary* (London: Duckworth, 1990), 119. The situation is further complicated by the fact that—perhaps surprisingly—even Latin terms such as *esse* and *essentia* are translated into English in very inconsistent ways, not only by different authors but even, sometimes, in the same author. John F. Wippel notes that even in Aquinas, the

of course, begs the question as to what each of these terms means and how they are to be related to each other. Are they synonyms, such that Being 'is' identical with nature, essence, or substance? That is the question that this chapter seeks to address, a question we can reformulate as follows: Is Being exhaustively knowable in its manifestation as nature, essence, and substance? Or, does the knowledge that we can attain of nature, essence, and substance give us a full and adequate knowledge of Being-Itself?[65] And, even if it doesn't, what could we know of Being at all if it was not revealed to us as a certain definite something, a certain 'what'? But in that case, what are the limits of that 'what'? How far is knowing 'what' a being is also a revelation of that being itself? And, with specific regard to the question of thinking about God, how far would a concept—any concept of God—designed to answer the question 'What is God?' be capable of revealing to us the God who is Being/Being-Itself?

The basic terms in which these questions are posed are already set out in Aristotle's *Metaphysics*, a text which would shape the way in which Christian theology itself developed its thinking about the Being of God, despite significant changes such as those resulting from the Christian emphasis on creation out of nothing. One starting point, then, is to look to the memorable definitions found in the *Metaphysics*, such as that given at the start of Book IV (Γ) where Being (*to on*) is defined as the supreme subject of metaphysical enquiry 'There is a science which studies Being qua Being (*to on hē on*)' (1003a21).[66] At the start of Book XII (Λ), the subject of metaphysics is further specified in terms of substance (*ousia*): 'Our enquiry is concerned with substance (*ousia*)' (1069a18). Why? Because, as Aristotle argues in Book VII (Z), 'Now of all these senses which "being" (*to on*) has, the primary sense is clearly the "what" (*to ti estin*), which denotes the "substance" (*ousia*)' (1028a14) and: 'the question which was raised long ago, is still and will always be, and which always baffles us—"What is Being?" (*to on*)—is in other words;

---

same principle can variously be described as 'a being [*ens*], or as "that which is," or as substance, or as essence, or as form, or as a creature, or as a thing, or as nature, or simply as that which participates' (in his article 'Metaphysics' in N. Kretzmann and E. Stump (eds.), *The Cambridge Companion to Aquinas* (Cambridge: Cambridge University Press, 1993), 99–100). There may be contextual justifications for such variations, but when they are not made explicit they can generate some confusion. These issues are, of course, made even more complex if we draw on sources written in other modern European languages where the same freedom of translation (especially with regard to the Greek terms) is employed.

[65] Such questions sound formidably abstract. However, the soteriological interest has not been and will not be forgotten in what follows, even if I do not further advert to it.

[66] References to Aristotle's *Metaphysics* are based on the Loeb edition, edited by H. Tredennick (Cambridge, Mass.: Harvard University Press, 1961–2). The numbers given in brackets after each quotation are the line references given in that edition.

"What is substance?" (*hē ousia*)' (1028b2). The substance of something, then, is *what* it really is, or, to use what seems the obvious Latin term, its essence. As Gilson summarizes Aristotle: 'The true Aristotelian name for being is substance, which is itself identical with what a being is . . . All we have now to do is to equate these terms: what primarily *is*, the *substance* of that which is, *what* the thing is. In short, the "whatness" of a thing is its very being.'[67]

We shall return to some of the questions that this seemingly self-assured assertion might appear to gloss over, but the robustness of the Aristotelian pronouncements should not blind us to the fact that what is being set out in Aristotle himself is not a once-and-for-all set of answers to a recognized problem: rather, it is the opening of a field of enquiry that would be developed and expanded over many centuries, and, in the course of this development, would criss-cross both the developing boundaries of divergent religious traditions (Judaism, Christianity, and Islam) and epochal shifts within philosophical traditions. Gilson himself is deeply aware of this and, as a Thomist philosopher, is concerned to show that Thomas transforms his Aristotelian heritage in a way that is distinctly Christian (as opposed, say, to the Islamic transformation of Aristotle in Avicenna and Averroes) and that is also adequate to both its theological and philosophical intentions (as opposed, say, to the alternative Christian transformations of Aristotle in, e.g., Siger of Brabant, Duns Scotus, or Suarez). All these religious developments of Aristotelian thought inevitably reflect what has been revealed of God in their respective Scriptures, and, not least, the fact that these Scriptures represent the world as existing only as the result of a divine act of creation.[68] All of them obviously desire to honour the unique sovereignty of God, but (according to Gilson and other Thomists), only Thomism does so in a way that is both true to its philosophical inheritance and to the revelation of God as creator. How, then, does it achieve this, and in what ways is it different from other versions of theistic Aristotelianism?

Gilson himself was one of the most distinguished of the twentieth-century interpreters of Thomism, and in the following pages I shall be largely guided by his particular version of Thomism, which I regard as exemplary not only in terms of the breadth and depth of his knowledge of the sources, but also because he combines an understanding of the religious and soteriological aspects of the question with a grasp of the philosophical issues.[69] Gilson

---

[67] *Being and Some Philosophers*, 46.

[68] In the Christian version, there is a particular emphasis on this act of creation being 'out of nothing', an emphasis that is reflected in certain aspects of Thomist Aristotelianism.

[69] On the continuing relevance of Gilson see, e.g., F. Kerr, *After Aquinas: Versions of Thomism* (Oxford: Blackwell, 2002), especially ch. 5 'Stories of Being' (pp. 73–96). Kerr suggests that it is essentially Gilson's Thomism that is expressed in the 1998 Papal Encyclical *Fides et Ratio*. I shall

characteristically sees Thomism as steering a path between two opposite dangers that nevertheless have the same outcome. The first is the inability properly to assure the independence of the world, whilst the second is a failure to account for the knowability of both world and God in their mutual distinctiveness. Crucial to this challenge is the conviction that the world we live in, the world we know, is a real world and that the way in which we apprehend it in a more or less common-sense realist way, as an ensemble of actually existing entities, is basically reliable. This, Gilson believes, is intrinsic to the basic Aristotelian impulse that to know something is to know some real thing and not its abstract 'idea'. Yet this is not to be confused with the post-Humean view that the things we encounter are merely inferred from the barrage of sensations in which we are enveloped in the world. It is not as if there is first of all a blur of optical stimuli that my mind sifts and organizes into an experience of green and brown shapes that I then interpret as a tree: rather, I see the tree—even though I cannot see it otherwise than as this particular material tree with its brown wood and green leaves. The world is constituted out of actually existing things (trees, rocks, animals), and when I know something these are what I know. This basic conviction means that when we know something, we know it in accordance with its Being. Gilson again: 'If to know is to know things as they are—for otherwise they are not known at all—to know them is to reach, not only their form, but their very "to be."'[70] In knowing we are not just reflecting on the appearances of things: we are dealing with the things themselves in a manner appropriate to their being. Knowledge is not just a construct placed on an indifferent reality: it is the mind's reception of the self-revelation of beings as the beings that they are.[71]

---

also be referring to the French philosopher Jacques Maritain, often linked with Gilson as, in their generation, the pre-eminent representatives of 'existential Thomism'. (On the differences between them see G. Prouvost, 'Étienne Gilson–Jacques Maritain', *Revue Thomiste*, 3 (1994), 380 ff.). Both were also defining figures for the Anglican Neo-Thomism of Eric Mascall. See the latter's books *He Who Is: A Study in Traditional Theism* (London: Longman, Green and Co., 1943) and *Existence and Analogy: A Sequel to 'He Who Is'* (London: Longman, Green and Co., 1949) and his Gifford Lectures, *The Openness of Being: Natural Theology Today* (London: Darton, Longman and Todd, 1971).

[70] *Being and Some Philosophers*, 187.

[71] A similar point is made by Maritain in writing of knowledge as 'immersed in existence': 'That is why', he explains, 'the pattern of all true knowledge is the intuition of the thing that I see, and that sheds its light upon me . . . Sense delivers existence to the intellect; it gives the intellect an intelligible treasure which sense does not know to be intelligible, and which the intellect, for its part, knows and calls by its name, which is *being*' (J. Maritain, *Existence and the Existent* (New York, Image Books, 1948), 21).

According to Aristotle's doctrine of categories, to say something meaningful—something that can be either true or false—about a given entity is to be able to say something specific about it, such as what it is, or where it is, or when it occurred. There are ten such 'categories' of knowing that Thomas takes over from Aristotle, and he further follows the Greek thinker in recognizing that although these could be understood merely as a way of formulating meaningful propositions their more important function is to refer to realities or purported realities. It is in this regard (and only in this regard, he claims) that issues of essence arise. Only something real can have an essence. To talk about essences is to talk about things we suppose to be real. Quoting Averroes, Thomas states that 'being *(ens)*, in the first sense, is what signifies the essence of a thing',[72] going on to note how essence is also taken to be synonymous or near-synonymous with such terms as the quiddity ('what the philosopher frequently terms what it is to be a thing'), form, and nature.[73] Moreover, essences have a distinctive relation to substances (the first of the ten categories), as opposed to accidents (the rest), and it is the question of essence that is in play when, in the case of a given substance (i.e., a given being), we ask, for example, whether it is a horse or a human being, as opposed to whether it is white or black, running or lying down. Both horses and human beings can be either white or black, running or lying down, but to say of a given object that it is human being and not a horse tells us something more basic and more important than that it is, e.g., white or lying down.

In each case, knowledge occurs only in relation to what is really there, and this means also what is not merely possibly there or potentially there, but what actually is there: in the Aristotelian-Thomist vocabulary, only what is in act, only what actually is what it is, is knowable. I can only know what it is for a tree to be a tree, a horse to be a horse, or a human being to be a human being on the basis of encountering actual trees, horses, and human beings in the world.[74] This act, as Gilson puts it, is not 'above' being (as, in his view, occurs in Platonism, where the reality of a given being is identified with its idea or form), but 'in being', it is 'the very reality of being'.[75] Yet, even though this

---

[72] Thomas Aquinas, *On Being and Essence*, trans. A. Maurer (Toronto: Pontifical Institute of Medieval Studies, 1971), ch. 1, 30 (translation amended).

[73] Ibid. 31 (translation amended).

[74] Of course, the Thomist scheme does not limit our knowledge to what can be known solely through bodily experience and also allows for knowledge of immaterial substances, such as angels.

[75] *Being and Some Philosophers*, 44. Gilson notes that there is also a kind of residual or potential Platonism in Aristotle himself, which he ascribes to a failure to distinguish adequately between what a thing is and that it is. This means that although on Aristotle's own account forms ought only ever to be knowable as the forms of actual beings they do in fact sometimes function rather similarly to Platonic forms. Consequently, the priority of knowing the actual

'escapes definition' it does not drift off into some kind of metaphysical or experiential space above or beyond the world: it is always reality shaped by and as a determinate 'what'. The task of the Christian philosopher is to keep this fusion of reality and essence in view, but that is not so easy.

In Avicenna, according to Gilson, existence becomes a mere accident, separate from the 'what'. On this Avicennan view essences are eternal in the mind of God, and it is solely God's will that decides whether or not they exist: their existing is not intrinsic to their being the essences that they are, it is merely a supplement, a kind of add-on that involves no essential change. If, on this basis, existing things are more or less reduced to the status of accidents, the opposite seems to occur in Averroes where substance is defined with being, such that not only God but, in effect, everything that exists does so necessarily, as a kind of extension of the divine Being. But even though these seem like opposite positions, neither of them presents us with a world in which anything really significant ever happens. In the case of Avicenna, the world and all that is in it is merely a concatenation of contingencies, a world of fleeting, impermanent, shadows; in the case of Averroes nothing new ever arises or ever could arise. Christianity, however, requires the possibility of radical novelty, the kind of novelty evidenced in creation out of nothing and in the incarnation.[76] This means that existence must be characterized by a kind of freedom that is impossible if it is equated with substance, i.e., as if whatever has substantial being must be or if the world of eternal essences prescribes what can or can't come into existence. As Gilson makes the point with reference to Duns Scotus, the Christian God is free to choose which ideas are 'creable'.[77]

Essences show us the 'what' of substances, *what* x or y or z *is*. Yet if the substances we know by means of their essences are in this way dependent on the will of God for their existence, doesn't this take us back to the position that Gilson ascribed to Avicenna and make the world merely arbitrary? Gilson would say not, arguing that Thomas significantly nuances the relations between substances, essences, and existence in a way that Avicenna did not. The fact that existence is dependent on the will of God does not make it

---

thing itself is weakened in favour of knowing the form—whereas, for Gilson, the form tells us 'what' a thing is only as and when it is actualized in the concrete reality of that thing.

[76] Obviously it is no accident that Gilson opposes two Islamic thinkers to his favoured Thomist position. However, we should note that he sees some Christian thinkers as prone to similar errors, as in the Christian Averroism of Siger of Brabant, in Scotus' and Suarez's diverse failures adequately to distinguish between essence and existence (according to Scotus, Gilson says, existence is only a modality of essence (*Being and Some Philosophers*, 91), whilst Suarez denies to existence the possibility of being a 'what' (ibid. 105)).

[77] Ibid. 85.

arbitrary, since what is at issue is precisely the existence of substances that have a definite and knowable essence—known, primarily, by the mind of God but, once existing, knowable also by human minds. From the standpoint of human beings' knowledge of the world existent things may appear to be evanescent, contingent, and corruptible, but that is a perspectival error. All composite substances, i.e., substances composed of matter and form, are indeed decomposable, but simple substances, such as those of human souls, angels, or God himself, are not. It is not the fact of being a created substance nor even (despite Augustine) the fact of existing in time that exposes a being to corruption. Whether or not it is thus exposed depends precisely on the kind of being it is, not on whether it exists or not, and there is therefore no inconsistency in positing the existence of non-corruptible created substances.

With regard to created beings, then, we find ourselves placed in a world in which we can have confidence. Ours is a world full of things that are knowable and worth knowing (God, after all, has freely chosen to know them as the existent things that they are, so why shouldn't we?). The outcome is eloquently stated by Maritain:

> God creates existent subjects or supposita which subsist in the individual nature that constitutes them and which receive from the creative influx their nature as well as their subsistence, their existence and their activity. Each of them possesses an essence and pours itself out in action. Each is, for us, an inexhaustible well of knowability. We shall never know everything there is to know about the tiniest blade of grass or the least ripple in a stream . . . This is why ours is a world of nature and adventure, filled with events, contingency, chance, and where the course of events is flexible and mutable whereas the laws of essences are necessary.[78]

This, the claim goes, is significantly different from the non-theistic Aristotelian vision, according to which the fact that something existed was attributable only to the fusion of form and matter. On that model, since matter was without specific distinctions in itself and was therefore entirely indifferent to whatever form was stamped upon it (so that, once abstracted from its form, there would be no distinction between the matter of a diamond, a tree, or a human brain), knowledge would still have a quasi-Platonic tendency to focus on the form at the expense of the matter. On the Christian view, however, each individual substance is properly knowable only as the distinctive matter-form unity it is. The matter of a creature really is integral to its being and to its being knowable as the thing that it is. Existence is not the mere materialization of form but the act whereby a form comes into existence. Just as matter is simply potentiality unless it becomes something through the imprint of a

---

[78] *Existence and the Existent*, 74.

form, so, analogously, form is merely potential—it is not the form of any-thing—unless it is made actual in existence. Rather than seeing existence as the descent of form into matter, Christian metaphysics therefore sees it as the ascent of form into actuality and existence.

All of which may be true of created and composite substances, but what of simple substances and, especially, of that supremely simple substance, God, whose Being is Being-Itself (*ipsum esse*)? How does this help us know God and, no less importantly, find assurance that it really is God we know in such divine knowledge? Passing over the specific questions relating to human souls and angels[79] (the chief examples of simple and immaterial created sub-stances), what, then, of God?

As I have expounded the Thomist position thus far, it might seem as if God's role was chiefly to provide a kind of guarantee for the knowability of the world. According to Thomists such as Gilson and Maritain, that is indeed what he does—but not in the manner of a convenient metaphysical hypothe-sis. God is not simply a means of underwriting our knowledge of the world: God is himself the supreme object of knowledge and all acts of knowledge in relation to creatures are ultimately directed towards God. Of course—and as we have already seen with regard to the direct vision of God that, according to Thomas, only becomes possible once the earthly body has been sloughed off in favour of the heavenly body—we do not and cannot have a direct vision of God in this life. We do not see God 'in' creatures, yet in seeing creatures as the beings that they are, in knowing them according to their being, we see that created being that provides us with a distant analogy for the divine being itself.

Maritain again:

[A]t the root of metaphysical knowledge, St. Thomas places the intellectual intuition of that mysterious reality disguised under the most commonplace and commonly used word in the language, the word *to be*... It is being, attained or perceived at the summit of an abstractive intellection, of an eidetic or intensive visualisation which owes its purity and power of illumination only to the fact that the intellect, one day, was stirred to its depths and trans-illuminated by the impact of the act of existing apprehended in things...[80]

---

[79] But noting Maritain's splendid comment that 'He who has not meditated on the angels will never be a perfect metaphysician' (J. Maritain, *The Degrees of Knowledge*, trans. B. Wall and M. R. Adamson (London: G. Bles, 1937), 221).

[80] *Existence and the Existent*, 28–30. It has been objected that Maritain's emphasis on a direct intuition of being is contrary to Gilson's view, according to which we only ever see 'Being' as an abstraction from sensory experience. Yet Gilson too speaks of our knowledge of Being as issuing from 'a simple seeing that is, for an instant, immobile'. See Prouvost, 'Étienne Gilson–Jacques Maritain'.

But what is this *Being*? *What*, i.e. what essence, do we know in apprehending 'Being' as such as the ultimate ground and goal of beings? It would seem that unless this question can be answered, talk about God as Being is simply going to grind to a halt in tautology, as if all we could say about God is that God is God—'I am that I am'—and nothing further. At one point this seems to be Gilson's conclusion: 'all that can be said about Him is, *He is*'.[81]

To say of something that it 'is' may seem to be the most basic thing we need to say about anything. We cannot say anything about cows, unless we know that cows 'are', and whatever else we say about cows will necessarily depend on what we can find out about actually existing cows. And yet merely to say of something that it *is* without saying anything more about *what* it is really to say nothing at all. We can imagine a conversation with a 3-year old that might go something along these lines: 'Hello, what's that you're looking at?' 'It's a cow.' 'Oh! And how do you know it's a cow?' 'Because that's what it is.' 'Yes, but what makes it a cow and not a crocodile?' 'Because that's what it is, silly.' If it is indeed a 3-year old being talked to, we might assume that the reason he or she won't say anything more about it is because they really don't know any more about it. If we were speaking with an adult, we would assume that they were wilfully concealing what they know about the differences between the specific properties of cows and crocodiles. We would assume that, even if the average adult couldn't come up with a specialist definition of what it is that makes a cow a cow and not some other kind of animal, they would nevertheless know enough about a cow to tell us that, for example, it's a four-legged, cloven-hoofed, herbivorous, horned mammal, etc.—which means that it therefore can't be a crocodile, since crocodiles share only one of these attributes with cows. Simply to define something in terms of its being what it is, is tautological: a cow is a cow because it's a cow; a rose is a rose is a rose. This might be the ultimate fall-back position of the 3-year-old and might occasionally work as poetry, but it is to confuse the existential use of 'to be', as when we say that something is or exists, with a predicative use, when we predicate, say, piebald-ness or hornedness of the cow, or pinkness and a divine scent of the rose, thereby extending our knowledge beyond the bare assertion of being.

The point could be made more formally by saying that a pure ontology, the pure determination of knowledge in terms of Being, would also be pure tautology.[82] This, however, seems unsatisfactory, and not only with regard

---

[81] *Being and Some Philosophers*, 180. However, note Anthony Kenny comment that '"God is…" …is just an incomplete sentence. So interpreted, the incommunicable name… seems to be just an ill-formed formula' (*Aquinas on Being*, 111).

[82] Heidegger interestingly acknowledges and accepts the charge of tautology which, he says, is precisely connected with the need of phenomenological description. See M. Heidegger, *Seminare* (*Gesamtausgabe*, vol. xv) (Frankfurt am Main: Klostermann, 2005), 399.

to cows and roses. It also seems to underperform in the case of less tangible topics, such as God: for when we talk about God, don't we want to say *something*, and not merely to reiterate an empty tautology? How can talking about God as Being be saying anything? So what can we say more precisely about the relationship between the ineffable divine substance and the divine essence that defines the substance and makes it known *as God, as this actual, real Being who is not any other kind of Being but precisely this unique divine Being?* One aspect of the answer to this question is the Thomist principle of the absolute simplicity of divine Being. However, the key issue is found in further reflection on the relationship between Being, essence, and existence.

If we return to the 'hermeneutics of suspicion' that Gilson practises on the varieties of philosophy that he surveys in *Being and Some Philosophers*, we see that despite their many differences the common deficiency of all those philosophies that in one way or another fall short of the Christian ideal—from Plotinus to Kierkegaard via Avicenna, Scotus, Suarez, and Hegel—is that they fail to demonstrate the intrinsic intelligibility of being, whether because they divide essence from existence or subsume the one into the other. If we are to be thoroughly assured as to the reliability of our knowledge we need to be able to close the circle of essence and existence in such a way that we see the one in the other and the other in the one. To borrow from the Christological formula of Chalcedon, we need to see essence and existence united but without confusion. Underlying and making possible all other acts of knowing there has to be a knowledge of *something*, some unique thing, in which essence and existence were not united as the result of an external will bringing a certain substance into existence (as occurs in creatures) but intrinsically—which, of course, is what Thomism finds in God. The divine name 'He who is', 'does not signify any particular form, but rather existence itself', says Thomas.[83] This, as he indicates, points back to what he has already established in *Summa theologiae* 1a.3.3 and 4; that 'God is to be identified with his own essence or nature' and that God is 'his own existence' or that 'God's substance is his existence' (. . . *quod subsistit in Deo est suum esse*). In these terms the divine Name tells us both *who* God is and *what* God is and in such a way that a certain definite content, a 'what', is ascribed to the 'who' whilst the 'what' is itself qualified in a distinctive and unique way.

The implication of this for the relationship between God and creatures is not that God is a kind of common being underlying or implicit in all creaturely relationships, but precisely the reverse, that, as Gilson puts it,

---

[83] *Summa theologiae*, 1a.13.11.

'supreme and unique individuality necessarily belongs to Him, and He *is* He, precisely because He alone is "to be" in its absolute purity'.[84] Only in this distinctness and individuality is God to be known both as creator in the beginning and as the object of the eternal beatific vision in the end. As such, God cannot be regarded as a kind of passive essence that simply is what it is but, as Kerr expounds Gilson, as being somehow verbal, 'a *doing* word, a word that designates an *act*.'[85] It was precisely the fault of how Thomism developed after Thomas, e.g., in Cajetan and Suarez, that it forgot this distinctness and individuality and reduced 'Being' to a kind of general term—a tendency that would, in Gilson's view, lead to a neglect of the proper relation between God and world.[86] As the sole being whose essence is 'to be' God does not stand in the same relation to essence as do creatures. Divine being is therefore not to be subsumed under some kind of essentiality:

> If God is *esse*, He is He Whose own 'to be' constitutes His own essence. Hence both His unicity and His singularity. Fully posited by its 'to be,' essence here entails neither limitation nor determination. [Whereas] finite essences always entail both limitation and determination, because each of them is the formal delimitation of a possible being.[87]

As we have already seen, genuine knowing is never simply a matter of a mental operation in which an essence is conceived without reference to the actual or possible existence of what I know. If I really know something (and don't just surmise it), I know its being 'in' its essence. It is not a case of 'my intellect conceives its essence', but, quite simply, 'I know it.'[88] At the same time it is the 'limitation' and 'determination' of the essence that make it possible for my knowledge to be articulated in a distinct and coherent way. This is not only true of things such as trees and cows, but also of human beings in their

---

[84] *Being and Some Philosophers*, 177. Karl Barth, of course, wished to put Reformed Dogmatics on a properly theological basis and to distinguish it from what he saw as the Catholic subservience to human philosophy. But Gilson also insists on the distinctiveness and priority of knowledge of God in relation to knowledge of creatures and there would seem to be nothing in his argument that would contradict Barth's insistence on God's Being as truly knowable only in the light of his self-revelation.

[85] *After Aquinas*, 83. The understanding of God's being as flowing from God's act would be a further point of commonality with Barth. See the whole §28 of *Church Dogmatics* II.1 (pp. 257–321).

[86] This, of course, is also a view more recently popularized by Radical Orthodoxy. Gilson's view raises the interesting further question as to whether Heidegger's account of the history of the forgetting of Being in the West is right to see Thomas as guilty of having overlooked the 'ontological difference' or whether, in this case, Heidegger is confusing a degenerate version of Thomism with the thing itself. For further discussion of Heidegger's relation to Thomism, see Ch. 3 below.

[87] *Being and Some Philosophers*, 183.

[88] See *Being and Some Philosophers*, 206–7.

personal reality. To be a person is possible only in association with 'an essence, an essential structure', a person is a substance, and is real and knowable only as such.[89]

But what about knowledge of God? Again, only even more radically, we encounter the twofold claim that whilst God's actual Being is not reducible to, nor limitable or determinable in terms of, any particular essence, nature, or quiddity, a certain 'what' is nevertheless going to have to be brought into play if we are to be able to say anything about God and, indeed, to say anything *true* about God. Therefore, whilst Gilson's entire argument can, on the one hand, be seen as arguing against the reduction of knowledge of God to knowledge of a mere essence or concept of God, it is also, on the other hand, a vindication of the possibility of knowing God in a concrete, propositionally articulated way. 'In fact, being itself is neither existence nor essence; it is their unity', Gilson writes.[90] Or, as Maritain puts it, existence is not an essence, but knowledge directed towards essences gives an analogy for what he calls the 'super-intelligible' knowability of existence.[91] Nevertheless, existence, above all divine existence, cannot be defined: commenting on Siger of Brabant's misreading of Thomas, Gilson remarks that in addressing the question 'What is existence?' Thomas 'gives the impression of trying to define existence, although as a matter of fact he is merely pointing to it'.[92]

But what links such pointing to that which is being pointed to? How does the statement ('x is y') relate to, represent, or make present to me, to the actual I who knows, the reality of that which is said in it? A similar question arises in relation to Maritain's statement that every judgement, including the kinds of judgements involved in any statements about God, 'affirms existence, it projects into it, as effected or effectible outside the mind, the objects of concept apprehended by the mind. In other words, when the intellect judges, it lives intentionally...'[93] But, then, how are we to know whether the

---

[89] *Essence and the Existent*, 87.

[90] *Being and Some Philosophers*, 209.

[91] *Essence and the Existent*, 28 and 43–4. Again, this seems to be entirely congruent with the position of Lonergan, who asserts that 'being is intelligible. It is neither beyond nor apart nor different from the intelligible. It is what is to be known by intelligent grasp and reasonable affirmation. It is the objective of the detached and disinterested desire to inquire intelligently and to reflect critically; and that desire is unrestricted' (*Insight*, 652). The full significance of this statement is seen when, a few pages later, Lonergan states that 'it is one and the same thing to understand what being is and to understand what God is' (ibid. 658).

[92] *Being and Some Philosophers*, 67.

[93] *Essence and the Existent*, 27. It has been objected to me that the implication that I draw from these statements by Gilson and Maritain, namely, that there is a kind of 'distance' between the knowing mind and its intentional object, is alien to Thomas himself, since, on his account, when the mind knows something it actualizes the object's essential knowability so as to unite knowing and being in a single event. However, given that the human mind is never itself purely

intention involved in any particular statement is fulfilled, whether the projection of the statement into existence is more than projection, whether it is, in fact, a statement of what is the case?[94]

Such questions force themselves on us even in the case of purely this-worldly knowledge, and both science and philosophy have developed complex strategies for dealing with them. If I want to know whether this is 'really' a tree of the species 'x', the botanist will explain to me how species 'x' may be differentiated from all other species of tree so that I can be assured that 'Yes, this really is an x'; or, if my anxiety is about whether there really is anything at all out there at all, non-sceptical philosophers are also at hand to offer their services. But because of the uniqueness of the relationship between existence and essence in the case of God, something rather more would seem to be demanded in matters of theology.

APOPHATICISM

At this point, and in order to do justice to both Augustinian and Thomist traditions, we need to address the question of apophaticism or negative theology. Even a rather common-sense approach might object—and might

---

active in relation to the divine mind, but always in some degree merely potential, the inhabitants of the sublunary world would seem condemned always to be falling somewhat short of an absolute identity of thought and being in any given act of knowledge. This would be the case even with regard to knowledge of creatures, since fully to know a creature would be to know it as it is according to the knowledge with which God knows it for what it actually is. Creatures really are and only really are what God knows them to be. *Summa theologiae* Ia, Q. 85.2, which has been cited against my position, seems rather to support it, in that it argues against the idea of any 'pure' knowing on the part of human beings that might dispense with a process of abstraction. Our knowledge is always mediated, and to that extent held at a distance from its object. In relation to Gilson, it is moreover central to his thought that the individual stands in a relation of real difference both to other creatures and pre-eminently to God. I really do know the creature for what it is and I may, one day, really come to know God as he is, but this does not collapse the ontological difference between myself, other creatures, and God.

[94] Similar questions arise for Tillich when he tries to account for how we know the presence of Being-Itself. His answer involves distinguishing between two ways of communicating meaning. The first is that of signs, purely conventional means of signification that, in relation to the Aristotelian tradition, could be said to serve the definition of the 'what' of an entity. The second is that of the symbol, of which Tillich says that 'the symbol participates in the reality of that for which its stands', so that a specifically religious symbol would participate 'in the power of the divine to which it points' (*Systematic Theology*, i. 265). For discussion of the relationship between the Thomist doctrine of analogy and Tillich's theory of the symbol see George F. McLean, 'Symbol and Analogy: Tillich and Thomas', in T. O'Meara and C. D. Weisser, *Paul Tillich in Catholic Thought* (London: Darton, Longman and Todd, 1965), 145–83.

have been objecting for some time—that the argument that Christian theology requires any kind of metaphysical underpinning obscures the theologically basic recognition of what Kierkegaard would call the 'infinite qualitative difference' between God and human beings. Whether we start from faith or from the standpoint of what our contemporary world understands as science, the most important thing we are able to say about God is surely that we cannot know God. But although Barth's adoption of Kierkegaard's phrase as a key to his interpretation of Paul's Letter to the Romans would make it one of the defining topics of early to mid-twentieth-century theology, the thought is not new. At the beginning of Book V on the Trinity (a text we have already visited in connection with Augustine's doctrine of being), Augustine acknowledges that 'From now on I will be attempting to say things that cannot altogether be said' and asks for his readers' forgiveness for the inadequacies that will necessarily dog his account.[95] Similarly, having supposed that in order to seek God we must in some way already know of him, like the woman in the biblical parable searching for her lost coin,[96] Augustine concludes that, after all, God is not 'in' the memory, but it is only 'in' God himself, 'above' us (*in te supra me*), that divine truth illuminates the mind.[97]

Augustine, as he acknowledged, drew many of his philosophical resources from Neoplatonism, and Neoplatonism itself already shows a strongly marked tendency to apophatic or negative theology (i.e., 'knowing' God by drawing attention to the difference between God and creatures). However, the negative theology of Neoplatonism develops Plato's statement in *The Republic* that the Good is even 'beyond' Being (*epekeina tēs ousias*)[98] in such a way as to suggest that since the realm of beings and the realm of the knowable are coterminous,[99] the supreme principle is unknowable because it is beyond Being or has no Being.[100] Being itself is only an approximation to this first principle. In this vein, the author generally referred to as Pseudo-Dionysius might be taken as reflecting a Platonizing influence when, in his work *The Divine Names*, he asks:

How then can we speak of the divine names? How can we do this if the transcendent surpasses all discourse and all knowledge, if it abides beyond the reach of mind and of being, if it encompasses and circumscribes, embraces and anticipates all things while

---

[95] *The Trinity*, 189.
[96] *Confessions*, X, 18.
[97] Ibid. 27. One amongst many virtuoso statements by Augustine of the paradoxes to which this situation leads is found in *Confessions*, I, 4.
[98] Plato, *The Republic*, 509b6.
[99] Plotinus, *Enneads*, III, 8.
[100] See, e.g., ibid. VI, 8.

itself eluding their grasp and escaping from any perception, imagination, opinion, name, discourse, apprehension, or understanding? How can we enter upon this undertaking if the Godhead is superior to being and is unspeakable and unnameable?[101]

Although Scripture offers an abundance of divine Names, even the divine Name given to Moses at the burning bush—so decisive for Augustine and for Aquinas—is to be understood as intrinsically incomprehensible, as a name above every name, and therefore no name.[102]

Dionysius' mystical theology would have a pervasive effect on the theology of the Middle Ages, an effect discernible in works of a practical and devotional kind, such as *The Cloud of Unknowing*, as well as in more formal theological work, including that of Thomas himself. Taking seriously Dionysius' objection that, since 'it is the knowledge we have of creatures that enables us to refer to God', Thomas seems to accept that 'these words do not express the divine essence as it is in itself'.[103] Nevertheless, he persists in asking whether any of the names we apply to God can be applied to the divine substance. He concludes that words such as 'good', 'wise', 'life', and 'Being' do apply in this way, although because our understanding of what is meant in such an application is constricted by the horizons of our creaturely being, we understand what we are meaning by them only imperfectly. They do properly apply to God, only in a 'more excellent' manner than we can understand—which Thomas takes to be the point of Dionysius' denials.[104] 'It is impossible to predicate anything univocally of God and creatures'—yet we can speak of God analogically or in a twofold manner (*dupliciter*).[105]

Thus Thomas hopes to escape having to reject Being as a proper name for God and, for Gilson, it was crucial that he did so. If God is beyond Being and Being is thereby reduced to the status of the highest creature, this, he says, is 'absolutely inconsistent with the mental universe of Christian thinkers, in which being cannot be the first of all creatures for the good reason that it has to be the Creator Himself, namely, God...logically speaking, one cannot

---

[101] Pseudo-Dionysius, 'The Divine Names', in *The Complete Works*, trans. C. Luibheid (New York: Paulist Press, 1987), 53.

[102] Ibid. 54. See also idem, 'The Mystical Theology', '[The supreme Cause] falls neither within the predicate of nonbeing nor of being. Existing beings do not know it as it actually is and it does not know them as they are. There is no speaking of it, nor name nor knowledge of it' (*The Complete Works*, 141).

[103] *Summa theologiae*, 3, Q. 12, 13.1.

[104] *Summa theologiae*, 3, Q. 12, 13.3. Whether this is a correct understanding of negative theology is relevant to Derrida's denial that deconstruction was, in fact, a form of negative theology. Curiously, one might conclude that Thomas and Derrida are in agreement that the 'negative' element in Dionysius is not really the ultimate point of his discourse. For further discussion see Ch. 5 below.

[105] *Summa theologiae*, 3, Q. 12, 13.5.

think at one and the same time, as a Neoplatonist and as a Christian'.[106] This, Gilson says, marks the fault-line that runs not only between Platonism and Christianity and between various forms of Islamic philosophy and Christianity, but within Christianity itself, when Christian theologians absorbed too much Plotinus, starting with Plotinus' Latin translator Marius Victorinus.[107]

Yet the matter still seems under-explained. In any case, whilst not forgetting the apophatic markers that accompany both Augustinian and Thomist traditions, two distinct possibilities for understanding the analogical relation of beings and names to God immediately present themselves. According to the first, which Gilson sees as Augustine's view, there is said to be a kind of intuition of the divine Being in creaturely being, although it is a confused and distorted intuition. Thus, whenever we see some truth, we also see Truth, i.e. divine Truth, in, with, and under it. We do so because only in the power of divine illumination is it possible for us to know anything at all.[108] According to the second way of understanding analogy, our knowledge of creatures has a relative independence vis-à-vis the knowledge of God, but provides the material out of which we weave our representations of God.[109] But in each case, since what we know when we know any entity is above all its Being, it is precisely this knowledge of Being in, with, and under our experience of creatures that—to go back to Gilson's appeal to an act of pointing—points us in the right direction.

But how far does this really take us? Mindful both of the original difference between creature and Creator and also of the further difference in their relationship brought about by the Fall, how can we know what is preserved and what is lost when words are 'transferred' from the creaturely to the divine realm? How can we ever know in just what respect God's Being is like worldly being, and in what respect unlike? Both the negations we might invoke at this point—immortal, invisible, infinite, etc.—and the positives—more excellent, pre-eminent, etc.—seem too general to convey anything concrete. Wouldn't it be not only more consistent but more meaningful to stick with the denials of the Platonists? Hasn't the Thomist set himself too hard a task? Maritain, at least, is candid enough to say that as far as this life is concerned, the only

---

[106] *Being and Some Philosophers*, 31.

[107] Ibid. 31 ff.

[108] See E. Gilson, *The Christian Philosophy of St Augustine*, trans. L. E. M. Lynch (London, Gollancz, 1961). This seems to be a point of tension between Maritain and Gilson, since the former also appears to affirm some kind of 'intellectual intuition' such that in knowing the creature one also intuits something of the divine Being, thereby providing a sure ground for knowledge in general. However, see n. 80 above.

[109] Although, NB, de Lubac's insistence that the true Catholic view never allows for a sphere of creaturely existence entirely independent of God.

assurance we can have that we are pointing in the right direction is the testimony of the mystics, i.e., of those who have been blessed with a direct vision—but they in turn speak only of an 'unknowing' that transcends all possible knowledge.[110]

We are in a realm of paradoxes. For whether we start from the Platonic-Augustinian or from the Thomist model, God, qua Creator, is the basis of all possible knowledge of creatures and truly to know creatures would be to know them as God knows them.[111] Real knowledge of creatures is possible only because creatures have been made knowable by God, and really to know them as they are is to know them as they are known by God. This suggests that we ought to begin with God and that we can make no real progress until we know something of God and of the divine Being. Yet God is unknowable, infinitely, qualitatively different. So how are we to break out of this circle? Where to begin? Where could we begin—except where we are, in the midst of the created order? To the extent that we have the possibility of knowing Being, it would seem that in the first instance—and, again, this would be equally true of Augustinian and Thomist models—we must therefore direct our attention to the beings that encounter us in our creaturely, worldly way of being. Where else, how else might we begin? But how can we even know the being of creatures? This question is philosophical because, as the history of philosophy demonstrates, it has always been possible to question just what it is we know in knowing entities and to ask whether what we know is the entities themselves or our mental images of them: how, then, might we find assurance as to the being of those creatures we seem to know?[112] But this question is also theological since, if God is the ground of all possible Being, it seems that we can never adequately know the being of anything without first of all knowing the being of God.

One answer that the history of philosophy has given is that Being can be known only on the basis or in the light of Being's own presence to us. The

---

[110] It is noteworthy that in *Method in Theology* Lonergan incorporates 'unknowing' more prominently into the bases of his theological programme. Thus, he writes that 'the primary and fundamental meaning of the name God...is the term of an orientation to transcendent mystery...So far from lying within the world mediated by meaning, it is the principle that can draw people out of that world and into the cloud of unknowing'—only he immediately adds that the fact that the world is mediated by the questions posed to it by our intelligence nevertheless gives us confidence in its having an intelligent ground. See B. J. F. Lonergan, *Method in Theology* (London; Darton, Longman, and Todd, 1971), 342.

[111] See Augustine, *Confessions*, XII, 38: 'We therefore behold these things which you have made because they are, but they are because you see them.'

[112] Of course, the 'answer' to the question encompasses virtually every twist and turn of the West's two and a half thousand years of philosophizing, a task we seem to be still far from finished with.

ultimate ground of knowledge is or can only ever be an actual encounter with what is there to be known. With regard to the knowledge of creatures, this might seem questionable. After all, I don't have to have been there myself to have known that John was in Paris yesterday since there are all sorts of other ways by which I could arrive at the correct judgement that John was indeed in Paris yesterday. Without launching into a possibly endless sequence of responses and counter-responses, however, it seems that, for the kind of theological view found in both Augustine and Thomas, some such appeal to presence is, in the end, unavoidable. Someone has to have seen John there or some DNA trace left on a park bench if I am to be assured of the fact of his having really been there. But this is all the more so in the case of God since, if salvation is defined in terms of a direct vision of God capable of transforming our very being into an immutable joy in the image and likeness of God's own eternal joy, then the real presence of the divine Being is indeed the ultimate term and ground of all possible knowledge.

Yet, starting from where we are now, it seems that whether we are thinking of creatures or of God the presence of what is to be thought is elusive. 'What' it is we know can be defined and debated, but how do we ever know whether this 'what' is grounded in the actual existence, the real being of an entity or ensemble of entities? We have heard Gilson and Maritain referring to the verbal sign as pointing to or intending the Being that gives it meaning, but it seems that there is a certain distance to be traversed between the sign and what it signifies, between our intention and its object. Is this distance merely an empty space such that it presents no obstacle or distortion in our view of Being? Thus understood, our verbal signs might well be taken as pointing—under optimal conditions—directly to what they serve to make present or to what is indeed actually present and to which they direct our attention. But is it so simple or does the distance to be traversed introduce an element of opacity into our relation to Being? Does it invite or obstruct, facilitate or undermine the progress of our minds towards Being? And how great a distance is it? Is the Being at which we aim near at hand or far away? And if it is far, is it so far as to be altogether beyond our horizon of knowing? What lies between us and the kind of openness to the presence of being in which the creature is known for what it is and a passage is opened towards knowledge of divine Being, whether by way of intuition or analogy? What possibilities do we really have here and now to experience and to know Being in its self-authenticating presence? Such questions will guide the following enquiry and, in giving them this role, I suggest that they properly take precedence over the question of analogy itself. For how can we extol an analogy of Being between created and uncreated Being if we do not yet know how Being can at all be represented, spoken, or known?

2

Presence and Distance

INTRODUCTION

We are seeking to clarify the possibility of a presence to Being that might provide a foothold for an analogical knowledge of the saving vision of God.[1] In the last chapter we saw how the topic of Being did not become central to the Christian theological tradition solely by virtue of its metaphysical credentials but also because it contributed to understanding the meaning of human salvation. In a similar manner, we shall see how, although it too can be formulated in purely philosophical terms, the theme of presence also carries a certain religious charge. In a very preliminary manner this can be discerned in the way in which, as we have been seeing, coming face to face with the presence of the God has been widely understood as defining the final state of redemption to which all Christian souls aspire. A further indication of the kind of religious force the term is capable of arousing can be seen in debates as to the nature of Christ's presence in the Eucharist or in the role of relics in making the healing power of the saint present in the community.[2] It can almost seem as if a 'sense of presence' is somehow salvific of itself. And, as George Steiner has argued, this is likely to be especially true when a culture (such as ours) feels itself as pervaded by a quality of 'secondariness' that, in turn, seems indicative of a deep spiritual malaise.[3] 'Presence' in this sense can also be taken as expressing what many feel has been lost to modern society by what Max Weber called the disenchantment of the world subsequent

---

[1] Or, in Augustinian terms, finding within such presence an implicit intuition of the divine Being in, with, and under the creaturely appearance—a divine Being that would be nearer to us than we are to ourselves.

[2] See Peter Brown, *The Coming of the Saints* (Chicago: Chicago University Press, 1981), ch. 6 'Potentia' (pp. 106–27).

[3] See George Steiner, *Real Presences* (London: Faber, 1989). For a theological discussion of Steiner's argument see Ingolf U. Dalferth, *Becoming Present: An Inquiry into the Christian Sense of the Presence of God* (Leuven: Peeters, 2006), 43–52. An earlier theological treatment from which much can still be learned is John Baillie, *The Sense of the Presence of God* (London: Oxford University Press, 1962).

on the Industrial Revolution, but still sought by those who look for its 're-enchantment'.[4]

But what is 'presence'? In the third of his lectures on *The Varieties of Religious Experience*,[5] 'The Reality of the Unseen', William James speaks of human consciousness as having 'a sense of reality, a feeling of objective presence, a perception of what we may call "something there," more deep and more general than any of the special and particular "senses" by which the current psychology supposes existent realities to be originally revealed'.[6] If religion is able convincingly to appeal to this 'reality-feeling' (as he also calls it) then it would be able to command belief, even though (as he also says) the objects of that belief might be indefinable in terms of 'whatness'. However, it soon becomes clear that although this *sense* for reality is supposed to be deeper and more general than any of the particular senses at play in the normal cognition of objects, it is nevertheless active only in relation to quite specific objects. Thus James's examples begin with the case of hallucinations, in which the subject may have a 'consciousness of a presence'. But this is not a matter of an everyday object (as, e.g., in Heidegger's example of the tree[7]) or of the world itself—experiences that belong to the common life-world of human beings—becoming present in a more than usually vivid and unmediated way. Rather it seems to be a way of gaining access to a peculiar class of objects that can only be cognized through this particular capacity: it is the presence of what subjects describe as 'the thing', or a deceased person, or a 'foreign presence'—and it is to the series of such experiences of presence that James adds the sense of the presence of God.

In contrast to the kinds of instances of presence adduced by James, the experiences of presence we are now about to examine are not such as to require us to suppose a peculiar class of objects or exceptional capacities on the part of those who have them. On the contrary, they are experiences that are, in principle, always and everywhere open to all of us. In a world characterized by secondariness and disenchantment, claims to experiences of presence seem to promise the possibility of a more original, elementary, primordial or even just a more simple relation to the world and to ourselves. But even if, as a matter of fact, such experiences of presence are, for the most

---

[4] See, e.g., James Elkins and David Morgan (eds.), *Re-enchantment* (London: Routledge, 2008); Gordon Graham, *The Re-enchantment of the World: Art versus Religion* (Oxford: Oxford University Press, 2007); Suzi Gablik, *The Reenchantment of Art* (London: Thames and Hudson, 1992).

[5] This does not preclude the possibility that James too, in his own way, represents a basically Romantic sense of presence.

[6] William James, *Varieties of Religious Experience* (London: Collins, 1960), 73.

[7] See 'Presence in Philosophy: Categorial Intuition' below.

part, exceptional, those who invoke or witness to them typically believe that this is a more or less accidental state of affairs, and that whether we know it or not, the presence of being is always already with us, if only we knew how to see it.

ROMANTIC PRESENCE

Perhaps one of the most familiar occurrences of the term 'presence' in English literature is that found in Wordsworth's 'Lines composed a few miles above Tintern Abbey, on revisiting the banks of the Wye during a tour, 13th July 1798'. This full version of the title clearly underlines the point that those who bear testimony to a sense of presence do so as human beings utterly identifiable in terms of a particular time and a particular place. But if the title identifies the who, where, and when of the poem, what of the sense of presence itself? We read

> And I have felt
> A presence that disturbs me with the joy
> Of elevated thoughts; a sense sublime
> Of something far more deeply interfused,
> Whose dwelling is the light of setting suns,
> And the round ocean and the living air,
> And the blue sky, and in the mind of man:
> A motion and a spirit, that impels
> All thinking things, all objects of all thought,
> And rolls through all things.[8]

It is easy to read these lines as attempting to convey a 'religious' or 'spiritual' experience. Yet no special revelation on the part of some transcendent being is mentioned—only the sun, ocean, air, sky, and the 'mind of man'. Nor does the poem call on us to separate ourselves from the world. On the contrary, it leads to an increased love for 'meadows', 'woods', 'mountains', 'all that we behold of this green earth' and for what eye and ear receive and imagine. As Wordsworth will say several lines later, it is 'nature and the language of the sense' that lies behind such revelations, anchoring and guiding them. Wordsworth's 'Nature' is no abstract principle: it is *presence*, giving itself to the poet, pouring in through his sense organs, and irradiating his mind with the joy and the

---

[8] Quoted from W. Wordsworth, *Poems*, vol. i (London: Dent, 1955), 32–5.

light of simple presence. Nature is present in the 'beauteous forms' that, in an earlier passage of the poem, are said to grant

> That blessed mood
> In which the burthen of the mystery,
> In which the heavy and weary weight
> Of all this unintelligible world,
> Is lightened:—that serene and blessed mood,
> In which the affections gently lead us on,—
> Until, the breath of this corporeal frame
> And even the motion of our human blood
> Almost suspended, we are laid asleep
> In body, and become a living soul:
> While with an eye made quiet by the power
> Of harmony, and the deep power of joy,
> We see into the life of things.

Yet even this clairvoyant state does not imply a separation from the world: quietened by the beautiful forms of nature, 'we' are led on by the affections to a bodily sleep in which the 'living soul' by no means leaves the body (as in Paul's account of a mystical ascent to the 'third heaven') but continues to participate in the 'life of things'. It is a vision of the 'within' of things that reveals the reality of their worldly being or their very life. Far from involving a rejection of the world it invokes a return to the world's original source in nature and finds there an intelligibility that is lost in the social and political distortions of contemporary life—yet this 'intelligibility' in nature is not an intellectual act in any narrow sense, but a 'mood', a 'sense', produced by the 'affections' and powered by 'joy'.[9]

I shall return to this remarkable poem, but first I wish briefly to examine another key Romantic text, published the following year, namely, Schleiermacher's *Speeches on Religion*. Schleiermacher's *Speeches* offer a passionate statement of the immediate experience of the presence of Being and, as the sub-title indicates, do so as a specific counter to the world of the 'cultured despisers' of religion. In a key passage of the Second Speech, Schleiermacher describes what he calls 'the natal hour of everything living in religion'[10] which, he says is something potentially implicit in all experience: it is 'that first mysterious moment that occurs in every sensory perception, before intuition and feeling have separated, where sense and its objects have, as it

---

[9] It is, however, 'intellectual' in the very specific sense with which both Wordsworth and Coleridge endow the term.

[10] F. D. E. Schleiermacher, *On Religion: Speeches to its Cultured Despisers*, trans. R. Crouter (Cambridge: Cambridge University Press, 1988), 113.

were, flowed into one another and become one...'[11] As such, it is beyond language, inexpressible and utterly fugitive. 'It is as fleeting and transparent as the first scent with which the dew gently caresses the waking flowers, as modest and delicate as a maiden's kiss, as holy and fruitful as a nuptial embrace: indeed, not *like* these, but it *is itself* all of these.'[12] It is an 'image of the universe' that the soul embraces 'as the holy essence itself'.[13] As in Wordsworth's 'blessed mood' it is a moment of clairvoyance in which a vision of the very 'life of things' is granted: 'I lie on the bosom of the infinite world. At this moment, I am its soul, for I feel all its powers and its infinite life as my own; at this moment it is my body...'[14] and yet 'with the slightest trembling the holy embrace is dispersed, and now for the first time the intuition stands before me as a separate form; I survey it, and it mirrors itself in my open soul like the image of a vanishing beloved in the awakened eye of a youth.'[15]

Although Schleiermacher identifies such moments as the source of 'everything living in religion', his critics have from the beginning accused him of falling short of what Christian theology needs to say about the transcendent God and have asserted that the 'religion' of the Speeches is no more than the worship of the universe, intuited[16] and, as Schleiermacher also puts it, 'tasted' as an infinite source of life and joy. Leaving the quarrel between Schleiermacher and the dogmatists to one side, however, it is clear that, in these speeches at least, Schleiermacher is affirming what the Romantic poet also affirms: that in experiencing the lived 'presence' of nature or the infinite universe there is always an excess of experience and meaning over any purely theoretical content: thought and conceptualization always come too late to 'catch' the vanishing aura of presence.

In their closely related ways Wordsworth and Schleiermacher promise a way of accessing the fluid space between essence and being—but in doing so they also acknowledge that, by definition, it is not a space in which language will find it easy to operate. Everything that happens here seems to frustrate the attempt to say 'what it is', other than in the non-scientific language of poetry and art. What Schleiermacher certainly knows is that whatever he *says* is going

---

[11] F. D. E. Schleiermacher, *On Religion: Speeches to its Cultured Despisers*, trans. R. Crouter (Cambridge: Cambridge University Press, 1988), 112.

[12] Ibid. 112–13.

[13] Ibid. 113.

[14] Ibid.

[15] Ibid.

[16] He himself says that 'intuition of the universe' 'is the hinge of my whole speech' (ibid. 104), adding that 'to accept everything individual as part of the whole and everything limited as a representation of the infinite is religion. But whatever would go beyond that and penetrate deeper into the nature and substance of the whole is no longer religion, and will, if it still wants to be regarded as such, inevitably sink back into empty mythology' (ibid. 105).

on here will be a matter for continuing and open-ended ventures of interpre-tation.[17] When we have once let go of the primacy of essence and definition, we are released into an infinitely fluid, infinitely interpretable world—but his premiss is also that just because our experience cannot be condensed into single, simple, univocal statements, this does not mean that we can say nothing, a conviction to which his whole literary and pedagogical productivity bears witness.

ROMANTIC PRESENCE AND MODERNITY: THREE PARADIGMS

Wordsworth and Schleiermacher stand at the source of the theme of Roman-tic presence that pervades the literary, artistic, and religious culture of mo-dernity, and they did much to define the way in which it was subsequently experienced and articulated. I shall now follow this theme further by briefly examining three significant examples from the later nineteenth and early twentieth centuries: the poetry of Gerard Manley Hopkins, the paintings of Paul Cézanne, and the interpretation of Zen Buddhism popularized by D. T. Suzuki, taking them as representative of the understanding of presence in three of the great streams of modern culture: poetry, art, and religious experience.[18]

In addition to his importance as a poet—although precisely with reference to his poetry—Hopkins continues to have a classic status in modern religious thought.[19] That Hopkins's poetry is guided by and attempts to guide the reader towards an immediate sense of the being of entities in their bodily presence might be inferred from such programmatic-sounding statements as the following: 'Each mortal thing does one thing and the same: | Deals out that being indoors each one dwells; | Selves—goes itself; *myself* it speaks and

---

[17] This is evidenced not only at many points of the *Speeches*, but also in Schleiermacher's innovative contribution to modern hermeneutics.

[18] Other examples could, certainly, have been found, including references to such experiences in the writings of Tolstoy, Dostoevsky, and many other modern novelists and poets. It is, of course, by no means accidental that each of the three examples I have taken bears a more or less explicit affiliation to the inheritance of Romantic poetry and thought. This includes Suzuki, deeply imbued with the thought-world of German Idealism, not least of Schelling.

[19] See, for example, Hans Urs von Balthasar in idem, *The Glory of the Lord*, iii: *Lay Styles*, ed. J. Riches et al., trans. A. Louth et al. (Edinburgh: T. & T. Clark, 1986), 'Hopkins', 353–99. On von Balthasar's interpretation see the essays by Bernadette Ward and Fergus Kerr in O. Bychkov and J. Fodor (eds.), *Theological Aesthetics after von Balthasar* (Aldershot: Ashgate, 2008). See also P. Sheldrake, *Spaces for the Sacred* (London: SCM Press, 2001), 23–5.

spells, | Crying *Whát I dó is me: for that I came*' (from 'As kingfishers catch fire . . .'). But the poem is not simply the vehicle for a certain knowledge as to what 'each mortal thing' does: it also seeks to enact or to show how we experience beings as calling out to us what they are. The opening line conjures the fiery moment of perception in which the poet glimpses the dazzling presence of kingfishers and dragonflies, before, in its second stanza, the poem turns towards a vision of humanity as a revelation of Christ. Note that, in this second stanza, the 'just man' who is what he is by 'justicing', by enacting justice, is not simply an image or analogy of Christ but 'Acts in God's eye what in God's eye he is—Christ'.

What is programmatically explicit in 'As kingfishers catch fire . . .' is reflected in the way in which, throughout his poetic work, Hopkins strains words and phrases to and beyond breaking point in order (it seems) to show us the thing itself: the world 'charged with the grandeur of God', flaming out, 'like shining from shook foil' ('God's Grandeur'); 'The glassy peartree leaves and blooms, they brush | The descending blue; that blue all in a rush | With richness . . .' ('Spring'); 'Brute beauty and valour and act, oh, air, pride, plume, here | Buckle! AND the fire that breaks from thee then . . .' ('The Windhover'). Or, as if overwhelmed by the impossibility of finding words that might force us to see what he is saying, he simply pleads to us to look and see for ourselves: 'Look at the stars! look, look up at the skies! | O look at all the fire-folk sitting in the air', he urges us in 'The Starlight Night', going on in the second stanza to implore us to 'Look, look,: a May-mess, like on orchard boughs! | Look! March-bloom, like on mealed-with-yellow sallows!' It is as if the poet is trying to get us to relive our original experience of the tree, even if all he can ultimately do is exhort us to look, look, look, look, look, look, and look again.

That such verbal extravagance is strategically intended and is not just an accidental by-product of a kind of poetic intoxication with the sheer effervescence of language is widely believed to be evidenced by the poet's study of Duns Scotus. Summarizing those points of Scotist philosophy that are most relevant to Hopkins, W. H. Gardner writes in his introduction to the Penguin edition of Hopkins's selected poems and prose that 'Scotus attached great importance to individuality and personality. The difference, he said, between the concept "a man" and the concept "Socrates" is due to the addition to the specific nature (*humanitas*) of an individualizing difference, or final perfection, which makes "this man *this*" and not "that". To this final individualizing "form" . . . Scotus gave the name Thisness (*haecceitas*).'[20] Furthermore, he

---

[20] W. H. Gardner, 'Introduction' to *Poems and Prose of Gerard Manley Hopkins* (Harmondsworth: Penguin, 1953), pp. xxiii–xxiv. Although Gardner's comments certainly do not express

adds, Scotus allows the possibility that the mind cognizes this *haecceitas*, the singularity of the thing, prior to and indeed as the basis of any further universalized knowledge of it (i.e., of its essence, as opposed to its singular 'thisness'). Gardner associates this with Hopkins's distinctive theoretical and poetic concept of 'inscape' and the related term 'instress'. '... [I]nstress is not only the unifying force *in* the object; it connotes also that impulse *from* the "inscape" which acts on the senses and, through them, actualizes the inscape in the mind of the beholder... Instress, then is often the *sensation* of inscape—a quasi-mystical illumination, a sudden perception of the deeper pattern, order, and unity which gives meaning to external forms.'[21] It is not stretching a point to see this as close to what we shall later in this chapter hear in Heidegger's discussion of 'categorial intuition'[22]—but the point is not simply the theoretical position at issue but how it is performed when the poet attempts to make explicit or to re-enact the dynamic of inscape-instress in the poetry itself. He does not just recall those moments when he experienced such epiphanies but strives to make 'the dearest freshness deep down things' present to the reader. Yet, as Wordsworth already knew, such moments of vision are exceptions in the world as it is, for ours is a world in which 'men' habitually ignore the revelation of God's grandeur and 'all is seared with trade; bleared, smeared with toil; | And wears man's smudge and shares man's smell: the soil | Is bare now, nor can foot feel, being shod' ('God's Grandeur'). So much the more must the poet strain against the expectations of readers by transforming the very language in which he seeks to call them to a face-to-face with the sheer radiance of beings.

Turning now to Cézanne, Joachim Gasquet's *Memoir with Conversations* ascribes a not dissimilar concern with the 'thisness' of his subject matter to the Provençal painter. Although his expressed desire to 'copy nature' was nothing new in itself, Cézanne seems to have given it a particular force and urgency:

You either see a picture at once or you never see it at all. Explanations are no help. What's the point of making comments?... To write below a person what he's thinking and what he's doing is to admit that his thought and his intention are not conveyed by

---

the latest scholarship on Hopkins or Scotus, the multiple impressions through which this edition has passed probably make it one of the most influential texts in shaping how the poet has been received in the last sixty years. For a useful philosophical introduction to Scotus see Richard Cross, *Duns Scotus* (Aldershot, Ashgate, 1999).

[21] *Poems and Prose of Gerard Manley Hopkins*, p. xxi.

[22] Heidegger himself wrote his Habilitation thesis on Duns Scotus' doctrine of categories (although the text on which he based his study is now generally regarded as having been by Henry of Ghent); see M. Heidegger, *Die Kategorien- und Bedeutungslehre des Duns Scotus*, in idem, *Frühe Schriften* (*Gesamtausgabe*, vol. i) (Frankfurt am Main: Klostermann, 1978), 133–353.

the drawing and the colour. And wanting to force nature to say things, making trees twist and rocks frown, as Gustav Doré does, or even painting it like da Vinci, that's literature too. There's a logic of colour, damn it all! The painter owes allegiance to that alone. The stuff of our art is there, in what our eyes are thinking... If you respect nature, it will always unravel its meaning to you.[23]

Yet Cézanne seems also to have been painfully aware that, as a man of the nineteenth century, such a direct relation to nature was problematic. 'I'm no longer innocent,' he admits. 'We're civilized beings. Whether we like it or not, we have all the cares and concerns of classical civilization in our bones ... it's no longer possible to be ignorant today ... We start breathing our profession at birth. And do it badly.' As he says in the same passage, 'One no longer is. We come into the world armed with facility. Facility is the death of art and we must rid ourselves of it.'[24] But getting rid of facility seems to mean abandoning anything like what is customarily called an 'artistic' approach to the world. On the contrary, Cézanne suggests that we (he!) would do better to live in the world and relate to it like the Provençal peasants amongst whom he lived.

These people know what's been sown here and there along the road, what the weather will be like tomorrow, and if Sainte-Victoire has its cap on or not; they can smell it, the way animals do, just as a dog knows what a piece of bread is when he sniffs at it. They register only what's important to them. I don't really believe that most of them either know or sense that trees are green, and that this green is a tree, that this earth is red, and that these disintegrating reds are hills ... Without losing any part of myself, I need to get back to that instinct ... Confronted by a yellow, they spontaneously feel the harvesting activity required of them, just as I, when faced with the same ripening tint, ought to know instinctively how to touch in the corresponding colour on my canvas in order to obtain a square of waving corn. Touch by touch the earth would thus come alive. By tilling my field, I would start to grow a lovely landscape.[25]

Somehow, Cézanne hopes, he can get behind 'explanations', 'literature', and 'facility', to a face-to-face with things and that out of that face-to-face he can make something that will recreate it also for the viewer of the painting (as long as the latter doesn't in turn explain it or transform it into literature!). What he sees and what he shows in his painting is the moment before the advent of the 'what', the moment of vision prior to what is simply there to be seen being overlaid with essentiality. Yet, although Cézanne generally resists

---

[23] J. Gasquet, *Joachim Gasquet's Cézanne: A Memoir with Conversations*, trans. C. Pemberton (London: Thames and Hudson, 1991), 161. The 'conversations' are not, of course, stenographic records but what, in his translator's introduction, Christopher Pemberton calls 'an amalgam of first-hand and borrowed material' (p. 25). On the genesis and reliability of the text, see also Richard Shiff's introduction.
[24] *Cézanne*, 155.   [25] Ibid. 162.

Gasquet's repeated attempts to theorize his work, he does occasionally allow himself to use allusions to philosophy to clarify what he is about. Recalling a conversation about Kant, he adds:

What is there in common between a pine as it appears to me and a pine as it is in reality? If I were to paint that . . . Wouldn't it be the realization of that part of nature which lies before our eyes, presenting us with a picture? . . . Conscious trees! . . . And in this picture wouldn't there be a philosophy of appearance more generally accessible than all the tables of categories, all your noumena and phenomena. Seeing it, one would feel how everything is related to oneself, to man . . . nature isn't at the surface; it's in depth. Colours are the expression, on this surface, of this depth. They rise up out of the earth's roots: they're its life, the life of ideas.[26]

Whereas impressionist painting is popularly thought to have aimed at capturing the absolutely momentary fleeting sensory perception, Cézanne seems to have been seeking something more akin to Hopkins's revelation of the inscape. He speaks repeatedly in these conversations about sensation, yet the colour that he seeks to recreate in his work is not a simple product of the play of light and shade on the optic nerve: it is the revelation of the 'depth', the 'roots' of our lived relation to the earth. It is life, not just as an evanescent process, but as given to us in and as an always specific thisness—*this* colour, *this* set of relations between colours, Sainte-Victoire, as it is *this* day in *this* particular light but also as it *is*: its depth revealed in its colour. Nor is it accidental that earlier in the passage just cited, Cézanne speaks of that which he is seeking to contact and to communicate in his work as a 'cosmic religious feeling, which moves and improves me'.[27]

These religious and artistic experiences of two nineteenth-century Catholics seem to be in accordance with some of the central insights of Zen Buddhism, as expounded by D. T. Suzuki, who perhaps did more than anyone to popularize Zen in the West in the twentieth century. The theme we have been considering in such terms as inscape and thisness comes to expression in Suzuki's treatment of the Buddhist term *tathatā*, which is variously translated 'thatness',[28] 'suchness',[29] 'isness',[30] and, as translating the Japanese equivalent of *tathatā*, *kono-mama*, 'I am that I am'—a translation that is especially thought-provoking in the context of reflections on the Western tradition of

---

[26] Ibid. 166.
[27] Ibid. 166. It is hard not to be reminded of Arnold's definition of God as 'a power, not ourselves, that makes for righteousness'. We shall return to Cézanne and to his significance for Maurice Merleau-Ponty's philosophical contribution to the question of Being in Ch. 6 below.
[28] D. T. Suzuki, *Studies in Zen Buddhism (First Series)* (London: Ryder, 1958), 92.
[29] Idem, *Studies in Zen Buddhism (Second Series)* (London: Ryder, 1985), esp. 231–5.
[30] Idem, *Zen and Japanese Culture* (New York: Bollingen, 1969), 16–17.

thinking of God as Being.[31] In formal terms, it is what is revealed in the moment of enlightenment (*satori*), the 'meaning hitherto hidden in our daily concrete experiences, such as eating, drinking, or business of all kinds'. And, Suzuki goes on to say, this meaning 'is not something added from the outside. It is in being itself, in becoming itself, in living itself . . . [It is] the "isness" of a thing, reality in its isness.'[32] Anthony Kenny would scoff—but Suzuki himself is well aware that such statements are open to charges of vacuity.

Some may say, 'There cannot be any meaning in mere isness.' But this is not the view held by Zen, for according to it, isness is the meaning. When I see into it I see it as clearly as I see myself reflected in a mirror. This is what made Hō Koji (P'ang Chü-shih), a lay disciple of the eighth century, declare: *How wondrous this, how mysterious! I carry fuel, I draw water.* The fuel-carrying or the water-drawing itself, apart from its utilitarianism, is full of meaning; hence its 'wonder,' its 'mystery.' Zen does not, therefore, indulge in abstraction or in conceptualization . . . *Satori* is emancipation, moral, spiritual, as well as intellectual. When I am in my isness, thoroughly purged of all intellectual sediments, I have my freedom in its primary sense.[33]

Living one's own isness is not only the basis of the specifically 'religious' manifestation of Zen, it also, as Suzuki adds, 'opens to the artist a world full of wonders and miracles'[34] and it is in Chinese and Japanese poetry, painting, craftwork, and martial arts that he finds some of the most expressive realizations of the relation to one's own isness. It is in relation to a haiku poem by the eighteenth-century Japanese poet Bashō that Suzuki makes an especially striking contrast between the vision underlying Western and Eastern ways of life. Bashō's poem concerns a small, flowering wild plant called the *nazuna*. It runs

> When closely inspected,
> One notices a nazuna in bloom,
> under the hedge.

Suzuki contrasts this with what might seem the not dissimilar vision and sentiment expressed in Tennyson's poem 'Flower in the Crannied Wall':

> Flower in the crannied wall,
> I pluck you out of the crannies,
> I hold you here, root and all, in my hand,
> Little flower—but *if* I could understand

---

[31] Idem, *Mysticism: Christian and Buddhist* (London: George Allen and Unwin, 1957), 143–58.

[32] *Zen and Japanese Culture*, 16.

[33] Ibid. 16–17.   [34] Ibid. 17.

> What you are, root and all, and all in all,
> I should know what God and man is.[35]

Suzuki suggests that Tennyson's frame of mind seems to have been close to the kind of vision counselled by Eckhart and other mystics. That is, it is an outlook on the world that is freed from the differentiation and relativity imposed by human concepts and categories and is thus able to see all things in their interconnectedness, yet, at the same time, sees them as focused in the immediate presence of just one manifestation of the world's 'wondrous' being. The Japanese poet too 'simply looks at the nazuna so insignificant and yet so full of heavenly splendour and goes on absorbed in the contemplation of the "mystery of being," standing in the midst of the light of eternity'.[36] Yet Suzuki also detects a decisive difference between the two poets and their underlying world-views. Tennyson's mind, he says, works analytically. The direction of his thinking is toward the externality or objectivity of things. Instead of leaving the flower as it is blooming in the cranny, Tennyson feels compelled to pluck it out and hold it in his hand. And, Suzuki adds, 'If he were scientifically minded, he would surely bring it to the laboratory, dissect it and look at it under the microscope; or he would dissolve it in a variety of chemical solutions and examine them in the tubes, perhaps over a burning fire.'[37] By way of contrast Bashō 'does not "pluck" the flower, he does not mutilate it, he leaves it where he has found it. He does not detach it from the totality of its surroundings, he contemplates it in its *sono-mama* state...'[38] In a concluding comment, Suzuki adds that the poet 'does not say a word about his inner feeling, every syllable is objective except the last two syllables, "*kana*." "*Kana*" is untranslatable into English, perhaps except by an exclamation mark, which is the only sign betraying the poet's subjectivity.'[39]

PRESENCE IN PHILOSOPHY: CATEGORIAL INTUITION

Can the kind of poetic, painterly, and mystical testimonies to the power of presence—'Romantic presence', we might call it—help us with regard to the

[35] Quoted from Alfred Lord Tennyson, *A Collection of Poems*, (ed.) Christopher Ricks (New York: Doubleday, 1972), 318.

[36] *Mysticism*, 101.

[37] Ibid.

[38] Ibid. 102.

[39] Ibid. 102–3. It is striking that the first personal pronoun occurs four times in six lines in Tennyson's poem, and on three of those four lines it is emphatically placed at the beginning of the line.

more philosophical question as to how we might imagine Being as being present in the act of knowing? One important attempt to answer this question is found in the philosophical investigations of Martin Heidegger. Especially pertinent are his 1925 lectures on *History of the Concept of Time*.[40] These not only helped prepare the ground for *Being and Time*, they also set out some of the basic philosophical clarifications that are presupposed but not in every case explained in that later work. In these lectures we see Heidegger offering an interpretation of phenomenology, but this is also a period in which he is repeatedly lecturing on Aristotle, and even if Aristotle is only rarely mentioned in the lectures it is clear that Heidegger has one eye on questions bequeathed to philosophy by the Greek thinker and on the way in which these questions were taken up in the Christian philosophy of the Middle Ages.[41] Indeed, as *Being and Time* will itself make clear, he is precisely trying to free the question of Being from what he regards as scholasticism's 'hardened tradition', in which the original possibilities of Greek ontology have been turned into a 'fixed body of doctrine'.[42] However, Heidegger's intention is not merely negative or polemical. Rather, he is precisely trying to get behind what has become hardened and fixed in scholasticism in order to arrive at a more adequate account of the situation of concrete knowledge of Being. If his path rapidly diverges from that of scholasticism, there is nevertheless a significant proximity in terms of the questions being asked. And, we may add, Heidegger is also a significant inheritor of the Romantic tradition, including not only the

---

[40] The theme is taken up again at the end of Heidegger's career in the 1973 Zähringen Seminar. See Martin Heidegger, *Seminare* (*Gesamtausgabe*, vol. xv) (Frankfurt am Main: Klostermann, 1986), especially 373 ff.

[41] With regard to his engagement with medieval Christian philosophy, Scotus has already been mentioned (see n. 19 above), but see also M. Heidegger, *Einführung in die Phänomenologische Forschung* (*Gesamtausgabe*, vol. xvii) (Frankfurt am Main: Klostermann, 1994), 'Rückgang auf die scholastische Ontologie: Das verum esse bei Thomas v. Aquin', 163 ff.; idem, *Geschichte der Philosophie von Thomas von Aquin bis Kant* (*Gesamtausgabe*, vol. xviii) (Frankfurt am Main: Klostermann, 2006). It is striking that another of Husserl's assistants, Edith Stein, explicitly embraced scholastic theology (or, as she called it, the 'perennial philosophy') and argued against Heidegger that his account was vitiated by not taking into account the division of body and soul, by confusing creatureliness with thrownness, by an inadequate account of sociality (including authority), by neglecting the possibility of life beyond death and of an eternal Being beyond time. Stein also draws attention to the fact that Christian doctrine does not merely ask the question of Being but has a certain definite teaching to give. See E. Stein, *Endliches und Ewiges Sein* (*Gesamtausgabe*, vols. xi/xii) (Freiburg: Herder, 2006), 445–99. Unfortunately the appendix in which this response is to be found is not translated in the English edition.

[42] M. Heidegger, *Being and Time*, trans. E. Robinson and J. Macquarrie (Oxford: Blackwell, 1962), 43, 44/22 (the last page number refers to the pagination of the first German edition, printed in the English edition).

poetry of Friedrich Hölderlin but also, amongst many other sources, Schleiermacher's *Speeches*.[43]

The relevant part of these lectures focuses on issues of intentionality and categorial intuition. Heidegger sees intentionality as one of the defining concepts of phenomenology and sees it as breaking the log-jam of a number of problems of philosophy clustered around questions about how we can be sure that knowledge 'really' represents the world as it is in itself, 'out there'. Whereas standard epistemology seems to assume a subject 'in here' and a world 'out there' and thus saddles itself with the problem of how they can be brought together, Heidegger claims that intentionality is not simply a matter of a certain subjective or epistemological comportment vis-à-vis the world but is 'a structure of lived experience'.[44] As such it precedes the abstract division of experience into subject and object, knower and known—divisions that burden the theory of knowledge with a sequence of insoluble dilemmas and have done so since at least the scholastic definition of truth as the adequation of the intellectual act and the thing itself (*intellectus* and *res*). But what, more specifically, can we say about this 'structure of lived experience'? '*Intentio* literally means *directing-itself-toward*. Every lived experience, every psychic comportment, directs itself toward something.'[45] Acknowledging that this may seem a merely trivial observation, Heidegger sees it as undercutting the kind of abstract divisions that have just been mentioned. The challenge, on this basis, is not how to bring together a subjective consciousness and a world of things or how to connect the knower with the thing known, but how to unfold and describe a 'relationship' that is always already given and that we cannot get back behind.[46]

Heidegger sets about showing the further dimensions of this relationship by looking at what he calls 'the exemplary case of naturally perceiving a

---

[43] See T. Kisiel and T. Sheehan, *Becoming Heidegger: On the Trail of his Early Occasional Writings, 1910–27* (Evanston, Ill.: Northwestern University Press, 2007), 86–91. Alexander S. Jensen, 'The Influence of Schleiermacher's Second Speech on *Religion* on Heidegger's Concept of *Ereignis*', *Review of Metaphysics*, 61/4/244 (June 2008), 815–26.

[44] M. Heidegger, *History of the Concept of Time*, trans. T. Kisiel (Bloomington, Ind.: Indiana University Press, 1985), 29. German edition: *Prolegomena zur Geschichte des Zeitbegriffs* (*Gesamtausgabe*, vol. xx) (Frankfurt am Main: Klostermann, 1979).

[45] *History of the Concept of Time*, 29.

[46] The word 'relationship' might, of course, be construed as already conceding too much to standard epistemology, since it implies a level of differentiation that is not, in fact, given in the intentional phenomenon itself. In this connection it is interesting that Heidegger himself notes that phenomenology need not be seen as refuting the medieval understanding of truth as the correspondence (*adaequatio*) of what is in the mind (*intellectus*) and the matter itself (*res*), but as deepening it (see ibid. 51). In other words, the medieval definition itself can be read as a particular interpretation of the structure of intentionality. See *Geschichte der Philosophie von Thomas von Aquin bis Kant*, 55–63.

thing',[47] i.e., looking at something such as a chair. The intentional act is not primarily about delivering a representation of the chair to consciousness: it is simply looking at the chair; it is the chair it is interested in, toward which it projects itself, which, quite simply, it intends. What I see when I see the chair is 'the chair itself. I see no "representations" of the chair, register no image of the chair, sense no sensations of the chair. I simply see *it*—it itself.'[48] At this point the person seeing the chair might be challenged to say *what* it is he sees, i.e., which chair it is, whether it is large or small, where it is situated, whether it is standing upright or has, perhaps, fallen over—i.e., to answer the questions that are reflected in the traditional Aristotelian list of categories. But one can also ask—and this is the question Heidegger is more interested in pursuing—how it is seen, or, as he puts it, 'in the way and manner of its being-perceived'.[49]

Aware that this probably sounds somewhat abstruse, Heidegger offers a simple example. I envisage a certain bridge. I can do this in a number of ways. I might, for example, be standing there looking at it. Or I might simply allude to it in a sentence such as 'the other day when I was crossing the bridge'. These are said by Heidegger to express, respectively, the bodily presence of the self-givenness of an entity and empty intending. When he further says that bodily presence is a 'superlative mode of the self-givenness of an entity'[50] this is not to denigrate empty intending, nor should the expression itself be taken as indicating an absence of content. On the contrary, the reference certainly refers to the bridge (the bridge itself, as in the previous example of the chair itself), but this reference lacks 'intuitive fulfilment', i.e., it's not 'there' when I talk about it to you today in the same way that it was 'there' when I stood and looked at it yesterday. Intuition, Heidegger says later, is the 'simple apprehension of what is itself bodily found just as it shows itself', although, as he immediately emphasizes, this is not to be taken as implying that sense perception is the only way in which we can intuit things.[51] Intuition and apprehension do not mean the influx of a mass of sense data into consciousness: they are the perceiving of the thing, the chair, the bridge, or, indeed, of a theoretical statement or mathematical formula. But for this to happen, it must be the case that even in its most primitive moments perception is never uninterpreted. I always see what I see in a certain way, as a certain thing, as this tree, as the meaning of this sentence. The intentional relation towards what is intended is always implicitly meaningful but this meaning is not the product of a subject reflecting on dumb experience 'after the event': rather, the meaning is what I intend, the thing I perceive or that is being said.

---

[47] *History of the Concept of Time*, 37.
[48] Ibid.   [49] Ibid. 40.   [50] Ibid. 41.   [51] Ibid. 47.

The resonances with the scholastic insistence on knowing as knowing an actual being are distinctly audible, nor is Heidegger so far from what is often referred to as the 'common sense' realism of Aristotle.[52] In any case, the basic conviction that is being articulated here would be an abiding feature of Heidegger's thought, as we can see if we turn to the lectures entitled *What is Called Thinking?* from 1951–2. There he traces the meaning of the word 'idea' back to the Greek *eidō* and explains that this means 'to see, face, meet, be face-to-face', a definition which he applies to a kind of encounter with the world that he contrasts with scientific and philosophical paradigms of knowledge: 'We stand outside of science. Instead we stand before a tree in bloom, for example—and the tree stands before us. The tree faces us. The tree and we meet one another, as the tree stands there and we stand face to face with it. As we are in this relation of one to the other and before the other, the tree and we *are*.'[53] We have, as he goes on to say, 'leapt' out of science and philosophy onto 'that soil upon which we live and die... the soil on which we really stand'.[54] 'Judged scientifically,' he adds, 'it remains the most inconsequential thing on earth that each of us has at some time stood facing a tree in bloom'[55]—and yet, he suggests, this rather 'inconsequential' commonplace experience is that it is not science and philosophy that determine the validity of our experience of the tree but rather vice versa. Since the dawn of philosophy in ancient Greece and down to the most advanced science and technology of the present day, 'thought has never let the tree stand where it stands'. But this, he seems to be proposing, is precisely the task of thinking today: to remind ourselves of the face-to-face awareness from which all our knowledge proceeds and to which—if it is to have any human value—it must be able to return.

Yet something seems to elude us in any such intentional act. When I see the yellow chair 'I can see the color yellow but not the *being*-yellow, *being*-colored... [a]nd this "being"... cannot be perceived.'[56] Even in the case when the entity is given in bodily presence, when I am standing there looking at it, seeing it as it is and for what it is, there is a dimension, referred to by such terms as 'is', 'being', 'unity', and 'thisness', that I do not see—or, Heidegger says, that I do not see in the manner of sensory perception. Yet, if the

---

[52] Heidegger gave many series of lectures on Aristotle in the 1920s. Some aspects of these will be considered in Ch. 4 below.

[53] M. Heidegger, *What is Called Thinking?*, trans. J. Gray and F. Wieck (New York: Harper, 1968), 41. German edition *Was Heißt Denken* (*Gesamtausgabe*, vol. viii) (Frankfurt am Main: Klostermann, 2002). For further discussion of this passage see A. Rudd, *Expressing the World: Skepticism, Wittgenstein, and Heidegger* (Chicago: Open Court, 2003), ch. 12.

[54] *What is Called Thinking?*, 41.

[55] Ibid. 42.

[56] *History of the Concept of Time*, 58.

basic principle of intentionality holds good, such categorical terms are given to us not as some kind of subjectively produced framework that we impose on events but as the matter of a certain kind of intuition that Heidegger calls 'categorial intuition'.

Let us go back a step. The simple intuition of the tree—the tree out there, in my garden—is, in Heidegger's parlance, the founding act. In relation to this found*ing* act, categorial intuition is describable as a found*ed* act, i.e., an act that presupposes or serves to articulate the primary act of simply seeing the tree. But the primacy of the founding act in its self-givenness and bodily presence is not 'presupposed' in a temporal sense, as if I first had an intuition of the tree and then subsequently interpreted it by passing my perception through the filter of a categorial intuition. In seeing the tree, I see it as this tree, as the tree that's there and, indeed, as 'a' tree and not a forest. The 'this', the 'there', and the singularity of the tree are not add-ons but are integral to the primary act. As Heidegger comments, these constitute an aspect of what has become known, thanks to Husserl, as the *Gestalt* of perception. Yet they are not simply that perception itself: they are features of the *how* of that perception, its 'as' (as in: I see that thing *as* a tree). Furthermore—and the question as to the relationship between essence and existence now starts to come back into view—there is a further kind of categorial act, namely, the acts that Heidegger calls 'acts of ideation', of which he says that they give 'the intuition of the universal', 'the idea', 'the species'. And, again, such acts of ideation are not simply added on to perception but give 'what is seen in the matters first and simply'.[57] Although it is the bodily presence of the tree (which, NB, comprises also my bodily presence to the tree, as well as the tree's presence to me) that fulfils my intention in a superlative way, I only see it as a tree by virtue of seeing it as an individual instantiation (*a* tree) of a universal essence (i.e., the concept 'tree'), as 'a' (i.e. one, singular) 'tree' (species, universal). Yet the universal is only ever given as founded in what Heidegger here calls the 'exemplary foundation' of a 'concrete individuation'.[58]

Reflecting on the significance of categorial intuition, Heidegger suggests that it offers an approach to understanding the reality of our experiences and to knowing them as experiences of beings, of things that *are* in a strong sense. He states: 'phenomenological research which breaks through to objectivity arrives at the form of research sought by ancient ontology. There is no ontology *alongside* a phenomenology. Rather, *scientific ontology is nothing but phenomenology.*'[59] As he then further argues, this also allows for a certain rethinking of the nature of the a priori. Whereas, at least since Kant, the a

---

[57] *History of the Concept of Time*, 66.   [58] Ibid. 67.   [59] Ibid. 72.

priori element in knowledge has been attributed to the mental forms that human beings spontaneously impose on their experience, the phenomenological approach offers a way of seeing the a priori as rooted in the structure of intentionality in such a way that it yields something more basic than the standpoint of the abstract epistemological subject, the seeker desiring to *know* Being. As Heidegger puts it, it is a 'title for being', 'a feature of the structural sequence in the being of entities, in the ontological structure of being'.[60] Does this then mean that we have answered the question as to the relationship between essence and existence and succeeded in showing how essence arises from and points to or articulates the being of the existing substance of which it is the essence? If so, then understanding the analysis of intentionality as an explication of the *how* of perception would mean that it was in this *how* that the *what* found its proper place and ground: that it was in seeing the thing *as it is* that I thereby see *what* it is—and vice versa: that in seeing *what* it is, I see it *as it is.*

Yet something still seems to be missing and we still seem to be operating in the domain of a set of claims rather than persuasive demonstration. As has been said, phenomenology does not seek to offer demonstrations of the kind that might satisfy analytic philosophers: phenomenological method relies not so much on analysis and argument as on description, and perhaps it is simply that the description given thus far remains too thin, too abstract really to do justice to anything that could really be called a categorial intuition of being. What we need—and what Heidegger himself knew he needed—is a thicker, more grounded description of the basic scenario in which Heidegger is setting his account of intentionality. In doing so, however, we encounter—as Heidegger himself encountered—features of this scenario that call its basic configuration into question.

PRESENCE-TO-BEINGS AND PRESENCE-TO-SELF

We have heard artistic, mystical, and philosophical testimonies to the possibility of experiencing the world in a mode of direct, unmediated presence that is also understood as an eminent source of artistic and religious living and, as such, is contrasted with the habits of mind formed by Western philosophical, scientific and civilizational concepts and practices. For the poets and the mystics, at least, reconnecting with the unmediated presence of the world is

---

[60] Ibid. 74.

already a kind of redemption, a return to Being in its plenitude and a radical conversion of the self from an isolated ego-consciousness towards a participative sense of the interconnectedness of the whole of reality. Yet this does not involve the obliteration of the self. In 'As kingfishers catch fire . . .' Hopkins makes clear that the ultimate instance of inscape is the revelation of what Dostoevsky called 'the man in man'. Cézanne speaks of his responsibility as an artist for the painterly transformation of the lived presence of things. Even Suzuki, whose Buddhism involves the denial of the substantial self of Western philosophy, allows a minimal sign of the poet's subjectivity—despite the fact that this can only be translated into English by an exclamation mark! Thus, in all three cases there is an implicit acceptance that attempting to communicate the experienced presence of the world will involve a self that communicates with other selves, whether in poems, paintings, or religious and philosophical expositions. Arguably, a thoroughly consistent advocate of a life lived in the sheer unmediated presence of Being would teach only by keeping silent, since the very process of putting presence into words would seem however minimally to overlay immediate experience with abstraction and differentiation, thereby falsifying the reality of presence. We shall return in a later chapter to issues of language and Being, and for now I note only that whether or not silence would be an exemplary response to presence, once one begins to speak about, to write of, or perhaps even to paint the experience of presence one has already broken the silence. Didn't Schleiermacher and Wordsworth already warn us that concepts, thinking, and language always come too late? As thinking and speaking beings, isn't our relation to the full presence of Being a case of something that is 'always already lost'?

The issue here is essentially that of the relationship between presence and selfhood, and to examine the interrelationship of these two topics more closely and to see how this might also relate to the possibility of a sense of the presence of God, I turn now to the later religious writings of the Danish Christian writer and thinker Søren Kierkegaard and, in particular, to the discourses entitled *The Lily of the Field and the Bird of the Air* and to *The Sickness unto Death* (both published in the summer of 1849). Kierkegaard is, of course, often cited as an extreme advocate of subjectivism for whom the God-relationship is developed in terms of a pure, unmediated face-to-face between the self and God that he also construes in exclusively negative terms, as the despair of the self unable to find its rest in God.[61] However, as *The Lily of the Field and the Bird of the Air* makes unequivocally clear, Kierkegaard is strongly committed to the kind of experience of presence we have just been

---

[61] As what follows will, I hope, show, this is in fact something of a travesty of what Kierkegaard actually said.

exploring and, in this period at least, his thought offers a model for thinking the interrelationship of presence, selfhood, and God.

In these discourses Kierkegaard takes as his text the section of the Sermon on the Mount (Matt. 6: 24–34) in which Jesus points his disciples to the lilies of the field and the birds of the air as exemplifying a way of living that is not corrupted by the anxieties to which human beings are so chronically vulnerable—anxieties about food, drink, housing, or, simply, 'the morrow'. Kierkegaard contrasts the kind of model offered by the lilies and the birds with the sort of sentimental cult of nature found in some representatives of Romanticism. A contemporary application of the Gospel imperative to become like the lilies and the birds would not mean merely indulging in occasional experiences of the beauty or sublimity of nature. Rather, the Gospel calls for a radical reorientation of the self that Kierkegaard deals with under the three headings of silence, obedience, and joy. In silence we suspend the theorizing habits of our modern Western minds, in obedience we abandon the self-assertion inculcated by our modern Western pursuit of autonomy, and in joy we establish a new relation to the source of our existence by becoming present to ourselves.

What is joy, or what is it to be joyful? It is truly to be present to oneself; but truly to be present to oneself is this *today*, this *to be* today, truly *to be today*. The more true it is that you are today, the more completely present you are to yourself today, the less the day of trouble, tomorrow, exists for you. Joy is the present time with the whole emphasis on: *the present time*. Therefore God is blessed, he who eternally says: Today, he who eternally and infinitely is present to himself in being today.[62]

Such presence-to-self is, however, possible only on the basis of also silently and obediently attending to God—but where do we find God in order to attend to him? In these discourses, Kierkegaard's answer is that we find him by going out and 'beholding' the lilies and the birds, by reminding ourselves of and re-situating ourselves in the original God-relationship of creature to creator. Of course, as he points out, neither the lilies nor the birds *think* about God. They merely are what they are, but it is precisely by being themselves that they fulfil God's purpose for them. In principle, at least, it is no different in the case of human beings. As Kierkegaard had argued in an earlier set of discourses on the same text, one thing we learn from the lilies and the birds is the glory of simply being human and being content with simply being human. But, obviously, human beings are not flowers or birds. Human beings have a kind of consciousness, manifest in thinking and willing,

---

[62] S. Kierkegaard, *Without Authority*, trans. E. H. and H. Hong, SKS 11 (Princeton: Princeton University Press, 1997), 39.

that neither flowers nor birds appear to have. Flowers and birds are as they are, but we are able to choose who we are—or, for that matter, to choose not to be who we are and to try to become something or someone else and renegotiate our place in the order of creation. In other words, the self-relation inherent in our human way of being means that something more is required of us than is required of the lilies and the birds.[63]

It is to this self-relation—and the various pathologies to which it can give rise—that Kierkegaard devotes his study of *The Sickness unto Death*, a biblical expression that he defines, simply, as 'despair'. But what is despair? Kierkegaard's answer to this question takes the reader through a sequence of ever more intense forms of despair. All of them, however, are described in terms taken from the basic definition of the self that Kierkegaard gives in the opening chapter:

A human being is spirit. But what is spirit? Spirit is the self. But what is the self? The self is a relation that relates itself to itself or is that aspect of the relation in which the relation relates itself to itself: the self is not the relation but is the relation's relating itself to itself.[64]

This is, of course, a highly intricate and much debated passage.[65] However, one thing it is fairly clearly seeking to establish is that the self is not understandable simply as a datum or a fact, a given part of the furniture of the world. We cannot say of the self that it simply 'is' in the way that a rock or a table 'is' or even in the way that the lilies and the birds are. Whatever the self is, it is that by virtue of how it relates itself to itself. I may be naturally endowed with great physical strength, good looks, or exceptional intelligence, but who I am, the kind of person I become, depends not on these gifts in themselves but on what I do with them.

But where does this 'self', this possibility of relating oneself to oneself, come from? If it is not a part of the furniture of the world, if it is not an entity amongst entities, how could it have come about? As Kierkegaard puts it, 'Such a relation that relates itself to itself, a self, must either have established itself or

---

[63] Of course, from Suzuki's point of view, Kierkegaard's way of interpreting the experience of the immediate presence of God in nature with human self-relation may seem to betray the latter's incurably 'Western' cast of mind.

[64] S. Kierkegaard, *The Sickness unto Death*, trans. H. and E. Hong, SKS 11 (Princeton: Princeton University Press, 1980), 13 (translation adapted).

[65] For discussion see, *inter alia*, M. Theunissen, *Der Begriff Verzweiflung: Korrekturen an Kierkegaard* (Frankfurt am Main: Suhrkamp, 1993); Robert L. Perkins (ed.), *International Kierkegaard Commentary*, xix: *The Sickness unto Death* (Macon, Ga.: Mercer University Press, 1987); N.-J. Cappelørn and H. Deuser (eds.), *Kierkegaard Studies Yearbook 1996* (Berlin: de Gruyter, 1996) and *Kierkegaard Studies Yearbook 1997* (Berlin: de Gruyter, 1997).

have been established by another.'[66] His view is that the self is indeed 'established by another', so that the optimum state of the self would be when 'in relating itself to itself and in willing to be itself, the self rests transparently in the power that established it',[67] that is, when the freely chosen self-relation in and through which we each become what we are is the free choice of what God wills for us.[68]

Thus, while in his own way restating the Romantic invocation of presence, Kierkegaard also draws attention to the way in which the self-relation and self-understanding of the human self is inescapably involved in any possible experience of the presence of Being—even if that self-relation and self-understanding takes up no more space than Suzuki's untranslatable exclamation mark! Anything else, of course, would not be an *experienced relation* to presence but merely the reversion of the dumb reality of the world to being—being-in-itself but no longer for-itself.[69]

Looking back from this Kierkegaardian perspective to Wordsworth and Schleiermacher, we can see that they too already understood the involvement of the self in the experience of presence, and in instructive ways. Thus, one of the most striking features of Wordsworth's 'Lines' is that it does not in fact presume to offer a direct transcription of the original experience but contextualizes that experience in the interplay of memory and anticipation. The poem does not witness to an experience of presence on 13 July 1798, but to an experience ('And I *have felt...*') associated with this place that the poet has not, at the time of writing, visited for five years. Moreover, the account of the 'blessed moods' in which he has seen 'into the life of things' is offered as a memory of a memory, of what the memories of nature's 'beauteous forms' meant to him when he was far away from them 'in lonely rooms, and 'mid the din | Of towns and cities'. But he also emphasizes how, thinking of these pictures, 'the mind revives again...not only with the sense | Of present pleasure, but with pleasing thoughts | That in this moment there is life and food | For future years'. Most subtly, the conclusion of the poem both takes up the anticipation of the future and inscribes a moment of loss and remembrance in this same future, when the poet appeals to his sister that if they are

---

[66] *Sickness unto Death*, 13.

[67] Ibid. 14.

[68] This would seem to be implicit in a number of biblical passages dealing with the presence of God in the act of calling and commissioning his prophets. See, e.g., the narrative of the call of Moses, which not only involves the question as to the name of God (as we have already seen), but Moses' further question, 'Who am I that I should go to Pharaoh and bring the Israelites out of Egypt' (Exod. 3: 11). See also Isa. 6: 1–8, Jer. 1: 4–10, 20: 7–18, as well as God's dialogue with Job, many psalms, and texts relating to Paul's conversion.

[69] On the meaning of this distinction see below.

separated in time to come, then she too will remember and her memory 'be as a dwelling-place | For all sweet sounds and harmonies', giving her 'healing thoughts | Of tender joy'. In such ways, the poem is not a re-enactment of the immediate and pure experience of presence, but a remembrance of presence: it is presence internalized into the living, growing life of the mind.

This is a duality that German idealism was able to combine into the one term *Erinnerung*, signifying both the internalization of experience in subjective consciousness and remembrance. It is not presence alone that gives insight, consoles, or heals, but presence that has been internalized, reflected on, remembered, and understood. In this way, the meaning of presence becomes inseparable from the whole life and self-consciousness of the one who has sensed the 'something far more deeply interfused' and is able to make of it a continuing creative power in his life. So too for Schleiermacher, as the Third Speech makes especially clear. What is experienced in the 'natal hour of everything living in religion' is not to be taken as an isolated or abstract event, but as something that feeds into and shapes the whole course of a human life: 'In the mind in which [religion] dwells it is uninterruptedly active and living, making everything into an object for itself and every thought and action into a theme of its heavenly imagination.'[70] And for Schleiermacher (as for Coleridge) imagination was a power that chiefly showed itself in bringing order, harmony, and joy into the life of the living human being.[71]

Kierkegaard's version of the interrelationship of presence and selfhood is more fragile, fractured, and potentially tragic than that of the first generation of Romantics. Whilst he affirms the possibility that we may choose ourselves in a presence-to-self that is also at the same time and transparently a presence-to-God, the ineluctability of our having to choose induces an anxiety in which we may—and, he seems to suggest, mostly do—fail to choose that possibility. And when we fail to be the selves we are, transparent to the ground that posits us (however that power is construed[72]), we are, he says, in despair. The

---

[70] *Speeches*, 144.

[71] A further point, to which we shall return in Ch. 6, is that both Wordsworth and Schleiermacher interpret their experiences of presence as indissociable from experiences of human love. Wordsworth's 'Lines' are addressed specifically to his sister; it is in her that he longs to 'behold . . . what once I was' and hear again 'the language of my former heart' and it is to her future memory of him that he entrusts the meaning of the 'sublime sense' of which he has been speaking. Similarly in the *Speeches*, Schleiermacher makes it clear that it is love that is the privileged instance of the revelation of the infinite universe.

[72] It is not perhaps self-evident that the power that establishes the self has to be identified with God. Habermas, for example, has given a non-theistic reading of this passage, according to which this power is to be interpreted as the language community by which each human self is formed (see J. Habermas, *Die Zukunft der menschlichen Natur* (Frankfurt am Main: Suhrkamp, 2001), 25–6). One might imagine alternative naturalistic interpretations or, e.g., a Buddhist

Romantics' sense of the power of presence would (and does) continue to mould the self-consciousness of the modern world, but it is Kierkegaard's more anguished vision that has more greatly impacted the philosophy of the twentieth century, anticipating that century's experiences of a separation from the spontaneous sources of a happy, joyful, creaturely life that no rhetoric of simple presence could heal. Yet this is not just an issue of setting hope and despair against each other. For Kierkegaard's analysis and the twentieth-century experience make explicit a tension within the idea of presence itself. This tension can be formulated as the question whether, once we have admitted that the presence of Being is meaningful only to and for a subject for whom it is meaningful, presence itself is still possible. Doesn't the advent of self-consciousness open up a fissure in our relation to Being that we have no resources for filling? Doesn't the introduction of the self-conscious subject introduce a moment of 'difference' into the undifferentiated continuum of pure Being in such a way as to make the kind of failure that Kierkegaard called despair a likely, if not an unavoidable feature of human life in the world? Sartre would take Kierkegaard's view as to the actual prevalence of despair as indicative not simply of the possibility of multiple failed choices but as disclosing a universal and inescapable aspect of the human condition—precisely because of the role of presence-to-self as the basis for the experience of the presence of the world or of Being. As he puts it in *Being and Nothingness*, the very structure of self-presence 'supposes that an impalpable fissure has slipped into being. If being is present to itself, it is because it is not wholly itself. Presence is an immediate deterioration of coincidence, for it presupposes separation.'[73] And 'the for-itself must be its own nothingness. The being of consciousness qua consciousness is to exist *at a distance from itself* as a presence to itself, and this empty distance which carries its being is Nothingness.'[74]

We shall return to these claims shortly, but before doing so I wish now to turn once more to Heidegger and to see how Heidegger too developed the question of presence in such a way as to make it inseparable from the question as to the being of the one to whom Being is or might become present, the being he would call *Dasein*.

---

interpretation in which the 'power' is identified with the absolute emptiness out of which all beings originate. At this point in our enquiry it is not important to decide this issue, although we shall need to return to it at a later point: see Ch. 7 below 'On the Field of Nihility/Khôra (?)'.

[73] J.-P. Sartre, *Being and Nothingness*, trans. H. Barnes (London: Methuen, 1958), 77.
[74] Ibid. 78.

DASEIN AND THE TURN TO THE SUBJECT

We have been wrestling with what Heidegger called the superlative mode of bodily presence that occurs face to face with the self-givenness of the entity—standing there, looking at the tree—and how we not only know that what we are seeing is a tree but also that there really is a tree there and that our vision engages its reality. Or, to put it another way, we have been considering the question of how, in, with, and under knowledge of a given essence, we can be assured that the essence points to or indicates something real: that essence reveals the existence of that of which it is the essence, in short, that essence discloses Being.

At a certain level it seems possible—perhaps it seems best—simply to cut through this tangle of issues by an appeal to the straightforwardness of our normal, everyday experience: don't we all know that there really is a tree there and that only fools or philosophers would ever think to doubt it? Isn't this what the poets and mystics are also aiming at: bringing us back once more to the self-evidence of our face-to-face encounter with things? Yet these simple appeals are, after all, appeals to some*one* and if certain forms of doubt are indeed exclusive to fools and philosophers it is only beings such as we are, beings endowed with consciousness, who are capable of seeing that there is something there to be seen. The tree will continue to be there after we have gone away and the tree in the wilderness is surely there, even though there is no one to see it, but the revelation of any tree as tree is possible only when there are conscious beings to whom it might be revealed.

One thought prompted by this observation is that getting assurance as to the being-there of what I see as a tree is not so much a matter of somehow getting behind my perception of the tree and finding a way of knocking against its 'reality' (perhaps like Dr Johnson kicking the stone to disprove Berkeleian idealism) but, instead, looking more closely at that being to whom the being of beings is revealed. This, essentially, is what Heidegger attempts in *Being and Time*. It has already been mentioned that in the period leading up to *Being and Time* Heidegger was working through the inheritance of Aristotelian philosophy and doing so with an explicit awareness of the questions associated with the medieval appropriation of Aristotle. That the question posed at the start of *Being and Time* is congruent with the kind of theological reflection on Being we have encountered in the Thomist tradition is therefore no surprise. This relationship is, indeed, clearly testified by the first numbered paragraph of the first chapter. It begins: 'The "essence" [*Wesen*] of this entity lies in its "to be" [*Zu-sein*]. Its being what-it-is [*Was-sein*] (*essentia*) must, so

far as we can speak of it at all, be conceived in terms of its Being (*existentia*).'
To which Heidegger adds: '*The essence of Dasein lies in its existence* . . . So when
we designate this entity with the term "Dasein", we are expressing not its
"what" (as if it were a table, house or tree) but its Being.'[75]

If these clarifications already broach issues we are not yet ready to deal
with—not least what that most characteristically Heideggerian term 'Dasein'
itself means!—the choice of words signals a clear affiliation to the sort of
discussion we have been encountering in the modern reception of medieval
philosophy. If Gilson left us with 'essences' that 'pointed to' the beings or
Being of which they were the essence but without having clarified what was
involved in that 'pointing', Heidegger seems here to be promising an exploration of just this relationship, i.e. how a certain being might reveal itself as the
Being that, in its 'essence', it is. This might prompt the thought that one thing
Heidegger is doing in *Being and Time* is attempting to solve—or to give
a more satisfactory account of—the question of Being as that had been
formulated in scholasticism. Indeed, we have already noticed how he offers
the phenomenological account of intentionality as explicating the scholastic
notion of truth as the adequation of thing (*res*) and idea (*intellectus*).[76]

The point there was not simply to refute the scholastic account, but to
ground it in a fuller description of the structures at play in the act of knowing.
So too, we might expect, *Being and Time* will set out to provide a basis for
understanding what scholastic thought was attempting to address although,
on a Heideggerian view, it did not in the event tackle it in an adequate way. In
fact, Heidegger describes his task precisely as 'loosening up' the 'hardened
tradition' that has resulted from the medieval 'uprooting' of Greek ontology
and making it into a 'fixed body of doctrine'.[77] There will therefore be some
continuity with scholasticism in terms of the question to be addressed, but we
are also to expect important differences in the Heideggerian approach from
that of the scholastics, important not least with regard to the question of God
and Being. It is worth taking some time to note these differences, especially
(1) what we might call the 'turn to the subject', and (2) the distinctive
relationship between existence and essence in the Heideggerian account,

---

[75] *Being and Time*, 67/42. Of course, this might also be read as provocative, not to say
blasphemous, in relation to scholasticism, since Heidegger seems to be saying of human beings
what Thomas taught could only be said of God! This is in fact one of Edith Stein's first criticisms
of her former colleague (see *Endliches und Ewiges Sein*, 463). However, as we shall see, Heidegger
gives a different meaning to the German *Existenz* from what he takes to be the standard meaning
of the Latin *existentia*.

[76] See n. 41 above.

[77] *Being and Time*, 43, 44/22. See also the comments on Thomism, Scotism, and Hegel in
Being and Time, 22/3.

and, in connection with this, the place of the question about God and Being. This will also involve us in considering Sartre's radically anti-theistic extension of Heidegger's analysis and his argument that the structure of subjectivity is such as to make human beings necessarily and utterly self-contradictory and to render the verdict on human life that it is a 'useless passion'.

First, however, we follow Heidegger's revision of Western thinking by focusing the question of Being on just one particular being, the being that he calls 'Dasein'. Without attempting to resolve all the issues that cluster around the interpretation of this key term, it is clear that, at one level at least, Heidegger takes Dasein as referring in a quite specific way to human beings. As the first sentence of this first chapter states succinctly: 'We ourselves are the entities to be analysed.'[78] One reason for this is the particular configuration of the relationship between existence and essence that he discerns in the specifically human way of being. We shall return to this point shortly, but there is another reason that Heidegger has already indicated in the introduction, namely, that 'Dasein is an entity which does not just occur among other entities. Rather it is ontically distinguished by the fact that, in its very being, that being is an *issue* for it.'[79] In other words, Dasein—the human being—is able to and, as a matter of fact does, raise the question of its own being. Dasein can and does ask 'Who am I? What kind of being am I?'[80] Even 'ontically', i.e., in normal, everyday life, human beings of all educational and cultural backgrounds, even children, find themselves puzzled by and asking about the distinctiveness of human existence about the individual's own consciousness of being an utterly unique being, someone who has never existed before and who will never exist again. We are beings whose being is an issue for us and thus, Heidegger suggests, our being, even our normal, everyday being, provides a most appropriate place to begin asking about being. Where else might we have access to Being if not in our own, everyday experience of the question as to our own being, here and now?

---

[78] *Being and Time*, 67/41.

[79] Ibid. 32/12.

[80] One translation of Dasein I have heard offered is 'Here I am!?', a formulation that condenses both the Aristotelian wonder at my being here, conscious of myself and my world (indicated by the exclamation mark), and the biblical-existentialist *question* as to the fearful and problematic aspect of our self-experience. It is important, however, to distinguish what Heidegger is highlighting here from other interpretations of the self-reflective nature of human consciousness, in which, for example, it might be my ability to feel or to do that is more pronounced. On Heidegger's departure from Husserl with regard to the accentuation of Being in self-reflection see the helpful discussion by J.-L. Marion in the introduction to his *Reduction and Givenness* (Evanston, Ill.: Northwestern University Press, 1998).

In a broad historical perspective this focus on Dasein, the human being capable of asking 'Who am I?', might seem to put Heidegger in the modern paradigm of the 'turn to the subject'. By this is meant the reformulation of ancient and medieval philosophical questions in terms of the knowing capacities of the human subject. The defining moment of this turn to the subject is generally taken to be Descartes's attempt to refute scepticism by interrogating what Bergson would call the 'immediate deliverances of consciousness' and, on that basis, to develop a set of foundations for all possible knowledge. A further refinement was Kant's use of what he called 'transcendental apperception', i.e., a 'pure original unchangeable consciousness' that is prior to all particular experience (including experiences of the self) and, as such, is the basis on which Kant develops his distinctive system of categories of knowing.[81] Further instances of this turn to the subject could be cited from subsequent versions of German idealism and also from amongst its critics—as in Hegel's assertion that 'the subject is substance' or Kierkegaard's statement that 'subjectivity is truth'.

Hegel's expression 'being-for-itself' is perhaps especially worth noting at this point. He introduces it to signal what he calls the essential idealism of all philosophy. What he means by this is that even where a particular school of philosophy calls itself realist and rejects one or other version of idealism, and even where it is some material substance that is identified as the one true substance out of which everything is made (as in early Greek systems that identified Water or Atoms as the raw stuff into which everything else could be dissolved or reduced), philosophy is nevertheless idealistic. In what sense? In the specific sense that qua philosophy it is always in pursuit of universal structures of knowledge and these, as Hegel puts it, 'are *thoughts*, universals, ideals, not things as they occur immediately, i.e., in sensuous singularity'.[82] He illustrates his point by referring to Thales' view that Water was the universal substance, commenting that although this did indeed include 'empirical water' (i.e., the water in the river, the puddle, or the bath) this was not simply identifiable with the 'universal' Water that Thales judged to be the 'true' substance of mountains, rocks, and living bodies.[83] But if all philosophy is idealistic or is an occurrence in and for (and only in and for) a self-conscious life that not only 'is' but is 'for itself', the formulation Being-for-itself also

---

[81] I. Kant, *Critique of Pure Reason*, trans. Norman Kemp Smith (London: Macmillan, 1933), 135–40.

[82] G. W. F. Hegel, *Wissenschaft der Logik I*, in *Werke*, v (Frankfurt-am-Rhein: Suhrkamp 1969), 172.

[83] When contemporary physics makes use of mathematical procedures it is being 'idealistic' in Hegel's sense.

implies that what is made conscious in philosophy is, after all, *Being*. Knowing is always knowledge of some *thing*, of some entity, or some intentional object.

Yet whilst Heidegger does, at one level, presuppose this turn to the subject, he does not endorse it entirely—thus, in the introduction, Descartes himself is seen not so much as the initiator of a new era of philosophy but as a representative of the 'hardened tradition' that has lost sight of the original Greek approach to the question. And whereas the philosophy of existence associated with *Being and Time* was seen by its opponents as essentially subjectivistic,[84] Heidegger would claim that this was a misreading and that the question of Being especially associated with his later philosophy was already at the centre of *Being and Time* itself.[85] Heidegger himself did not use the term, but what he is saying might be taken as effectively condensed into the Hegelian expression 'Being-for-itself' in which, as we have seen, 'Being' counts as much as does 'for-itself'.

Heidegger may be pursuing metaphysics in *Being and Time* and he may be doing so in a way that has continuities both with the scholastic tradition and with his own later meditations on the history of Being, yet he clearly differs from the former in terms of his decision to focus specifically on the everyday consciousness of just this being, the human being. And even if Heidegger's Dasein is not to be equated with the Cartesian ego or the Kierkegaardian subject that is still a significant difference. But Heidegger also seems to differ from the scholastics in his distinctive configuration of the relationship between essence and existence. If the kind of Christian Aristotelianism we have encountered in Thomas (interpreted by Gilson) joins Aristotle in seeing the 'what it is' as the primary meaning of *ousia* or substance and therefore as what defines a given existing entity, Heidegger's formulation seems almost to invert this relationship: 'Its [i.e. Dasein's] Being-what-it-is [*Was-sein*] (*essentia*) must, so far as we can speak of it at all, be conceived in terms of its Being (*existentia*)'.[86] Indeed, the whole point of focusing on Dasein is to give us a point of access to Being/*existentia* that is in some sense prior to whatever knowledge of 'what a thing is' gives us of its being.[87]

This striking inversion is followed by another swift definitional move that is equally decisive for the subsequent argument of *Being and Time*. Having

---

[84] As, e.g., in the Marxist Georg Lukács's reference to it as 'the Good Friday of parasitic subjectivism'.

[85] For further discussion see, e.g., G. Pattison, *The Routledge Guidebook to the Later Heidegger* (London: Routledge, 2000), 6–14.

[86] *Being and Time*, 67/42.

[87] And remember: this is also why we have at this point turned to Heidegger to see if he can help us find a way of understanding the relationship between *essentia* and *existentia* that might throw light on the, thus far, merely empty formulation that essence 'points to' existence.

proposed the scholastic *existentia* as a point of reference for the modern German *Sein* (Being), Heidegger immediately adds that, if the Being of Dasein is best spoken of as 'existence' (using the German *Existenz*) 'this term does not and cannot have the ontological signification of the traditional term "*existentia*"; ontologically *existentia* is tantamount to *Being-present-at-hand*, a kind of Being which is essentially inappropriate to entities of Dasein's character'.[88]

There are several points to tease out here. First, *existentia* is taken as denoting what Heidegger will call Being-present-at-hand. But what does that mean? Whilst the full force of this Heideggerian neologism will take a long time to be unfolded, Heidegger will shortly afterwards make an important clarification. The terms *existentialia* and categories, he says, refer to 'the two basic possibilities for characterizing Being'.[89] But whereas a doctrine of categories sets out the ways in which we explicate 'what is sighted and what is visible'[90] in our encounters with entities, *existentialia* are structures specific to Dasein. As Heidegger sums up: 'any entity is either a "who" (existence) or a "what" (presence-at-hand in the broadest sense)'.[91] This final parenthetical remark, however, implies that Being-present-at-hand corresponds to the 'what' of a thing, i.e., to its *essentia*—at least 'in the broadest sense'.[92]

As we have seen in Chapter 1, there is some justification for the view that in the Aristotelian-scholastic tradition essence is seen as expressing what a given substance is: the substance of an entity is 'what' it is—'what' it is is what it *is*, we might say. Therefore, to the extent that we know the essence of something, we know its being. On Heidegger's view, however, this is basically reductive. The role given to knowledge of essences in scholastic philosophy occludes the possibility of other kinds of knowing. Knowledge of existence is limited to what can be formulated in terms of essence as a 'what' or as a proposition or series of propositions made up of terms defined as specific 'whats'. For this reason too, knowledge of persons (of the 'who') is dealt with in scholastic thought in the inappropriate medium of knowledge of essences. In other words, the outcome of the 'hardened tradition' of Western metaphysics is

---

[88] Ibid.
[89] Ibid. 71/45. Translation amended.
[90] Ibid. 70/45.
[91] Ibid. 71/45.
[92] This may seem to conflict with the statement previously cited that 'ontologically *existentia* is tantamount to Being-present-at-hand, a kind of Being which is essentially inappropriate to entities of Dasein's character'. However, despite its Latin '*existentialia*' is to be taken as referring to what Heidegger regards as the distinctive features of *Existenz*, which, as we have noted, he distinguishes from *existentia*.

precisely the (to Heidegger's mind) unsatisfactory situation that essence is made the measure of existence and there is no procedure for interpreting the personal, human existence that Heidegger here calls Dasein.

But if both essence and existence are in this way identified with the 'what', with presence-at-hand, what exactly is presence-at-hand, and what kind of relations to Being (if any) might we have that are not reducible to presence-at-hand? To give a full account of this crucial term and of the questions associated with it (let alone to explore Heidegger's alternative approach) would probably divert us too greatly from the main course of this enquiry and require a further addition to the constantly growing library of Heidegger literature, but it is nevertheless to our purpose to make some further comments on it.

Early on in part I of *Being and Time* Heidegger will set out what would become one of his most original contributions to modern philosophy, namely, his account of being-in-the-world. To some extent we have been prepared for this by the analysis of intentionality,[93] since the core insight articulated in the expression being-in-the-world is that when we encounter human beings (ourselves!) in existence we do not encounter the beings with whom philosophical enquiry typically concerns itself, that is, beings who know themselves in the first instance as conscious subjects who only subsequently become troubled as to the reality and reliability of their mental representations of a supposedly 'external' world. In existence, in life as it is lived, we are 'always already' involved in the world, in the midst of it, absorbed in it, struggling with it.

Let us take some relatively simple examples. An infant grabs the spoon and stuffs some porridge into its mouth, smearing a considerable quantity on its face. If it subsequently refines this process into a more or less well-mannered analogue of adult eating, it may have been helped by having the nature and function of spoons and the distinctions between edible and non-edible gooey matter explained to it, but such explanations only occur and only make sense to a being who is already embarked upon an existence that involves eating with implements. Heidegger's own main example, it should be said, is the somewhat more adult example of a person hammering.[94] But in none of these

---

[93] See above 'Presence in Philosophy: Categorial Intuition'.

[94] In earlier lectures Heidegger had approached the question through Augustine's account of temptation in which, as Heidegger expounds it, we see that we only ever get to become the selves that we are by the constant struggle to free ourselves from a 'world' that we find pressing upon us. See M. Heidegger, *Phänomenologie des Religiösen Lebens* (*Gesamtausgabe*, vol. lx) (Frankfurt am Main: Klostermann, 1993). See also my article 'Heidegger, Augustine and Kierkegaard: Care, Time and Love', in C. De Paulo (ed.), *The Influence of Augustine on Heidegger: The Emergence of an Augustinian Phenomenology* (Lewiston, NY: Edwin Mellen Press, 2007).

cases do we initially encounter entities such as the spoon and porridge or hammer and nails as a 'what' that we first learn about and only then get to use or to resist. Rather, Heidegger suggests, beings are first of all disclosed to us as what he calls readiness-to-hand: my environment is revealed to me as I get on with living in it, grabbing my spoon and eating my porridge, fixing the fence with my hammer, etc. Our interest in the 'what' of the entities with which we have to do is only secondary. It is only when I can't find the hammer, when one or other piece of equipment for dealing with my environment breaks down, or (to revert to the example of the infant) I can't use it in the right way that I am provoked into reflecting on the thing in isolation from the total context in which it normally works for me. It is at this point, Heidegger says, that we begin to see the object as something present-at-hand. Instead of just getting on with life, I have to reflect on it or perhaps (in the case of the infant learning to eat) be taught about it in a formal way. Instead of just rushing on, I stand back and look at it—and, as Heidegger reminds us, the 'look' of something, how it looks, is etymologically at the root of that most basic of all Greek philosophical terms, idea.[95]

This suggests that the most original form of theoretical knowledge is the kind we associate with master craftsmen, farmers, or mariners, that is, with those who are not just good workers but who know what each bit of their equipment is for, how it works, and how one might mend or substitute for it if it goes wrong or gets lost. Yet the scope of such primitive theoretical knowledge is still circumscribed by the range of involvements (porridge-eating, wall-mending, etc.) in which things have disclosed themselves as ready-at-hand. Nor, as Heidegger's later writings on technology will show, does the quantitative improvement and complexification of our instrumental dealings with the world change the picture in any essential way. Furthermore, although all of this belongs to the primary lived context out of which being-in-the-world emerges, a life that merely oscillated between encountering beings as ready-to-hand (pragmatically) and present-to-hand (knowingly) would not yet be all that even a rather ordinary human life is.

If the kind of involvement with the world disclosed in beings as ready-to-hand and present-to-hand is necessarily integral to existence there is nevertheless something more—a 'more' that is indicated by the possibility of asking what it is all *for*. This possibility is especially prominent in those moments when my equipment fails me. Unable to find the hammer, I'm provoked to ask what I'm fixing the fence for anyway. Yet it is also implicit, if unspoken, in the activity of hammering itself. If someone asks me, I have

---

[95] *Being and Time*, 88/61.

no hesitation in telling them that I want to fix the fence because I want to make the homestead secure and attractive, and if I am questioned further I can go on to explain that I want the homestead to be secure and attractive because I envisage it as a home for my family, where my children can grow up in a secure and attractive home so that they will become happy and serviceable members of society, etc.[96] Maybe I didn't think any of this explicitly. Maybe I just looked out of the window and thought 'the fence needs fixing'—but my behaviour, my 'comportment', as Heidegger might say, i.e., my way of dealing with my world, is both intentional in the phenomenological sense and also meaningful, no matter how limitedly I express this meaning in words. The whole complex of pragmatic action and knowledge of how things work is shaped and guided in every case by a tacit understanding of the larger horizon in which my dealings with the things around me become meaningful.

Following this clue, it is not hard to picture a series of such horizons, such as the horizon of my life as an individual, as a member of a family, a local community, a *polis*, a cosmos brought into being by God or gods for a divine purpose beyond all our human purposes. Yet Heidegger is not attempting to construct a kind of hierarchy of horizons or lead us towards a world-view in which our manifold horizons are ordered and arranged. For his purposes it does not especially matter if one person understands their lives as devoted to their family, another to the service of the city, another to the service of the gods. Each will have their own 'ultimate concern', but whatever a person's proximate or ultimate concerns, their involvement with the world is always marked by a 'for which', a 'for the sake of', or a 'towards which',[97] and it is in this 'for which' that Dasein's own being becomes an issue for it. Whether I understand myself primarily as a family man or a servant of the city, I myself am at stake in the welfare of my family or the triumphs and disasters of my city. If, in the one case, my family falls apart or, in the other, my city is defeated by its enemies, my life too is ruined. On the other hand, if I live to celebrate my golden wedding and see my children successfully pursuing their chosen careers or see my city go from strength to strength in prosperity and esteem, then I too see my life as fulfilled. I may not see this clearly myself, I may be too absorbed in my family or my city to raise the question of my own participation in it all, but it is nevertheless revealed in the way in which

---

[96] My extension of Heidegger's argument deliberately develops what might be seen as its implicitly (and even unfortunately) gendered character: one senses that Heidegger assumes it will be the 'father of the house' who is doing the hammering here. The use of the porridge-eating infant is partially intended to counter the potentially exclusive tendencies of Heidegger's own example.

[97] *Being and Time*, 114–21/83–7.

I throw myself into mending the fence or canvassing for my chosen political party.

And perhaps we can reach the same point even more simply. 'How are you?' someone asks me. 'Fine', I reply. 'Why's that?' they enquire. Maybe it's just because it's a sunny day and I'm in good health. Maybe it's because yesterday I fixed the fence that had been broken all summer, maybe it's because the latest opinion polls suggest a landslide for the political party I favour. But the interesting point is that the question is about how *I am*—not just about what mood I'm in, what sort of weekend I had, or the state of the world. And, quite spontaneously, in a multitude of everyday encounters, we do all constantly ask about and reveal how we are putting ourselves, our very being, at issue in one or other worldly involvement. We could, of course, easily imagine the question being posed in a less personal way, such as 'How's life?' or 'How are things?', and, in fact that would make the point even more clearly: that my response would not just be a matter of reporting some more or less fleeting subjective state but a comment about 'life' as such or 'things' as such. My response would then reveal not just how I think I am, but how I relate myself to the whole world in which I find myself existing.[98]

All of this is occurs at what Heidegger calls the 'ontical' level, i.e., in our pre-philosophical, pre-reflective life in the world—the level of reality in which babies eat porridge, family life is enjoyed and endured, and politics and religion are practised. Taking account of what happens in this ontical world is only preparatory to the more rigorous philosophical work of analysing and ordering the structures that ontical life reveals and which, in turn, make ontical life intelligible. At the level of the ontical, each of us is different and there is no obvious end to the ways in which we can throw ourselves into our lives and live out the human condition, tragically or comically as the case may prove to be. What Heidegger hopes his phenomenological analysis will do is to lay bare the ontological structures that are determinative for all possible human existences. But to do so, his starting point has to be precisely existence itself, i.e., the point at which, whatever our differences, we relate ourselves to our world-as-a-whole or to our life as such.[99]

This, then, is the Heideggerian existence: it is not, as in the scholastic *existentia*, about whether or not a given entity (a 'what' defined as a certain *essentia*) 'exists'; instead, it is about *how* I am, *how* I find myself to be in my

---

[98] On 'life' and 'things' as implicit metaphysical categories see Don Cupitt, *The New Religion of Life in Everyday Speech* (London: SCM Press, 1999) and idem, *The Meaning of It All in Everyday Speech* (London: SCM Press, 1999).

[99] We shall return to the importance of the interplay between ontical life and ontological analysis later in this chapter.

relation to my existence (*Existenz* not *existentia*) as such. The question of existence thus becomes: *how do I experience my being?*

We shall not now follow any further how Heidegger proceeds to address that question. The point here is merely to indicate how Heidegger places his enquiry into the meaning of Being on the ground of human being itself, Dasein, the being that we are, that each of us is. This may be depicted as an example of the modern 'turn to the subject', but in Heidegger, at least, it is argued as pointing beyond the subject to the Being that reveals itself to the subject, the Being toward which we find the existing human subject directing his or her existence.

EXISTENCE, ESSENCE, AND GOD

I now wish to look at the meaning of Heidegger's interpretation of the relationship between existence and essence (inclusive of his distinction between *existentia* and *Existenz*) in relation to (a) one of his closest predecessors and (b) one of his philosophical heirs, namely, Kierkegaard and Sartre. Doing so will help clarify further the bearing of the Heideggerian sense of existence on the revelation of Being, i.e., the question as to how an understanding of existence might lead to a revelation of Being that would have the kind of assurance that was lacking in the formula 'essence points to existence'.

Werner Brock, one of Heidegger's teaching assistants in the 1930s, stated that it was specifically from Kierkegaard that the distinctive and decisive modern sense of existence was derived. For Kierkegaard himself the theme of existence was especially developed in the context of his critical response to German idealism.[100] He was certainly aware of Kant's claim that existence is not a predicate and that to add 'existence' to a notional 100 dollars adds nothing to the concept of 100 dollars. Nevertheless, he was also convinced that there is all the difference in the world between the mere idea of something and its actually existing. Precisely for that reason he rejected what he understood to be the Hegelian claim that existence can be derived from a purely logical analysis of pure thought. In alliance with the Aristotelian logician Trendelenburg he argues that to the extent that Hegel does indeed deal with issues of existence it is because he has subverted his own rules and introduced—'smuggled in', as Kierkegaard puts it—a knowledge of reality that does not derive from logic. However, if it is not a case of intellectual

---

[100] For a fuller discussion of the range and implications of Kierkegaard's discussion of existence see my *The Philosophy of Kierkegaard* (Aldershot: Ashgate, 2005), 12–45.

disingenuousness, this simply reveals another aspect of the same basic confusion between what is merely thought and what actually exists, a confusion that he regards as endemic in Hegelianism. This basic confusion provides Kierkegaard with the opportunity for some of his most scathing and most satirical remarks on Hegelianism (or as he also refers to it, 'the systematic idea' or 'the speculative point of view').[101] The speculative thinker is absent-minded (he has forgotten to take note of his actual existence in constructing his system); he is like a dancer who leaps so high that he imagines he could fly; he confuses himself as an individual with humanity as such; he believes that he can contemplate life *sub specie aeternitatis* (and Kierkegaard would certainly have embraced the designation of such philosophical absent-mindedness as a 'view from nowhere'). He is, Kierkegaard concludes, a 'fantastical' being. The ambition of the Hegelian systematician is to demonstrate the unity of subject and object, and the unity of thinking and being is possible only if existence itself is left out of the equation since, far from revealing the unity of subject and object, existence means their separation. As Kierkegaard quickly adds, 'it by no means follows that existence is thoughtless, but existence has spaced and does space subject from object, thought from being'.[102] One cannot argue from thought (or logic) to existence and, once one steps outside of the realm of purely formal relations (as in logic or mathematics), once one begins to think a definite content, one can only do so on the basis of existence.[103]

On Kierkegaard's understanding, then, to exist is precisely to be separated from one's idea or essence—which, for human beings, means that existence will always involve striving to become what one is, or, more simply, to become oneself. But there is a further twist since the goal of existence, the self we are to become, is characterized in terms of infinite possibility, i.e., the possibility of an eternal life or a God-relationship. In this respect human existence is very different from the case of, e.g., a purely botanical or biological entity. Any plant or animal can realize its essence simply by becoming what it is: each tree, each insect, and each fox is what it is by instantiating the characteristics of its species. This particular cherry tree, this particular ant, this particular fox is simply a singular instance of its species.[104] In the case of human beings,

---

[101] On the legitimacy of Kierkegaard's use of humour as a philosophical tool see John Lippitt, *Humour and Irony in Kierkegaard's Thought* (Basingstoke: Macmillan, 2000).

[102] S. Kierkegaard, *Concluding Unscientific Postscript*, trans. H. and E. Hong, SKS 7 (Princeton: Princeton University Press, 1992), 123.

[103] S. Kierkegaard, *Philosophical Fragments*, trans. H. and E. Hong, SKS 4 (Princeton: Princeton University Press, 1985), 40.

[104] This is not unproblematic post-Darwin, but for present purposes I am accepting the frame of reference that Kierkegaard and his contemporaries assumed.

however, the individual is not defined by the species but is what—or who—it becomes through its conscious, chosen, and responsible relation to itself and its being. Moreover, Kierkegaard (unlike the speculative thinkers) does not think that the infinite or the eternal can be incorporated into the horizon of human theorizing. Our relation to the infinite and eternal is to an open horizon that transcends our actual existence and, consequently, our specifically human existence is marked by a lifetime of striving: 'continued striving is the expression of the existing subject's ethical life-view.'[105]

Now it may seem that this already assumes too much, i.e., that it presupposes a religious understanding of life. Certainly Kierkegaard's whole argument is directed towards vindicating a specifically Christian understanding of existence, but it by no means relies on presupposed dogmatic principles. Key aspects of the particular issue around the separation of thought and existence and the exigency of continued striving are already focused in the human being's relation to its death. Of course, we can know a great deal about death, a point Kierkegaard makes with his customary humour: 'I know what the clergy usually say; I know the stock themes dealt with at funerals. If there is no other hindrance to moving on to world history, then I am ready; I need only buy some black cloth for a clerical gown, and then I shall deliver funeral orations as well as any ordinary clergyman. I readily admit that those with velvet panels do it more elegantly, but the difference is not any more essential than the difference between a five- and a ten-rix-dollar hearse.'[106] Nor would the point be significantly different if, instead of the knowledge about death associated with the clergy, we were to appeal to the very different knowledge about death associated with morticians or medical practitioners. The issue is not the particular knowledge, but the stance of knowing itself. Thus, Kierkegaard immediately adds that 'despite this almost extraordinary knowledge . . . I am by no means able to regard death as something I have understood'.[107] This is above all the case with regard to my own death, where, even before we wrestle with the impossibility of imagining ourselves dead, we are confronted by the uncertainty of death, which could come tomorrow or in twenty years'

---

[105] *Postscript*, 121–2.

[106] Ibid. 166. An example of a Kierkegaardian funeral sermon is the discourse 'At a Graveside' in the small collection *Upbuilding Discourses on Imagined Occasions*. Here, Kierkegaard expands on the brief formulations of the *Postscript* by illustrating many of the ways in which we depict or conceive of death and showing how, nevertheless, these all fail to think death itself. For discussion of the relationship between this discourse and *Being and Time* see M. Theunissen, 'The Upbuilding in the Thought of Death: Traditional Elements, Innovative ideas, and Unexhausted Possibilities', in Robert L. Perkins (ed.), *International Kierkegaard Commentary: Prefaces and Writing Sampler and Three Discourses on Imagined Occasions* (Macon, Ga.: Mercer University Press, 2006), 321–58.

[107] *Postscript*, 166.

time. Even talking about the uncertainty of death can confuse the issue, not least in the case where an oration on the uncertainty of death ends with urging the listener to live purposefully—since, Kierkegaard suggests, this is a sign of having forgotten the main point, i.e., the uncertainty, and more specifically the uncertainty of *my* death. 'To think this uncertainty once and for all, or once a year at matins on new year's morning, is nonsense, of course, and is not to think at all . . . If death is always uncertain, if I am mortal, then this means that this uncertainty cannot possibly be understood in general if I am not also such a human being in general. But this I am not.'[108] Thinking my death is impossible—and yet my whole identity is shaped by my having to die. Consequently, my existence will always elude the possibility of being thought through.[109]

Kierkegaard is, of course, the first to acknowledge that uncertainty of this kind is extremely harrowing. It would be much easier to define our lives according to the principles of one or other world-view—seeing ourselves as Christians, as representatives of the forward march of history, as fighters for political freedom. Such choices offer relief from what would otherwise be an incessant state of anxiety, but all such attempts are nevertheless marred by what Kierkegaard sees as the unavoidable 'dialectics' of thought and existence, i.e., that thought and existence must always be separate *in existence*.

This, in a sense, is the challenge that *Being and Time* picks up and, as many commentators have noted, some of the key terms or situations used there to show both how human beings typically conceal from themselves their actual relation to their own existence and how they might, nevertheless, break through to a more authentic attitude are derived from Kierkegaard (including idle talk, anxiety, guilt, the moment of vision, resolution, repetition, and, as we have been seeing, the confrontation with death).[110] Heidegger accepts Kierkegaard's view that, for the most part, human beings as we encounter

---

[108] Ibid. 166–7. This passage contains the nub of a Kierkegaardian critique of a Heideggerian programme of living authentically towards death. See comments on M. Theunissen in n. 65 above.

[109] Death offers Kierkegaard a pre-eminent instance of this separation and its implications. However, the relational structure of the self set out in *The Sickness unto Death* means that the possibility of despair—i.e. of failing to be the self that one is—is an unavoidable accompaniment of human existence.

[110] Of course, to acknowledge a Kierkegaardian influence is not to reduce Heidegger to a mere commentator on the Dane. Shestov's accusation that *Being and Time* merely translated Kierkegaard into the language of phenomenology is provocative, but does not do justice to the full range of sources that are taken up into and also transformed in that work—including, as we have been seeing, a certain critical transformation of the Aristotelian-scholastic heritage (see the letter to B. Fondane published in N. Baranova-Shestova, *Jiizn' L'va Shestova* (The life of Lev Shestov) (Paris: La Presse Libre, 1983), ii. 17).

them in existence (not absent-mindedly forgetting to include ourselves in this accounting) do not relate decisively or truthfully to that existence, to their life as a whole or as such, but, as he puts it, constantly fall short of their own possibilities. Nevertheless he argues for the possibility of Being becoming revealed in an open and authentic confrontation with the uncertain and conflicted evidence of our—Dasein's—existence. Existence lies beyond or is prior to essence, but it stands in a relation to Being that offers a way towards interpreting Being in an authentic existential manner.

Such a revelation might seem to parallel Kierkegaard's account of faith. Despair is the prevalent condition of human beings, but despair, failing to be all that we could be, is not a fate or necessity and it is possible not to be in despair. But Kierkegaardian faith is surely different again from the Heideggerian vision of Being. As Heidegger himself puts it, Kierkegaardian faith is a matter of *existentiell* decision, not existential understanding. And this seems to be right. The kind of self-commitment that Kierkegaard describes as faith is not offered as a way of addressing the question of Being, nor as requiring any specific intellectual development or preparation. It is simply a matter of a certain kind of passion: it is faith, hope, and love—not knowledge. Yet if the issue as to whether you or I are able to find faith is in this way pre- or even non-philosophical, Heidegger's point is that the possibility of faith is itself dependent on or presupposes a more general possibility of an authentic disclosure of Being. It is this general possibility that the analysis of Dasein sets out. Although Heidegger himself does not put it like this, we could see *Being and Time*'s analysis of Dasein and of Dasein's relation to Being as what Kierkegaard might call a thought-experiment, that is, as an answer to the question: were an authentic relation to Being on the part of an existing entity such as Dasein to be possible, how would it look? In a possible allusion to Kierkegaard's complaints about Hegelianism, Heidegger acknowledges that this might seem to be 'fantastical'[111] and, if he is insistent that the possibility of an *existentiell* resolution of the questions of authentic self-commitment presupposes a more general ontological understanding of existence, he also acknowledges that 'The fact that an authentic potentiality-for-Being-a-whole is ontologically possible for Dasein, signifies nothing, so long as a corresponding ontical potentiality-for-Being has not been demonstrated in Dasein itself.'[112] In other words, the ontological possibility of human beings achieving an authentic and open relation to Being is purely empty unless there are some human beings who actually do realize such a possibility in

---

[111] *Being and Time*, 311/266. See also the reference to '"idealistic" exactions soaring above existence and its possibilities' on 358/310.

[112] Ibid. 311/266.

their lives. However, from Heidegger's point of view, the kind of Christian faith advocated by Kierkegaard would be only one way in which this might occur. Other kinds of religious faith might also demonstrate it, as might certain non-religious commitments. The philosopher's interest is merely in the formal structure that any such realization would presuppose. Yet there must be some cases of *existentiell* realization if the philosopher's account is not to be either empty or fantastical and the philosopher cannot derive existence from an analysis of existential possibilities. Whatever else is to be said for or against the author of *Being and Time* he has understood Kierkegaard's critique of speculative thought and he knows that philosophy remains empty unless or until it is able to cite the 'testimony'[113] of Dasein itself, i.e., how you and I actually live and experience our lives. But, then, in what way, even in the light of a maximal level of self-knowledge and self-commitment, might we say that what we know in knowing ourselves is *Being*? If Dasein (the being whose being is an issue for it, the being who is being-for-itself, you and I) is as Kierkegaard and Heidegger describe it, if 'proximally and for the most part' we are shown to be falling short of our own possibilities and immersed in our worldly preoccupations and failing to get a grip on our life as a whole or our existence as such, how can we have any confidence in the deliverances of some supposed 'moment of vision' in which Being is disclosed to us in a decisive and unambiguous way? Isn't this simply like asking the divided self of Augustinian anthropology to give itself the grounding in Being that it lacks, i. e., asking it to save itself? And isn't this to embroil it in still further self-contradiction? If the philosopher's account of the ontological possibility is 'fantastical' as long as it lacks ontical testimony, how can we be assured that such testimony is anything other than empty? Whom could we trust to tell us what Being was really like?

Is the possibility of an authentic disclosure of Being at the ontical level a possibility that Heidegger's more narrowly philosophical assumptions should not really allow him to endorse? Does the analysis of Dasein actually allow us to suppose that any pure 'moment of vision' ever actually occurs? Perhaps Heidegger would be more consistent to say that, on the basis of what we do know about Dasein, such a disclosure would, in fact, be impossible. Dasein, thus described, could not have an authentic relation to Being: Dasein would be self-contradiction 'all the way down'.

This is just what Heidegger is wanting to avoid, yet it was the direction in which his thought was developed in the radically anti-religious existentialism of Sartre. Sartre's famous slogan 'existence precedes essence' is not intended to

---

[113] Ibid. 311/267.

imply that existence might provide a basis from which to approach knowledge of the human essence. Rather, it means that there is no human essence, no human nature. 'We are the sum of our actions' or, as he also puts it, 'You are nothing but your life.'[114] The cry, ascribed to Dostoevsky, that 'if God does not exist, then everything is permitted' becomes the starting point of this kind of existentialism.[115] There is no source of values, no criteria against which human life is to be measured, apart from human freedom itself. The heavens are empty and the future is open to however we choose to make it. The issue is not that of an authentic relation to Being, since that is impossible, but simply the readiness to take responsibility for my own free acts without excuses. But why is an authentic relation to Being impossible?

As Sartre describes it, being-for-itself can only arise as a 'nihilation' of the givenness of being-in-itself. In a world devoid of consciousness, a world that was simply and utterly being-in-itself, there would not be 'the slightest emptiness in being, not the tiniest crack through which nothingness might slip in.'[116] Consciousness enters this scene as 'a decompression of being'[117] such that being no longer coincides with itself. The very structure of self-presence that is given with being-for-itself 'supposes that an impalpable fissure has slipped into being. If being is present to itself, it is because it is not wholly itself. Presence is an immediate deterioration of coincidence, for it presupposes separation.'[118] And 'the for-itself must be its own nothingness. The being of consciousness qua consciousness is to exist *at a distance from itself* as a presence to itself, and this empty distance which carries its being is Nothingness.'[119] Whereas Dasein's ability to raise the question of its own being allows Heidegger to hope that he will eventually escape the labyrinth of inauthenticity and come face to face with Being itself, Sartre sees this ability as bringing about

---

[114] J.-P. Sartre, *L'Existentialisme est un humanisme* (Paris: Nagel, 1970), 58.

[115] Ibid. 36.

[116] *Being and Nothingness*, 74. I am taking Sartre as a guide to the critique of presence rather than the more recent critique found in Derrida because, in the first instance, the latter's argument is quite specifically focused on issues of sign and signification, rather than on more general characteristics of human life in the world. Of course, a concern with such 'more general characteristics' might seem naive, now that we know that such a concern can never come to expression outside language and therefore cannot occur without signs, i.e. language. Nevertheless, I think it also the case that Derrida's critique can, from a certain angle, be seen as a development within the Sartrean paradigm rather than simply as an alternative to it. See, for example, the useful comments by Christina Howells in her 'Conclusion: Sartre and the Deconstruction of the Subject', in C. Howells (ed.), *The Cambridge Companion to Sartre* (Cambridge: Cambridge University Press, 1992), 318–51. Derrida's critique of the longing for presence—which he likens to the flight of Icarus—is first worked out in his *La Voix et le phénomène: Introduction au problème du signe dans la phénoménologie de Husserl* (Paris: Presses Universitaires de France, 1967).

[117] *Being and Nothingness*, 74.   [118] Ibid. 77.   [119] Ibid. 78.

an inexpungible nothingness at the heart of human existence: 'Nothingness is the putting into question of being by being—that is, precisely consciousness or for-self'.[120] Thus 'Human reality is being in so far as within its being and for its being it is the unique foundation of nothingness at the heart of being.'[121] Nothingness is inherent in the structure of presence-to-self that is a condition of consciousness as such. Even more basic than freedom is the basic structure of presence-to-self: 'man is free because he is not himself but presence to himself.'[122] Yet such Sartrean 'presence', constituted as it is by an 'empty distance', is surely more accurately described as 'absence'.

This situation is one that human beings find anguishing. We flee the freedom that reveals the nothingness within and we develop infinitely varied strategies of avoidance (and Sartre's descriptions of the various modes of 'bad faith' whereby we thus avoid taking responsibility for who we are and what we are doing make a large contribution to the force of his philosophy and is also explored in many his plays and novels as well as in his more purely philosophical works[123]). This is a situation from which we long to be delivered. We do not experience freedom as a gift to be enjoyed but as a kind of condemnation. Freedom forces us to confront our nothingness (or would do, if we were not consumed by bad faith), and humiliates our desire to be. For, basically, what we want is simply, to be: 'man is the desire to be . . . The original project which is expressed in each of our empirically observable tendencies is then the *project of being*.'[124] But this project could only be fulfilled if the for-itself were able to find or to give itself a basis in being such, in being-in-itself, i.e. to be or to be the guarantor of its own foundation. That, however, is contradictory, a contradiction expressed in the statement that 'The for-itself arises as the nihilation of the in-itself and this nihilation is defined as the project toward the in-itself.'[125] The maximum that being-in-itself can be for the conscious subject is the contingent and ephemeral occasion of its becoming conscious of itself in this or that situation. How it then interprets and acts towards that situation depends entirely on itself (on consciousness, on freedom). If the self wants more than this, if it wants really to be what it is, to have its being secured in a ground of being beyond all contingency and ephemeral chance,

---

[120] Ibid. 79.   [121] Ibid.   [122] Ibid. 440.

[123] Indeed, one could argue that the subtlety and many-layered nature of such strategies of avoidance forces existentialist thinkers from Kierkegaard to Sartre to go beyond a narrowly philosophical discourse into literature, psychoanalysis, and other forms of representation better able to deal with the fugitive and shady subterfuges of human self-deception. Heidegger too will find himself forced to retreat from the scholastic idiom of Husserlian phenomenology to, e.g., the poetry of Hölderlin, in order to attend more closely to what he takes to be the call of Being.

[124] *Being and Nothingness*, 565.

[125] Ibid.

then what it actually wants is not merely to exist authentically but, Sartre says, to be God: 'To be man means to reach toward being God . . . man fundamentally is the desire to be God.'[126]

This is not a mere caricature of Christian theology. As we have seen in Chapter 1, the Christian tradition itself portrays the human being as marked by a fundamental lack with regard to its own being. This lack is revealed in the self's experience of itself as exiled from the realms of true being and in the restlessness of the heart that longs for reunion with the lost plenitude of the divine Being. It might, however, be objected to Sartre that although Christian theology has sometimes spoken of the ultimate end of human life as 'divinization', that is, as a full participation in the divine life itself, it does not express a desire to *be* God, merely to be in union with or to participate in God in such a way that the divine pre-eminence is always recognized and honoured. Even so, we have to acknowledge a certain formal correspondence between the Sartrean account of wanting to be God and the Christian account of the ontologically deficient self seeking its fulfilment in God.

In fact, on Sartre's own premises, even if God existed, he would be subject to the same paradox as the human subject that wanted to be its own foundation. If God is defined, as classical Christian metaphysics defines him, as, e.g., cause of himself (*causa sui*), then this involves God in a causative act that, according to Sartre, 'is a nihilating act like every recovery of the self by the self'[127] and which, as such, presupposes a prior givenness of the self that, since it is ungrounded, is merely contingent. Whether it is a human being or God, a being that is both 'self-consciousness and the foundation of himself'[128] is a contradiction in terms. Of course, the theological reader would object that Sartre has not done justice to the uniqueness of God and that Christian theology very well understands that, from the point of view of human reason, a Being who is ground and cause of his own Being will appear paradoxical. Isn't the kind of ontological disproof of the existence of God that Sartre is offering here an expression if not of bad faith, then at least of malice? Yet, from another angle, Sartre might merely be seen as highlighting a problem with which, as we have seen, Christian theology itself is familiar. For this is once again the problem as to finding assurance as to the being of the God to whom we relate in thinking—as, for example, in the unresolved question as to how we can be sure that *what* we know of God is knowledge of what God *is*. Isn't every reduction to essence a 'decompression of being', the manifestation of the self putting itself at a distance from its being? Nor would Sartre be without Christian theological allies in seeing the attempt to move beyond the impasse

---

[126] *Being and Nothingness*, 566.   [127] Ibid. 80.   [128] Ibid. 90.

indicated by this question on the basis of an analysis of human existence as self-defeating—at least on a philosophical level. This might, after all, be one way of interpreting the impact of Kierkegaard's critique of philosophy. In a not entirely unappreciative discussion of Kierkegaard, Gilson concludes that Kierkegaard leads directly to existentialism, since the 'full meaning of Kierkegaard's philosophical message' is that 'he has turned existence itself into a new essence, the essence of that which has no essence . . . It is *not* knowable from without, and it can *not* be known from without, but it can at least know itself, and, when it does so, what existence discovers in itself, as the ultimate ground, is that it is in itself a radical lack of being.'[129] Religion (faith in the possibility of a living experience of God) and philosophy (the attempt to articulate the metaphysical basis on which discourse about God would be possible) are consequently driven apart. Kierkegaardian faith, then, would seem to have some common cause with Sartre against traditional Christian metaphysics.

But a separation of this kind between faith and philosophy would not only be objectionable to Catholic theology. It would also seem to confound Heidegger's claim that the ontological account of Dasein that was sought in *Being and Time* could allow for and even appeal to *existentiell* testimonials as to the possibility of the self becoming wholly present to itself, including the testimonials of such religious thinkers as Augustine, Luther, and Kierkegaard on whom Heidegger relies rather heavily. Yet it might seem as if Sartre is being the more consistent thinker on this point, since if we once accept the condition of an existence separated from essence as the starting point for philosophical investigation, then how can we reach anything outside or beyond the scope of such an existence, and how then can we ever know the 'what' of God? Perhaps we might reach a kind of apprehension of transcendent power in a pure apophatic revelation, but that, by definition, would be a 'knowledge' of God that was no knowledge and that could only with difficulty find expression in coherent doctrinal exposition.[130] Should we then conclude that a would-be theology that took existence (in the sense of *Existenz*) as its starting point would be condemned to end as it began, as a simple expression of subjectivity, and nothing more? To use the expression applied by Don Cupitt to his own theological experiments of the 1980s and 1990s, wouldn't

---

[129] *Being and Some Philosophers*, 152–3. I say 'not unappreciative' because Gilson acknowledges the Christian motivation of Kierkegaard's authorship that, as he puts it, was 'the exasperated protest of a religious conscience against the centuries-old suppression of existence by abstract philosophical thinking' and the 'main responsibility' for the negative outcome of this protest 'lies, not with Kierkegaard, but with the abstract speculation about possible essences which has so obstinately refused to unite essence and existence in the unity of being' (p. 153).

[130] Even on his own non-theistic premises, Heidegger is led at several points to speak of reticence and silence as modes of authentically articulating the moment of vision of Being.

such a theology end up as a 'non-realist' theology, a theology that no longer asked the question of the being of the God it addressed?[131]

Has the Heideggerian attempt to approach Being by means of an analysis of existence then led us into a cul-de-sac? Or are we perhaps taking Sartre's objection too seriously? Does the notion of presence, by involving the for-itself of human consciousness (even if only in the minimal form of Suzuki's exclamation mark!), necessarily lead to the kind of decomposition of onto-logical unity that Sartre depicts? We might concede to Sartre that the structure of the for-itself introduces a gap, a space, or, at any rate, an element of distance into the continuum of Being-in-itself. But, once we recognize the metaphorical nature not only of 'distance' but of 'fissure', 'nihilation', 'deteri-oration', and all the other terms in which Sartre describes what happens to Being under the impact of the 'upsurge of nothingness' that consciousness brings about, then we are surely free to question the implications that he reads into them. We shall later have occasion to consider whether even 'nothing-ness' is best thought of as a 'negative' way of characterizing a certain mode of Being.[132] The more immediate point, however, is simply to issue a reminder that 'distance' can be understood at one and the same time in contrary yet ultimately identical ways: for 'distance' is not only indicative of separation, but also of the possibility of relationship. To become distant from the beloved may entail anguish and distress, yet without distance there could be no love: the total fusion of lovers (were it possible) would be an end of love, an end of relationship—the 'two' would be absorbed into a single glutinous ego. Whether 'distance' is interpreted in terms of the anguish of separation or the distance that allows relationship itself to occur will therefore depend on the kind or degree of distance in any given case. Thus Heidegger himself is able to interpret this 'distance' not as Dasein's alienation from Being but as its possibility of becoming open to Being. Twenty years on from *Being and Time* (and implicitly responding to Sartre) Heidegger would argue that already there (i.e. in *Being and Time*) the term 'existence' meant 'a way of Being; specifically, the Being of that being which stands open for the openness of Being in which it stand in enduring it'.[133] Care and being-towards-death are

---

[131] See Don Cupitt, *Taking Leave of God* (London: SCM Press, 1980). For a while, Cupitt did seem to allow something like the Heideggerian question of Being into his thought (see *The Religion of Being* (London: SCM Press, 1998)), but he has consistently decided the question either in terms of an autonomous subject who chooses his own religious goals and values or a certain kind of vitalistic celebration of 'life' that just carries us along.

[132] See Ch. 7 'On the Field of Nihility (Khôra?)' below.

[133] M. Heidegger, 'Introduction to "What is Metaphysics?"', trans. W. Kaufmann, in W. McNeil (ed.), *Pathmarks* (*Gesamtausgabe*, vol. ix) (Cambridge: Cambridge University Press, 1998), 283–4 (translation amended—GP).

said to be not so much modes of subjectivity turning in upon itself but as modes of 'the ecstatic essence of Dasein'. As such this 'ecstatic' way of existing precedes consciousness, which 'does not itself create the openness of beings, nor is it consciousness that makes it possible for human being to stand open for beings'.[134]

Such openness to Being does not, of itself, legitimize each and every way of interpreting beings. Indeed, although any historical revelation of Being will also involve a certain occlusion or distortion of what is revealed, inevitably foregrounding a particular aspect of Being or set of beings at the expense of Being-as-a-whole, there are ways of interpreting Being that are especially problematic in this regard. For Heidegger it is clear that the technological mind-set of modernity is a salient example of such a distorting interpretation. Openness to being does not imply a straightforward access to a certain 'what'. Rather, it is the possibility of entering into a questioning, enquiring, interpreting relation to Being that, as such, precedes any particular doctrine of essence (in the sense of *essentia* found in Thomism).[135] In a sense, nothing is said, nothing is revealed in the bare possibility of such openness. It is empty—not as 'deterioration' or 'nihilation', or not as these only but as readiness, waiting, attention. It is the unknowing that precedes and grounds all possible knowing. As such it is not hard to see it as possibly resonating with the apophatic pole of theology and these resonances have been reflected in some theological responses to Heidegger.[136] Something analogous seems also to be happening in Gabriel Marcel's idea of 'fidelity' to the revealed yet mysterious presence of Being, of which he says that 'presence is mystery in the exact measure in which it is presence'.[137]

As yet we are far from being in a position to decide between these alternative ways of understanding the 'distance' that inheres in the self-relation of human being, the being that is uniquely able to question itself as to the kind of being that it is and that, through this possibility of questioning, stands out—ecstatically—from the realm of beings in which, as a biological and historical individual, it lives. Even to begin to see all that is at issue in such a choice we

---

[134] Ibid. 284. See also the 'Letter on "Humanism"', trans. F. A. Capuzzi, in the same volume. The theme of 'openness to being' is a pervasive theme in the later Heidegger.

[135] Heidegger does refer here to the 'ecstatic *essence* of Dasein': however, he is using the term 'essence' in a distinctive manner that is implicitly distinct from what he takes essence to mean in the Aristotelian-Thomist tradition. For more on this distinctive doctrine of essence see the following chapter.

[136] See, e.g., C. Yannaras, *On the Absence and Unknowability of God: Heidegger and the Areopagite* (London: T. & T. Clark, 2005).

[137] G. Marcel, *The Philosophy of Existence*, trans. M. Harari (London: Harvill, 1948), 22. These ideas are treated fully in his Gifford Lectures, *The Mystery of Being* (vol. i: London: Harvill Press, 1950; vol. ii: Harvill Press, 1951).

need to go far more deeply and far more extensively into the structures of the for-itself (i.e., of Dasein: the subject that we ourselves are) and to see whether these argue more for the annihilation of any intrinsic relation of human existence to Being or for a subtler and more complex relation to Being than the simple dualism of the Sartrean model of being-in-itself/being-for-itself. In this latter case (to which the following argument will, perhaps unsurprisingly, tend), there will inevitably be further decisions as to how far the Augustinian-Thomist modelling of Being can serve an approach that has fully internalized the kind of questions brought to the fore by modern philosophies of existence. We shall find a spectrum of approaches to Being that runs from speaking of the concealment of Being through revision or 'weakening'[138] to the simple abandonment or movement 'beyond' Being.[139] It is too early as yet to judge the respective merits of these approaches and there is a sense in which the remainder of this book is an extended meditation on the various possibilities they offer contemporary reflection on God and Being. As we proceed through the themes of temporality, spatiality, language, relations to others, and embodiment we shall see more of what is involved in the 'distance' separating the subjective self from Being but also how this distance might indicate a certain relation as well as a certain separation. In the light of these meditations, we shall then consider whether the refusal of Being that we find in Sartre—and that has been taken up, reworked, and extended by Sartre's philosophical heirs[140]—is finally justified or whether it remains possible to speak of a certain God *and* Being. In other words, is Being still possible as a theological category 'after' the critique of ontotheology, and does Being still have a place, however transformed, however radically re-envisioned, and maybe however 'weakened' in interpreting the ways of human beings, the world, and God?

---

[138] The notion of a 'weakening' of Being is especially associated with Gianni Vattimo. See, e.g., G. Vattimo and A. Rovatti (eds.), *Il pensiero debole* (Milan: Feltrinelli, 1983). On the application of Vattimo's idea of 'weak thought' to religion see G. Vattimo, *Belief,* trans. L. D'Isanto and D. Webb (Cambridge: Polity Press, 1998); idem, *After Christianity,* trans. L. D'Isanto (New York: Columbia University Press, 2002); idem, with John D. Caputo, *After the Death of God* (New York: Columbia University Press, 2007). For general discussion see S. Zabala (ed.), *Weakening Philosophy: Essays in Honour of Gianni Vattimo* (Montreal: McGill-Queen's University Press, 2007).

[139] Associated in theology with Jean-Luc Marion. See J.-L. Marion, *Dieu sans l'être* (Paris: Presses Universitaires de France, 1991). For further discussion see Ch. 7 below.

[140] I am referring here specifically to practitioners of deconstruction. However, I am not implying that Derrida and others merely 'repeat' Sartre. An 'heir' is not a pupil, but one who is entitled freely to avail himself of what he has inherited and, in doing so, may and often does quite transform it. In this sense, Kierkegaard and Marx might both be said to be heirs of Hegel, without it being implied that either of them are 'Hegelian'.

3

Time and Space

INTRODUCTION

Time, as we have had several occasions to learn, has long been central to the question of human beings' relation to and understanding of Being. Within Christian theology, however, it has been widely construed in largely negative terms. For thinkers such as Augustine, time, non-being, and death flow together into a single figure associated with human fallenness and our alienation from the selfsameness of true Being. Subsequently, within and outside Christianity, different schools and thinkers would continue restating the issue in comparable terms. In the twentieth century, however, a very different view became standard, a view hinted at in the very title Heidegger's *Being and Time*. As Heidegger would argue in that work, time is now seen as constituting the essential horizon for the interpretation of the meaning of Being, suggesting that outside of or apart from time Being can mean nothing at all. *Being and Time* is an extraordinarily original work but there is nevertheless a sense in which what Heidegger is doing here is essentially drawing out and bringing into a coherent form what seems to be a widespread shift in the evaluation of time that occurred at some point in the modern period and that achieved its first definitive philosophical expression in Hegel. Broadly, this can be associated with what has been called the rise of the historical consciousness in early modernity and a view of history in which the passage of time is not merely a story of the decline and fall of ancient virtues or the unendurable anxiety of exile from the soul's true eternal home but the occasion of significant progress in the amelioration of the human condition. Yet, despite the Augustinian suspicion of time, this discovery of history and of time was guided at a number of key points by intellectual imperatives drawn from Christian and biblical thought. This, of course, is a story that has often been told, and I shall not retell it here, other than as it bears on the understanding of Being and, in particular, of the implications of temporality for the human relation to Being and, especially, to divine Being.[1]

---

[1] Bultmann's *History and Eschatology* remains a useful account of this development as seen from within a theological perspective that is also conscious of existential philosophy

We have arrived at the question of time from reflecting on the meaning of being-for-itself and the turn to the subject as articulated in the modern existentialist tradition of Kierkegaard, Heidegger, and Sartre. It would be entirely out of the question even to attempt to establish some general theory of time mid-way through an enquiry such as this, nor is there scope even to do justice to some of the key texts that will be guiding us. It is therefore extremely important to bear in mind that this virtually infinitely extendable topic is being addressed here within very narrow boundaries and is focused exclusively on exploring and interpreting the implications of the difference or distance that the structure of self-relationship introduces into human beings' relation to Being and, by analogy, to divine Being. And that is already more than enough.

Even on a cursory view of the question it becomes clear that reflecting on the 'place' of time in the structure of the for-itself can only deepen the problematic aspects of this structure vis-à-vis its possible openness to Being. If the contemplation of time's effect on the external world—the passage of the seasons, the decay of empires, the wastage of physical powers—already seems to weaken confidence in a unitary and sustaining power of Being present in, with, and under all that is, then how much more when it is a matter of time as a dimension of our self-relation? Already in childhood we find ourselves spontaneously wondering at how we seem to have come into being out of a past that our conscious memory cannot retrieve and as we grow older we see more and more clearly that our future will disappear into an oblivion that cannot be fathomed by either thought or feeling and that even the past we have ourselves lived through is becoming barely recuperable in memory. To be in time and to exist as a temporal being is to be always in a process of coming into and passing out of being and therefore to be a relative and transient being. Even in the more immediate time-experiences of everyday life we have no difficulty in recognizing that whatever continuity there may be in our self-consciousness, we are not exactly the same today as we were yesterday and that what we were yesterday has, in a sense, vanished irrevocably. To paraphrase Thomas Hardy, the experience that we are not as we were is an experience we can have any day, any time. If, then,

---

(R. Bultmann, *History and Eschatology* (Edinburgh: Edinburgh University Press, 1975)). For a comprehensive anthology of key sources see R. M. Burns and H. Rayment-Pickard, *Philosophies of History: From Enlightenment to Postmodernity* (Oxford: Blackwell, 2000). An especially thought-provoking treatment of the subject is that of Michael Theunissen, who argues with his customary textual detail and analytical rigour that a negative view of time is already implicit in Parmenides and continues to mark the philosophical tradition not only up to but also including Heidegger. Christian theology, which takes its starting point in faith in the redemptive power of God, has, he contends, a fundamentally distinct approach to the whole question. See M. Theunissen, *Negative Theologie der Zeit* (Frankfurt am Main: Suhrkamp, 1991).

temporality is integral to who we are, if we are beings who are what and as we are as beings in time, as historically acting and suffering beings, then it would seem hard, if not impossible, to imagine how we might embrace and hold fast a lasting and saving relation to the fullness of selfsame and immutable divine Being. How could a being who was radically and thoroughly temporal ever come to the joy that Kierkegaard saw in the moment of self-presence figured in the lilies of the field and the birds of the air? For such a being every moment of presence would already be slipping away into the past, every 'Now' would already be gone.

Of course, there has been a long tradition of understanding the human soul as essentially timeless. In Plato's *Phaedo* the soul is not only imperishable and immortal but is unaffected by anything external to it; it is a life-giving power that cannot be touched by change and is not subject to death. A similar teaching is found in the *Bhagavad Gītā*.[2] Within Christianity, as we have seen, a central and normative tradition sees the soul as capable of sloughing off at least those aspects of bodily existence associated with its entanglement in temporal change. There may still be philosophical arguments that might persuade some to affirm these or similar views. However, I shall assume that this is not a view of the self that comes naturally to those living this side of the nineteenth and twentieth centuries.[3] This is because in this period a broad range of influences converged to shape an understanding of human existence as utterly historical and utterly temporal. Romanticism already knew that 'the child is father to the man', and from the 'novels of education' of the eighteenth century through to psychoanalysis there has been a steady and incremental strengthening of the view that we are the individuals that we are only in, through, and as patterns of temporal development. Such insights were further backed up by the new understanding of human culture and values as historically formed, and, on a still larger canvas, by the evolutionary view of human origins, which thus epitomized and sealed rather than revolutionized the understanding of human life that had been emerging on many fronts over the previous half-century. The outcome was that life in time was no longer seen as something to be merely endured but was reconceived as offering a potential plenitude of life-enhancing experiences—a view for which Nietzsche was perhaps the most eloquent spokesman. As a result, we now mostly feel that to live our lives as historical beings, who are changed by and

---

[2] See, e.g., *Phaedo*, 79B–80E; *Bhagavad Gītā*, II. 11–30.

[3] This point is not about belief in life after death but about a conception of the soul as essentially atemporal. It is striking that more recent restatements of belief in life after death often incorporate an element of becoming, as in the vision presented in John Hick, *Death and Eternal Life* (London: Collins, 1976).

who develop through their adventures, decisions, and sufferings, is richer, more satisfying, and more precious than to envisage ourselves as self-enclosed spheres, passing unaltered through the ebb and flow of temporal occurrences—even if we are at the same time aware that this exposes us to risks of nihilism and relativism.

Against this background, to speak of Being as being-in-time is to say that, for us, nothing 'is' what and as it is other than as we are able to experience it in time. But is this also applicable to the God-relationship and, if so, in what way? One line of theological reflection—classical theism—would want to call a halt at this point, since, even if it is prepared to concede that human beings are temporal through and through, it is precisely the supreme excellence of the divine Being that it is above and beyond all possible change. Insofar as time enters into the God-relationship, it can do so (the claim is) only as a feature of mortals who turn to God in need and joy. Even in heaven we may perhaps remain somehow temporal, but in himself God is timeless, above and beyond all orders of time. Again, there might be narrowly philosophical arguments that might lead us to accept this view,[4] but the pre-philosophical assumption guiding this present chapter is that the view that God is without time and that salvation must involve some kind of relation to what is extra-temporal depends largely on a negative evaluation of the meaning of life in time that no longer comes naturally to us. Yet old habits die hard and to formulate an understanding of life in time that might be capable of satisfying human beings' religious longings is not easy, whilst appropriate and forceful symbolic expressions for such temporal fulfilment remain elusive or tenuous. A tragic view of life might offer one alternative to a non-nihilistic affirmation of historical existence.[5] But whilst such a tragic view may resonate with much in the Christian tradition, the two can only with difficulty be entirely con-flated.[6] Nevertheless, unless or until it might be shown that life in time was capable of fulfilments of an equal or greater excellence than those that a non-temporal immortal soul was capable of enjoying; unless or until we become capable of modelling salvation as an event in time that we could experience as

---

[4] We shall shortly look more closely at the classic presentation of this case in Augustine's *Confessions*. For a recent defence of the timelessness of God see B. Leftow, *Time and Eternity* (Ithaca, NY: Cornell University Press, 1991).

[5] The expression 'tragic view of life' is associated with the Spanish philosopher Miguel de Unamuno, but whilst Sartre claims Unamuno as an ancestor of his existentialist tragic view of life, Unamuno himself stresses the inextinguishable longing of human beings for immortality and the transcendence of tragedy. See M. de Unamuno, *Tragic Sense of Life*, trans. J. E. C. Flitch (London: Macmillan, 1921).

[6] For a discussion of many of the key questions arising at the intersection of tragedy and Christianity see Kenneth Surin, *Christ, Ethics, and Tragedy: Essays in Honour of Donald Mackinnon* (Cambridge: Cambridge University Press, 1989).

what was most worth striving for—unless or until then, the Christian mind will probably continue to feel the need for connecting salvation to some kind of supra-temporal reality. There might be many possible ways of bringing about such a revaluation. The divine being itself might, for example, be re-envisaged in such a way as to allow an element or analogue of temporality in the divine life.[7] Or, if we reached the conclusion that any meaningful concept of Being does, after all, require the exclusion or suppression of time, we might simply opt to disconnect theology from ontology and on that basis argue that God is to be thought of as 'without being'[8] or, as has been quite widespread in modern Protestant thought, to declare that the biblical, historical understanding of existence never did have anything in common with the supposedly 'Greek' cult of timeless Being anyway.[9] Or we could simply replace the category of God with that of 'life! life!'[10]

It should at once be emphasized that I do not hope to achieve more than merely to touch the hem of the mystery to which our reflections are leading us in this matter. Nevertheless, we might hope to go some way towards drawing out and clarifying the meaning of human temporality with regard to the God-relationship and to exploring the possibility of human beings and God somehow sharing a common horizon of lived time. Especially, of course, we shall be concerned to probe how such a possibility might affect the claim that theological truth is grounded in an experienced presence of Being that might provide an analogical pointer to divine Being itself. In the conclusion of the previous chapter, we saw how modern existential thought

---

[7] This view is represented in a number of strands of modern theology and religious philosophy. One is associated with Jakob Boehme and was developed in modern European philosophy through German idealism (principally Schelling) and such inheritors as N. A. Berdyaev. Another is process thought, originating with A. N. Whitehead and influencing a considerable number of late twentieth-century theologians, e.g., J. Moltmann, *The Trinity and the Kingdom of God* (London: SCM Press, 1981). Apart from Whitehead's own works, a useful source book for process thought in its relation to theology remains Charles Harsthorne and William L. Reese, *Philosophers Speak of God* (Chicago: Chicago University Press, 1953). The influence of such thinking can even be discerned in a certain interpretation of Karl Barth; see E. Jüngel, *God's Being is in Becoming: The Trinitarian Being of God in the Theology of Karl Barth* (Edinburgh: T. & T. Clark, 2001). However, see Colin Gunton's statement of the differences between Barth and process thought in his *Becoming and Being* (London: SCM Press, 2001).

[8] See Jean-Luc Marion, *Dieu sans l'être* (Paris: Presses Universitaires de France, 1991).

[9] See the comments on Theunissen in n. 1 above.

[10] Nietzsche might be seen as having attempted this from an anti-Christian and anti-religious perspective. More recently, the English philosopher of religion Don Cupitt has tried something similar, especially in works from the 1990s and the third millennium—see, e.g., *The New Religion of Life in Everyday Speech* (London: SCM Press, 1999); *Life! Life!* (Santa Rosa, Calif.: Polebridge Press, 2003). However, whilst Cupitt is eager to present his philosophy of life as in some sense answering human beings' need of religion, he is clear that he is no longer attempting to combine this new religion of life with the inheritance of Christian theology.

argues that human beings' self-relation opens up a rift in the continuum of being-in-itself that entails a weakening of the classic theological model of divine Being, although I suggested that this does not immediately require us completely to abandon that model (which is why I have preferred at several points to speak with Gianni Vattimo of the 'weakening' rather than the 'annihilation' of Being). In these terms we might be led to think less of the simple presence or absence of God qua Being-Itself and more of a fluctuating interplay of nearness and distance, in which God might appear most distant, withdrawn, and mysterious even and perhaps especially when he is most near.[11] But can the tension involved in such a relationship be sustained and what might that mean?

Those, essentially, are the questions that this chapter will now explore further. My procedure will be as follows. First, I shall revisit the Augustinian interpretation of the relationship between divine eternity and human temporality; then I turn to Kierkegaard's introduction of the idea of the 'moment of vision' as the conjunction of time and eternity and explore further what this means with the help of another Kierkegaardian concept, repetition, also drawing in Paul Tillich as a significant conversation partner; this, in turn, leads to Heidegger's adaptation of the 'moment of vision' and repetition as key elements in the interpretation of time in *Being and Time*, and we shall also follow some of the transformations of these ideas in Heidegger's later thinking; a critical perspective on Heidegger's approach is developed in dialogue with Emmanuel Lévinas, which leads into a brief discussion of utopistic time. I shall then illustrate the expression of two of the main views considered in the chapter as they are found in the writings of two British poets, T. S. Eliot and Edwin Muir. Finally, I shall offer some comments on the experience of space as a necessary complement to that of time. As previously stated, I do not anticipate this yielding anything like a fully worked-out ontology of time but I do hope to indicate how we might learn to view time not merely in negative terms but also as offering a way, a form, or an opportunity of experiencing truth—although whether or how such truth might be construed as a true revelation of Being will remain undecided. To put the argument in more graphic terms, alongside the image of time the destroyer, Father Time whose sickle and hourglass blend into the iconography of the Grim Reaper, our cultural inheritance also offers the image of time the revealer, vindicating the

---

[11] It is characteristic of the experience of biblical prophets that the manifestation of God is precisely the revelation of his awesome mystery. A classic treatment of the interrelationship of epiphany and transcendence is R. Otto, *The Idea of the Holy*, trans. J. W. Harvey (Oxford: Oxford University Press, 1923).

truth of virtue, innocence, and love 'in the end' or 'the long run'.[12] Perhaps these enigmatically contradictory aspects of time cannot finally be separated, but if the power of time the destroyer is only too obvious, we must all the more take care to remember that this same time may serve as revealer—and perhaps such remembrance will turn out to be especially well served by Heidegger's reformulation of truth not as the correspondence of idea and thing but as the unconcealment of Being, that is, Being made manifest even in the midst of its ceaseless coming-into-being and passing-away. As we shall see, Heidegger especially associates such a manifestation with a poetic word to which he attributes the power of uttering a utopian promise to a world suffering the distress of alienated temporal existence. First, however, we turn once more to Augustine, for whom it is especially the negative aspects of life in time that are to the fore and where the truth of time is not to be found in time itself but only in what necessarily and inherently transcends time.

AUGUSTINE

The discussion of time found in Book XI of Augustine's *Confessions* remains a major point of reference even for modern philosophical treatments of the subject.[13] It occurs in the context of an exposition of the creation story of Genesis 1: 'Let me hear and understand, how you made heaven and earth in the beginning,' Augustine prays on opening the Scripture.[14] As he launches his enquiry, he is immediately faced with what seems to be the self-evident truth that heaven and earth themselves proclaim that they are created 'for they are changed and altered from what they were. Whereas whatsoever is not made, and nevertheless is, contains nothing that was not in it before, such as could be changed and altered' (XI, 4). The distinction between the mutable and the

---

[12] As explored in Panofsky's study of 'Father Time', with particular reference to Bronzino's *Allegory of Innocence*. See E. Panofsky, *Studies in Iconology* (New York: Harper and Row, 1962), 83 ff. As Panofsky suggests, this becomes an especially prominent theme in the Baroque era. In addition to the visual arts, we might also think of, e.g., Handel's oratorio *Il triomfo del tempo* or Edward Young's *Night Thoughts*.

[13] See, e.g., E. Husserl, *Zur Phänomenologie des Inneren Zeitbewußtseins*, ed. R. Boehm (*Husserliana: Edmund Husserls Gesamte Werke*, vol. x) (The Hague: Martinus Nijhoff, 1966), 3. Also P. Ricœur, *Time and Narrative*, trans. K. McLaughlin and D. Pellauer, vol. i (Chicago: Chicago University Press, 1984), ch. 1 'The Aporias of the Experience of Time: Book 11 of Augustine's *Confessions*'.

[14] Augustine, *Confessions* (XI, 3). Further references are given in the text by book and chapter number.

immutable is thus the most basic of all the distinctions that can be drawn between created and uncreated Being. There follows a series of reflections on the difference between divine and human making, with particular reference to how God creates by means of his Word. This leads to the question of time and, especially, of the difference between divine eternity and creaturely temporality, since when Genesis says that God 'spoke' Augustine cannot imagine that this meant he uttered 'sounding' words that 'pass away' but rather that he spoke an 'eternal word, which is in silence' (XI, 6). Otherwise there would have had to be corporeal bodies for measuring the passage of time prior to the creation, but this is an absurdity.[15] Instead, 'that which was spoken was not spoken successively, one thing spoken ended that the next might be spoken: but all at once and unto everlasting. Otherwise there should be time and alteration, and no true eternity, no true immortality' (XI, 7). The enquiry into time now intensifies as Augustine faces a set of questions that are aimed at ridiculing the Jewish and Christian idea that creation occurred at a particular moment in time (as opposed to the view that the world itself had existed eternally). On the one hand, the objectors ask what God was doing before the creation; on the other, they ask why, if God had willed the creation from eternity, the world had not existed from eternity.

It is in responding to these questions that Augustine begins the extended meditation on time that takes up most of the remainder of Book XI. First of all, he says, those who ask such things show that although they may desire to know eternal things 'their heart runs to and fro between the motions of things past and to come' (XI, 11). But instead of trying to understand and to judge eternity by the standards of temporal life, they should judge time by the light of that 'ever abiding [*stantis*] eternity' (XI, 11). If they were to do that, they would see that there is no comparison. For in the eternal, 'nothing becomes past, but all is at once present, whereas no time is all at once present' but time 'flows out of that which is always present' (XI, 11). Thus the eternal 'gives the word of command to the times past or to come, itself being neither past nor to come' (XI, 11). Since there is therefore neither future nor past in eternity, there was no time 'before' the creation, 'there was no "then" when there was not time' (XI, 13). God could not 'precede times in time' since his years 'neither go nor come' but 'abide all at once because they abide ... Your years are one day; and your day is not every day, but today ... [and] your today is eternity' (XI, 13).

But if God is in this way utterly beyond time, the question still remains as to what time itself is—a question that, in this context, is doubly important. On the one hand, it is important because (on Augustine's reading) time is one of

---

[15] Although later, as we shall see, Augustine rejects the idea that the movements of bodies in space can provide a basis for measuring time.

the basic features that distinguish creation from the uncreated heaven of the divine life. On the other hand, it is itself a spur to the longing heart that seeks, in time, to know what is above and beyond time—thus the failure to ask about eternity in the right way is repeatedly associated with the confusion and misdirection of the enquiring heart. Creatures in and of time, we nevertheless strive to find and to know that which is above time, but how is this possible? The more one looks into it, the harder it seems to find an answer and, as Augustine himself famously comments, so long as no one asks me about it, I know what time is, but as soon as anyone asks me, I cannot explain it (XI, 14). The past no longer is, the future is not yet, and the present passes away in the moment we become aware of it. Where, then, is time? How can we know it? How can we measure it?

It is not to the purpose of this chapter to go into the detail of Augustine's argument, but several points require attention. To begin with, Augustine explicitly rejects the view that time is determined by the movements of the heavenly bodies. For if we are to know these movements as having a temporal character, we already have to have a certain understanding of time. In preference to such physicalist explanations, Augustine sees time as a product of the human mind. Putting it somewhat anachronistically, we might say that he portrays it as a kind of a priori form of intuition (for human beings, though not for God). It is in the mind that the past exists, as the memory of the past, and it is in the mind that the future exists, as the anticipation of the future. The mind 'expects, and attends, and remembers' (XI, 18), and it is through such expecting, attending, and remembering that it first becomes possible to conceive and measure time. 'It is in you, o my soul, that I measure my times' (XI, 27). This measuring occurs on the basis of the soul's ability to 'distend' itself across the three modes of time, whilst holding them together in the unity of a single mental act. But precisely the unity of this mental act indicates that time is not determined or measured by anything that is itself temporal. Indeed, the exemplary instance of such an act is the knowledge that God himself has of temporal things and this cannot be temporal. Just as when we sing a psalm we hold the whole together as a single act extended through time, so too, only in an infinitely more sublime manner, God knows all that is past and all that is to come in the manner of his eternal and unchanging divine way of being. Compared with the kind of knowledge we have of temporal things, 'far be it from us to think, that you, Creator of this universe . . . should no better know what were past and what were to come. Greatly, greatly more wonderfully and greatly more secretly you know them' (XI, 31). For God's knowledge of temporal things, unlike those things themselves, is a knowledge 'without variety' (XI, 31). Therefore, the true interest of the human mind should not be in the things of time, but 'forgetting what is past' and not being distracted by 'what shall be and shall pass away' it extends itself to those things that are before (XI, 29).[16]

The ambiguity of such knowledge as we can have of temporal things is focused in this passage in one of Augustine's key terms, namely, 'distention'. For whilst the capacity to distend itself across the three modes of time is the key to the mind's ability to know time at all, this distention also marks or even enacts a certain dissolution of the mind's inner unity. Thus, in the passage alluding to Philippians 3, William Watts's translation 'not distracted but attracted . . . not, I say distractedly, but intently' interprets *distentio*—without which knowledge of temporal phenomena would not at all be possible—as 'distraction' and contrasts it with the 'attraction' (*extentus*) of the mind towards its proper object ('the things that are before') or its 'intention' (*intentio*) in seeking the 'garland of the supernal calling', namely, the heavenly delights that 'neither come into being nor pass away' (XI, 29). And, in the event, it seems that for Augustine himself the attraction of these delights and his capacity for being steadfast in seeking them intently cannot resist the counter-pressure of temporal distraction: 'I fall into dissolution amid the times whose order I do not know, and my thoughts are torn asunder by tumultuous vicissitudes, even the inner parts of my soul, unless I merge with you, purged and melted by the fire of your love' (XI, 29).[17]

But is it entirely congruent with Christian doctrine to suggest, as Augustine seems to, that life in time is somehow intrinsically separated from God? Since time is intrinsic to creation, should it not be viewed as God's handiwork and therefore as intrinsically 'good'? Our suspicions on this point might increase if we note how, interestingly, Augustine does not limit the class of supra-temporal realities to the divine life. When Genesis 1: 1 speaks of God creating 'heaven and earth' Augustine takes 'heaven' to refer to what he calls 'some intellectual creature; which, although in no way co-eternal with you, the Trinity, nevertheless participates in your eternity' (XII, 9). Or, it is 'that intellectual heaven, where it is the property of the intelligence to know all at once, not in part, not, darkly, not through a glass, but in whole, clearly, and face to face . . . without all succession of times' (XII, 13). It is created wisdom, a 'sublime creature', 'the house of God', 'a spiritual house and partaker of your eternity', 'that chaste city of yours, our mother which is above' (the New or Heavenly Jerusalem) (XII, 15). If human destiny is to become incorporated

---

[16] This last phrase is a reference to Paul's comparison of the longing for heaven with the efforts of an athlete racing towards the finishing line (Phil. 3: 13).

[17] On the Augustinian understanding of distention see *Time and Narrative*, vol. i, especially pp. 19–21. Note Ricœur's conclusion that Augustine's account of the soul's ability to engage itself with the temporal data that it establishes in the act of distention constitutes 'the most impenetrable enigma' of all the aporias of time with which Augustine wrestles.

into this heavenly city, partaking in the divine eternity, then we must become capable—without losing our humanity—of shedding our temporality and achieving that focused intention on the divine nature that is so easily and typically lost here, in time. Temporality, then, would not be an essential or defining feature of human existence but a mark of our failure to be what and as we should be. Meanwhile, in time, as long as we are in time, our temporality is a mark of our distance from the simplicity of eternal divine Being.

But, to repeat, this scarcely seems to do justice to the biblical account itself, in which it does not seem to be the fact that human beings live, and move, and act, and suffer in time that is at fault, but the particular character of the decisions they make. Biblically, to have to make a particular choice for or against God in a specific historical moment is precisely what decides whether we are living faithfully or not. History and time would seem to be a necessary condition not only of being human but of being in a right relation to God. And this would seem to be implicit in the very structure of having-to-choose with which the divine commandment confronts human beings. Where such having-to-choose is taken seriously, it would seem that temporality is going to have to receive a very different treatment from what we find in Augustine. It is in this respect scarcely coincidental that one of the most significant modern revisions of Christian thinking about time and eternity occurred in a post-Kantian Protestant context, that is, a context shaped by an interpretation of Christianity in which moral responsibility was given a pre-eminent role in the human God-relationship and a context in which the historical aspect of biblical faith was likewise stressed in an unusually high degree. This revision finds paradigmatic expression in the work of S. Kierkegaard.

KIERKEGAARD

As so often, and without taking a position on the question as to how specific Kierkegaard's knowledge of Hegel was, it is useful to draw attention to the development of the topic in the thought of Hegel before turning directly to Kierkegaard himself.

There seems to be little doubt that, with regard to the question of temporality and, especially, the implications of a developed concept of time for the understanding of essence and Being, Hegel represents a watershed in the history of Western thought. Basically, his move is an extremely simple one. It is to suggest that, far from time meaning a falling away from the fullness of original Being, nothing is what it is other than through a process of becoming. Thus, to know something is not to be able to define its essence but is to show

how it became what it is: it is to know the whole process whereby it emerged into and sustains itself in being. In the introduction to *The Phenomenology of Spirit* Hegel made the point by means of a simple botanical illustration:

> The bud disappears in the bursting-forth of the blossom, and one might say that the former is refuted by the latter; similarly when the fruit appears, the blossom is shown up in its turn as a false manifestation of the plant, and the fruit now emerges as the truth of it instead. The forms are not just distinguished from one another, they also supplant one another as mutually incompatible. Yet at the same time their fluid nature makes them moments of an organic unity in which they not only do not conflict, but in which each is as necessary as the other; and this mutual necessity alone constitutes the life of the whole.[18]

It is not the end-state that is the object of knowledge, but the movement of the whole. A. N. Whitehead's philosophy of process rested on a very similar insight, and Whitehead's statement 'that *how* an actual entity *becomes* constitutes *what* the actual entity *is*... Its "being" is constituted by its "becoming"'[19] captures what Hegel too is saying. The effects of this insight are discernible in every part of Hegel's thought, from logic through to art, philosophy, and religion. In logic, it relates to the distinctive role he gives to the category of movement, which he introduces at the very foundation of the system of logic as a designation for the alternation of Being and Nothing as the two most basic forms of Being.[20] From there on, movement pervades the whole system: thus the doctrine of essence appears only after the movement from being, through nothingness and becoming, to being-for-itself has been completed. Essence, as Hegel puts it, 'is the truth of Being'.[21] Knowledge of such truth, however, because it presupposes the sequence of 'movements' initiated by the dialectic of Being and Nothing, presupposes a certain temporality. Temporality is therefore engrained in the very structure of consciousness as such. Thus, Hegel would argue that in knowing the essence, I know *what* the object of knowledge *really* is (in a fairly conventional sense I know that that conglomeration of green and brown impressions is a tree and not a cat), but I *know* it only in an act of consciousness (since only for consciousness can truth be an issue at all). In other words, essential truth is both true in itself (the tree really is a tree) and for itself (it is known as a tree only in its

---

[18] G. W. F. Hegel, *Phenomenology of Spirit*, trans. A. V. Miller (Oxford: Clarendon Press, 1977), 2.

[19] A. N. Whitehead, *Process and Reality* (New York: Harper and Row, 1960), 34–5.

[20] Early critics, including Trendelenburg and Kierkegaard, already saw this as a piece of audacious sophistry.

[21] G. W. F. Hegel, *Wissenschaft der Logik II*, in *Werke*, vi (Frankfurt am Main: Suhrkamp, 1969), 17.

reflection in conscious life). But the in-itself is known to the for-itself only as a result of the process whereby the knowing mind has stripped away the accidentalities of the empirical object and identified what is truly essential in the tree, a 'movement' in which the conscious mind 'negates' the purely external elements of what is to be known, thereby also replicating the movement of the object itself (as in the life-process of the tree that runs from bud to blossom to fruit). Thus, in response to the question posed at the conclusion of Chapter 2 as to how essence might 'point to' Being, Hegel's answer would seem to be that before there can be a knowledge of essence, there must be a more original experience of Being *as time* or as temporal.

However, implicit in the claim that we do, after all, arrive at an adequate and reliable essential knowledge of the truth is the assumption that the process can be completed, that we can follow the life-cycle of the object under consideration through to its end—whether it is a tree, the history of philosophy, of art, or of religion. 'The true is the whole,'[22] and Hegel's confidence in our capacity to know the truth depends on both the world and our knowledge of it being able to complete the process whereby things become as they are.

It is precisely this assumption that Kierkegaard would challenge, especially in his *Concluding Unscientific Postscript*. There, in addition to a merciless assault on Hegel's claim that the principle of 'becoming' can be deduced from the relationship between Being and Nothing, Kierkegaard insists that, as least as far as human beings are concerned, the process is necessarily inconclusive. Until the moment of death we cannot know what our life has been all about. More fundamentally, since we cannot know with certainty whether we are actually immortal souls—as both philosophy and religion then taught—or mere congeries of matter that dissolve at the point of biological death, we are in a state of essential ignorance as to who or what we really are. Yet nothing is more important for us than to know this. The contradiction of being unable to know what is most important to us as individual, existing human beings therefore means that existential thinking, thinking about one's own life, will be marked to an extraordinary degree by passion—as opposed to the detached contemplation of the philosophical sage who believes himself to be in possession of a vision of the whole. The philosopher speaks as if he believes that he is able to consider the world and all that therein is *sub specie aeterni*, from the perspective of the eternal. The introduction of movement as a logical category is in effect retracted by the holism that enables him to grasp the movement as a start-to-finish whole and that thereby abstracts what is known

---

[22] *Phenomenology*, 11.

from time.[23] 'But', as Kierkegaard puts it, 'where everything is in a process of becoming' (as it is for the existing human subject), everything comes down to passionate decision, not to knowledge.

At the same time, Kierkegaard acknowledges that unless there is some kind of continuity in time, there can be no meaning in existence that does not dissolve into the flux of becoming. That is the conclusion reached by the pseudonym Constantin Constantius in the novella *Repetition*. Having decided that repetition, i.e. continuity, is impossible, Constantin concludes his reflections with a eulogy of the coach-horn, since, as he says, it never plays the same note twice. Elsewhere, he recalls the disciple of Heraclitus, who capped the master's saying that one cannot step twice into the same stream by adding that if there is only a continual and universal flux then one cannot step into it even once, since neither the stream nor the person stepping into it would have any coherent identity. However, in the *Postscript* Kierkegaard allows that there is something that transcends the flux,[24] something he calls 'the eternal'—but this is not present to the existing individual as a basis for knowledge (*sub specie aeterni*), but 'only so much of the eternal is present that it can have a constraining effect in the passionate decision, where the *eternal* relates itself as the *future* to the *person in a process of becoming*—there the absolute disjunction belongs. In other words, when I join eternity and becoming, I do not gain rest but the future.' And, Kierkegaard adds, 'this is why Christianity has proclaimed the eternal as the future, because it was proclaimed to existing persons, and this is why it also assumes an absolute *aut/aut* [either/or]'.[25] Because I cannot *know* the future—my future—I therefore have to take responsibility for my understanding of it in an act of courageous self-choice and commitment that is necessarily marked by objective uncertainty.

Kierkegaard's most philosophically detailed treatment of the relationship between time and the eternal is found in the third chapter of *The Concept of Anxiety*, where he is exploring the relationship between anxiety and sin. Anxiety is here depicted as a generic state in which the self is, as it were, suspended in a kind of neutrality vis-à-vis the possibilities of choosing good

---

[23] Husserl also makes the point that all comparison and relationship seem to presuppose a 'timeless comprehensive knowing' in which the data dispersed through time or across the relational field is drawn together into an indivisible time-point. See *Zur Phänomenologie des Inneren Zeitbewußtseins*, 19–21. This invites comparison with Augustine's insistence on the unity of the mental act in which the threefold structure of time is known as a single fact.

[24] 'Inasmuch as existence is in motion, it holds true that there is indeed a continuity that holds the motion together, because otherwise there is no motion.' S. Kierkegaard, *Concluding Unscientific Postscript*, trans. E. H. and H. Hong, SKS 7 (Princeton: Princeton University Press, 1992), 312.

[25] Ibid. 307.

and evil. Everything depends on how this state is resolved in action and decision, whether I succumb to my anxiety and fail to realize the existential possibilities awaiting me (the most typical outcome of anxiety's vertigo) or whether I arouse in myself the 'courage to be' and go to meet my future in confidence and faith, thereby choosing the good. The question, then, is what happens in the moment in which the indeterminate state of anxiety is resolved into one or other outcome (sin or faith/the good). Once again, Kierkegaard tosses off some mocking comments on the Hegelian system, in particular on the way in which it reduces the category of transition to a purely logical move. Against this, Kierkegaard insists on the importance of 'the moment' in which the existing individual realizes one or other existential possibility and becomes what she or he is. Even if one assumes that the human being is not only 'a synthesis of soul and body, but ... also a *synthesis of the temporal and the eternal*',[26] this is not to be understood as some timeless attribute of the human essence but as a state that has to be achieved or chosen and therefore actualized in time. But this raises Augustine's question as to where, in time, one might find a foothold by which to understand time. For each present moment immediately vanishes into the past (it is an 'infinite vanishing', as Kierkegaard puts it), and in the moment in which we begin to think about it, it is no more. Thus, for the most part, we do not really think the moment in an appropriately temporal way but rather 'spatialize' it, representing it in a way that suits our capacities of thinking but that betrays the thing itself.[27] Summing up thus far, then, 'if ... time and eternity touch each other, then it must be in time, and now we have come to the moment'.[28]

Really to understand the significance of the moment requires that we move beyond the merely abstract terminology of logic, and Kierkegaard is swift to point out that '"The moment" is a figurative expression, and therefore it is not easy to deal with'—but, he continues, 'it is a beautiful word to consider'.[29] In fact, rather than being inconvenienced by the inevitably figurative character of a term such as the moment, we cannot think about temporal existence without figuration. If meaning is the yield of a sequence of occurrences, then it cannot be comprised in the simplicity of an abstract definition but must reflect in itself something of the composite reality of which it is the meaning. It must engage and reveal (and not abstract from or occlude) the articulated variety of what it represents—thus, 'the moment'.

---

[26] S. Kierkegaard, *The Concept of Anxiety*, trans. R. Thomte, SKS 4 (Princeton: Princeton University Press, 1980), 85.

[27] Ibid.

[28] Ibid. 87.

[29] Ibid.

Kierkegaard's Danish term, *Øjeblikket*, literally means 'the glance of an eye'[30] and may therefore be rendered 'moment of vision',[31] and he himself goes on to interpret it by means of a dramatic moment of separation between two lovers in a well-known contemporary poem. As the heroine, Ingeborg, looks across the sea toward her departing lover her look gains in intensity because she knows that she will be forced into marriage during his absence: it is not simply a 'moment' of nostalgia for the loss of a beloved presence but the marking of an irrevocable rupture in the defining relationship of her life—and her 'look' comprises also her knowledge of this (although, as Kierkegaard insists, it is a knowledge too all-embracing, too existential, for it to be adequately articulated in anything she might possibly have said).[32] That, Kierkegaard suggests, is how life in time is, and our awareness of time is always both an awareness of its passing (its 'infinite vanishing') and, paradoxically, the realization that what happens in time is utterly decisive for our lives, for who and what we are. Only so, only in the moments of vision that reveal our future—or at least our next step—does our 'eternal' identity get revealed.

The experience of Ingeborg is an experience of a lost future and a lost happiness. Yet Kierkegaard does believe that it is possible, in time, to relate in a fulfilling and happy—or, as his expression might also be rendered, 'blessed'—way. This is because, beyond human beings' proximate future (i.e., what we will be doing tomorrow, next week, or next year), there is an eternal future with God. However we cannot enter into relation to this eternal future other than by the choices we make in time—and we might note that, despite the very real difference that separates Kierkegaardian thinking about time from that of Hegel, this twofold assumption closely reflects Hegel's view that knowledge of what exists in time involves both the in-itself and the for-itself. But how are the possibility of a relation to the eternal and the ever-to-be-repeated 'moment' connected? How can the entirely temporal moment of decision also disclose or even bring about a relation to the eternal?

Fully to answer this question we must go back several steps and look more closely at Kierkegaard's analysis of the development of the religious consciousness in a human being. In one of his upbuilding discourses Kierkegaard describes the first step on the way from the existing individual's everyday way of being to living in the light of the eternal as beginning in the moment when

---

[30] Although sometimes it is rather misleadingly translated as 'the blink of an eye', which, of course, suggests closing rather than opening the eye, which is the point!

[31] This is also the Macquarrie/Robinson translation of Heidegger's *Augenblick*.

[32] The best commentary on this passage is N. N. Eriksen's *Kierkegaard's Category of Repetition: A Reconstruction*, Kierkegaard Monograph series 5 (Berlin: de Gruyter, 2000), 69–76.

'there awakens in [a person's] soul a concern about what meaning the world has for him and he for the world, about what meaning everything within him by which he himself belongs to the world has for him and he therein for the world'.[33] This awakening of 'concern' is also described as 'a deeper reflection that makes [the person] *older* than the moment' since it 'lets him grasp the eternal' and thereby 'assure himself that he has an actual relation to a world, and that consequently this relation cannot be mere knowledge about this world and about himself as a part of it'.[34] In such a moment of awakening to concern about the meaning of his existence, the individual becomes older than the moment (the ephemeral moment that is nothing but an infinite vanishing) and acquires a certain continuity, even if it is only the continuity of the question or the concern, that is, in the fact that he goes on being concerned by it, day after day. We can thus distinguish a double sense in the Kierkegaardian 'moment': on the one hand it is the merely 'momentary', the vanishing instant: on the other, it is the moment of vision, the moment in which I extend my self-awareness across a passage of time. In such extension the self, as he puts it, becomes 'older' than the moment. Or, as he develops this idea in a later discourse, one acquires one's soul 'in patience', i.e., by allowing oneself to be formed in and through one's acts of self-choice and self-commitment extended through time.[35] In its more developed form, this hopeful concern becomes what Kierkegaard calls the 'expectation of an eternal happiness', which he illustrates by such examples as the biblical prophetess Anna, who waited on the revelation of God's kingdom for sixty years after being widowed and losing her earthly happiness,[36] and the apostle Paul, whose confident relation to a future blessedness enables him to confront and overcome all earthly obstacles and doubts.[37] Kierkegaard seems here to resemble Augustine in that he is both defining the truth of human existence by means of the relation to the eternal and finding the basis for what he calls the meaning of time in human subjectivity—but note the difference: time, for Kierkegaard, is no longer a mere distraction from the relation to the eternal but the way in which this relation becomes actual; the possibility of distending the soul in time coincides with the possibility of becoming a 'soul' or self at all

---

[33] S. Kierkegaard, *Eighteen Upbuilding Discourses*, trans. E. H. and H. Hong, SKS 5 (Princeton: Princeton University Press, 1990), 86.

[34] Ibid. For a fuller discussion of Kierkegaard's 'upbuilding' writings see my *Kierkegaard's Upbuilding Discourses: Philosophy, Literature and Theology* (London: Routledge, 2002).

[35] See the discourse 'To Gain one's Soul in Patience' in *Eighteen Upbuilding Discourses*, 159–75. Also the discourse 'To Preserve one's Soul in Patience', ibid. 181–204.

[36] See the discourse 'Patience in Expectancy', ibid. 205–26.

[37] See the discourse 'The Expectancy of an Eternal Salvation', ibid. 253–73. For further discussion of these discourses see *Kierkegaard's Upbuilding Discourses*, 39–51.

and is therefore the necessary condition of any possible life with God. For Kierkegaard no less than for Hegel, the being of the human being is constituted by its becoming—but, against Hegel, this 'becoming' is not a process that we could ever regard as completed and, as such, recuperable in an act of theoretical cognition; rather, it is actual only in the moment of vision that enables us to commit ourselves to becoming who we believe ourselves to be called to be.

Kierkegaard's account lays particular weight on the future, which, as he puts it, is 'the possible' and therefore 'the first expression of the eternal, and its incognito'.[38] Nevertheless, even regarded as the incognito of the eternal, the future only reveals its meaning when it is chosen in the moment, which means in the present, the 'now'. Qua possibility, the future can be figured either as breaking open a present that is closed in on itself or as giving prospective continuity to an infinitely vanishing present that would otherwise fall away into nothingness, yet it is still in this present that the future must be grasped and affirmed. Here we might recall the analysis of the present found in Kierkegaard's discourse on the lilies and the birds discussed in Chapter 2 above, where he answers the question 'what is joy, or what is it to be joyful' in terms of the present: 'It is to be present to oneself, but truly to be present to oneself is...truly *to be today*...Therefore God is blessed, he who eternally says: Today, he who eternally and infinitely is present to himself in being today.'[39]

This priority of the 'Now' is also emphasized by Paul Tillich in, e.g., his sermon on 'The Eternal Now'. Yet Tillich's formulation of this priority raises a question that we can turn back on Kierkegaard, namely, as to whether time has been thought through in such a way as really to do justice to its properly temporal character. The charge is familiar from one of *Being and Time*'s several ambiguous footnotes on Kierkegaard, where Heidegger says that Kierkegaard 'clings to the ordinary conception of time, and defines the "moment of vision" with the help of "now" and "eternity"', which, for Heidegger, is to fall into the misapprehension of within-timeness, i.e., of thinking of time as a kind of external container of human action rather than realizing all that is involved when a 'moment of vision' is truly decisive for the meaning of time.[40] But to return to Tillich. As he states the case, 'The mystery of the future and the mystery of the past are united in the mystery of the present'—but, he asks, can we have 'presence'? 'Is not the present moment gone when we think of it?' Yet, he says, we *do* have a present, and, because of this, we also have a relation to the future and to the past. And we can have this

---

[38] *Anxiety*, 91.
[39] *Without Authority*, 39.
[40] *Being and Time*, 497/338.

present because time is not simply flux or, rather, the flux of time is not all
there is. There is also 'that which comprises all time and lies beyond it',
namely, 'the eternal'. In saying 'Now' we are able to 'stop the flux of time'
and we can do so 'because every moment of time reaches into the eternal . . . It
is the eternal "now" which provides for us a temporal "now"', which, as he
says, 'not everybody, and nobody all the time, is aware of'—but 'sometimes it
breaks powerfully into our consciousness and gives us the certainty of the
eternal, of a dimension of time which cuts into time and gives us our time'.[41]

But if it is only possible to find a course across the trackless and constantly
shifting ocean of becoming through our own acts of self-choice and self-
commitment—what Kierkegaard sometimes calls 'repetition'—what basis do
we have for seeing the continuity that such acts are able to provide as
manifesting 'the eternal'? What enables us to say that there is anything
more than an always provisional, always risky 'leap' into an always unknown
future? Kierkegaard and Tillich both accept that there is no knowledge of the
eternal that could be established independently of the confidence in which we
are enabled to make such provisional and unsecured leaps. Yet what, then
(apart precisely from its Christian vocabulary), makes this Christian existential relation to the mystery of time different from, e.g., the Nietzschean *amor
fati*, the daring affirmation in which the individual says of all that has
occurred in his or her experiences of the infinite flux of time that 'I willed it
thus'?[42] What ground, other than subjective conviction, is there for the
assertion that the eternal *is*?

What we are in search of—if we are to remain within the terms of the kind
of enquiry being pursued here—cannot at this point be any kind of demonstration or proof, nor can we simply appeal to the data of revelation (since the
way in which we would be able to receive and to understand such data is itself
at issue). Rather, we are seeking a more adequate account than any we have
heard so far of how life in time might be more than an infinitely vanishing
sequence of transitory moments sporadically 'redeemed' by moments of
vision and decision, and might, instead, be experienced as the very ground
and possibility of the God-relationship. If Kierkegaard and Tillich took the
moment of vision more seriously than did Augustinian theology, they might

---

[41] P. Tillich, 'The Eternal Now', in *The Boundaries of our Being* (London: Collins, 1973), 106–7.
Tillich's embrace of a kind of epiphanic view of time here stands in a certain tension to the
more prophetic, future-oriented view characteristic of the writings of his Religious Socialist
period.

[42] F. Nietzsche, *Also Sprach Zarathustra, Werke*, ii (Frankfurt am Main: Ullstein, 1972), 669.
This would seem also to be the standpoint implicit in Heidegger's adaptation of Kierkegaard's
'moment of vision' to describe the authentic temporality achieved in anticipatory resoluteness
(*Being and Time*, 370–82/323–33). See the following section for further discussion of this.

nevertheless be seen as understanding it as no more than the occasion or opportunity for coming into relation to the eternal. What I am asking now is whether we can go further than this, so as to arrive at an understanding of the God-relationship as thoroughly temporal—and, were we to do so, what this would mean for thinking of God as Being. Putting it in theological terms, must a Christian understanding of time and history always remain determined by the model of epiphany, i.e., the revelation of the eternal in time, or might it be capable of encompassing a view of the eternal *as time*? In pursuit of this question we now turn to what has proved to be the most influential of all modern philosophical treatments of time—a treatment involving an explicit reference back to both Kierkegaard and Nietzsche— namely, Heidegger's *Being and Time*.

BEING, TIME, AND DEATH

We have previously seen how, in *Being and Time*, Heidegger attempts to reopen the question of Being and to do so by getting behind what he regards as the 'hardened tradition' of scholasticism to a more fundamental experience of Being. This involves him not only in exploring what it might mean to experience the bodily presence of the intuited object prior to that object getting defined in terms of a certain 'what', but also in setting out the characteristic ways in which we find ourselves 'being in the world' other than those formalized in the knowledge-relationship that has for the most part been the primary preoccupation of philosophers. In the course of these explorations it becomes clear to Heidegger that human life is guided by a fundamental desire to live and to experience oneself as a whole, that is, fully and wholly to be the person that I am. But, he says, this desire will inevitably be frustrated by the fact of death. Death makes it impossible for us to be-as-a-whole—unless we prove to be capable of somehow anticipating our death and folding our understanding of death back into our lives here and now 'mid-way upon this course of life'. An authentic potentiality for being-a-whole is therefore one in which we resolutely incorporate into our self-understanding the nothingness that we are by virtue of being thrown into an existence that is a constant and ineluctable falling towards death. Crucially, Heidegger regards this as involving what he calls an *existentiell* act of coura-geous self-choice, i.e., a real event in individual life,[43] but this also provides

---

[43] As an example he gives the experiences of the eponymous hero of Tolstoy's *Ivan Ilych*. For further discussion of this reference, see below.

the only possible basis for a proper, existential (i.e., philosophical) under-standing of the distinctive being revealed in human Dasein. The human task of finding a right (i.e., utterly honest and unblinking) orientation toward death and the philosophical task of laying bare the fundamental structures of Being are intertwined—and even if it is perhaps finally unclear how this intertwining occurs, it is crucial for Heidegger's argument that it does.[44] For what the relation of the one Kierkegaard would call the 'actually existing individual' to death discloses is that the distinctive being of Dasein cannot be encompassed or expressed in any kind of 'what'. As Heidegger puts it: 'Its [Dasein's] "subsistence" [*Bestand*] is not based on the substantiality of a substance but on the "Self-subsistence" [*Selbstständigkeit*] of the existing Self, whose Being has been conceived as care'[45]—or, as he puts it shortly afterwards, 'the substance of man is existence'.[46] This distinguishes Dasein from any kind of object in the world and from anything that is knowable in terms of its essence, the kind of knowability associated with those entities he calls present-at-hand. Consequently, the mental act of resolutely anticipating death cannot be construed as an act of knowledge in any normal sense. Rather than being a kind of retrieval of a sense of self from the annihilating jaws of death, it is a kind of openness or readiness for regaining the sense of self that has been imperilled by the anticipation of its own annihilation. Resoluteness, therefore, is less of a once-for-all act of heroic self-affirmation and more a matter of continuing to hold oneself open, a 'resoluteness which resolves to keep on repeating itself'.[47] It is this ecstatic openness of the self to a future it cannot surpass that reveals authentic temporality, of which Heidegger says that 'it is not but temporalizes itself',[48] i.e., it is nothing but time.[49] Here, then, the claim is, we have a basis for self-understanding in which the utterly temporal character of human existence is fully accepted and internalized, but

---

[44] In ¶61 of *Being and Time*, Heidegger speaks of the distinction between the *existentiell* experiences of individuals and the existential reflections of philosophers as based on the fact that the latter 'think these possibilities through to the end' (*Being and Time*, 350/303), a phrase he takes up several times in the following pages. However, it is open to question whether here or elsewhere he really provides a satisfactory account of how we might know when a given possibility has been thought through 'to the end'!

[45] Ibid. 351/303.

[46] See also the assertion on p. 152/117 that 'Dasein's "Essence" is grounded in its existence . . . Dasein is itself only in *existing* . . .'; also p. 318, where it is said that Dasein's essence 'lies in' its existence.

[47] Ibid. 365/308. Cf. the comments above about patience in Kierkegaard's upbuilding discourses, and also, of course, Kierkegaard's notion of repetition as the mode in which the self might establish itself in a counter-move to the otherwise endless flux of sheer temporality.

[48] Ibid. 377/328.

[49] Again, this 'openness' can be related to Heidegger's understanding of truth as *alētheia* or 'unconcealment'. For further discussion see the following chapter.

in which there is no recourse to anything like 'the eternal', outside of, anterior to, or in any way beyond time.[50] Heidegger uses the Kierkegaardian expression 'moment of vision' to define the kind of authentic temporality characteristic of resoluteness, but he is clear that this is to be understood as a willed synthesis of past, present, and future without reference to anything 'eternal'.[51] And, having established this basis, Heidegger then proceeds to retrace his steps through the various forms of everyday care that he has analysed in the earlier part of the book, showing how the principle of temporality can be used to provide a more adequate explanation of these phenomena.

But has Heidegger really achieved what he wanted? Questions might be raised from a number of angles.

We might, for example, see Heidegger's project as a way of reconciling his double inheritance from, on the one hand, Kierkegaard (and, more broadly, from Christian theology)[52] and, on the other, Nietzsche. With Kierkegaard (and Christian theology) he wants to be able to affirm the possibility of meaning in time, and to do so without reliance on the 'hardened tradition' of scholasticism and what he regarded as its reified concepts. As the basic question guiding *Being and Time*, the question as to the meaning of Being supposes that 'Being' is not, as such, entirely dissolved by the vision of a thoroughly temporalized world, even if it now has to be thought in a manner other than that of traditional metaphysics.[53] With Nietzsche, on the other hand, Heidegger wants to affirm that time is all-encompassing and that it is impossible to identify any source of meaning outside of or apart from what we can experience in time itself. Whatever meaning can be given to Being will be a meaning that can only be formulated in, with, and under the conditions of life in time. But can these different perspectives be reconciled? Is there a philosophical meta-narrative that could allow them both to be, somehow, 'true'? If it is once conceded that the meaning of Being is to be found in its Becoming, do we not become committed simply to letting Being go? Isn't the affirmation of meaning and self-commitment found in Kierkegaardian repetition ultimately purely subjective and, as such, incapable of grounding

---

[50] This, however, is one of the points at which Edith Stein criticizes the assumptions behind *Being and Time*. See *Endliches und Ewiges Sein*, 472–81.

[51] See, e.g., *Being and Time*, 376–7/328–9; also 497/338.

[52] Especially, in this connection, the experience of the human condition as being determined by its relation to an anticipated eschaton or 'end of the world'. See his lectures on Paul in *Phänomenologie des religiösen Lebens*.

[53] In this connection we may note the impulse that Heidegger gives to modern (and postmodern) hermeneutics, since radical hermeneutics would seem to be committed to following the model of *Being and Time* by finding the ground for possible human meaning in—and solely in—the interpretation of the historical record of human beings' self-understanding.

any more general understanding of Being (or, as Kierkegaard might have put it, incapable of being transformed into a knowledge-relationship)?[54]

But, in any case, is Heidegger's treatment of death in fact capable of providing the foothold for the meaning of Being that he is seeking? One issue here is that the kind of anticipation of death he describes ultimately involves a certain equivocation. On the one hand, he insists on distinguishing between one's own death and that of others. Yet do we actually have means for envisaging our own death that are essentially different from those whereby we envisage the death of others? If I think of my own death, do I not essentially picture it in the same way as I picture someone else's death—only projected into an unknown future? It is striking that in describing the need to break away from the tranquillization that society offers the individual in the face of death Heidegger alludes to Tolstoy's novella *The Death of Ivan Ilych*, and further consideration of this reference will help us identify a problem with Heidegger's position.

Ivan Ilych is a successful lawyer, who has lived a life in conformity with what might be expected of a successful lawyer and householder—until he becomes terminally ill. Then, he realizes that 'The syllogism he had learned from Kiezewetter's Logic: "Caius is a man, men are mortal, therefore Caius is mortal," had always seemed to him correct as applied to Caius, but certainly not as applied to himself.'[55] Notionally, he now acknowledges its truth, but existentially he cannot make sense of what he experiences as this incomprehensible 'It' means:

And what was worst of all was that *It* drew his attention to itself not in order to make him take some action but only that he should look at *It*, look it straight in the face: look at it and without doing anything, suffer inexpressibly. And to save himself from this condition Ivan Ilyich looked for consolations—new screens—and new screens were found, and for a while seemed to save him, but then they immediately fell to pieces or rather became transparent, as if *It* penetrated them and nothing could veil *It*.[56]

Increasingly aware that he had not, in fact, lived as he ought to have done, it is only at the end of the last three pain-tormented days of his life that a moment of compassion for his son takes him outside himself 'and it was revealed to him that though his life had not been as it should have been, this could still be rectified'.[57] Ivan Ilych is no longer physically capable of communicating this insight to those around him, but it completely transforms his inner being:

---

[54] Note Heidegger's concern to distance his own project from that of Kierkegaard, which, he says, fails to grasp the existential, i.e., ontological issue.

[55] From L. Tolstoy, 'The Death of Ivan Ilych', trans. A. Maude in *The Death of Ivan Ilych and Other Stories* (New York: New American Library, 1960), 131.

[56] Ibid. 133.

[57] Ibid. 155.

'And death . . . where is it?' He sought his former accustomed fear of death and did not find it. 'Where is it? What death?' There was no fear because there was no death. In place of death there was light. 'So that's what it is!' he suddenly exclaimed aloud. 'What joy!' To him all this happened in a single instant, and the meaning of that instant did not change. For those present his agony continued for another two hours. Something rattled in his throat, his emaciated body twitched, then the gasping and the rattle became less frequent. 'It is finished!' said someone near him. He heard these words and repeated them in his soul. 'Death is finished,' he said to himself. 'It is no more!' He drew in a breath, stopped in the midst of a sigh, stretched out, and died.[58]

In these words, Tolstoy dramatizes what Heidegger describes as Dasein's being 'face to face with the "nothing" of the possible impossibility of its existence'.[59] In his last moments, Ivan Ilych exemplifies what it is to tear free from the 'concernful solicitude' of others and he experiences 'an impassioned freedom towards death—a freedom which has been released from the Illusions of the "they" . . .'.[60] But Tolstoy's narrative presupposes a kind of authorial insight into the dying man's consciousness that is, surely, superhuman. A third party could not know—as none of those at Ivan Ilyich's deathbed knew—what was going on in the dying man's soul. But if we are content for novelists to cheat in this kind of way (it is, after all, 'only fiction'), should we allow the same indulgence to philosophers? Can authentic dying in fact be represented in any other way than what a third-person narrator would be able to narrate were such a one to have insight into the thoughts of the dying man? And how would that be altered if I myself was both the narrator and the subject of the narration? Is there really the kind of essential difference between the deaths of others and one's own death that Heidegger presupposes? And what if Ivan Ilyich were to have a last-minute recovery and be returned to life, would it necessarily follow that he could thenceforth live with an 'anticipatory resoluteness' of death?[61]

It is on just this question of taking the consciousness of death back into our lives that Michael Theunissen's appreciative but critical treatment of Heidegger's contribution to the question of death focuses. The problem that Theunissen sees is that a radical recognition of the inconceivability of death brings with it an accompanying recognition of the impossibility of 'anticipating'

---

[58] From L. Tolstoy, 'The Death of Ivan Ilych', trans. A. Maude in *The Death of Ivan Ilych and Other Stories* (New York: New American Library, 1960), 155–6.

[59] *Being and Time*, 310/266.

[60] Ibid. 311/266.

[61] This question is, however, raised in Dostoevsky's novel *The Idiot*, in the story of the man who has a last-minute reprieve as he awaits death by firing squad (something Dostoevsky himself experienced)—and, as Dostoevsky makes clear, it proved impossible to live in the light of the intense experience of time lived in those moments.

death. What Heidegger does, in fact, is to let slip the inconceivability of death and to dissolve death back into life as a part of the process of life. In the mode of 'anticipatory resoluteness', death is no longer the absolute end that confronts Dasein with its utter nullity but a dimension of life.[62]

But why the exclusive emphasis on death? Heidegger's basic assumption that death constitutes a uniquely privileged focus for Dasein's face-to-face with its own temporal finitude would seem to be eminently challengeable. As we have seen, Sartre already finds nothingness in the basic self-experience of consciousness and, from a rather different point of view, Emmanuel Lévinas too challenges the Heideggerian preoccupation with death. There will be more to say of Lévinas's way of opposing the ethical demand to doctrines of Being.[63] Here I note only Lévinas's comment on Heidegger's reduction of the question of death to the subjectivity of individuals confronting their own death that 'for Heidegger... the fear of becoming a murderer would not be able to surpass [i.e. in existential seriousness] the fear of dying'.[64] Of course, as Lévinas candidly admits, Heidegger does not exactly say that and the objection seems exaggerated—but it is well made: that if we are to think death, there may be more to think of than our own future decease.

As an alternative to Heidegger (whose work he nevertheless calls an 'obligatory passage') Lévinas turns to the Marxist thinker Ernst Bloch. For Bloch, as summarized by Lévinas, the starting point for understanding history is human beings' common concern to overcome the concrete forms of historical suffering. In the history of humanity's journey towards a definitive surmounting of such suffering, the true Being of human beings emerges most clearly in work and in hope. The relationship between work and hope can in turn be seen in terms of an interplay between fulfilment and non-fulfilment: human beings' life in the world is always incomplete as long as there is still work to be done, whilst the summons to work is itself motivated by the unconditional hope of a future and common fulfilment. The spirit of utopia thus drives human beings to work for each other's betterment and to exist in a genuinely historical way. To Heidegger's analysis of Dasein as a nullity that consistently fails to realize itself as a whole, Bloch opposes the role of all the work that is still to be done in the world, and to Heidegger's anticipatory resoluteness in the face of death he opposes the spirit of utopia. From which Lévinas

---

[62] See M. Theunissen, 'The Upbuilding in the Thought of Death: Traditional Elements, Innovative Ideas, and Unexhausted Possibilities in Kierkegaard's "At a Graveside"', in Robert L. Perkins (ed.), *International Kierkegaard Commentary*, vols. ix and x: *Prefaces and Writing Sampler* and *Three Discourses on Imagined Occasions* (combined volume) (Macon, Ga.: Mercer University Press, 2006), 337ff.

[63] See Ch. 5 below.

[64] E. Lévinas, *Dieu, la mort et le temps* (Paris: Grasset, 1993), 107.

concludes that time is not defined by death, but by hope.[65] Ultimately this means that far from thinking of time in the singular light cast by death, death itself is to be thought in the perspective of utopistic time—i.e., an envisaged redemption not just of the individual, but of humanity.[66]

But even on his own premisses, we might ask the philosopher of *Being and Time* whether the phenomenal life of his thoroughly temporalized self is in fact sufficient to provide a basis for finding some meaning in Being. Or must the search for such meaning ultimately appeal—as we have heard Kierkegaard and Tillich appeal—to something from beyond this world, a super-temporal power, the eternal, that would alone be capable of giving meaning to being in time? Humanly, we might rephrase this question in something like the following terms: if we are alone with time and death, who can have the courage to hold out for ten, twenty, or thirty years or more in a state of courageous openness to death? On that basis, doesn't authentic existence—a genuine human existence—become the preserve of a few exceptional spirits? But are we really on our own, having to will ourselves into authenticity? Is there no one to help? Is there no word to guide us? Even on Lévinas's revision of the Heideggerian question, we might still want to ask—and not least in the light of the tragic sequence of the modern world's failed utopias—who can we trust to lead us in the right direction? Which prophet of which utopia are we to heed?

As is well known, Heidegger himself was by no means convinced that he had reached the end of his enquiry with the conclusion of the book published as *Being and Time*. The ways in which he would subsequently develop his 'path of thinking' are complex and various. For the present, I wish only to point to one of the ways in which the 'heroism' of *Being and Time* is importantly moderated in the later work. Especially in relation to his writings on Hölderlin, on whom he regularly lectured from the 1930s onwards, Heidegger is able to distance himself from the scenario of the isolated individual striving to keep open an anticipatory resoluteness in the face of his ineluctable death and to explore how such openness can be communicated in a way that allows for inter-subjectivity and even for forms of community (since community is no longer identified with the anxious suppression of the thought of death typical of the 'they').

---

[65] E. Lévinas, *Dieu, la mort et le temps* (Paris: Grasset, 1993), 109–11.

[66] Ibid. 122. A comparable move is that made by Theunissen in *Negative Theologie der Zeit*, where he argues that—in this case—the Christian conception of the relationship between time and eternity is fundamentally dissimilar from that presupposed in the Western philosophical tradition, in which time is seen primarily in terms of its evanescence and corrosiveness vis-à-vis substantial Being. The Christian eternity is not adequately figured by the eternally recurrent circular movement of the Greek divinity, since it is the power of a redemptive action that has meaning only in relation to those living in time. See n. 1 above.

In the next chapter, as we come to focus on the question of language, we shall have more to say about further aspects of Heidegger's philosophical poetics. Here, I shall point solely to the poet as the bearer of a 'word' that is able to call human beings to an authentic historical existence and, thereby, provide an alternative point of access to such existence than that provided by the anticipation of death.

TIME AND THE POET

Heidegger develops his understanding of poetic vocation in a number of lectures and lecture series on Hölderlin, whom he regarded as the poet of the modern world par excellence and whose writing expresses most succinctly the peculiar tension of a poetic existence in this 'barren time'.[67] It is the particular vocation of the poet, as revealed in Hölderlin, to awaken a sense for the holy in the midst of the profane and godless world of the modern West, a time and place marked by the 'forgetfulness of Being'. In this connection the poem 'Remembrance' gives the philosopher particular occasion to reflect on the role of the poet in relation to feast-days and festivals. Having been called by a divine summons to speak the word of the holy, the poet's word is essentially festal, calling his hearers to step out of the rhythms and the tasks of the everyday into the celebratory rhythms of the sacred festival. This is not just a matter of having a day off work in which to relax, but of renewing the basic order of society: it is the cycle of festivals and not the cycle of work that determines the calendar, the passage and structuring of time. Although the festival is properly a time for celebration, for dancing, for turning the night into day and for disrupting the order of ordinary time, it—like poetry itself— gives a deeper order and measure to time and existence. In this way the world of the festival that the poetic word reveals is 'the ground and essence of history'.[68] As such it can also be described as the wedding feast of mortals and deities, the time and place where humans and their gods meet and are

---

[67] For a fuller discussion of Heidegger's relation to Hölderlin see my *Routledge Guidebook to the Later Heidegger* (London: Routledge, 2000), 159–86.

[68] M. Heidegger, *Hölderlin's Hymne 'Andenken'* (*Gesamtausgabe*, vol. lii) (Frankfurt am Main: Klostermann, 1982), 68. See pp. 59–90 for the general exposition of the idea of the festal. Heidegger's thinking about festal time here is strikingly similar to that of Mircea Eliade, although I know no reason to suppose any influence of either one on the other in this regard. See, e.g., M. Eliade, *The Sacred and the Profane: The Nature of Religion* (New York: Harcourt, Brace and World, 1959), esp. ch. II 'Sacred Time and Myths' (pp. 68–115). A further aspect of Eliade's thought will be discussed in the final section of the present chapter.

united in a common time and a common action, a kind of liturgical world. The intoxication of the festival is therefore not mere drunkenness, but a rapturous elevation that bestows a clearer sense of the peculiar dignity and possibilities of human being. The truly festal element in the feast is the experience or discovery of the true relationship of human beings and gods: 'the festal is what gives an original accord', Heidegger comments.[69] This 'accord', he adds, is enacted in the mutual greeting of gods and mortals, a reciprocal act of welcome in which human beings learn that they are not alone in the world but are blessed by, responsible towards, and encompassed by the holy world of the gods—and thereby also participants in a common human world. Although occurring in the midst of times, festal time is utopian time, a release from mundanity into the fullness of human possibilities. It both refounds the community and reconciles the community with itself and its gods. Elsewhere, Heidegger will speak of this event as the 'round dance' of earth, sky, mortals, and their gods, and it is important to underline that— precisely qua utopia—it is not a particular place or time or even 'moment' in history, but a movement that precedes, grounds, and thereby holds open the possibility of historical movement. As the one who calls to and gives voice to the world revealed in festal time, the poet therefore is the one who 'founds what abides in time' and can even be said to be 'the founder of Being [*Seyn*]'.[70]

Connected with this event is a new understanding of essence as being effected or brought about by the poetic word. Heidegger's comments play on specific possibilities of the German language, but this does not mean that they are unintelligible to non-Germans (as his critics sometimes object). The standard German term for essence is *Wesen* (as in Feuerbach's *The Essence of Christianity: Das Wesen des Christentums*), and Heidegger connects this to the perfect participle, *gewesen*, of the verb 'to be' and to the noun *Das Gewesene*, which we might translate as 'the past' in the sense of 'what has been'. He contrasts this with another term for the past, *Die Vergangenheit*, commenting that although these are often used interchangeably in everyday discourse, they can be understood as pointing to two very different ways of experiencing the past. *Die Vergangenheit*, we might say, refers to what has 'come and gone', to what is irretrievably past. It is, Heidegger says, a kind of store room for everything that belongs in the past which, even if it can still be recalled, can never again become present in the way that it did as and when it occurred.[71]

---

[69] 'Andenken', 69.

[70] M. Heidegger, *Erläuterungen zu Hölderlins Dichtung* (*Gesamtausgabe*, vol. iv) (Frankfurt am Main: Klostermann, 1996), 45–6.

[71] M. Heidegger, *Hölderlins Hymnen 'Germanien' und 'Der Rhein'* (*Gesamtausgabe*, vol. xxxix) (Frankfurt am Main: Klostermann, 1989), 108.

By way of contrast, the essence of *das Gewesene* continues to be effective in the present: it is what, having been essential in the past, remains essential in the present and therefore also opens a path into the future.[72] The poet, then, is one who, by remembering what is most worth remembering in the past and making what is essential in the past present to his hearers, also reveals the way to the future. The festal time of the poetic song anticipates a time to come when the union of gods and mortals and of mortals with each other will no longer be merely an annual remembrance but a new and lasting golden age. Time thus represented will no longer be primarily conceived as a more or less rapid plunge into nothingness but as the occasion for mortals and gods to enter into mutual relations.

We have, it seems, come a long way from the situation of the isolated individual fleeing or heroically confronting the prospect of his own unthinkable death. But even though historical life now seems to be being very differently grounded from what was envisaged in *Being and Time*, Heidegger has not abandoned his guiding question as to the meaning of Being. Yet now it seems that it is not Being that gives meaning to what happens in time but that what happens in time—in the sacred time inaugurated by the poetic word—gives meaning to Being and is itself the event of the meaning of Being. Of course, both Hölderlin's poem and Heidegger's interpretation invoke the pre-Christian world of Greek polytheism, a world of gods and mortals rather than of God and creatures, and whilst Hölderlin himself at times explicitly heralds the Christian gospel of the incarnation as completing the historical movement of Greek religion and the 'flight of the gods' that is experienced in the later stages of that religion, this seems to be a possibility Heidegger resolutely avoids.[73] If his later poetic thinking offers a kind of utopian thinking, it is very different from the historical utopia of Jewish and Christian hope for a coming Kingdom of God. Rather, it seems to be a kind of natural and ethnic utopia, the gathering of a particular people in their unique historical place and time in a liturgical celebration of an exclusive identity,[74]

---

[72] Ibid.

[73] See my discussion in 'Heidegger's Hölderlin and Kierkegaard's Christ', in S. Mulhall (ed.), *Martin Heidegger* (Aldershot: Ashgate, 2006), esp. 403–4.

[74] Whatever one makes of the fact, it is striking that the lectures on the poems 'Germania' and 'The Rhein' date from the Winter Semester of 1934–5, i.e. from an early period in the history of the Third Reich when the new regime is itself enacting its reaffirmation of the Fatherland in such liturgical rites as the Nuremberg Rallies. Knowing this, and knowing Heidegger's own political choices, it is very hard not to read such sections of the lectures as the discussion of 'The "Fatherland" as the Historical Being of a People (*Volk*)' without connecting them in some way. Does this mean that there is nothing in these lectures but a kind of ideological gloss on the then current German nationalism, as argued in E. Faye, *Heidegger: L'Introduction du nazisme dans la philosophie* (Paris: Albin Michel, 2005)? For a

and not a message of freedom, equality, and fellowship for the world. It is therefore easy to see why, in addition to the specific charge of Nazism, such thinking can also be accused of a kind of paganism that has little in common with Judaeo-Christian thinking about God.[75] Yet in purely formal terms there seems also to be a significant analogy to the relationship between liturgy and prophecy on some accounts of the biblical history, whether it is the annual autumnal celebrations of the Kingship of Yahweh or the more historically oriented Passover festival that are seen as providing the liturgical blueprint for the new order that the prophets applied to the concrete historical circumstances of Israel.[76] Like Heidegger's Hölderlin, such prophets can be interpreted as speaking what is essential in the memory of the past as giving meaning to the present and providing a directive vis-à-vis the future.

Against any such assimilation of Heidegger's poetics to biblical prophecy, it might be objected that Heidegger's view, even if it has now acquired a more 'religious' aura than the atheistic rhetoric of *Being and Time*, still presupposes a kind of human self-assertion that is suspect from the point of view of Christian theology. Whereas the prophet is called by God to deliver a 'word from the Lord' the poet merely offers his own imaginative vision. However, as we shall see further in the next chapter, it is essential to Heidegger's view of the poetic word that the poet too is elected and called by the gods and that it is only on the basis of his being thus called that his word is empowered to bring about the reconciliation of gods and mortals. The issue then becomes an issue as to which is the true God—even if the formal structure of divine calling and commission is the same in both cases.

In order to explore further dimensions of some of the issues that have been addressed in the present chapter, I turn now to two British poets, T. S. Eliot and Edwin Muir. My suggestion is that whereas the relation to time expressed in Eliot's *Four Quartets* is akin to kairotic or epiphanic relationship of time and eternity that we found in Kierkegaard and Tillich, a number of Muir's poems adumbrate an understanding of time that approximates more to elements of Heidegger's interpretation of Hölderlin.[77] In transposing the

robust response to Faye see, e.g., J.-F. Mattéi, 'Emmanuel Faye: L'Introduction du fantasme dans la philosophie', in *Heidegger: La Pensée à l'ère de la technique et de la mondialisation = Le Portique* 18 (Strasbourg, 2006), 53–81.

[75] See, e.g., John D. Caputo, *Demythologizing Heidegger* (Bloomington, Ind.: Indiana University Press, 1993), esp. ch. 9 'Heidegger's Gods' (pp. 169–85).

[76] See, e.g., J. H. Eaton, *Vision in Worship: The Relation of Prophecy and Liturgy in the Old Testament* (London: SPCK, 1981).

[77] This is scarcely surprising, in that Hölderlin was a significant point of reference in Muir's own poetic journey: see the essays on Hölderlin in E. Muir, *Essays on Literature and Society* (London: Hogarth Press, 1965).

discussion into this British context, I hope that much that is perhaps strange and remote in the Heideggerian way of questioning may become more accessible—not in the sense that one might wish to make what is genuinely mysterious and difficult to think about easier than it actually is, but rather so as to see more clearly just where the genuine mystery and the really puzzling riddle lie. Moreover, because this is a matter of poetry and not philosophy, the differences between these poetic visions to which I shall draw attention are not simply to be construed as 'opposed' or 'exclusive', but more as differing in the tone, the tenor, and the nuance of their approach to what both poets would surely concede stretches both thinking and language to breaking point. However, the poets not only offer rhetorically powerful imaginings of the issues we have been considering, but, as we shall see, Muir in particular helps us to formulate a question that may prove of decisive significance with regard to a possible Christian appropriation (or, if we take Hölderlin's own Christianity seriously, re-appropriation) of Hölderlin's festal eschatology, as interpreted by Heidegger.

THE *FOUR QUARTETS* AND 'THE JOURNEY BACK'

The opening section of *Four Quartets*, 'Burnt Norton', begins by squarely stating one of the many aporias with which time confronts those who once begin to ponder its mysteries:

> Time present and time past
> Are both perhaps present in time future,
> And time future contained in time past.
> If all time is eternally present
> All time is unredeemable.[78]

Here and throughout the cycle of poems the narrative voice of the poem is that of a man approaching old age. Threatened by nostalgia for the unfulfilled possibilities of his past, he sees his contemporary world very much in terms of the 'fallenness' of the 'average everyday' life of the 'man without qualities' of modern urban existence: it is 'a place of disaffection...neither daylight Investing form with lucid stillness...Nor darkness to purify the soul'(I, 91, 93–4, 97); the 'time-ridden faces' of his contemporaries are 'filled with fancy and empty of meaning...Men and bits of paper, whirled by the cold wind That blows before and after time'. It is a 'twittering world', a 'waste sad time'

---

[78] All quotations are from T. S. Eliot, *Four Quartets* (London: Faber and Faber, 1944), I, 1–5. Part and line number of subsequent quotes are given in brackets in the text.

(I, 100, 102, 104–5).[79] If this is all the time there is, then the poem might be read as an invocation of despair, but already in 'Burnt Norton' another possibility is broached. This is a possibility revealed 'At the still point of the turning world' (I, 62), 'where past and future are gathered' (I, 65). It is not to be imagined as a point of 'fixity' (I, 64), but as a 'dance' (I, 63, 67), which, although it does not take place anywhere or occur in any time, nevertheless has the power to make 'a new world' (I, 75) and to make the 'old' 'explicit' (I, 76), releasing the self from both action and suffering. Yet it can be 'known'—or, rather, glimpsed—only in a manner as ineffable and as fugitive as the most transient of moments: 'Quick now, here, now, always—' (I, 73) urges the poet in the closing lines of this first part.

The instability of this 'conclusion' is made clear when the second quartet, 'East Coker', opens with the comment that 'In my beginning is my end' and, as the following lines suggest, this is to be taken in the sense that every beginning is already under way to dissolution and decay. We human beings are, it seems, part of a natural cycle of reproduction and death that has its poetry and its time, but that does not essentially rise above the time of mere animal life. From within that kind of cyclical time-experience, all that can be expected is the final destruction of all things in an all-consuming fire (II, 67). Order is only ever the imposition of a pattern which falsifies what it seems to know (II, 84), and, in the end, 'all go into the dark' (II, 101).

Yet now the poet also begins to speak of another possibility, a moment of submission, of waiting. In the first instance this must be a waiting without hope, without thought, without love, yet it is in this waiting that we find the beginnings of faith and hope and love. Section 4 of 'East Coker' makes yet more explicit the Christian intention that is being developed. Submission is not simply submission to time, but to the 'wounded surgeon' (II, 147), the Christ who feeds us with his 'dripping blood' and 'bloody flesh' in the self-surrendering death of Good Friday (II, 167, 168). Thus strengthened, the narrator of 'East Coker' ends with a note of hope: 'Old men ought to be explorers . . . In my end is my beginning' (II, 209).

The next of the Quartets, 'Dry Salvages', begins with an evocation of the river, 'a strong brown god' (III, 2), 'destroyer, reminder Of what men choose to forget' (III, 8–9). The river and the sea are, of course, amongst the most ancient and accessible figures of time and of the power of time to unravel and destroy all human achievements and happiness. Life in time is an ambiguous sequence of destruction and preservation, but though it seems again and again to bring us to the moment of death (and to nothing beyond that), time's

---

[79] This is also the world of Eliot's earlier work *The Waste Land*.

voyagers are even here urged to say 'Not fare well, But fare forward...' (III, 167–8).

But is this really all? Is there only the ebb and flow, the all-embracing, all-consuming flux of time, to which our best response is a heroic resoluteness in face of an unknown future? The opening line of 'Little Gidding' offers a new and paradoxical perspective in the midst of death and decay: 'Midwinter spring is its own season' (IV, 1). This suggests rebirth and new life and, as such, epitomizes the experience of the time-bound pilgrim journeying to Little Gidding, the place where once, in the past, 'prayer has been valid' (IV, 46); where, once, there occurred 'the intersection of the timeless moment' with 'England and nowhere' (IV, 52, 53). Yet even if this intersection occurred in a specific place at a specific time in the past, its timelessness means that it can become available also to inspire and move others in other times and places, providing the basis or possibility for what Kierkegaard would call a 'repetition'. In the power of that possibility we see that we might hope for more than the isolated and fugitive epiphany of the individual and look toward a common and open history. This would be history as 'a pattern of timeless moments', occurring wherever the once-lived openness to the timeless moment of prayer is repeated, appropriated, and re-lived. There is no cessation from the journey, no end of exploration, until we 'arrive where we started And know the place for the first time' (IV, 241–2). Here, we know that all shall be well, yet—reminding ourselves that the logic is not that of a philosophical argument or a dramatic narrative—we recall that 'where we started' is also a beginning, the first step on a new round of journeying, wayfaring, wandering, pilgrimage. But, to revert to Kierkegaard's language, this is a repetition at a newer level, a repetition in which it is not forgotten that we belong in a history in which 'all shall be well'.

There are several parallels between Eliot's vision and that of the later Heidegger, not least concerning the way in which the sacral or ritual action to which both poets call their readers is seen as giving a decisive meaning to life in time. Clearly, Eliot does not think that time simply comes to a stop as a result of such experiences, yet—and again not unlike Heidegger—the future possibilities of time are focused on the destiny of national community that is to be defined and understood with reference to the ritual order inaugurated by the poetic word. But the moment of intersection of time and eternity already gives to those who are open to it the realization that 'here' and 'now' are also 'always'. There is no history to come that can ultimately be closed off from the promise of such moments of vision. If the opening lines of the poem stated that the eternal presence of all time would make time irredeemable, the end seems to suggest that once one has grasped the 'eternal now' this is no longer true: the future has nothing new that is not already given 'at the still point of the turning world'.

There are also many lines of convergence joining Eliot's treatment of time in *Four Quartets* with that of his contemporary Edwin Muir, yet the latter also offers certain perspectives that point beyond Eliot's formulation of the 'eternal now' theme. From early on, Nietzsche's vision of eternal recurrence haunted Muir's personal and poetic journey. In 'The Recurrence', explicitly alluding to Nietzsche, the poet notes that, if this vision is indeed how things are, then 'the prison clock | Will toll on execution morning, | What is ill be always ill, | Wretches die behind a dike, | And the happy be happy still' (29–33).[80] The poet finds this vision intolerable, and cannot accept that what is ill should always continue to be ill. What, for example, would be the implications of this for the crucifixion? If the vision of eternal recurrence is true, then 'the Actor on the Tree | Would loll at ease, miming pain, | And counterfeit mortality' (44–6)—lines that Muir almost repeats in the poem 'Antichrist' a decade later: 'Ingeniously he [the Antichrist] postures on the Tree | (His crowning jest), an actor miming death, | While his indifferent mind is idly pleased | That treason should run on through time for ever' (24–7). Yet the knowledge that the man who died on the cross was not simply one more in history's long line of innocent victims of injustice but 'a God' cannot be read off from the surface of the event. In 'The Killing' 'the day they killed the Son of God | On a squat hill-top by Jerusalem' (1–2) is described from the point of view of a passing traveller. 'I was a stranger,' he comments, 'could not read these people Or this outlandish deity. Did a God | Indeed in dying cross my life that day | By chance, he on his road and I on mine?' (41–4).

In terms of historical time and of the events that appear in the course of history it is impossible to penetrate to a level at which we might know whether such an encounter was more than chance. But Muir is tireless in pursuing the possibility that time, and life in time, can also be understood as a rhythm of creation, incarnation, and redemption. In 'The Journey Back' he undertakes a kind of retrospective metempsychosis, envisaging his life as reaching back into the lives of his ancestors, passing back through known human history with its many dark and mean episodes, experiencing himself as 'rich and poor | Victor and victim' (1, 58–9), concluding that 'In all these lives I have lodged, and each a prison' (1, 60). There seems to be no end to the possibilities of such journeying back and forth through time, and consequently the individual lives and the interweaving of individual lives that constitutes our common history seem to have no direction, no purpose, no true end, and no true beginning. Yet there is also the possibility: 'that some day | I know I should find a man who has done good | His long lifelong and is | Image of

---

[80] All references are to Edwin Muir, *Collected Poems* (London: Faber and Faber, 1984). Line numbers are given after quotations in the text and, where the poem is not clearly identified, the title.

man from whom all have diverged' (1, 67–70). As he puts it in a later section of the poem 'Without the blessing cannot the kingdom come' (5, 173).

One possibility of what that blessing might mean is sketched in part 6 of 'The Journey Back', a vision of a world ordered by immortals living in unbroken blessedness.

> They walk high in their mountainland in light
> On winding roads by many a grassy mound
> And paths that wander for their own delight.
> There they like planets pace their tranquil round
> That has no end, whose end is everywhere,
> And tread as to a music underground . . . (6, 1–6)

This is an order of temporal movement higher than that of historical time. It depicts time as a blessed dance, tranquilly progressing through a measured sequence of changes that involves no essential change or break in the luminous silence of the ritual-like movement. But, the poet adds, 'This is the other road, not that we know' (6, 12). The path we know is the path on which our fates are inescapably involved with all possible forms of human violence and perfidy. But we are not abandoned to the meaningless violence of history. We cannot escape our embodiment and will never have the kind of freedom of 'the eternal spirits' but we can know revelations of fulfilled time, a hope that Muir focuses on the incarnation. For the incarnation gives the possibility of an experience of time other than that revealed in the twisted tale of an infinitely recurring historical violence. This other way is announced in Gabriel's greeting to Mary:

> See, they ['the angel and the girl'] have come together, see,
> While the destroying minutes flow,
> Each reflects the other's face
> Till heaven in hers and earth in his
> Shine steady there. ('The Annunciation', 6–10)

Time continues on its way—like a barrel organ, as verse 3 suggests—but in the time during which the angel and girl meet, divine and human are united.

As the poem 'One Foot in Eden' declares, we are fallen from Eden's perfection, and time further tears and ravages what was broken in that original fall, but time, and quite specifically fallen time, is also the condition of the blessing that is the promise of the kingdom:

> Time takes the foliage and the fruit
> And burns the archetypal leaf
> To shapes of terror and of grief
> Scattered along the winter way.
> But famished field and blackened tree

> Bear flowers in Eden never known.
> Blossoms of grief and charity
> Bloom in these darkened fields alone.
> What had Eden ever to say
> Of hope and faith and pity and love
> Until was buried all its day
> And memory found its treasure trove? (16–27)

Life in time alone makes memory of Eden possible and memory of Eden is in turn the possibility of the blessing of the kingdom. And so, in 'The heart could never speak', the poet addresses time itself: 'Time, teach us the art, | That breaks and heals the heart ... Time, teach us the art | That resurrects the heart' (5–6, 11–12), before turning to God: 'Time, merciful lord, | Grant us to learn your word' (17–18).[81] In the light of such a possibility, we may, finally, learn what Muir calls 'the old saw', that 'Love is exempt from time' ('Love's Remorse', 10), or, as the poet restates it, although time is the condition of lovers being given to each other 'we who love and love again can dare | To keep in his despite our summer still, | Which flowered, but shall not wither, at his will' ('Love in Time's Despite', 12–14).

Crucially, the interrelationship of time, loss, memory, and hope concerns not only individuals but also communities. 'All we' is a phrase that gives the title and opening words of just one poem, but, in a sense, it could stand as a motto for much of Muir's work, which is not solely the record of an individual journey but also a reflection on the convulsions that befell 'the good town' of European civilization. 'Look at it well. This was the good town once' the poem entitled 'The Good Town' begins, before it goes on to list the 'mounds of rubble, | And shattered piers, half-windows, broken arches | And groping arms' that 'were once inwoven in walls | Covered with saint and angels ...' (22–6). But, as the poet acknowledges, 'It was not time that brought these things upon us, | But these two wars that trampled on us twice' (54–5). And whilst it might have seemed to many that it was some kind of terrible chance or fate that brought this destruction upon the peoples of the good town, the more reflective find themselves asking 'Could it have come from us | Was our peace peace? | Our goodness goodness?' (80–1). The collective fate, and the possibility of re-enlivening the memory of a better world, an Eden, are matters of human responsibility, and peace will not come if we do not love.

Poetry here pushes against the ultimate ambiguities of our experience of time, revealing that what is truly desperate about life in time is not the constant

---

[81] It is arguable that it is time itself and not God that is being addressed here or that the prayer is deliberately ambiguous. However, in the overall context of Muir's poetic vision and of this poem in particular, reading it as referring to God seems at least justifiable.

erosion of the biological basis of our existence, the inevitability of our powers failing us and, in the end, our being annihilated, but that it destroys hope and faith in love. Yet, if we are to believe in love, do we need to deny, transcend, or otherwise roll back the surge of time? Do we not rather need to be in time and to live in time otherwise than in the manner of violence and betrayal? The challenge is not to escape time, to transcend time, or to find a kind of centre to time, but to live out a different kind of time, a time turned towards justice, forgiveness, and peace rather than to an endless vanishing into nothingness.

These comments mark the first point on a narrative arc that leads to questions we must take up in a later chapter. First, however, we must briefly restate the point at which the enquiry has now arrived, and indicate the next step to be taken. Beginning with the Augustinian view that time is meaningful only when lived and understood in the light of 'the eternal now' of divine Being, we have traced a number of modern views—from Hegel, through Kierkegaard, Tillich, and Heidegger—in which the attempt has been made to do justice to our human time-experience. All, in their differing ways, see 'Being' as refracted in the mirror of 'becoming'—yet none of them maintains that Being simply dissolves into mere flux. But what is the ground of this resistance to dissolution? Is it something arising from within our time-experience itself? Or is it the intimation of an 'other power' entering into and sustaining our lives in time? Where Kierkegaard and Tillich—though each radically qualifying the Augustinian evaluation of time—still wish to speak of or to point to 'the eternal' as the ground of this resistance (a view also found in Eliot's 'pattern of timeless moments'), Heidegger appears to suggest that the very possibility of a relationship of gods and mortals is a product of time, specifically the festal time announced and celebrated in the poetic word. Yet the suspicion still lurks that the way in which the poetic word invokes a sacred time somehow predestines time itself and, what is worse, replaces the redemptive power of the eternal with the 'redemptive' power of a particular ethnic and historical community. Muir, notwithstanding the distinctively Scottish spirit of his work, does not write of the sacralization of time for a given ethnic community, but, in a more biblical tenor, of time being redeemed for all the victims of violence, terror, and untimely death. Nor is it accidental in this respect that where Heidegger obscures the Christian elements in his own sources, Muir draws explicitly on the Christian story of fall, incarnation, and redemption. The seriousness of life in time is that it is the only possible site of a redemption that is achieved through incarnation, crucifixion, and resurrection and that is to be appropriated in individual lives in and only in love. But would such a redemption of time still be thinkable within the paradigm of God as Being? Could a God, could any God, enter so deeply into time as to suffer and die and still be a God who could be named Being-Itself? Or should we say that although such a historicization of the divine–human relationship sets the relation to Being at the greatest possible distance from the living and suffering of *existentiell* time, this is still not such a distance as to be synonymous with the complete negation of Being (as Sartre, for one, supposed)? We are not yet in a position to decide the question, but to follow it further we shall now approach it from a related but distinct angle. Heidegger's own reflections on the poetic vocation indicate, and the introduction of such doctrinal terms as fall, incarnation, and resurrection also suggest, that the question of meaning in time points to the complementary question of how meaning might at all be communicated, and how language ('the word') might serve—or transcend—the communication of Being to those who can live in no other way than as beings of time. In the following chapter we shall therefore take up the question of language. First, however, it is necessary briefly to supplement what has been said about time with some remarks about space.

SPACE, PLACE, AND TIME

In beginning our enquiry into the dissolution of claims concerning an experienced presence of Being by focusing on time we may appear to have overlooked a principle no less fundamental than that of time and without which the discussion of time itself must appear curiously lop-sided, namely, the principle of space. Such a neglect of space in favour of time is by no means uncommon in modern theology and philosophy. On the contrary, it has seemed to some to be a necessary consequence of Judaeo-Christian ideas of prophecy and historicality. Tillich, for example, understands the relationship between space and time as inherently conflictual and sees this conflict as reflected in paganism and biblical religion respectively, where paganism means 'the elevation of a special space to ultimate value and dignity'[82] and biblical prophecy points instead to a God who is a God of time and history. Paganism, he argues, is inherently polytheistic and inherently tragic: it is polytheistic because it defines its gods in terms of their relation to a particular locale and it is tragic because it is incapable of transcending 'the circle of genesis and decay'.[83] He also connects this with the Greek conception of the supreme God as an immovable being, symbolized in 'the sphere or the circle, the most perfect representation of

---

[82] Paul Tillich, 'The Struggle between Time and Space', in idem, *Theology of Culture* (London: Oxford University Press, 1959), 31.
[83] Ibid. 33.

space'.[84] Judaism marked a definitive break with such conceptions by affirming a God who was primarily revealed in the historical events of the Patriarchal histories and, supremely, the Exodus from Egypt. This historical emphasis was then reiterated in the prophetic call to the nation to see God's hand in the convulsive histories of the divided kingdoms of Israel and Judah and in the hope of a future return from exile and the ultimate reign of God on earth. Judaism and subsequently Christianity 'break the claims of the gods of space who express themselves in will to power, imperialism, injustice, demonic enthusiasm, and tragic self-destruction'.[85] The gods of space are ultimately the gods of ethnicity, whilst the Lord of history is also, as such, the God who is and who demands justice.[86]

A similar taxonomy is also found in the work of one of the defining figures of the modern study of religions, Mircea Eliade, and the distinction between forms of religion that centre on a basically spatial conception of the world and the 'historical' religiousness of Judaism and Christianity is basic to his conception of religion and the sacred. Those who inhabit a world experienced as 'sacred' are precisely those whose world is defined by its relation to 'an absolute fixed point, a center' or a 'central axis' around or upon which this same world is ontologically founded.[87] Myth and ritual repeat and re-enact this foundation in their 'construction of sacred space'[88] and their manner of

---

[84] Ibid. 34.   [85] Ibid. 39.

[86] However, Tillich sees Judaism as itself succumbing to the temptation of space by limiting its hope to that of the nation (ibid.). The question has, of course, acquired a new force in the light of the more recent history of the State of Israel and the role of claims to land as being integral to Israel's nationhood—new force, but by no means new clarity! For an important (Christian) commentary on some of the issues see W. Brueggemann, *The Land: Place as Gift, Promise and Challenge in Biblical Faith* (Philadelphia: Fortress Press, 1982). From a Jewish perspective, Franz Rosenzweig insisted that 'in contrast to the history of other peoples, the earlier legends about the tribe of the eternal people are not based on indigenousness. Only the father of mankind sprang from the earth itself, and even he only in a physical sense. But the father of Israel came from the outside . . . To the eternal people, home never is home in the sense of the land . . . In the most profound sense possible, this people has a land of its own only in that it has a land it yearns for—a holy land. And so even when it has a home, this people . . . is not allowed full possession of that home. It is only "a stranger and a sojourner." God tells it: "The land is mine"' (F. Rosenzweig, *The Star of Redemption*, trans. W. H. Hallo (Notre Dame, Ind.: Notre Dame Press, 1970), 300). These issues re-echo, of course, in the opposition of a 'jewgreek' demand for justice the preoccupation with discerning a 'history of Being' in the flux of time. See, e.g., Caputo's writings on Derrida and Heidegger: *Demythologizing Heidegger* and *The Prayers and Tears of Jacques Derrida: Religion without Religion* (Bloomington, Ind.: Indiana University Press, 1997).

[87] Mircea Eliade, *The Sacred and the Profane: The Nature of Religion*, trans. W. R. Trask (New York: Harcourt, Brace, and World Inc., 1959), 21. Eliade is no longer a fashionable figure amongst students of religion. However, his thought was not only highly influential on the mid-twentieth-century development of the field, but it is also characteristic of a certain kind of taxonomy of religions prevalent then.

[88] Ibid. 22.

organizing time as a perpetually recurring cycle of liturgical occasions. In contrast to this the modern experience of freedom and history takes the Jewish and Christian narrative of the expulsion of humanity's progenitors from paradise to its logical conclusion. In this perspective human beings are robbed of the stability provided by the ritual repetition of archaic archetypes and exposed to what Eliade calls 'the terror of history'.[89] This historical world is essentially profane, outside of and alien to the sacred space of myth and ritual. Perhaps unsurprisingly, Eliade correlates the experience of the sacred with Being. Outside of time, a spatially constructed world is a world of stasis, a world without change, a world that simply *is*. As he puts it in an essay on sacred architecture, 'The Sacred is something that is altogether other to the Profane. Consequently it does not belong to the profane world, it comes from somewhere else, it transcends this world. It is for this reason that the Sacred *is* the real par excellence. A manifestation of the Sacred is always a revelation of *being*.'[90]

The disorientation and bewilderment consequent upon modernity's loss of a sense of place are undoubtedly present in the interest contemporary spirituality shows in reinvigorating 'spaces for the sacred' in the midst of modernity's wasteland.[91] In this regard we might also note that the tropes of Romantic presence were frequently focused on *place*: we have considered the role of time and memory in Wordsworth's *Tintern Abbey*, but also, and perhaps more obviously, this is a poem about place and about places of presence that are capable of counteracting the loss or imperilling of such presence in the convulsions of modernity's historical experiences. And we could say the same of Cézanne's Mont Saint-Victoire and even Hopkins's Oxford. We might note too that Eliot presents the experience of 'the intersection of the timeless moment' as inseparable from the concrete experience of a sacred place such as the church at Little Gidding, whilst Muir figures the quest

---

[89] See M. Eliade, *The Myth of the Eternal Return or Cosmos and History*, trans. W. R. Trask (Princeton: Princeton University Press, 1954), especially the closing chapter 'The Terror of History' (pp. 139–62).

[90] M. Eliade, *Symbolism, the Sacred, and the Arts*, ed. D. Apostolos-Cappadona (New York: Crossroad, 1986), 107. The whole section 'Sites of the Sacred' is worth reading as a further working-out of this remark.

[91] The allusion is to the title of Philip Sheldrake's *Spaces for the Sacred* (London: SCM Press, 2001). This might also be connected with the theme of 'the re-enchantment of the world' as developed in some currents of contemporary writing about art. See, e.g., James Elkins and David Morgan (eds.), *Re-enchantment* (New York: Routledge, 2009). The topics of sacredness or sacramentality, place, and the dis- and re-enchantment of the world are extensively and elegantly discussed in David Brown's *God and Enchantment of Place: Reclaiming Human Experience* (Oxford: Oxford University Press, 2004).

for the time of love as also a quest for a certain elusive place—and offers a whole series of poems in which the word 'place' recurs in each title.[92]

In this connection it is not accidental that pilgrimage and journeying are significant themes in both poets. Both are undertakings that involve both space and time and, at least since Einstein and Heisenberg, no one questions that space and time can be ultimately disconnected. On the contrary, they are now widely understood as intrinsically interconnected, even if—despite the widespread use of the expression 'space-time'—their interconnections continue to challenge scientific theorizing as well as poetic and artistic representation. In this regard it would be erroneous to suppose that Heidegger—the twentieth century's philosopher of time par excellence—was neglectful of issues of space. On the contrary, several of his reflections on Hölderlin concentrate on the role that the poet gives to the great German rivers the Rhein and the Danube as defining the 'space' of German identity. These rivers, as Heidegger reads Hölderlin, are not to be taken as mere symbols for what the poet is 'really' writing about: they are themselves the content of the poems and they are themselves constitutive of the world that the poems call into being.[93] As William McNeill and Julia Davis translate, 'The river "*is*" the locality that pervades the abode of human beings upon the earth, determines them to where they belong and where they are homely [*heimisch*]. The river thus brings human beings into their own and maintains them in what is their own.'[94] The rivers, in other words, found and give to human beings their place or 'abode'.

As Heidegger's meditations develop, they involve allusive but careful interweavings of such key terms as the neologism *Ortschaft*, translated here as 'locality' but incorporating the humble term *Ort*, an everyday word for 'place'. The relationship between the two invites being construed as analogous to that between 'science' (*Wissenschaft*) and simple 'knowing', where the former indicates the formal possibility rather than the concrete act but, as such, grounds the latter: whilst I may know various things without knowing them scientifically my knowledge is only fully secure when it is grounded in a full and adequate scientific account. I may know that the battle of Waterloo happened in 1815, but I have never myself investigated any of the contemporary

---

[92] 'The Unfamiliar Place', 'The Place of Light and Darkness', 'The Solitary Place', 'The Private Place', 'The Unattained Place', 'The Threefold Place', 'The Original Place', 'The Sufficient Place', 'The Dreamt-of Place'.
[93] For Heidegger's critique of a 'symbolic' interpretation of the poems see M. Heidegger, *Hölderlins Hymne 'Der Ister'* (*Gesamtausgabe*, vol. liii) (Frankfurt am Main: Klostermann, 1984), 24–31; cf. M. Heidegger, *Hölderlin's Hymn 'The Ister'*, trans. W. McNeill and J. Davis (Bloomington, Ind.: Indiana University Press, 1996), 21–31.
[94] *Der Ister*, 25 (*The Ister*, 21).

documentation that demonstrates this fact of history—but such investigation
of primary sources is precisely the business of a 'scientific' grounding of what is
otherwise merely opinion (even if, in this case, it is also a correct opinion). In
this sense, then, when it is said that 'the river "*is*" the locality that . . . brings
human beings into their own' the point is that *Ortschaft*—in this case instan-
tiated in the flow of the river—provides the general possibility of there being
such a thing as 'place' at all.[95] But note also that we are now speaking not of
'space' but 'place', terms between which Jeff Malpas draws an important
distinction in his treatment of Heidegger's 'topology' (or 'discourse on
place'). 'Space', according to Malpas, is best understood in relation to the
abstract, universal space of Cartesian thinking, whereas 'place' is something
more obscure and elusive. Yet, whilst space may be conceived as containing all
possible experience (such that there could be no human experience that was not
somehow already 'in' space), place will always relate to the very specific place
in which we experience the presence (or, we might add, the loss) of Being.[96] In
this regard, it is also significant that the term translated here as 'their own' (i.e.,
human beings' 'own' place) is closely related to the key Heideggerian term
conventionally translated as 'authenticity', which, in *Being and Time*, denotes
the individual Dasein's 'ownmost' owning of its own being. The rivers, then,
establish the *place* in this specific, local, concrete sense, where mortals (in this
case the Germanic peoples) are given a possibility of dwelling and knowing
themselves as the distinct and particular people whom the poet summons into
an encounter with the divinity that is to ground and guide their historical
destiny.[97] The association of poet, place, and nation is also revealed in the
language in which the poet speaks to those who dwell in the place marked out
by the rivers and which, as their mother tongue, confirms their identity as a
nation—a set of relationships which indicates why, for Heidegger, the rivers are
not to be understood as mere 'symbols' but are eminently what and as they are
when they are 'spoken' by the poet whom they (the rivers) have themselves
called to be *their* poet. In this connection the river, qua *Ortschaft*, not only gives
mortals a place (*Ort*), but also gives them the means of discourse—a point

---

[95] In the light of these comments, I am tempted to suggest 'topicality' as a less misleading
translation of *Ortschaft*, since locality in English can mean, precisely, a particular place, 'a
locality'. Unfortunately, the current usage of the term bears no relation to Heidegger's discussion
and, rather than connoting a relation to place, actually suggests a certain relation to time!

[96] See Jeff Malpas, *Heidegger's Topology: Being, Place, World* (Boston: MIT Press, 2006). Even
if it were not the only English-language book adequately to address this important topic in
Heidegger's thought, the lucidity of Malpas's exposition and the sureness of his grasp of
Heidegger's texts make this an indispensable work for anyone wanting to engage with the topic.

[97] Malpas is, of course, alert to the problematical associations with National Socialism that
this complex of ideas potentially betrays. See *Heidegger's Topology*, 18–27.

Heidegger makes by highlighting the etymological force of the German term *Erörterung*, conventionally translated as 'discussion' but which itself contains the root *Ort*, suggesting that 'discussion' is interpreted as the presentation or relation of what is said to a determinate 'topic'.

This is a dense grouping of terms and themes and Heidegger by no means makes matters easy for his readers. However, in a further twist, he reminds us that the flow of the river is by no means accidentally a figure for time, and that, as Hölderlin's poems make especially clear, the river is not only characterizable as 'locality' but also as 'journeying'. And, as Heidegger notes, 'Locale and journeying belong together like "space and time".'[98] However, he is concerned—indeed, it is central to the thrust of his whole preoccupation with Hölderlin's poetry—that the unity of space and time that comes to the fore in the belonging together of locality and journeying is not the kind of space-time unity that is explored by modern physics nor is it even susceptible to the kind of mathematical symbolization that the physicist's work presupposes. The experience of place and of historical existence that the poetic word discloses is, for Heidegger, more original than the experience that draws time and space into the scientific and technologically oriented ordering of the world as a system of causally interconnected functions.[99] Here again the particular connotation of 'place', as opposed to 'space', plays an important role. This is especially sharply expressed in a later essay, 'Building—Dwelling—Thinking', where Heidegger contrasts the modern, post-Cartesian way of defining a thing in terms of its location 'in' a uniformly extended space with the way in which those 'things', such as a bridge, that belong to human beings' fundamental way of inhabiting their world actually determine how we experience space. This, he suggests, was already understood implicitly by the Greeks, for whereas modern thought understands a boundary as limiting or defining a given entity (the aquatic nature of the fish reflects its limitations with respect to being able to live on land), the Greeks did not see a boundary as 'that at which something stops but... [as] that from which something *begins its presencing*... Space is in essence that for which room has been made, something that is allowed to be within its boundaries' and this occurs 'by virtue of a place (*Ort*), that is, by such a thing as the bridge. Accordingly spaces receive their being from places and not from "space".'[100] In the age of the aeroplane and radio, however (and, had he lived longer,

---

[98] *Der Ister*, 46, *The Ister*, 39.

[99] Although he also insists that it is not necessarily opposed to the scientific understanding, merely that it precedes it and is not reducible to or exhaustively accounted for by it.

[100] M. Heidegger, *Poetry, Language, Thought*, trans. A. Hofstadter (New York: Harper and Row, 1971), 154 (adapted); M. Heidegger, 'Bauen Wohnen Denken', in *Vorträge und Aufsätze* (Stuttgart: Neske, 1954), 149.

Heidegger would surely have been able to add 'the internet'), the original uniqueness of 'place' is dissolved or obscured in the universal calculability and manageability of time and space.

The point, therefore, is not simply to invert the conventional ranking of time and space, and, in modernity, both are in fact exposed to parallel distortions in the alienating medium of technology. Likewise, the reconnection to what is most authentically one's ownmost way of being that occurs when we attend to the poetic invocation of the river is not an alternative to the authenticity arrived at by the one who achieves a decisive moment of vision in face of the annihilating power of time. Ultimately, both time and place must be in play—as Heidegger explores in one of the more difficult passages of his philosophical notebook published as *Contributions to Philosophy*. Here he speaks of time-space in their original unity as constituting the abyss that 'is the original occurrence of the essence of groundedness' that is also as such coterminous with the occurrence of the essence of truth.[101] What matters, then, is to be open to both space and time in their original unity, a unity that, as the cases of the rivers and the bridge show, is not some sort of metaphysical or transcendental unity behind appearances but is given in the concrete, local, lived moment.

The experience of place is not a shortcut by which alienated moderns can reconnect with their primordial Being. Because its truth is indissociable from its occurrence in conjunction with time, place does not give us an unqualified entrance into stasis, into a pure experience of Being freed from the flow of becoming: space is always already temporal and time is always already localized—a point that Heidegger's focus on the 'locality' and 'journeying' of the rivers especially brings to the fore. If 'presence' can be read as either temporal or spatial, the decomposition of presence can also occur as either temporal or spatial—or, in each case, as both. From Heidegger's point of view this does not simply rule out time or space (or time-space) as allowing for a certain relation to Being: on the contrary (and as we have just seen), the occurrence of time-space is the only possible ground on which the truth of Being might be known by human beings. Yet, equally, from the standpoint of classical theism this must nevertheless seem to mean accepting a certain loss of Being. In this regard, although much less commented on than his discussion of time, it is striking that Augustine registers his discovery that God is not a spatially extended being ('some corporeal substance, taking up vast spaces of place: and that, either infused into this world, or else diffused indefinitely

---

[101] See M. Heidegger, *Beiträge zur Philosophie (vom Ereignis)* (*Gesamtausgabe*, vol. lxiii) (Frankfurt am Main: Klostermann, 1989), 371–88.

without it') as a key moment in his journey towards Christianity.[102] It is therefore axiomatic for Augustine that the God who is Being-Itself is neither temporally distended nor spatially extended and the reason is essentially the same in both cases, namely, that such distention or extension would diminish, weaken, or corrupt the self-identical immutability condensed in the divine name 'I am that I am'. But is Augustine—here once more in curious proximity to Sartre—right to suppose that the relation of selfsame being to space and time is thus a relation of either-or and that to know ourselves as inseparable from the movement of time-space is *ipso facto* to have lost the possibility of a true knowing of Being?

In his *Poetics of Space*, Gaston Bachelard explores the poetic images in which human beings concretely experience their space, images such as those of houses, nests, shells, corners, and roundness. Such images, he suggests offer a phenomenological route to what he calls a 'direct ontology'.[103] Amongst these images, those that figure 'home' have a special privilege: 'all really inhabited space bears the essence of the notion of home,' he writes.[104] The home is the house that first allows the 'I', the self, to experience itself protected and supported by the non-I. It is the model, the ground-plan of all subsequent relations between self and world: 'the house thrusts aside contingencies, its councils of continuity are unceasing. Without it, man would be a dispersed being . . . It is body and soul. It is the human being's first world. Before he is "cast into the world" . . . man is laid in the cradle of the house'— and, he adds, this shows that 'Being is already a value. Life begins well, it begins enclosed, protected.'[105]

Presumably, Bachelard's allusion to the view that the primal experience of existence is that of being 'cast into the world' (a view ascribed to 'certain hasty metaphysics') refers to the notion of 'thrownness' developed in *Being and Time*. This allusion is taken further when, rather than seeing our original relation to existence in terms of anxiety, Bachelard insists that the imaginary of house and home demonstrates that thrownness and anxiety belong to a merely 'secondary metaphysics' that 'passes over the preliminaries, when being is being-well, when the human being is deposited in a being-well, in the well-being associated with being'.[106] Whilst a metaphysics that attended only to consciousness would indeed have to confront alienation, anxiety, and the fallenness of the world, a phenomenology that was attentive to what is given in basic images—reading them not psychoanalytically but with regard

---

[102] See Augustine, *Confessions*, VII, 1 (Watts's translation). Augustine acknowledges the role of Platonism in helping wean him from such ways of imagining God—see *Confessions*, VII, 20.
[103] G. Bachelard, *The Poetics of Space*, trans. M. Jolas (Boston: Beacon Press, 1994), p. xvi.
[104] Ibid. 5.   [105] Ibid. 7.   [106] Ibid.

to what they reveal of our relation to Being—would learn of 'an enveloping warmth' 'in the being of within', a warmth that 'welcomes being', nourishing, gratifying, and comforting the human being *and doing so before we are driven to seek comfort and gratification by experiences of dread and deprivation*. But if Bachelard's analysis is polemically framed in relation to Heidegger and Sartre, its outcome is not so very distant from that of the Heidegger who writes of the poet, the rivers, and the edifices that welcome human beings into their original—but occluded—kinship with being. Furthermore, in his introduction Bachelard explains that he does not see the primordial images of space as straightforwardly denoting Being but as 'reverberating' with the 'sonority of being' and, like Heidegger, he rejects an approach that would see them as metaphors or as symbols for some purely psychological experiences.[107] We shall see further in the next chapter how this too reveals a certain—if unconscious—proximity to Heidegger's understanding of the relation of language and Being. But, looking once more from an angle arguably shared by Augustine and Sartre, the 'reverberation' of Being in the poetic image, above all in the imagery of house and home, is not a simple, pure, direct, or unmediated revelation of Being. Although Bachelard rejects the primacy of being-in-the-world for phenomenological investigation, it is hard to see how his own starting point, the home from which each of us goes out into the world, is not in its own way a form of being-in-the-world, albeit otherwise focused and interpreted than the being-in-the-world described by the Heidegger of *Being and Time*. Yet, once more, it is nevertheless—Bachelard, at least, claims that it is—the revelation of a human relation to (or, more precisely, a human rootedness in) Being. The reverberation and sonority of the image, we may say, reveal something both of the distance and of the nearness that characterize that relation and that rootedness. A closer account of both distance and nearness, however, requires that we now turn to a theme that has been running through much of this chapter, namely, language, for it is in language, whether in the word of the poet or the utterance of the basic image, that we articulate and communicate our experience of time and space as humanly meaningful.

---

[107] G. Bachelard, *The Poetics of Space*, trans. M. Jolas (Boston: Beacon Press, 1994), pp. xvi, 233.

4

Language

LANGUAGE AND ITS CRISES

Language is something with which all readers of this book along with the overwhelming majority of human beings who survive early infancy are familiar. This near universality of language, a phenomenon until very recently thought to distinguish human beings from all other animals, led Aristotle to define the human being as the *zōon logon echon,* the living being that has discourse or 'the word' (*Politics,* 1253a).[1] Yet, just as Augustine said that he knew what time was as long as no one asked him to define it, we too might say that, despite our extensive experiences of, in, and with language we cannot really say what language is. Is it at all appropriate even to refer to it as 'something', as in the opening sentence of this paragraph? If it is 'some thing', it is clearly a 'thing' of a very different kind from many of the other 'things' with which we have to do. The advent of language has been described as 'overrunning' the field of vision and the other senses like an invading army,[2] and whilst various sciences—amongst them grammar, linguistics, neuro-biology, and philosophy—can make language the object of their enquiries, our normal experience is not so much of language as an object but as a kind of atmosphere, an environment in which we live and move and, perhaps, have our being. Trying to step outside that atmosphere and look at it, as it were, from the outside would seem extremely difficult, if not impossible—a reflection that has led some contemporary thinkers to suggest that there is no 'outside' of language, that the world we live in is a world constructed by and as language.[3] Recalling that our enquiry is specifically

---

[1] Heidegger, however, points out on several occasions that *logos* does not mean language in the modern sense and that the Greeks had no word for what we call language.

[2] M. Merleau-Ponty, *The Visible and the Invisible,* trans. A. Lingis (Evanston, Ill.: Northwestern University Press, 1968), 155.

[3] Although this claim is sometimes made with reference to the later Wittgenstein, it would seem also to be an extension of the opening gambit of the *Tractatus*—that 'the world is the sum of facts, not of things'. It is also, of course, especially influenced by a certain reading of Derrida to whom this chapter will, some might feel inevitably, steer a course.

about Being and that we are here to consider language in its relation to the question of Being, the more language is seen as determining the totality of our existence the less it is seen as relating—or needing to relate to—any 'being' external to itself. 'Being' can itself come to be seen as no more than an epiphenomenon, a reflex of language, perhaps even more particularly of the grammatical structures specific to the Indo-European languages.

Leaving the questions that these remarks suggest to be taken up at a later point in this chapter, it would nevertheless seem uncontroversial to repeat that language is something we are all familiar with and, for the most part, proficient in. Even a 3-year-old can use the future conditional with great assurance, although adults learning a foreign language would regard themselves as quite advanced if they had got on to such parts of speech in the learned language. Yet even proficient language users will often find themselves frustrated or adrift in the ebb and flow of words. If we assume that the poets (to whom we shall have to turn at several points in this chapter) are exponents par excellence of language, then it is striking that even the poets—perhaps especially the poets—cannot always find the words to say what they want to say. Eliot (once more) described 'the intolerable wrestle | With words and meaning' (East Coker, 70–1) in paradigmatic phrases:

> Words strain,
> Crack and sometimes break, under the burden,
> Under the tension, slip, slide, perish,
> Decay with imprecision, will not stay in place,
> Will not stay still. (Burnt Norton, ll. 149–53)

Whether we think of language as a means of referring to external realities, as expressing inner states (thoughts or feelings), or as mediating social relationships, it often seems to fail us. It is alternately too hard, not sufficiently nuanced, or simply too strange. And even if we do not think of language as 'means' to anything but as the way we are, perhaps in the spirit of Hölderlin's invocation of 'the conversation that we are', then neither does this rescue us from the terrors and other aporia of language—and it was Hölderlin too who spoke of language as 'the most dangerous of gifts' of the gods to mortals. To say that 'we are' a conversation, that we live 'in language', only deepens the bewilderment we feel in the face of language, our inability to say what we want to say, or else saying what we didn't really want or mean to say. To paraphrase Derrida, we have only one language, and it is not our own, but—whether it is English, German, Chinese, or any other existing language whatsoever—a vast communicative system that did not develop with a view to facilitate 'my' expression of 'my' thoughts and feelings.[4] At one and the same time language seems to be both the pre-eminent organ of human communication and yet also the most insurmountable obstacle to such communication.[5]

The sense of there being a crisis in language is often seen as a very specific historical phenomenon. Today there is considerable anxiety about the effect on language of new electronic media. Are such phenomena as electronic mail, texting, the sound-bite culture of the contemporary media, the abandonment of traditional forms of language teaching (including grammar and the study of literary classics), and the prevalence of forms of language associated with management culture and scientific research leading to a reification of language, a flattening-out of its riches and possibilities for existential expression or serious ethical reflection? Are education, cultural activity, and political life being reduced to mere communication of information? As artificial intelligence researchers work towards the production of thinking robots, aren't there even more fast-moving and effective forces at work that will turn human intelligence itself into a simulacrum of AI? Yet whether our perceived contemporary crisis of language is entirely a product of forces effective only since (say) the 1980s, or whether it has a longer historical tail, it is clear that our age is not the first to sense that language is at risk.

If we turn back to the 1920s, Eliot's *Lovesong of J. Alfred Prufrock* and *The Waste Land* testify to the levelling of language amongst gallery-goers 'talking of Michelangelo' (*Prufrock*, 13–14), tourists chattering in the Hofgarten (*Waste Land*, I, 10), or the gossipy talk of the working classes (*Waste Land*, II, 139 ff.), phenomena for which Heidegger's account of 'idle talk' (*Gerede*) in *Being and Time* seems to give a philosophical explanation.[6] There we find the philosopher describing a sort of talk with which we are all certainly familiar and in which, as he puts it, 'there lies an average intelligibility . . . What is said in the talk gets understood but what the talk is about is understood only approximately and superficially.'[7] As Heidegger describes the situation, most of us most of the time have no real essential understanding of what is at issue in the topics that make up the most part of everyday conversation. Each of us can surely confirm this for ourselves: I have to admit that I have only a

---

[4] See J. Derrida, *The Monoligualism of the Other or the Prosthesis of Origin*, trans. P. Mensah (Stanford, Calif.: Stanford University Press, 1998). The point is perhaps analogous to Wittgenstein's claim that there is no such thing as a private language.

[5] See V. Jankélévitch, *Le Je-ne-sais-quoi et le presque-rien*, vol. ii (Paris: Édition du Seuil, 1980), 30.

[6] Another striking example is Hugo von Hofmannsthal's fictional letter from Lord Chandos to Francis Bacon. See G. Ebeling, *Introduction to a Theological Theory of Language*, trans. R. A. Wilson (London: Collins, 1973), 68 ff. Ebeling treats the crisis of language under the thought-provoking rubric of 'boredom with language'.

[7] *Being and Time*, 168 (translation adapted).

second- or fourth-hand understanding of the laws of economics that lie behind the economic debates of the day I hear discussed on the radio; I have no real expertise in the technical aspect of any of the sports I enjoy watching on television; I 'know' that x is a great actor, although I know little enough of the various schools of acting and their various aims, methods, or values—but I could talk to you intelligently enough about any of these topics. And I can do so, because I have been informed by what others (what Heidegger calls 'das Man', 'they' as his translators put it) have told me needs to be said about one or other subject.

This, then, is the situation in which we 'talk' by 'passing the word along', taking the word of another and relaying it as if it were our own. But this is not just a matter of 'gossip' in the superficial sense. It is also characteristic of much of our written culture, public discourse, and even academic study and teaching, e.g., when logic is taught as a system of rules for thinking but without any deeper investigation as to how or why such rules might be required or when they might be appropriate. A certain kind of scholar can relay in a more or less effectively organized way a multitude of assertions, sources, and even interpretations—but it by no means follows that the issues have been thought through to the point of really engaging with the issue, *die Sache selbst*. At whatever level we find ourselves talking without having the matter itself in view, we are engaged in 'idle talk'—whether it is a sports event, a political debate, or a discussion of, let's say, the philosophy of Heidegger. Such idle talk 'releases one from the task of genuinely understanding, but develops an undifferentiated kind of intelligibility, for which nothing is closed off any longer [i.e. one can talk about anything and everything in this way] . . . There are many things with which we first become acquainted in this way, and there is not a little which never gets beyond such an understanding. This everyday way in which things have been interpreted is one into which Dasein has grown in the first instance, with never a possibility of extrication.'[8] In this situation 'The "they" prescribes one's state-of-mind, and determines what and how one "sees".'[9]

We shall return to Heidegger's reflections on the origins of this situation, but note here that his account of 'idle talk' was widely interpreted both as a kind of commentary on the anomie of the urban civilization of early twentieth-century Europe and as a restatement of some of Kierkegaard's reflections on his own 'present age' eighty years previously. There, in a review of a

[8] *Being and Time*, 213/169.
[9] Ibid. 213/170. A striking counter-example to the literature on the crisis of language is Helen Keller's essay 'The Day Language Came into my Life', in Helen Keller, *The Story of my Life* (New York: Doubleday, 1903).

contemporary novel, Kierkegaard gave an account of the 'levelling' that he saw as characteristic of his present 'age of reflection', in which talking was systematically substituted for doing.[10] 'What is it to *chatter*?' he asked, replying that 'It is the annulment of the passionate disjunction between being silent and speaking. Only the person who can remain essentially silent can speak essentially, can act essentially. Silence is inwardness... [T]he person who can speak essentially because he is able to keep silent will not have a profusion of things to speak about but one thing only, and he will find time to speak and to keep silent.'[11] But this is just what his contemporaries are unable to do: 'Talkativeness gains in extensity: it chatters about anything and everything and continues incessantly. When individuals are not turned inward in quiet contentment, in inner satisfaction, but in a relation of reflection are oriented to externalities and to each other, when no important event ties the loose threads together in the unanimity of a crucial change—then chattering begins.'[12]

Kierkegaard ascribes a particularly significant role in the growth of chattering to the newspapers and the creation of a 'public' whose opinions the newspapers supposedly express. Yet because the public is everyone and no one, is not a real person capable of responsibility and decision, and because the newspapers are protected by the anonymity of their 'authors', 'The sum-total of all these comments does not amount to personal human discourse such as can be carried on even by the most simple man who is limited in subject but nevertheless does speak.'[13] If this continues, Kierkegaard predicts, 'eventually human speech will become like the public: pure abstraction— there will no longer be someone who speaks, but an objective reflection will gradually deposit a kind of atmosphere, an abstract noise that will render human speech superfluous, just as machines make workers superfluous'.[14]

But the tale could easily be extended back beyond the 1840s—many of Kierkegaard's complaints about chatter and the literary press would doubtless have elicited approval from Alexander Pope and other critics of Grub Street.

---

[10] The section on 'The Present Age' is only a small part of this review, but it has been published as a self-standing book in several languages, including English and German.

[11] S. Kierkegaard, *Two Ages*, trans. H. V. and E. H. Hong, SKS 8 (Princeton: Princeton University Press, 1978), 97.

[12] Ibid. 97–8.

[13] Ibid. 104.

[14] Ibid. For further, excellent, comment on 'chatter' as a theme running through Kierkegaard's work see Peter Fenves, *'Chatter': Language and History in Kierkegaard* (Stanford, Calif.: Stanford University Press, 1993). H. Dreyfus is only one who has argued that Kierkegaard's critique of the degradation of communication in 1840s Denmark anticipates precisely the issues in play in our contemporary experiences with IT. See H. Dreyfus, *On the Internet* (London: Routledge, 2001), especially ch. 4, 'Nihilism on the Information Highway: Anonymity and Commitment in the Present Age' (pp. 73–89).

Similarly, his critique of the moral vacuity underlying the superficiality and hypocrisy of 'the public' both echo and are anticipated by such commentators on the deceit and flattery of courtly French society as Pascal, La Rochefoucauld, Molière, and Laclos.[15] Kierkegaard himself suggested that his 'present age' resembled that of the Greek city states in the period of their decline and, especially, that of Athens in the age of Socrates.[16] That this too was a time of crisis in language is noted by, amongst others, Heidegger, who sees the very origins of philosophy as responding to the rise of the sophists and their skill in deploying language to deceive as well as to enlighten.[17] In such a situation the search for the grounds of true speech receives an added urgency, an urgency already registered in such Platonic dialogues as *Gorgias*, *Phaedrus*, and the *Sophist*, where Plato raises just this question and does so with a view to the specific threat coming from the professionalization of the art of speaking and the associated phenomenon of writing being integrated into the art of speaking.[18]

When George Steiner described contemporary culture as falling into a mire of secondariness and as marked by the loss of the 'real presence' that alone grounds and gives meaning to what we say, he believed he was describing a very particular cultural moment.[19] Yet—and not forgetting that 'presence' has proved a key category in our exploration of how Being might be revealed to historical human beings—it increasingly looks as if language itself engenders a kind of secondariness and a certain loss of presence. The crisis of language associated with the ills of modernity and postmodernity might actually prove to be a trans-historical experience, a crisis of language in itself and as such. Language seems perennially on the edge of slipping away from us or carrying us away from ourselves. Not so much a means of communication, language sometimes seems designed to frustrate or undo what fragile, ambiguous communication we are, in fact, able to have with one another.

If, then, language is inherently liable to limit or distort our possibilities of communicating with one another about the world in which we live, this might

---

[15] For Kierkegaard's familiarity with and use of all of these see, e.g., R. Grimsley, *Kierkegaard and French Literature* (Cardiff: University of Wales Press, 1966). It is striking that it was precisely France that provided 1840s Denmark with a model of a polite and cultured society (see my *'Poor Paris!' Kierkegaard's Critique of the Spectacular City*, Kierkegaard Studies, Monograph Series 2 (Berlin: de Gruyter, 2000)).

[16] This is, of course, to leap over many other possible times of crisis in the human experience of language, such as (for example) the age of Shakespeare, the invention of printing, late medieval nominalism, or the crisis of classical rhetoric and philosophy reflected in, e.g., Augustine.

[17] M. Heidegger, *Grundbegriffe der Aristotelischen Philosophie* (*Gesamtausgabe*, vol. xviii) (Frankfurt am Main: Klostermann, 2002), 108.

[18] We shall return to Heidegger's analysis of this situation later in this chapter. See 'Heidegger on Language in Aristotle' below.

[19] See G. Steiner, *Real Presences* (London: Faber, 1989).

be something we just have to accept, in the same way that we live with various other limitations to our physical powers, e.g., not being able to fly. In that case there would be no moral fault in our failure to achieve optimum communication through language, it would simply be a natural limitation of our powers. Nor would it be anything other than natural that we should seek to make up for such a limitation by the use of one or other technical prosthesis, from loudspeakers to speech production technologies. On the other hand, as in Eliot, Kierkegaard, Pascal, and Plato, it is hard to deny the sense that there is a kind of moral corruption in our failures of communication, epitomized in a quotation that Kierkegaard ascribed to Talleyrand but that was also found in the English poet Edward Young, who complained that 'men speak only to conceal the mind'. On this view, the sophist is not merely a technician of speech whose specific techniques (perhaps inadvertently) widen rather than narrow the gap between word and meaning. Rather, he is a moral danger to society. Even more dangerous, of course, is when the deliberate manipulation of language is practised on the grand scale, as ideology—fictionally in the 'newspeak' of Orwell's *1984*, historically in the totalitarian systems of the twentieth century, and, some would say, in the management-speak and political correctness that pervade contemporary institutions. But although these two aspects of the critique of language are in principle separable, they are often elided in practice, so that, for example, it is hard not to sense that, despite his own disavowal of any such intention, Heidegger's critique of the 'idle talk' of the 'they' does involve something like a moral disapprobation of those unable to raise themselves out of that situation.

I have mentioned the poets, and spoken of them as the practitioners par excellence of language, and the poets have, more than anyone perhaps, been aware of the fissures, slippages, and distortions seaming the common language in which they have to work.[20] We have already noted Eliot's testimony,

---

[20] Novelists too are aware of such issues. But what poets might most naturally experience as a challenge to the very possibility of their art becomes a rich vein of opportunity for the novelist. At least, for such a novelist as Dostoevsky, who so intently and consistently focuses on the way in which so many, perhaps the majority, of his characters live in a miasma of deliberate or thoughtless lies and 'idle talk', avoiding, deferring, or belittling the possibilities of meaning and commitment that their conversations open up. We shall later discuss the double-voiced nature of Dostoevskian fiction, its polyphony, and unfinishedness, but the novelist's sense for the non-communicative nature of so much human communication is not exhausted by such categories. Commenting on a passage in *The Gambler*, John Jones writes that 'The shifting, crumbling surface of this prose evokes ... circularities, equivocations, half-contradictions, where smells aren't exactly bad but slightly decaying, and convenience/comfort is juggled from hand to hand to avoid the downright lie. Here the overall pattern runs "I live in the kitchen, no really I sort of don't live in the kitchen, so you mustn't go on thinking that I live in the kitchen, but if you look at it like that I sort of do live in the kitchen". John Jones, *Dostoevsky* (Oxford: Clarendon Press, 1983), 23. Jones's sudy is full of such detailed studies of the way in

and he is only one amongst many. But if some poets might regard themselves as working towards a paradigmatically transparent mastery (or, some might say, *service*) of the word by seeking to order words in such a way as to allow Being in all its plenitude to become almost miraculously present to the reader, it is the same poets who are often seen by others (not least philosophers and scientists) as especially culpable with regard to the corruptions of language. For the poetic art, which puts in play the myriad possibilities of metaphor, musicality, and ambiguity that language has to offer, makes maximum use of precisely those features of language that make it so unserviceable for the simple, direct, and true expression of states of affairs and ideas. Some models of poetic practice even suggest that it is the aim of poetry not to refer at all or to refer only to itself, its language, and, in that way, to escape the demands of truth claims or of fidelity to being.[21] Would it, then, be better for language not to refer at all, or not to try to refer—since, in the end, it cannot succeed? But is the fact that reference, if it is at all possible, may have to be oblique, metaphorical, equivocal, or in any other way *difficult* the same as saying that it simply *isn't* possible or simply isn't worth it? And what of our everyday experiences of what we experience as successful reference, as when I tell you that the tree over there is in blossom or, in a different key, that I love you? And should reference primarily mean reference to a particular 'what', or might not the most successful act of referring be when the word simply summons us into the presence of what is spoken of, even if no particular 'what' is specified?

It has not been forgotten that we are now considering language specifically and exclusively as regards its relation to the question of Being and, more particularly, to the question as to whether or how the reflexive self-relationship of being-for-itself disables the possibility of simple openness to the sheer presence of Being. Language seems to reinforce or deepen this self-reflexive structure in such a way that in the moment in which we think of it or speak of it, 'pure' presence seems already to have slipped away to a certain distance. In this regard, language seems to extend the 'distancing' of humanity and Being already encountered in relation to time, and, of course, language and time are deeply interwoven. For example, I previously noted but did not then emphasize that Augustine's meditation on time was framed, at the start, by a meditation on the divine Word as the means of creation, and, at the finish, by reflecting on how we can think of the verse of a psalm as a single unit, prior to and as we sing

which Dostoevsky tracks the flawed, decaying interchanges of intentionality and reference both in the way in which he describes his characters and in their ways of talking.

[21] It is precisely this distinction that lies behind Todorov's analysis of the decline of rhetoric that occurred when the rhetorician adopted a literary and poetic model of language. See T. Todorov, *Théories du symbole* (Paris: Éditions du Seuil, 1977), 65 ff.

it. Language, it seems, presupposes time at every level, 'Words move . . . only in time' (Eliot—again: 'Burnt Norton', 137–8). But does the phenomenon of language extend the distancing of self-conscious life from the immediate presence of Being, pushing us even further away from the possibility of experiencing such presence? Or, given that we are always being carried beyond the simple presence of Being by the flood of becoming, does language perhaps provide a way of recalling or of turning ourselves back towards what, in time, is always passing away?[22] And, however we answer such questions, what further features of the relation of self-conscious life to its own being does the phenomenon of language bring to view?

I shall address these questions in the following way. I shall begin by summarizing Hegel's account of language in the section on psychology in his *Encyclopedia of the Philosophical Sciences*. This will give us a general view of an understanding of language which offers what might be called a success story regarding the possibility of language mediating the general experience of Being on the part of what Hegel calls 'subjective Spirit', i.e., self-conscious, thinking human beings. Following that, I turn, again, to Heidegger. In the first place, I shall briefly examine the treatment of language in *Being and Time* and in Heidegger's lectures on Aristotle from the early to mid-1920s that lay the groundwork for the discussion there. Then I turn to aspects of his later thinking about the poetic word and what the poetic word tells us about the essence of language, and the 'event' of language, that both reveals and conceals our relation to Being. This is then further discussed in the light of Derrida's approach to language, an approach that, despite his undoubtedly critical reception of Hegel and Heidegger, responds to and draws out some of the key features of Heidegger's own treatment of the event of language. This leads to the further question of language as a mode whereby we experience and express ourselves as personal and interpersonal beings, since it is only as a sociable, communicative being that I can be a 'being having language'. This question will be addressed with particular reference to Kierkegaard, Dostoevsky, and Dostoevsky's commentator, Bakhtin.[23]

---

[22] The intertwining of issues of time and language is reflected not only in the title of Paul Ricœur's *Time and Narrative*, but also in the way in which he adduces a notion of 'emplotment' drawn from a meditation on Aristotelian poetics, i.e., a specifically literary concept having its *Sitz-im-Leben* precisely in language, as a way of resolving, or at least reframing, the Augustinian aporias concerning time. See P. Ricœur, *Time and Narrative*, trans. K. McLaughlin and D. Pellauer (Chicago: University of Chicago Press, 1984), especially vol. i.

[23] It is perhaps appropriate at this point to comment on the relationship between this chapter and the treatment of religious language in British philosophy of religion from the 1950s through to the 1980s. In retrospect, the debates of that period (e.g., the famous 'University Debate') were rather naive in assuming that the kind of scientific language for which the principles of verifiability and falsifiability seemed to provide appropriate regulative principles

HEGEL

Why turn to Hegel at this point? First, because it was Hegel who established the paradigmatic structure of Being as involving both what he called Being-in-itself and Being-for-itself which, in turn, prompted the question as to whether it is possible to believe that self-conscious beings might ever experience Being in its sheer presence and fullness. As opposed to Sartre's negative answer to this question, Hegel consistently and even doggedly affirmed that despite the power of negation at work in thinking and history alike, the tension implicit in the twofold structure of Being is ultimately reconcilable. Indeed, if there were no reconciliation there would be no tension, merely chaos. This is true with regard to time, but also, and no less so, to language. Hegel allows that language occurs only as a continuing wrestling with what appears to be 'other than' the self, yet the basic structure of language assures him that this 'other' is in the end revealed as a form of self-othering. Consequently, what is represented in language as something 'out there' can be retrieved and internalized in an act of knowing in which there is a kind of double transparency: of sense-experience to word and of word to idea. In these terms Hegel is a superb exemplar of the logocentrism that will be the object of Derrida's critical grammatological scrutiny.[24] We shall return to Derrida in due course, but first we shall briefly

could and should be paradigmatic for all other kinds of language use. The later Wittgenstein certainly offered a way out of the extraordinary condition of one-dimensional stasis into which such an assumption had led reflection on God and language, and the fruits of this can be seen in the work of, e.g., Don Cupitt, D. Z. Phillips, and Fergus Kerr. Some of the issues addressed in that connection also relate closely to the *Fragestellung* of the present chapter. However Wittgenstein could also be used to lead theology into a rather uninspiring cul-de-sac, as in George Lindbeck's cultural-linguistic model of doctrinal language. Alongside this Wittgensteinian moment, hermeneutics, feminism, political theologies and/or deconstruction have allowed the contexts, tensions, displacements, obscurities, and paradoxes of human beings' attempts to speak to one another about God to be given their due. To the extent that the return to Thomas Aquinas and to the question of the analogy of Being offers the possibility of re-relating the question of religious language to the fundamental questions of metaphysics, 'Radical Orthodoxy' has made an important contribution. However, just as the more naive postmodernists seemed to assume that it was sufficient merely to repeat the key words of Derridean deconstruction (perhaps, dare we say it, in the manner of 'idle talk'!), so too the mantra that Thomas's teaching about Being, and especially about the analogy of Being, somehow provides us with an inerrant perspective on how to speak well of God cuts far too many corners to provide good answers. Indeed, it might be argued that one of the themes of this enquiry is that while Thomas engages the important questions, it remains entirely open to question as to how far he might help us with the answers—if, indeed, answers are what is to be sought.

[24] It is no coincidence that a quotation from Hegel prefaces the first chapter of *On Grammatology*.

delineate the outlines of the concept of language presented by Hegel in the section on psychology in the *Encyclopaedia of the Philosophical Sciences*.

'Psychology' is located in a part of the *Encyclopaedia* devoted to subjective Spirit. Under this heading Hegel deals with human life in abstraction from such concrete forms of social life as the family, property-owning, and the state and the cultural expressions that are focused in art, religion, and philosophy, all of which he refers to as 'Objective Spirit'. Objective Spirit, however, presupposes that there are individual human beings who can combine into families, states, etc., whereas the doctrine of subjective Spirit deals with the individual human being as such. This human being is both a phenomenon of nature, with bodily and affective dimensions on a par with other animals (what Hegel calls 'soul'[25]), but also a self-conscious, thinking being, i.e., Spirit. The doctrine of subjective Spirit spells out the relationships that connect these dimensions and how what is at one and the same time a part of nature and yet, also, 'spiritual' is nevertheless one being, a human being. It is perhaps striking—not least in the light of recent emphases on the total permeation of human being by language—that Hegel only arrives at the question of language after having traversed a sequence of preceding stages, including sensibility, perception, and the emergence of self-consciousness through the encounter with others. Only then does he begin to deal with Spirit proper, or theoretical Spirit, i.e., human life as intelligent and thinking.

All expressions of intelligent life aim at cognition, the mental activity in which we discover and make our own what is knowable in the objects that we encounter in the world.[26] This activity is set in motion when the intelligence becomes aware of itself as being determined by something outside it. This occurrence is more precisely defined as intuition, where the German term *Anschauung* (literally: looking-at) has important connotations of visibility. But *Anschauung* is not simply the effect in the mind of an external cause, it is itself an event within mental life: it is not just a matter of *seeing* but of the *I* who sees and, as such, it cannot occur without the activity of my mind. Therefore, Hegel argues, it is more properly definable as a representation— and, again, he has chosen his own words with care, since the German *Vorstellung* suggests the action of placing (*-stellung*) what I see in front of (*Vor-*) me, so that I can see it for what it is. In representing the object to myself, then, I make my own what might otherwise be a merely transient and insignificant sense-impression or mere impersonal occurrence. Representation is in this way a synthesis or double movement that is simultaneously an

---

[25] i.e., *Seele* as opposed to *Psyche*.
[26] The following is a resumé of the argument of §§ 444–68 of G. W. F. Hegel, *Enzyklopädie der Philosophischen Wissenschaften III*, in *Werke*, x (Frankfurt am Main: Suhrkamp, 1970), 240–88.

act of internalization and of externalization, an act in which I direct my mind towards what is external to it whilst at the same time taking what is externally given to me and incorporating it into my own consciousness. In the first instance what is given to me in intuition is given as an image (*Bild*), but images are transient, they flow into and out of consciousness without interruption. It is only when the image is held fast and recollected that we can really speak of a representation (and, again, the German term used by Hegel, *Erinnerung*, literally 'internalization', is significant). Representation is thus more closely defined as the synthesis of the recollected or internalized image or picture in the mind with that of which it is the representation.[27]

But what is it that enables us to form images in our minds? In the first instance, it is what Hegel calls the 'reproductive imagination', the *Einbildungskraft*, literally the 'power of imaging as one'. Hegel rejects the associationist theory that would base an entire theory of mind on the accumulated associations of images produced in the mind in this way, since, he argues, these only mean anything when they are invested with a universal significance that points beyond their immediate, sensuous shape, i.e., when I become capable of seeing each and every tree as a tree and not just my grandfather's apple-tree or the old oak on the common, etc. (i.e., a mere sequence of individual examples without a unifying sense of what each is an example of). Even in the reception of mental images, the mind is not merely reproductive but productive, so that the mental image is a synthesis of Being (insofar as the mind is affected by what is outside it) and universality, of object and subject.[28] This productive power is called 'fantasy, the symbolizing, allegorizing or poetizing imagination'.[29] This is not only the power to convert images coming into consciousness from outside into meaningful wholes, but also to produce new images to express and communicate the subject's own thought and to do so in such a way that this acquires a certain claim to being. As Hegel puts it, it is the activity in which 'it makes itself a being, a something (*Sache*). Actively determining itself in this way, it is externalizing, productive of intuitions—sign-making fantasy'.[30] It is therefore basic to Hegel's view of language that it is not simply the outworking of a cumulative association of ideas, but presupposes the subjective capacity for making—inventing—signs. The importance of this moment is further underlined when Hegel says that fantasy is the mid-point of the whole sequence of forms of self-consciousness, 'the

---

[27] See also the discussion of presence and memory in Ch. 2 above.

[28] The account of reproductive and productive imagination will be familiar to many English-language readers from the work of S. T. Coleridge.

[29] *Enzyklopädie*, 266.

[30] Ibid. 268.

mid-point in which universality and being, what is one's own and what is discovered, the inner and the outer are completely made into one'.[31] The sign produced by such active fantasy expresses the subject's own sense of being, its claim, as it were, to the meaningfulness of its experience. And yet, at the same time, the sign is a sign 'of' something, and its connection to what comes to us from intuition is maintained in its image-like character.

In the midst of this discussion Hegel makes a point that concerns the very place of language in philosophy. 'Normally,' he comments, 'the sign and language are shoved into some sort of appendix to psychology or also into logic, without thought being given to their necessity and their connection with the system of the activity of the intelligence.'[32] However, he suggests, the power of sign-making, language in the broadest sense, is properly understandable only as intimately connected with the a priori production of time and space as forms of intuition, the difference being that in language we determine the objects we intuit in time and space 'as our own', i.e., as humanly meaningful. This occurs more particularly in what he calls the 'productive memory' (*Gedächtnis*), which, he says, is distinct from recollection in that it has specifically and solely to do with signs. Language therefore belongs not only to the form but also to the content of philosophy.

Sign-making is inconceivable without time. The sign functions as sign precisely because of its capacity to outlive the vanishing of the object of which it is a sign. I can say and understand the compound sign 'the tree in my garden', even when I have not seen the tree for many years or long after it has been chopped down. Because of the sign's persistence through time it is able both to preserve the sensuous element deriving from intuition and to transcend it (in the characteristic double movement of the Hegelian *Aufhebung*). It does this through the vocalization (*Ton*) of the subject's inwardness and the articulation of this vocalization in specific representations (*Rede*—discourse) and, in this way, language (*die Sprache*) emerges as a 'higher' state of being (Hegel's term is *Dasein*) in which the sensations, intuitions, and representations derived from sense-experience find a new existence in a 'realm of representations'.

Yet the second reality constituted by the realm of representations that is language still has a certain external quality. Although we are now firmly established on the ground of representation, a word or a name still has something object-like about it. Language occurs in time and space as bodily produced sounds or written signs. How do we get from here to the pure transparency of thinking? This question leads Hegel to reflect further on

---

[31] Ibid. 268.   [32] Ibid. 270.

memory (*Gedächtnis*). Scorning mnemonic systems of mind-training that depend precisely on the relation to exteriority from which thinking needs to liberate itself, Hegel commends *Gedächtnis*-memory as recognizing 'the thing in the name and the name in the thing without perception or image'.[33] But the ability to understand the meaning of words is not yet the ability to understand the wider, larger, or deeper sense of what is said—a point Hegel makes by referring to what he regards as the familiar fact that young people have better memories than the old but, as he puts it, they still have to learn to reflect, to ponder, or to think over what has been said (*Nachdenken*). '*Gedächtnis*-memory is as such only the external mode, the one-sided moment in the existence of thinking,'[34] but thinking proper requires the active self-motivated engagement of the subject, i.e., reason.[35] This yields a double outcome. On the one hand, thought is now able to develop forms proper to its pure, ideal character, i.e. logic. On the other, it is capable of articulating and expressing the free activity of the mind.

Intelligence, which in its theoretical aspect was concerned to make what determined it in its immediacy its own, has now completely taken possession of this and is invested with what is proper to it; through the final negation of immediacy it has been established that it determines its own content. Thinking, as the free concept, is now also free with regard to its content. Knowing itself to be what determines the content, which is just as much its own as it is something determining it from outside, it is the will.[36]

Hegel is now prepared for the transition from theoretical to practical reason. We shall, however stop at this point and note some of the important and relevant features of his account.

As everywhere in Hegel, we have always to bear in mind the twofold aspect of the *Aufhebung* of every phenomenon by what succeeds it. On the one hand, this means that the preceding form or stage is negated, but rather than being simply annihilated is taken up or incorporated into what follows. As suggested by the term 'sublated', one of the standard English translations of *Aufhebung*, each new form is the 'sublimation' of the foregoing. So it is here. Language, as the realm of pure representation, sublimates the realm of sense-experience but not in such a way as simply to deny what was experienced at the lower level. Rather, language enables us to 'see' for ourselves what

---

[33] *Enzyklopädie*, 278.
[34] NB Hegel has yet again, and perhaps paradoxically, made use of the 'pictorial' qualities of the German language in helping his argument along at this point, since the central part of the term *Gedächtnis—dächt*—derives from the past participle (*gedacht*) of *Denken* ('to think').
[35] *Enzyklopädie*, 283.
[36] Ibid. 287.

the bodily sense gave us to 'see' in a merely external way. The double nature of *Aufhebung* therefore means that although the account of sense-experience precedes language in the unfolding of the system, the 'higher' form of language has a retroactive impact on everything that preceded it and the meaning of sense-experience only becomes apparent in and as language. This also implies that the progression from intuition to thought, which, as we have seen, is dependent on the sign-making powers of the productive imagination, is a continuum. Nothing essential is lost. On the contrary, it is precisely by following this continuous progression to its end that we get to be able to know what is essential in experience. What is essential is what can be said and what is truly essential in what is said is what alone can truly be thought. As Hegel makes especially clear in the comments on fantasy being the mid-point of the whole sequence of the phenomena of theoretical self-consciousness, language not merely requires the possibility of a correspondence between object (*res*) and thought (*intellectus*) but depends on and grows out of a kind of chiastic intercalation of thinking and being. In language we are able to say how we see the world as being. We are able to give utterance to what is the case. Language is translucent to everything that vision gives us to see. Indeed, only in language can we see what we do, in fact, see—because only in language can we *say* it and therefore only in language can we *think* it. From the other side, whilst 'signs' and language as a system of signs are produced by the active power of the mind and to that extent are 'subjective', language is not merely arbitrary. For whilst a certain arbitrariness would seem to be signalled by Hegel's closing invocation of the will as integral to thinking, this is modified by the fact that, first, the pure form of thinking occurs as logic, and, secondly, thinking has the capacity—which it constantly exercises in the activity of thinking—to incorporate into itself the deliverances of sense-experience. It thinks what is. As such it is therefore the most intense integration of subjectivity and objectivity.

Hegel's careful sequence of syntheses produces a complex whole in which the relations of its constituent parts are all delicately balanced. As such it is exposed to many different kinds of criticism. Moreover, it offers a particular view of language and of the relation of language to Being that would be thoroughly and fundamentally contested in the twentieth century, both directly and indirectly, by the two thinkers to whom we shall be turning next, Heidegger and Derrida. However—and perhaps not without a nod to the ambiguity of the Hegelian 'sublation'—neither of these understood themselves as simply 'rejecting' Hegel or the kind of metaphysical logocentrism his system set in place. Rather, it is as much the force of Hegel's belief that language does enable us to think the reality of the world we inhabit as the various possible shortcomings of his argumentation that provokes them to rethink the interrelationships of language, subjectivity, and Being in such a way as to unravel the intertwined threads of his all-harmonizing, all-unifying theorizing of the ontology of language.

HEIDEGGER ON LANGUAGE IN ARISTOTLE

We have already looked briefly at Heidegger's discussion of 'idle talk'. But his interest in 'idle talk' is not simply that it offers a striking example of the fallenness of the 'average everyday' life of the modern world. Rather, 'idle talk' is a primary form of human language and, as such, revelatory of Dasein's way of being-in-the-world.[37] As a study of Heidegger's lectures from the early to mid-1920s shows, it is not so much Kierkegaard and his critique of 'chatter' as Plato and Aristotle who stand in the background of Heidegger's discussion. These lectures covered parts of Aristotle's *Metaphysics*, *Physics*, and *Rhetoric* and Plato's *Sophist* (which also included an extended discussion of Aristotle's *Ethics*). We shall return to these lectures, but first we turn to *Being and Time* itself.

'Idle talk' is not the first kind of language addressed in *Being and Time*. On the contrary, Heidegger early on sets out an interpretation of *logos*-discourse as a part of his preliminary account of phenomenological method. He understands phenomenology itself as 'the science of the Being of entities—ontology'.[38] In this science, the Being of entities is not to be inferred, deduced, or explained otherwise than by attending to the way entities show themselves—and the way in which entities show themselves is, simply, as phenomena. This term, *phainomenon*, derives (Heidegger says) from a root that means 'that which is bright [i.e. luminous or shining]—in other words, that wherein something can become manifest, visible in itself': 'phenomenon' 'signifies that which shows itself in itself, the manifest'.[39] However, it is always possible that what shows itself is not in fact the thing itself, but a semblance. Similarly, what appears is not immediately identifiable with what is shown: the symptoms are not the disease, although they make the disease manifest. Heidegger several times notes that the

---

[37] Heidegger's translators note that the German *Gerede* does not have the pejorative tones of their rendering 'idle talk' and, indeed, perhaps it would have been better just to translate this as 'talk'.

[38] *Being and Time*, 61/37. Although I shall use *logos* and language interchangeably in the following pages, Heidegger himself several times points out that *logos* cannot be taken as meaning what we today mean by language and that, in a quite definite sense, the Greeks had no word for 'language'.

[39] Ibid. 51/28.

various meanings that can be attached to these terms are 'bewildering' and suggests that if we are to understand 'the phenomenological conception of phenomenon' then it is necessary first to understand the *logos* that is (literally) integral to phenomenology.

Again there are many—perhaps even a 'bewildering' number of—ways in which *logos* too has been understood. A basic meaning (and one which is subsequently presupposed in just about everything Heidegger says about language) is that 'Logos as "discourse" means rather the same as *dēloun*: to make manifest what one is "talking about" in one's discourse'.[40] 'The *logos* lets something be seen'[41]—which, as Heidegger indicates, once more puts in play the verb *phainesthai* from which 'phenomenon' itself is derived. Genuine discourse is itself apophantic, a phenomenologization in which we are enabled to see *what* is being said from the very process of talking and in such a way that what one person says is disclosed or made accessible to others.

Logos points us towards a certain something, towards 'what' is being talked about. But, precisely because it is not a dumb, gestural pointing it 'points' by letting what is being pointed to be seen '*as* something'. This 'as'-character of language means that it is inherently articulated: it has the character of a *synthēsis*, which, Heidegger notes, creates the possibility of what is being said being either true or false. Anticipating the fuller discussion of truth that will occur at a much later point in his argument, Heidegger indicates that the truth of *logos* is to be understood not in terms of its correspondence or agreement with things but as its capacity for making manifest and taking 'the entities of which one is talking . . . out of their hiddenness . . . [and] let [ting] them be seen as something unhidden'.[42] But this also means that *logos* is not itself 'the primary "locus" of truth'.[43] Truth is not, in the first instance, the truth of judgements. Rather, '*Aisthēsis*, the sheer sensory perception of something, is "true" in the Greek sense, and indeed more primordially than the *logos* which we have been discussing'.[44] *Logos* lets us see things, but what seeing discovers are not propositions but how entities are: 'Pure *noein* is the perception of the simplest determinate ways of Being which entities as such may possess, and it perceives them just by looking at them.' This *noein* is what is '"true" in the purest and most primordial sense'.[45]

But what is truth? Heidegger does not engage in an extended discussion of this question until the very final section of part I of *Being and Time*. There, having set out an account of Dasein's being-in-the-world that makes it clear

---

[40] Ibid. 56/32. Heidegger notes but does not dwell on other kinds of logos that do not have this apophantic function, e.g. 'requesting'.
[41] Ibid. 56/32.   [42] Ibid. 56/33.   [43] Ibid. 57/33.
[44] Ibid. 57/33.   [45] Ibid.

that Dasein is not the kind of entity that can be defined by traditional philosophical categories such as essence or substance, Heidegger responds to the implicit question as to how the understanding of Being from the perspective of existence can in any sense be regarded as true. At the beginning of ¶44 he notes that 'From time immemorial, philosophy has associated truth and Being.'[46] Now, however, he suggests that we need to revisit the conventional understanding of this association in order to arrive at a view of truth that would allow us to see how a phenomenological interpretation of *existentiell* phenomena can be understood as making a certain kind of truth claim. Initially, this returns us to what is already familiar from the discussion of *logos* and phenomenology: 'To say that an assertion "is true" signifies that it uncovers the entity as it is in itself. Such an assertion asserts, points out, "lets" the entity "be seen" (*apophansis*) in its uncoveredness. The Being-true (truth) of the assertion must be understood as Being-uncovering.'[47] However, 'Being-true as Being-uncovering, is in turn ontologically possible only on the basis of Being-in-the-world. This latter phenomenon, which we have known as a basic state of Dasein, is the foundation for the primordial phenomenon of truth.'[48] Why is this? It is because (as Heidegger believes he has shown in the preceding analyses of Dasein's Being-in-the-world) Dasein exists in a manner that is characterized by 'circumspective concern' or by the 'care' that puts Dasein always ahead of itself, understanding its own possibilities through its relations to entities or to its own intentions and projects. In other words (and as we have already seen in Chapter 2), its self-relational structure means that Dasein is not a simple entity to be defined in terms of a certain essence or 'what': Dasein is what it is as and by virtue of its multiple relational possibilities and it can be what and as it is only to the extent that it discovers—'uncovers'— these: 'hence only with Dasein's disclosedness is the most primordial phenomenon of truth attained . . . In so far as Dasein is its disclosedness essentially, and discloses and uncovers as something disclosed to this extent it is essentially "true". Dasein is "in the truth" . . . the disclosedness of its ownmost Being belongs to its existential constitution.'[49]

Logos has not been forgotten in this discussion and Heidegger notes that the phenomenon of truth in the sense of uncoveredness is already linked with *logos* in one of the fragments of Heraclitus. However, as another early thinker, Parmenides, indicated, the goddess of Truth shows the seeker two paths, 'one

---

[46] *Being and Time*, 61/37. Although I shall use *logos* and language interchangeably in the following pages, Heidegger himself several times points out that *logos* cannot be taken as meaning what we today mean by language and that, in a quite definite sense, the Greeks had no word for 'language', 256/212.
[47] Ibid. 261/218.   [48] Ibid. 261/219.   [49] Ibid. 263/220–1.

of uncovering, one of hiding'.[50] This Heidegger takes as showing that 'Dasein is already both in the truth and in untruth,' so that 'the way of uncovering is achieved only in the *krinein logo*—in distinguishing between these understandingly, and making one's decision for the one rather than the other'.[51] This double aspect of Dasein, Heidegger says, is what he has earlier called 'thrown projection': Dasein does not come to consciousness of itself as a fully formed sovereign intelligence, capable of seeing things (and itself) as they are in their Being; instead, it finds itself thrown into a world that it cannot immediately understand, that is ambiguous and alienating and in which it is 'sucked into the turbulence of the "they's" inauthenticity'.[52] However, one of the ways—if not the pre-eminent way—in which this 'inauthenticity' holds sway is precisely *Gerede* or 'idle talk'. What is said in *Gerede* possesses an 'average intelligibility', but, as opposed to apophantic discourse in which what is being talked about comes to view in what is said, the 'being-with-one-another' of the talkers is allowed to take precedence over the 'primary relationship-of-Being towards the entity being talked about'.[53] Even when there is no deliberate intention to deceive, such talk 'serves not so much to keep Being-in-the-world open for us in an articulated understanding, as rather to close it off, and cover up the entities within-the-world'.[54] And this can be as true of scholarly discourse as of street-corner gossip. It may be true to say that '*Being and Time* contains important discussions of language and truth' but the correctness of this statement does not of itself reveal what is really at issue in what is being talked about. The note-taker who has jotted down that '*Being and Time* contains important discussions of language and truth' may have very little conception of what is said in these 'important' discussions or why they are important and, what is worse, the very fact of being able to repeat this may make it harder for such a note-taker to move on to the next level because she or he already 'knows' what needs to be said about language and truth in *Being and Time*. The question of truth, then, is not just whether what is said is correct, but whether it genuinely serves to uncover the matter at issue.

In the course of this discussion, Heidegger noted that Aristotle is generally regarded as the source of the two main rival views of truth, namely, truth as a value of judgement and truth as correspondence.[55] However, it is also his view

---

[50] Ibid. 265/222.
[51] Ibid. 265/223. [52] Ibid. 223/179.
[53] Ibid. 212/169. [54] Ibid.
[55] *Being and Time*, 61/37. Although I shall use *logos* and language interchangeably in the following pages, Heidegger himself several times points out that *logos* cannot be taken as meaning what we today mean by language and that, in a quite definite sense, the Greeks had no word for 'language', 257/214.

that these views represent an impoverished reception of Aristotle and, in fact, his own researches on Aristotle, reflected in a sequence of important lecture series through the mid-1920s, can be seen to have played a crucial role in developing the interpretation of Dasein expounded in *Being and Time* itself. I want now to mention some points in these lectures that help to clarify several features of the role of language in *Being and Time* but that also indicate possibilities that are, in the event, less emphasized up until this mature expression of Heidegger's early philosophy.

In summer 1922 Heidegger lectured on 'Phenomenological Interpretations of Selected Treatises of Aristotle on Ontology and Logic', primarily focusing on sections from the *Metaphysics* and the *Physics*. He starts with the opening sections of the *Metaphysics*, which take him to basic questions about the nature of philosophical enquiry. His renderings of such terms as *epistēmē*, *theōria*, and *sophia* consistently emphasize their visual character. Thus the *theōrētikoi* are contrasted with the *poiētikoi* as those whose comportment more emphasizes 'the illuminative bringing into view than the productive preoccupation with things', whilst 982a1–3 of Aristotle's text is translated 'Understanding is a mode of illumination and, to be precise, that which brings into view and in which what is put in front of us [*zu Gesicht gebracht wird*] is shown in its character of why and whence.'[56] Philosophy arises only when other needs have been satisfied and is concerned solely 'with a pure desire to see without any other goal'.[57] This desire is already present in the Pre-Socratics, but Aristotle qualifies it in an important and, for Heidegger, decisive manner. Commenting on Aristotle's discussion of Parmenides in *Physics* A 2 185, Heidegger places especial weight on the philosopher's decision to interpret what his predecessor had to say about Being by 'looking at how they [the Eleatics] speak about it'.[58] The problem with Parmenides' saying *hen ta panta* is that Parmenides overlooked its *logos* character, imagining that his saying offers a direct and unmediated view onto the things themselves without seeing how the saying itself transforms his relation to the things. It is therefore precisely the *logos*-character of the Parmenidean saying that Aristotle makes the object of his critique. It is not that *logos* has no relation to Being or to beings. On the contrary, *logos* always expresses a relation to what is being talked about ('auf hin', as Heidegger puts it). That is why *logos* can have an apophantic character and bring to expression and

---

[56] Martin Heidegger, *Phänomenologische Interpretationen ausgewählter Abhandlungen des Aristoteles zur Ontologie und Logik* (*Gesamtausgabe*, vol. lxii) (Frankfurt am Main: Klostermann, 2005), 30. Compare Ross's translation: 'Wisdom is knowledge about certain principles and causes.'

[57] *Phänomenologische Interpretationen*, 39.

[58] *Phänomenologische Interpretationen*, 199.

view what is at issue in a given discourse. Yet (anticipating what we have already read in *Being and Time*), because *logos* represents the matter at issue in a certain way, 'as' *x*, the possibilities for seeing how things are that are given in and with *logos* are thus inherently articulated and stand in the midst of the play of truth and falsehood in such a way that the simplicity of Parmenides' identification of thinking and Being is impossible.

The crucial role of language in metaphysical reflection on Being is consistently emphasized in the lectures of the following years. It is also clear that both in his readings of Aristotle and in the insights he is gaining into language Heidegger believes himself to be arriving at a decisive breakthrough in philosophical thinking. The extent of the 'revolution' he believes to be in progress is indicated by the opening remarks of the lectures 'Introduction to Phenomenological Research' in 1923–4: 'I am convinced, that philosophy is finished. We are faced with completely new tasks that have nothing at all to do with traditional philosophy.'[59] But this revolution is inseparable from Aristotle and the theme of language, which is now perceived as inseparable from human beings' way of being: 'To the extent that human beings are in the world and want anything from it or from themselves they speak. They speak to the extent something like a world is disclosed to them as something they might be concerned about and therewith also themselves. But the word is not an instrument...Language is the being and becoming of human beings themselves.'[60] What language reveals is therefore a 'possibility of being for human beings.'[61] *Logos* discloses the world: 'speaking and perception are one' and only as *logos* is the world made accessible 'in its unitary articulatedness.'[62] With regard to its perceptual character, however, what *logos* shows, what I see in it and you see in my words, must be there: it must be present, here, now (i.e., as an act of fulfilled intentionality in the sense that Heidegger will expound in the lectures on *The History of the Concept of Time* that were given in the following year).[63] Yet, equally, perception, *aisthēsis*, already involves a judgement: it is not in itself a *logos* and yet it is 'something like a logos',[64] embracing a becoming-other, a suffering, a judging, and a mediation (since the perception of red is not itself the colour on the leaf). Perception itself has a language-like character and is found only in a being capable of language: 'with or without being given voice it is always in some way or other

---

[59] Martin Heidegger, *Einführung in die Phänomenologische Forschung* (*Gesamtausgabe*, vol. xvii) (Frankfurt am Main: Klostermann, 1994), 1.
[60] Ibid. 16.   [61] Ibid. 21.   [62] Ibid. 28.
[63] See Ch. 2 above for discussion.
[64] Ibid. 29.

a speaking.'[65] Yet, as we have seen, speaking itself already conceals the world and puts in play the possibility of falsehood.[66]

These comments help deepen our understanding of what Heidegger says in *Being and Time* when he insists that truth is not in the first instance a characteristic of propositions or language but has to do with the original encounter of self and world, *aisthēsis*: precisely because he is not starting with the epistemological challenges facing a Cartesian 'I' nor yet with the robust faith in the primacy of things of common-sense realism, he is saying *both* that language cannot be separated out from how the world itself comes to expression in it *and* that we have no experience of the world other than in language or in language-like perceptual experiences that present the world to us as speakable. In this respect he might also be understood as attempting, like Hegel, to do justice both to the claim of Being-in-itself and the role of being-for-itself in the constitution of language as well as interpreting language in the light of the phenomenological idea of intentionality.

However, even if we allow that he has not let himself be trapped in some version of Cartesian intellectualism, Heidegger seems to be envisaging knowledge (no matter how dramatically reformulated) as occurring in the traffic between self and world, as if the philosopher is engaged in a monological and introspective reflection on the complex interaction between mind and beings (trees, leaves, objects 'out there' in some way or other or, more metaphysically, 'Being' itself as the Being of those objective entities). Somehow or other, this seems to find a spontaneous expression in *logos*. Something seems to be missing, however, something we might call the social dimension of language. Maybe it is there implicitly—and we note Heidegger's insistence in emphasizing 'speaking' as integral to *logos*—but has it yet been sufficiently emphasized? Who is the philosopher speaking to and how? What does it mean that he 'speaks' his perception of the world rather than just silently observing it? What does the possibility of speaking show about the one who speaks and how does that inform or distort what he speaks about?

Heidegger implicitly addresses such questions in the 1924 lectures on 'The Basic Concepts of Aristotelian Philosophy'. Here, after reminding listeners that knowledge too is to be understood as a possibility of human existence and that, as such, it cannot detach itself from the historicity of such existence, Heidegger moves fairly swiftly to examine the interrelationship between *logos* and *ousia*. He comments that 'For the Greeks above all, every act of speaking is speaking to someone or with someone, with oneself or to oneself. In the concreteness of Dasein speaking—since we do not exist alone—is speaking

---

[65] See Ch. 2 above for discussion. 30.   [66] Ibid. 40.

with someone about something whilst speaking with someone about something is always an expression (a speaking-out) of myself.'[67] *Logos* can only be understood through the analysis of *ousia*: but that is not something 'out there'; it is the concrete Dasein of the one who speaks. Yet, at the same time, this Dasein can only be understood through *logos* and, for the Greeks, *logos* belongs to the very definition of being human. A human being is a *zōon logon echon*, a being having discourse. The way in which we are in speaking of ourselves is the way in which we are. Later in the lectures, Heidegger therefore turns expressly to 'the exposition of human Dasein with regard to the basic possibility of speaking-with-one-another' and does so following the 'guiding-thread' of Aristotle's *Rhetoric*. Language does not arise in the first instance in the encounter between human minds and non-human objects, but human beings exist as having discourse because they find the meaning of their lives in talking with one another, meeting in the agora (or, we might say, the bar) and talking to each other about everything that's going on in their lives—a point which Heidegger connects with an alternative Aristotelian definition of human being as the *zōon politikon*, the 'political animal'. Being together and speaking together are two sides of the same coin. This, however, leads to a qualification of the previous emphasis on seeing. If conversation, speaking with one another, is the primary *Sitz-im-Leben* of language, hearing—not seeing—becomes the original *aisthēsis*. Although seeing discloses the world, 'it is nevertheless hearing, because it is the perception of speaking and because it is the possibility of being with one another' that now takes precedence.[68] Moreover, in the kind of social life now being considered, what is of most interest is not whether a certain leaf is red or green but whether such-and-such an action or person is to be approved or blamed, encouraged or warned. Here the very ambiguity of language makes the speakers vulnerable to being deceived (and sometimes deliberately deceived) not just about the world but about themselves, their wishes and intentions. This is the situation that sees the rise of the rhetor. His is not a special science, such as medicine, but a power relative to anything that can become the matter of discourse and its exercise concerns the whole manner of human beings' being-together in the polis and therewith also their existence as historical (*geschichtlich*). The abstraction of 'nature' as a topic for disinterested contemplation is subsequent to and dependent on this primary phenomenon of human beings' way of living in the world as self-revealed in language. As will be the case in *Being and Time*, knowledge of entities that are present-to-hand in the world as

---

[67] Martin Heidegger, *Grundbegriffe der Arisotelischen Philosophie* (*Gesamtausgabe*, vol. xviii) (Frankfurt am Main: Klostermann, 2002), 17.

[68] *Grundbegriffe*, 104.

'objects' of knowledge is secondary to knowing—if such knowing can be achieved—who we ourselves really are in our distinctively human, self-relational being. However, the phenomenon of the rhetor warns us of the possibility of language being used to mislead human beings, to point them away from truth and entrap them in falsehood. But this is not just a fault of the malice or cynicism of the rhetor. It is a possibility that is latent in language itself. As Heidegger will emphasize in lectures given the following year on Plato's dialogue *The Sophist*, language is itself the medium in which truth and semblance meet. Thus, Heidegger comments, philosophy was, from the beginning, defined not only by its quest for truth, to show beings as they are in their being, but by 'the battle against idle talk', to which the struggle against sophistry by Socrates, Plato, and Aristotle bears witness.[69]

   The possibility that language might serve to cover up the way things are rather than being genuinely disclosive is, then, not just a matter of malpractice by sophists and others. Language itself contributes to displacing truth from the original encounter with 'the things themselves' and relocating it to a concern for the timeless and abstract 'being' of mere 'object' or entities. This development is tracked in the 1925/6 lectures on logic.[70] After dismissing popular ideas of logic as teaching techniques of thinking, as derivable from psychology,[71] or as a system of 'eternal laws' of thought,[72] and after an extensive discussion of Husserl's critique of psychologism, Heidegger arrives at two questions: why truth should be understood in terms of intuition as the 'immediate having of the bodily-present-to-hand'[73] and why what abides, the same ('what' is known in knowing), should be construed as timeless. These questions once more lead him back to the Greeks and to a consideration of truth and *logos* as found in Aristotle. And, again, this leads him also to ponder how it is that a *logos* can be *false*. Again, he connects this with the 'as'-character of any *logos*-utterance, which, as he puts it, 'moves a priori in the realm of the "as"'.[74] This is what distinguishes a speech-act of this kind from merely pointing. But from whence does this possibility of taking something 'as' something derive?

---

[69] M. Heidegger, *Plato's Sophist*, trans. R. Rojcewicz and A. Schuwer (Bloomington, Ind.: Indiana University Press, 1997), 11 (*Gesamtausgabe*, vol. xix).

[70] M. Heidegger, *Logik: Die Frage nach der Wahrheit* (*Gesamtausgabe*, vol. xxi) (Frankfurt am Main: Klostermann, 1995). On the title, see T. Kisiel, *The Genesis of Heidegger's Being and Time* (Berkeley and Los Angeles: University of California Press, 1995), 559 n. 23.

[71] As by J. S. Mill who relates, e.g., the law of non-contradiction to various preceding psychological experiences: *Logik*, 39.

[72] As in Lipps's remark that 'logic is the physics of thinking': Ibid. 41.

[73] Ibid. 103.

[74] Ibid. 135. This clearly bears comparison with Wittgenstein's interest in 'seeing-as'. Cf. L. Wittgenstein, *Philosophical Investigations*, trans. G. E. M. Anscombe (Oxford: Basil Blackwell, 1972), section II. xi, 193 ff.

Here, as throughout these lectures, Heidegger is especially emphatic that, in a certain sense, meaning precedes language and that the possibility of language disclosing the world rests on the world itself being disclosed in a yet more basic way, namely, in a fundamental and mutual openness of Dasein and world. These are lectures, and we should therefore not be surprised when Heidegger's example is taken from the lecture-hall itself. If, Heidegger says, the lecturer complains that 'the chalk is too hard' as he tries to write on the blackboard, this is not, in the first instance, an objective comment about the chalk but about how it's being used, its usefulness vis-à-vis what he's trying to do with it when he picks it up 'as' something to write with. This (doubtless trivial) example illustrates how the 'as' structure of language is already implicit in the way we are in our world—even though this is something that, in the first instance, we simply *live* rather than reflect on. It also illustrates how we are always 'ahead of ourselves', since our practical involvement in the world runs on ahead of our thoughts. I have to pick up the chalk and start scribbling before I am able to find out whether it is too hard or too crumbly for what I want to do with it. Having then to consider whether it is in fact fit for purpose involves me in a kind of reflex, coming back to what I was doing or wanting to do with it in the first place. And this, Heidegger suggests, means that the 'as'-structure of our involvement with the world is temporal from the ground up. However, in the way in which the *logos* represents this 'as' structure in a verbally articulated pronouncement characteristically presents it as a state of affairs, as a statement about a certain 'what' ('This chalk is too hard'), obscuring its originally practical context. *Logos* thus leads us away from the actuality of our present experience, toward a theoretical and timeless view of things.

Language gives us the very possibility of truth, since it is in language that the world is disclosed in such a way as to allow it to be a common and continuous world, in which we live together by talking about it together over time. Yet language abstracts its objects from a lived context that is practical and temporal. Philosophy, the search for the truth in language, is always a struggle—not only against those like the sophists who seek deliberately to deceive, but also against the tendency of language itself to cover up what it potentially uncovers. In this struggle, philosophy must therefore seek to tear the thinker away from the contemplation of his object as a certain timeless, selfsame 'what' and towards the thing itself as present. *Ousia*, he says, is not substance but presence—not the timeless presence, the *nunc stans*, of medieval philosophy, but the presence that I am able to live, thinkingly, in language, now. But this also suggests that language must be guided by something that calls from beyond language. In the case of Dasein itself—we ourselves—this call from beyond language will be identified in *Being and Time* with what

Heidegger speaks of as the 'call of conscience', a peculiar call that 'dispenses with any kind of utterance' and that 'does not put itself into words at all' but discourses solely and constantly in the mode of keeping silent.[75] The meaning of language is not to be found in language but in attention to the presence of Being and that, in the first instance, means attending to the singular kind of being—Being-towards-death—that I myself am. The silence in which conscience calls and in which our true Being is disclosed is, we may say, the silence of the grave. In such a silence the Hegelian attempt to hold language, Being-in-itself, and Being-for-itself within a single theoretical horizon comes apart. If language can, in the end, only point to a site of encounter with Being that is external to language itself, we will always find ourselves already distanced from Being in every word we ever say. Just by virtue of being the beings that have their Being in language, we are, it seems, always already 'beyond Being'.

LANGUAGE AND THE CONCEALING OF BEING

The paradox that language not only reveals but also conceals what is said in it continues to accompany Heidegger's reflections on language throughout his future development and I want now, briefly, to indicate two of the foci of this paradox in his later thinking. Here, much seems to have changed from the world of *Being and Time*. But much has also remained constant. Philosophers continue to struggle against the covering-over of the lived presence of Being by the scientific, humanistic, and theological world-views of the age and they continue to do so in an intense dialogue with the originators of philosophy in ancient Greece. But there are also new elements. The first of these is the emergence of the poet as a key figure in the relations of truth and Being, and the second is the emergence (or, better, the clarification—I take it to be already implicit in some of the lectures of the 1920s we have been considering) of the distinctive idea of 'the event' of the word. We have already seen in the previous chapter how Heidegger charges the poet with a special role in the grounding of historical experience. Called by the gods, the poet speaks the festal word that ordains the measure of time, and what needs special emphasis here is that it is precisely the poet, the one gifted in a special way with the power of the word, who is charged with this task: the calling of the poet, the ordering of the seasons, and the grounding of history occur as an event of language. But what is the nature of such an event?

---

[75] *Being and Time*, 318/274.

The expression 'event of language' points to one of the key terms of Heidegger's later thinking: *Ereignis*. Like so many key Heideggerian terms, it is virtually untranslatable. But this is not because it is an obscure technical term. On the contrary, it is a somewhat everyday word that we could, in some contexts, straightforwardly translate as 'event' or 'happening'. However, it also incorporates the term 'eigen', one's own, associating it with the key concept of *Eigentlichkeit* or authenticity in *Being and Time*. It is this association that presumably led the translators of Heidegger's *Contributions to Philosophy*, sub-titled *Vom Ereignis*, to translate *Ereignis* as 'Enowning', i.e., the process of making an experienced meaning one's own. The moment of 'owning' indicates that the occurrence of meaning in language cannot be simply an event or happening in which we, the speakers and hearers, are not involved. Rather, it is an event that is what and as it is precisely because in it we make the meaning that is proffered by the word our own.[76]

I shall now explore further how Heidegger understands this 'event of understanding' with reference to his lecture *Identity and Difference*, in which he sets out to consider the contemporary significance of the principle of identity, conventionally summarized in the formula A=A. As he interprets this, it does not mean that A is equal or equivalent to A, but that A *is* A. This doesn't seem to get us very far, until Heidegger turns to a Parmenidean fragment, translated by Kirk and Raven as 'for the same thing can be thought as can be'.[77] Glossing this saying, Heidegger interprets it as a statement of the belonging together of man (the one who thinks) and Being. He argues that for most of the Western philosophical tradition this has been understood to mean the 'togetherness' of thinking and being or that the truth of thinking is determined by its sameness or identity with what is. To speak truthfully is to state what is the case. Language is merely the instrument by which the selfsameness of the object being thought is enabled to appear in thought, as itself. This assumption, Heidegger claims, is one of the basic principles of Western European thinking and of Western science and technology. For even though science and technology do not waste time on such an abstract idea as the principle of identity, they nevertheless assume it—otherwise, Heidegger says, 'science could not be sure in advance of the identity of its object, it could not be what it is'.[78]

---

[76] See M. Heidegger, *Contributions to Philosophy (From Enowning)*, trans. P. Emad and K. Maly (Bloomington, Ind.: Indiana University Press, 2000). However, whilst I understand the reasons behind the translation, I don't think it helps the cause of understanding Heidegger to introduce ungainly neologisms for which there is no basis in the original text. If necessary, periphrasis is, in my judgement, to be preferred.

[77] M. Heidegger, *Identity and Difference*, trans. Joan Stambaugh (New York: Harper and Row, 1969), 269.

[78] Ibid. 26.

Heidegger does not directly attempt to refute this principle. Instead, he sketches an alternative approach, which, he hints, is attentive to dimensions of the Parmenidean saying that have passed unnoticed in the course of Western philosophical history. Instead of focusing on the 'togetherness' of thought and being, he suggests, we should think instead of 'the belonging together of man and Being'. Seen from the kind of representational thinking that is characteristic of philosophy, science, and technology this seems a rather imprecise and poetic formulation, and, from that standpoint, to make this move would seem like an unwarranted leap. Yet, if we are prepared to make that leap, then we discover that thought never is without Being, being never is without thought. Heidegger speaks here of a 'realm, vibrating within itself'.[79] Why 'vibrating'? Because there is no final fact, thing, or reality to which meaning could be reduced (along the lines of A (statement)=A (referent)) and, equally, no final logical requirement to which Being would have to answer to count as true. This, once more, brings us back to language. 'To think of appropriating as the event of appropriation (*Ereignis*) means to contribute to this self-vibrating realm. Thinking receives the tools for this self-suspended structure from language. For language is the most delicate and thus the most susceptible vibration holding everything within the suspended structure of the appropriation. We dwell in the appropriation inasmuch as our active nature [*Wesen*] is given over to language.'[80]

Language reveals Being as being open to language. Being 'is' as a linguistic 'happening' and only as such is it thinkable. This does not mean that we have no access to being apart from language and that, therefore, Being 'is' *only* what it is in and as language. Rather, Being 'is' *also* as it is in language—and language 'is' (i.e., functions as meaningful discourse) *also* as a revelation of what is given us in and by Being.

We have heard how already in the early lectures on Aristotle Heidegger briefly considered the primacy of hearing in relation to speaking and here too he emphasizes the acoustic metaphor implicit in the 'belonging' of humankind and Being, since the German term for belonging, *Ge-hören*, incorporates the everyday word for 'to hear', *hören*. Meaning is not constructed in language, but issues from the manner in which we listen or attend to Being. Language itself is the form that such listening and attention take in human existence. Moreover, even though all language is likely to contain some trace, however distorted or diminished, of its original belonging-together with Being, some forms of language express this in greater measure than others

---

[79] M. Heidegger, *Identity and Difference*, trans. Joan Stambaugh (New York: Harper and Row, 1969), 37.

[80] Ibid. 37–8.

and the poetic word especially resonates with the vibrancy of this belonging-together.

Yet, at the same time, even when it is said by the poet, what is said never simply *is* what it says. At the same time as the word reveals Being it also effects a certain withdrawal of Being. Every act in which Being is revealed is at the same time a concealing of Being such that truth occurs only in the context of this interplay of revealing/concealing, disclosure/covering-over. Many of Heidegger's statements about this are exceptionally oracular, yet the point is not perhaps quite as Delphic as he makes it sound. For when the word reveals or brings a given phenomenon into the open light of truth, it simultaneously allows or even causes whatever is not said to remain in or even to fall away into the background. If I focus my attention on what is to my right, I do not see what is on my left—and whether I focus to right or left, every act of focusing narrows or circumscribes my possible relation to the whole of my potential vision or experience. To become expert in a given field of study, I must surrender my cultivation of other competencies. Something like this seems to be what Heidegger means when, for example, he writes that 'The concealing of concealed beings as a whole holds sway in that disclosure of specific beings, which, as forgottenness or concealment, becomes errancy.'[81] In this sense, our pursuit of truth is itself a kind of errancy: 'errancy and the concealing of what is concealed belong to the originary essence of truth.'[82] Thus, even the poetic word, the supreme instance of the word's power to illuminate existence, will, in the end, speak in enigmas and hints rather than saying just what it means. The poet himself is no serene Olympian figure, but one who has been seared, broken even (as Hölderlin was broken) by the divine lightning-flash he is called to articulate in human words. Perhaps, then, the ultimate communion with what is communicated in the event of language is not itself 'in' the word but in silence, a possibility Heidegger several times recurs to. Perhaps language is ultimately not itself verbal but what, in commenting on a poem of Georg Trakl, he calls the 'peal of silence.'[83] Perhaps silence itself is the true voice of Being? Or perhaps, as in the experimental printing of Being 'under erasure' (B̶e̶i̶n̶g̶), we can only say Being by not saying it. Silence again: but divine—or simply inhuman?

In drawing to an end this brief abstract of Heidegger's lifelong attempt to hear what language is saying, I shall now offer an even briefer theological

---

[81] M. Heidegger, 'On the Essence of Truth', trans. John Sallis, in W. McNeill (ed.), *Pathmarks* (*Gesamtausgabe*, vol. ix) (Cambridge: Cambridge University Press, 1998), 150.

[82] *Pathmarks*, 151.

[83] See Derrida's comment on this expression in J. Derrida, *De la grammatologie* (Paris: Éditions de Minuit, 1967), 36.

reflection on what we have been reading before turning to one of Heidegger's most important contemporary inheritors, Jacques Derrida.

When Heidegger tells us that the world is fundamentally open to language and gives itself to be spoken, even if, in the same instant, Being also withdraws from its utterance in language, the Christian theological commentator might be tempted to see a possibility for resolving Heidegger's paradoxes theologically. For, such a commentator might say, if the world is open to being revealed in its truth in and as the event of language, might this not be because the world itself was created in and by *the* Word; the world is itself the utterance of God, what God's creative word 'lets be'?[84] But might this not, in turn, mean that although the world withdraws from being made totally transparent in language truth can be retrieved at the theological level, since what is left obscure in human language is or will be made clear in the light of divine discourse, divine revelation? The divine Word thus becomes both the basis of human language and also the means that liberates human language from its inability to say all that it strives to say. Edwin Muir again: 'The heart could never speak, But that the Word was spoken.'[85]

Yet such divine speaking would seem not to escape the basic tension of the creator/creature relationship and the mutual implication of analogy and apophasis considered in Chapter 1. Whatever is said by the divine Word can only attain expression in human words under the conditions of equivocation and unsaying. For if we are not using 'Word' here as a vivid metaphor for some kind of divine self-impartation that is essentially wordless, such as an intuitive vision of divine light, then that divine Word will need to be translated into and submit to the conditions of human language and to become audible in and as a fully human word. In doing so it may seem to lose much or all of what might be regarded as proper to a truly divine Word, a Word of which it could be said that it dwelt in the beginning with God. Nevertheless, not only Christian but also Jewish theologies witness to such a translation of the divine into the human word as a basic possibility of the divine–human relationship. Creation itself is described as having been effected by the Word, God speaks with Adam and Abraham and calls Moses and the prophets to become bearers of 'the Word of the Lord' in such a way that divine Words are portrayed as becoming human words and human words become capable of transmitting divine Words. In the New Testament this idea

---

[84] One might at this point also mention the Jewish mystical view that the divine language—the Hebrew alphabet—is itself the structuring principle of all that comes into existence. See G. Scholem, *Major Trends in Jewish Mysticism* (Jerusalem: Schocken, 1941).

[85] *Collected Poems*, 292.

is reiterated and even intensified: 'In the beginning was the Word' (John 1: 1), writes John, and it is precisely this 'Word', 'that was in the beginning with God, that was God', that is said to have taken flesh in the human life of Jesus of Nazareth. From start to finish, the biblical story is told as the story of the divine Word's journey into human language, as the only way in which it could ever be heard by and make a difference to us. This is the situation that makes it possible for Karl Barth to speak in one breath of the speech of God both as the mystery of God and yet as inherently secular. Once transposed into human language, the divine Word must share in and suffer the laws, constraints, and distortions of grammar, history, context, and, to recur to Heidegger, the 'withdrawal' of what is meant from what is said. As Barth puts it, 'The veil is thick. We do not have the Word of God otherwise than in the mystery of its secularity. This means, however, that we have it in a form which as such is not the Word of God and which as such does not even give evidence that it is the form of the Word of God.'[86] If, when God speaks with himself, his Word is entirely perspicuous to what is said in it, we cannot hear a divine Word other than as marked by the tensions, uncertainties, distances, and undecidable paradoxes that characterize human speech. It is therefore entirely appropriate that Muir's 'The heart could never speak . . .' concludes with the prayer: 'Time, merciful lord, | Grant us to hear your word.' It implies no deficiency in the one who is tasked with speaking the divine Word if that Word can only become meaningful in relation to the specific ontological, historical, and cultural situation of its hearer. What language in general can mean for the hearer of the Word is, then, going to be integral to any theological attempt to say how divine discourse can be humanly meaningful.[87]

---

[86] K. Barth, *Church Dogmatics*, i. 1, 165.

[87] In Barth's debate with Emile Brunner, he condemns any interest at all in the hearer of the Word as a kind of lèse-majesté in relation to the divine Word. This is connected with his Calvinist understanding of the utter ruination of human nature in the Fall. See K. Barth, 'No!', in E. Brunner and K. Barth, *Natural Theology*, trans. P. Fraenkel (London: Geoffrey Bles, 1946), 78–94. It is striking that Karl Rahner, writing from a Catholic perspective, has no hesitation or embarrassment in making 'The Hearer of the Message' a major topic of his theological work. In the first part of his exposition of *The Foundations of Christian Faith*, for example, he poses the question 'What kind of hearer does Christianity anticipate so that its real and ultimate message can be heard?' and comments that 'This is the first question we have to ask.' K. Rahner, *Foundations of Christian Faith*, trans. W. V. Dych (London: Darton, Longman and Todd, 1978), 24. Despite these differences, both Barth and Rahner suppose an emphasis on the 'event' character of the divine Word that strongly resembles that of Heidegger. In the case of Rahner this reflects a fairly straightforward pupillage at the feet of the master. In the case of Barth, it may be more appropriate to look to a subterranean dialogue with Buber—which may also be in the background of Heidegger's own thinking; see Hans Vium Mikkelsen, *Reconciled Humanity: Karl Barth in Dialogue* (Grand Rapids, Mich.: Eerdmans, 2010), 96–120.

DERRIDA

Derrida's critical relation to both Hegel and Heidegger is flagged on the very opening page of *On Grammatology*. In drawing attention to what he calls the ethnocentrism of the Western view of language and the unexamined privileging of speech over writing that this involves, Derrida remarks that assigning the origin of language to the logos and explaining 'truth in general' in terms of logos is a major contributing factor to this occlusion. That this has been the prevailing assumption of Western metaphysics—and, he adds, science, technology, and economics—determines the basic view of truth in the West, including the notion of truth as the correspondence between thought and Being. From Aristotle onwards this has also led to a downgrading of writing, since, it has been thought, written words are symbols of the sounds emitted by the voice, which are in turn symbols of the 'affections of the soul', the impressions made on the psyche in its interaction with the world about it. Writing is thus conceived as being at two removes from reality and when phonetic writing—the writing characteristic of the West—is seen as the best model for imitating speech in writing, then this merely underwrites the Aristotelian assumption. The spoken word thus occupies a kind of mid-point in a chain of transparencies that allows the mind to scrutinize the knowledge-yielding essences of things. Pointing in one direction to the thought or idea as the meaning of what is said and, in the other, to the thing or object 'out there' in the world, the spoken word has therefore been taken as the paradigmatic instance of signification. In the medieval development this further involves the idea that things themselves, the objects that make up the world and the world as a whole, have been created in accordance with the divine idea—and this divine idea itself is the 'what' that is understood in the communication of the divine Word.[88] Even in post-medieval and post-Enlightenment thought (and even where God is not specifically invoked) the basic model of signification that still prevails rests on the assumption that reality has a fundamental intelligibility that precedes and makes possible any given system of human signs. As Derrida writes, 'the sign and divinity are born at the same time and place, the epoch of the sign is essentially theological'.[89] This 'epoch of the sign' is what Derrida also calls the epoch of 'the book'. This may seem somewhat paradoxical, since the book is, rather obviously, a written artefact, but Derrida takes 'the book' as epitomizing a view of signification that sees the sign as referring beyond

---

[88] *Grammatologie*, 22–3.   [89] Ibid. 25.

itself or, more precisely, not only beyond itself as this particular sign, but to something that transcends the order of signs, to what the sign *means*. On this basis, a whole way of representing the world is developed, typically manifested in such apparently natural polarities as that between interior and exterior, ideal and non-ideal, universal and non-universal, transcendental and empirical.

In fact, Derrida claims, not only does the epoch of the sign and the book outlive its medieval Christian formulation, but it also received a renewed impetus in the seventeenth and eighteenth centuries. The idea of the world as a book, 'the book of nature', is already known in the Middle Ages,[90] but Derrida is able to cite a whole sequence of authors, from Rabbi Eliezer through Galileo, Descartes, Hume, and Rousseau to Karl Jaspers, who deploy this metaphor.[91] Whether it is 'nature' or the human 'heart' that is deemed to be the *Ur*-book, it suggests the superiority of the natural or 'good' writing written by God with the artificial writing derived from human convention that finds expression in writing in the everyday sense of the word. But, once again, the speaking voice occupies a kind of middle point in the system, since it has a natural and spontaneous quality, an assumption that also reflects a range of connotations that link the divine breath or spirit breathed into the first human being as the source and power of life with the breath that is the medium of articulated speech. It is specifically the conjunction of these ideas in Rousseau's essay on the origin of languages that makes that work a major

---

[90] Derrida refers to the discussion of this in E. R. Curtius, *La Littérature européenne et le Moyen Âge latin.* See *Grammatologie*, 27.

[91] He could, of course, have cited many others. It is, for example, central to Ruskin's theory of art, and has found extensive expression in popular piety, as, e.g., in the hymn 'There is a book, who runs may read | Which heavenly truth imparts, | And all the lore its scholars need, | Pure eyes and Christian hearts. | The works of God, above, below, | Within us and around, | Are pages in that book to show | How God himself is found.' In this connection, Derrida notes the fascination of the early modern period with Chinese calligraphy and such systems of writing as that devised by John Wilkins in his *Essay towards a Real Character and a Philosophical Language.* Although such systems of writing seem to break the bond linking voice and meaning, they also reveal the assumption that language is intelligible on the basis of its signifying an extra-linguistic (transcendental) order of signification. See *Grammatology*, ch. 3. A further examination of Wilkins's argument nicely illustrates Derrida's interpretation. Wilkins accepts that '*Writing* is but the figure of *Speech*', but whilst he then says that this is only true as regards the 'order of time' and that 'in the order of Nature there is no priority between these' and that '*voice* and sounds may be as well assigned to Figure as *Figures* may be to sounds' (p. 385), his whole project of a universal system of signs supposes the possibility of a 'full and adequate' '*Enumeration* and description of such things or notions as are to have *Marks* or *Names* assigned to them' and of taxonomy of signs 'exactly *suted* [*sic*] *to the nature of things*' (p. 21) that encompasses both the most general concepts of metaphysics and the minutiae of the natural order. (References to John Wilkins, *An Essay towards a Real Character and a Philosophical Language* (London: The Royal Society, 1668).)

focus of the second part of *On Grammatology*. Writing, seen from this perspective, is merely 'a technique in the service of language'.[92] Although the world of modern linguistics may seem to have moved on a long way from Rousseau's essay, Derrida finds evidence that Saussure too subscribes to the view that the proper object of a science of language is the 'natural' form of language found in speech, as do other defining figures of linguistics.[93] The same assumption can be seen in the kind of ethnographical research into language found in Lévi-Strauss.[94]

A fundamental trait of the era of the sign is the privileging of the presence of what is signified in the act of signification itself—a view that we have seen amply illustrated by both Hegel and Heidegger. Yet the very idea that we can speak of Being being present in the event of understanding is itself, Derrida believes, a manifestation of the assumptions of logocentrism. Heidegger is right to see that the questions of logos, metaphysics, and Being are all fundamentally interrelated, but he is not able entirely to let go of a belief in the transcendence of Being over representation as grounding the possibility of meaningful discourse. As we have seen, Heidegger does insist that even the most revelatory poetic word and even the most penetrating philosophical word cannot entirely transmute the world into infinitely illuminated intelligibility. Being always withdraws, even as it is spoken, and our best response to it may, in the end, be silence. Derrida notes Heidegger's reference to the 'peal of silence' as 'the voice of Being'. But this 'rupture' in the order of logos—this acknowledgement of the failure of logos ever finally to deliver on what it so tantalizingly seems to promise—'at one and the same time confirms a basic metaphor [i.e., the metaphor of the word being grounded in an act of signification that transcends the word itself] and exposes it to suspicion', a situation, he says, 'that well translates the ambiguity of Heidegger's situation in relation to the metaphysics of presence and logocentrism'.[95] When, in his later writings, Heidegger sometimes takes to writing Being 'under erasure', this, Derrida comments, 'is the final writing of an epoch'.[96]

Perhaps the gesture of erasure indicates a move away from the sign being understood as pointing to the presence of Being towards what Derrida (following Lévinas) calls the 'trace'. The trace is not a natural sign but a cultural product. It is a sign of the absence of its other. Of course, it is not news that a word isn't what it means. A poet such as Eliot was only too keenly

---

[92] *Grammatologie*, 17.
[93] See ibid., ch. 2, 'Linguistics and Grammatology'.
[94] See ibid., part 2, ch. 1, 'The Violence of the Letter'.
[95] Ibid. 36.
[96] Ibid. 38.

aware of the absence of what he was trying to express, rendering it as 'inexpressible': yet, somehow, that 'inexpressible' was there to be sought, wrestled with, and, in peak moments of poetic achievement, expressed. But the trace has no 'other' that (or who) could become present. That to which it points is necessarily, utterly, and irretrievably absent—so absent as not even to be in question. In the trace, the wholly other announces itself as wholly other.[97] The trace is the mark of that most Derridean of terms, *différance*: not the difference between sign and thing signified familiar from the standard view of verbal signification, but the endless play of positing difference, with no final 'thing signified' to bring the game to an end.[98] Against Heidegger's view that Nietzsche remained trapped within the assumptions of the metaphysics he sought to overturn, Derrida believed that Nietzsche very precisely anticipates such a play of *différance* by exemplifying a kind of philosophical writing that didn't presuppose any kind of anterior truth it was obligated to transcribe.

It is therefore in the endlessness of the world being opened up by the practice of writing as *différance* that Derrida believes we can see the era of the sign and of the book as declining towards its end. This 'eschatological' movement is anticipated both in Hegel's view of the end of history and Heidegger's grand narrative of the history of metaphysics as an unitary revelation of truth spanning the time from the Pre-Socratics to the advent of a globalized system of technological thinking and communication—and, as we have just seen, terminating in Heidegger's own writing of Being 'under erasure'. But Derrida also cites a number of other factors bringing about this end: the development or expansion of non-vocal communications including cinematography, choreography, pictorial, musical and sculptural forms of 'writing', and athletics. Nor is it accidental that both biology and cybernetics represent human existence as pro-grammed—and Derrida is quick to point out that this word itself incorporates the Greek *grammē*, the written mark. Moreover, as he goes on to point out, the kind of mathematical sign-writing that lies at the basis of contemporary science is precisely a form of writing that eludes the possibilities of phonetic transcription. However, the view that the era of the book is coming to an end does not mean that it is simply going to stop. Here, Derrida distinguishes between 'closure' and 'end'. The era of the book is closed, in the sense that we are now able to see it for what it is and to anticipate all the possibilities of which it is capable. However, this does not mean that the basic way of understanding ourselves and our world to which it has given rise will not carry on being powerfully formative

---

[97] Ibid. 69. Some of the further implications of this will be discussed in the next chapter.
[98] Derrida sees a certain analogy to this in the semiotics of C. S. Peirce.

for an indefinite time to come. Indeed, perhaps we may never be able entirely to shed it (just as we still speak of the sun rising, although we know it doesn't).

Derrida is by no means seeking to 'ban' a certain kind of (metaphysical) thinking and writing or to assert that 'we postmoderns' no longer do that kind of thing. Given the permeation of our habits of mind by the assumptions of metaphysics—and perhaps even by the basic structures of our own language and our continuing to write in a phonetic alphabet—we are not simply in the process of exiting the era of the book. We cannot get outside the system, but whilst we still remain within it, we do (he thinks) have possibilities of showing (by 'a discourse prudent and attentive to minute detail') how it is the system that produces such-and-such an effect and so reveal 'the glimmer of what is beyond closure'.[99] This means that the deconstruction of a metaphysical view of language would not so much involve simply denying the possibility of Being's presence being effected in language, but rather showing that even the promise of such presence was itself a reflection of our language: that Being is not 'out there' waiting to be found (or speaking to us from 'out there') but is itself a reflection or epiphenomenon of our language itself. And yet, even at this point, there is not simply nothing, not simply the play of language with itself, but something that has a certain analogy to signification—the announcement of the wholly other of language in the trace. To say this has a certain analogy to signification is not to say that 'the wholly other' is the 'meaning' of the trace, but it indicates that Derrida is not conceiving of language as a closed and self-referential system. However, between language—the trace—and what lies outside it, there are no threads to guide us from the one to the other. The wholly other is not the supreme Being that grounds all possibilities of meaning and to which all speaking and writing seek to re-ascend. It is neither before nor after and, strictly speaking, neither outside nor inside.

Let us recall the hope of modern Thomist philosophy that knowledge of essences reveals the truth of the substances of which they are the essences, and that, similarly, knowledge of divine essence yields a knowledge of God or, at least, 'points' (in a way that is never finally specified) to the divine Being. Derrida's venture of deconstruction seems to have rendered such 'pointing' and the whole relationship between essence and Being unreadable. But must this be understood as a simple nihilism?

From early on, Derrida was not only accused of nihilism but also of a kind of covert negative theology—and sometimes the two accusations were

---

[99] Derrida sees a certain analogy to this in the semiotics of C. S. Peirce. 25.

combined.[100] But whether or not one regards negative theology as a kind of intellectual crime, anyone familiar with the key texts of negative theology can scarcely avoid recognizing their apparent echo in some of Derrida's formulations. In his lecture 'How to Avoid Speaking: Denials', Derrida brushes off his accusers ('No, what I write is not "negative theology"'[101]), although he also immediately acknowledges that he has long been fascinated by negative theology and has had 'a long-standing wish: to broach—directly and in itself—the web of questions that one formulates prematurely under the heading of "negative theology"'.[102] This way of putting it already alerts us to the fact that, despite his disavowal of having written negative theology, the question 'Are you or aren't you a negative theologian?' is wrongly formulated. Rather than a nice simple category into which we can slot one or other thinker, negative theology is a premature formulation for a whole web of questions. If the title of the lecture hasn't already done so, this further specification of his 'wish' serves notice that there is going to be nothing direct or simple about what he is going to say.

One thing, however, is fairly clear: that what is mostly called negative theology is somewhat deceptive. It denies Being to God only in order to apply it in a more eminent sense: God may be beyond what we call Being, but that is because God and God alone truly 'is' and God alone is the true measure of real Being. As Derrida puts it, '"negative theology" seems to reserve, beyond all positive predication, beyond all negation, even beyond Being, some hyperessentiality, a being beyond Being'.[103] Furthermore, and not least in its appearance in such mystical texts as those of Pseudo-Dionysius and Meister Eckhart, the apophatic 'voyage' is typically accompanied by 'the promise' that the adept will be led through and beyond denial to an intuition or vision of the presence of that supreme, hyperessential Being beyond being.[104] As Derrida writes, quoting Dionysius, 'This mystic union, this act of unknowing, is also a "genuine vision and a genuine knowledge [*to ontôs idein kai gnôsai*]". It knows unknowing itself in its truth...'[105] Later, in a comment on Plato's statement that the Good is beyond Being, Derrida says

---

[100] See J. Derrida, 'How to Avoid Speaking: Denials', trans. K. Frieden, in H. Coward and T. Foshay (eds.), *Derrida and Negative Theology* (Albany, NY: State University of New York Press, 1992), 73–7. Curiously—or not—the lecture, which appeared in French, was originally spoken in English, a point which the English translation of the French text occludes. For the French version see J. Derrida, 'Comment ne pas parler: Dénegations', in idem, *Psyché: L'Invention de l'autre*, ii (Paris: Galilée, 1987/2003). The 'accusation' is mostly from those hostile to any theology, it seems: however, some years later theologians would *welcome* Derrida for just this same proximity to negative theology.

[101] 'How to Avoid Speaking', 77.   [102] Ibid.   [103] Ibid.77.   [104] Ibid. 79.

[105] Ibid. 80. Derrida notes a similar ambiguity in Wittgenstein's injunction that one must remain silent about that of which one cannot speak.

that the very logic of 'hyper' ('above') requires some kind of relationship between the two terms (in this case, between essential being and what is above essential being) and this is precisely what Thomas's notion of analogy insists on: 'what exceeds the border may be compared to Being; albeit through the figure of hyperbole.'[106]

Further features of negative theology that especially interest Derrida (without his taking a final position with regard to any of them) are that the negative theologian typically summons his reader to 'come apart', to find the 'place' or 'sanctuary' where, away from the world, genuine mystical knowledge is to be found. He connects this with Plato's treatment of *khôra*, the 'receptacle' that makes possible the creation of cosmos yet which is neither before nor subsequent to it.[107] Then, there is the theme of a 'secret' in which the would-be mystic is to be instructed and, in connection with this, a pervasive rhetoric of initiation, instruction, and hierarchy. Finally, there is prayer, which, as Derrida says, 'is not a preamble, an accessory mode of access. It constitutes an essential moment, it adjusts discursive asceticism, the passage through the desert of discourse, the apparent referential vacuity which will only avoid empty deliria and prattling, by addressing itself from the start to the other, to you.'[108]

That Derrida is far from simply denying all these features of negative theology is then made as explicit as anything ever is in this highly allusive lecture, so full of indirections and hesitations. 'In every prayer', he continues, 'there must be an address to the other as other; for example—I will say, at the risk of shocking—God. The act of addressing oneself to the other as other must, of course, mean praying, that is, pure prayer demands only that the other hear it, receive it, be present to it, be the other as such, a gift, call, and even cause of prayer.'[109] In other words, every address to 'the other as such' or every occasion when this same 'other as such' gives to the one who asks the gift of being willing to hear and attend to what they are asking, causes prayer to happen. Pure prayer demands nothing more 'than the supplicating address to the other, perhaps beyond all supplication and giving, to give the promise of His presence as other, and finally the transcendence of His otherness itself, even without any other determination.'[110]

---

[106] Ibid. 80. Derrida notes a similar ambiguity in Wittgenstein's injunction that one must remain silent about that of which one cannot speak. 102.

[107] This will be discussed more extensively in the section 'On the field of Nihility (Khôra?)' in Ch. 7 below.

[108] Ibid. 110.

[109] Ibid.

[110] Ibid. 111. I am unsure how well justified the translators' use of a capital 'H' in 'His' is here: does what Derrida is saying require that we immediately start speaking about 'God'?

Such 'pure' prayer is contrasted with what he here calls the encomium or hymn. For whilst neither the prayer nor the hymn are 'predicative, theoretical (theological) . . . constative' or 'attributive',[111] the hymn nevertheless names its object in such a way as to preserve 'an irreducible relationship to the attribution'.[112] Thus Dionysius names the God to whom he prays by hymning the Holy Trinity, thereby distinguishing his Christian God from, say, the Jewish or Islamic God. Such naming may not be propositional in form, yet it specifies true prayer as exclusively Christian. Although 'its attributions or naming do not belong to the ordinary signification of truth' they do belong to a 'hypertruth that is ruled by a hypersessentiality'.[113] Unlike prayer it speaks 'of' rather than 'to' God, even when it is also speaking to him.[114]

Derrida would return to the subject of negative theology in later work, as in the discussion of Angelus Silesius in *Sauf le nom*. As in the case of Dionysius he finds a certain ambiguity in the 'Cherubic Wanderer'. On the one hand, Angelus Silesius' hyperbolic paradoxes offer a radical contestation and critique of the tradition from which he comes, yet he does, nevertheless, insist on a certain naming of God that, after all, reinscribes him in a rather traditional theology in which God is essential as opposed to what is accidental and necessary as opposed to what is contingent. Nevertheless, there is a certain 'Gelassenheit'[115] in these poems that Derrida interprets as a readiness to make way for the other and to every other which is also hospitality.[116] This open

---

[111] Ibid. 110–11.

[112] Ibid. 111.

[113] Ibid.

[114] Buber is never mentioned in this text. Yet there seems to be an extensive congruence of thinking. I note, for example, the following lines from the beginning of the Third part of *I and Thou*, where Buber starts to reflect specifically on the religious dimensions of the I–Thou relationship: 'Men have addressed their eternal Thou by many names. When they sang of what they had thus named, they still meant Thou: the first myths were hymns of praise. Then the name entered into the It-language; men felt impelled more and more to think of and to talk about their eternal Thou as an It. But all names of God remain hallowed—because they have been used not only to speak *of* God but also to speak *to* him' (M. Buber, *I and Thou*, trans. W. Kaufmann (Edinburgh: T. & T. Clark, 1970), 123). Although Buber judges the hymn more positively than Derrida, he too sees the hymn as prone to slip into myth and, eventually, 'It-language', precisely because the moment of address *to* God is occluded by what is said *of* God. The whole of this third part would be worth reading alongside Derrida. Buber was, of course, also a seminal influence on Lévinas, who certainly was a constant point of reference in Derrida's thought. Cf. also Rosenzweig's comments on the 'vocativity' of a properly Jewish understanding of biblical language (discussed in Ch. 1 above).

[115] The term, found already in Meister Eckhart, re-entered modern thought through a lecture by Heidegger. It may be variously translated as 'abandonment', 'letting-be'.

[116] J. Derrida, *Sauf le nom* (Paris: Galilée, 1993), 102. The title *Sauf le nom* is only inadequately translated in the English version as *On the Name*. It seems to imply the paradox that whilst the name of God is the one name that cannot be named, nothing at all can be named unless God is.

welcome leads back to the question as to the place where the knowing/
unknowing of God might occur and, once more, to the Platonic *khôra*.[117]

Before leaving Derrida, there is a further point in the lecture 'How to Avoid
Speaking' that is worth drawing attention to. Here Derrida makes much of the
fact that this is a lecture delivered in Jerusalem, and he alludes several times to
the implicit messianic promise of the saying 'Next year in Jerusalem'. In the
light of this promise, Derrida wonders whether he is really 'in' Jerusalem, even
though he also acknowledges that, clearly, he is 'in Jerusalem' in a normal
everyday sense. But such 'being-in' misses the fullness of what is promised to
those who will be in Jerusalem when the Messianic promise is fulfilled. The
promise to speak of what cannot be spoken of is not simply a matter of
addressing a certain timeless question in epistemology, along the lines of
'How can we come to know what lies outside the scope of knowledge?' It is
also a question that has a certain temporal, historical shape: when will we be
able to speak of God, to speak *to* God, in a manner that is not distorted by the
violence and evil of human history? The question of how to speak of God,
then, is not separable from the question of justice, of a human community
liberated from the compulsions of what Marx liked to call pre-history but
which most of us know as just 'history', history as the war of all against all.
Apophatic theology, in this perspective, is not separable from the prophetic
theology that sees the decisive encounter with God as still to come.[118]

SPEAKING TO CONCEAL THE MIND

In thinking about the relationship between language and Being, we have largely
focused on the dimension of distance that separates words from that to which
they refer. Not least in the light of what we have been reading in Heidegger and
Derrida, it might seem that the popular idea of truth as the correlation of
thought and Being is simply too naive, since the very act of formulating truth in
and as language renders a direct and unproblematic relation to being impossible—to the point that ideas of representation themselves seem no more than
reflexes of grammatological structures and a direct relation to Being itself is
infinitely deferred. Even when, as in the later Heidegger, we find a hope in the

[117] Derrida's text *Khôra* was part of a trilogy that also included *Sauf le nom*. It will be
discussed further in Ch. 7.

[118] This is a prominent theme in John D. Caputo's interpretation of Derrida's 'religion
without religion'. See, e.g. his *The Prayers and Tears of Jacques Derrida: Religion without Religion*
(Bloomington, Ind.: Indiana University Press, 1997), especially ch. III, 'The Messianic'.

possibility of a word that might break free from the deadening weight of the idle talk that stifles the revelation of Being and, in doing so, break open a way into the presence of 'beings in Being', this is nevertheless an exceptional word, a divine gift, a word that could truly be spoken only in an eschatological moment that, as such, is only ever ambiguously related to the words we speak in the continuum of common life. There is, of course, scope to be more or less optimistic or pessimistic about this situation and its implications for the understanding of God as Being, but before reaching any provisional conclusion on that all-encompassing issue there are several further factors to be taken into account. For language is not a kind of film or membrane spread more or less tightly over the thing-like world of entities. Language exists as spoken, written, or recorded by human beings. It is a personal and a social event. Language involves speakers—indeed, it does not simply 'involve' them, it cannot occur without them: it is what they say, what they write, or what they otherwise articulate or record. The possibility that language might yield a direct saying and through that saying a direct seeing of Being, will therefore depend on whether or how the speakers themselves relate to Being: how Being is manifest in their lives—or how it eludes them.

Such an emphasis on the role of the speaker is implicit in the basic argument of *Being and Time*, since it would only be on the basis of an original and resolute act of self-commitment that the spell of idle talk could be broken. Even before *Being and Time*, as we have seen, Heidegger had located the origin of philosophical reflection on language in the day-to-day life of the Greek agora, where men talked with one another about what concerned them in their common life. Later too, he would emphasize that language always occurs as a *saying*, and not simply as a function of an autopoietic system. Nevertheless, and perhaps especially in the later Heidegger, the one who speaks seems somehow to recede. The poet, indeed, is central to the later writings, but he is no ordinary speaker—and even the poet disappears behind or is absorbed into the luminosity of the 'poetic word' itself. He exists only as the speaker of the poetic word. To turn now to consider those who speak language is not necessarily to turn away from Heidegger (nor even, it should be said, from Derrida) in principle, but it is to turn towards what Heidegger neglects and, in neglecting, arguably occludes.

Kierkegaard, for one, never forgot that language is *spoken*, that it exists only as the act of concrete human beings, bound to one another in complex and often conflicted ways.[119] A primary consequence of this is that the meaning of

---

[119] For further discussion see my *The Philosophy of Kierkegaard* (Chesham: Acumen, 2005), 76–82 and 'Representing Love: From Poetry to Martyrdom or Language and Transcendence in Kierkegaard's Works of Love', *Kierkegaardiana*, 22 (2002), 139–54.

what is said is not only—and not even primarily—determined by the formal relations between 'sign' and 'thing signified' but by the intention of the speaker. Kierkegaard thus repeatedly recurs to the possibility that saying one and the same thing or speaking one and the same word can mean very different things when spoken by different people in different contexts. Whatever may be said about its formal structures, language is essentially performative: it only ever communicates actual meaning as the act of a particular speaker in a particular context or relationship. In the opening meditation of *Works of Love* he tells us that

> There is no word in human language, not a single one, not the most sacred word, of which we could say: when a man uses this word, it is unconditionally proved thereby that there is love in him. Rather, it is true that a word from one person can convince us that there is love in him and the opposite word from another can convince that there is love in him also. It is true that one and the same word can convince us that love dwells in the person who uttered it and not in another who nevertheless also uttered the same word.[120]

As the author of *The Seducer's Diary* Kierkegaard well knew that words of love can be used to flatter, deceive, and betray, and as a reader of *King Lear*, he also knew that deep and genuine love is often speechless or inarticulate. As has been mentioned, he several times quoted the line from Edward Young that 'men speak only to conceal the mind' and, in his last years, he made it increasingly clear that virtually everything said from contemporary pulpits—no matter how consistent with traditional doctrine and in that sense 'correct'—was essentially false. Tough love may need to be heard as cruel by those who most need it, and emollient words, such as those Kierkegaard heard from the pulpit, may merely express the abnegation of responsibility.

Supporting this interpretation was a view of language that had much in common with that of Hegel since, like Hegel, Kierkegaard saw language as presupposing a reflective relationship between self and world. Also like Hegel and other German idealists, he laid emphasis on the active element in representation, such that language does not simply mirror the world but imaginatively recreates it. To exist as Spirit is therefore to exist as a being who is the active shaper of his world and who is therefore responsible for that world. It is perhaps in this regard that in his retelling of the biblical story of the Fall Kierkegaard dismisses the serpent as a mythical intrusion and suggests that it was Adam's own capacity for speech that seduced him: 'the speaker is

---

[120] S. Kierkegaard, *Works of Love*, trans. H. V. and E. H. Hong, SKS 9 (Princeton: Princeton University Press, 1995), 13.

language, and thus it is Adam himself who speaks.'[121] Why? Because language, is expressive of a free act of world-creation that transcends the passivity of mere sensation and reveals to Adam possibilities that he would not otherwise have known, including possibilities of obedience and disobedience to the promptings of his natural instincts. Language makes it possible for Adam to do what he could indeed do, but which, as a merely animal entity, he would never have dreamed of.

In *Works of Love* Kierkegaard proposes the view that the twofold character of language has to do with the fact that we learn to speak in infancy, at an age when we are unable to understand the full meaning of our words. At this stage we are largely sensuous-psychic entities, without the conscious self-reflection and responsibility that supervenes on our merely natural life when we become 'Spirit', i.e., self-conscious subjects. However, when the time comes at which Spirit wishes to express itself, it has only the language shaped by and for the needs of sensuous-psychic existence. In other words, we can only articulate and communicate our moral, spiritual, and religious aspirations and commitments by using the primary language of sensuous-psychic life in what Kierkegaard calls a 'transferred' or metaphorical sense. Thus—to take the particular example that occupies him at this point—even such a central religious term as 'edification' or 'upbuilding' has, as he points out, a primary material meaning that is radically transformed when used to describe an inward and spiritual process. The meaning of what we say—when we are talking about human meanings, values, and relationships—cannot be read off directly from what we say, since our words will always have evolved from experiences that are of an essentially bodily nature.[122]

Language thus means what it means because of the 'spiritual' intentions with which it is invested by the speaking subject. This not only presents a challenge to the speaker, who must select and arrange words in such a way as to make them transcend their own immediate meaning, it also presents a still more serious challenge to the successful communication of those meanings and the development of a coherent and continuing discourse in which our

---

[121] S. Kierkegaard, *The Concept of Anxiety*, trans. R. Thomte, SKS 4 (Princeton: Princeton University Press, 1980), 45.

[122] Kierkegaard's understanding of language seems close to that developed by Lakoff and Johnson in their *Metaphors We Live By*, in which they argue that even complex conceptual and religious ideas are metaphorical transformations of bodily experiences. As they say, 'The essence of metaphor is understanding and experiencing one kind of thing in terms of another' (G. Lakoff and M. Johnson, *Metaphors We Live By* (Chicago: Chicago University Press, 1980), 5). However, since they do not accept the hypothesis of a mind capable of existing independently of the body, they regard all mental and moral discourse as reliant upon relations primarily given through the sensorimotor activity of the embodied cognitive system. For further discussion see Ch. 6 below.

subjective interest in what we say is appropriately realized. For Kierkegaard himself, this understanding of language fed into his own strategy of 'indirect communication', since, he concluded, the subject's essential religious interest in existence could never be communicated directly.[123] Doubtless there is much that is idiosyncratic in Kierkegaard's further reflections on such indirect communication, but the central insight reaches beyond his own particular concerns. This is the insight that, to the extent that it involves human intentions, language will be exposed to possibilities of ambiguity, imprecision, and deception (including, of course, self-deception) that constantly imperil the speaking of truth and would do so even were the structures of representation embedded in language otherwise unproblematic.

A very similar approach to language can be found in the writings of Mikhail Bakhtin, probably not uninfluenced by Kierkegaard in this regard. In his early work *The Philosophy of the Act* he described the disjunction between what he calls the cognitive-significative theorization of life found in scientific and scholarly work and 'actual, individual experience'—a common view of the 'crisis of the European sciences' in the second decade of the twentieth century. These two forms of life have become so disjoined that they are in effect 'two worlds' that 'stand over against one another, absolutely lacking mutual communication and permeability'. The one is a world that is merely 'given', that simply 'is' what it is, whilst the other is a world that, through the active intervention of the self, is 'posited' or, as we might gloss it, 'owned'.[124]

Yet—again like many of his contemporaries—Bakhtin is seeking a point of unity, a common level 'where both aspects reciprocally define one another in relation to one unique unity', a 'being-as-a-whole' in which the world of scientific knowledge and cultural expressions would be integrated into the wholeness of the human being. This is often promised but cannot be delivered by science, scholarship, or the objective culture of society since, whilst these may strive towards and even attain a certain unity, this is never the 'individual historical unity of my life'. The 'I' who knows such-and-such a scientific truth is not identical with but is an abstraction from the I who is always 'some real, actual thinking human being'. This dualism is, in one respect, insuperable, yet if the cognitive and technical functions of consciousness are not brought into relation to the living 'I', then these functions become a 'fearful, destructive power'.[125]

---

[123] For further discussion see *The Philosophy of Kierkegaard*, especially 126–32 and 169–71.

[124] M. M. Bakhtin, *K Phiilosophiiii Postupka* (Towards a philosophy of the act), in *Chelovek b Miire Slova* (Man in the world of discourse) (Moscow: The Russian Open University, 1995), 22 ff.

[125] Ibid. 25.

The history of ideas shows that abstract thought has always attempted to become *prima philosophia*, but to the extent that it succeeds, it displays a weakened sense of what it actually is to exist, to be—a point that Bakhtin finds illustrated in Kant's assertion that there is no conceptual difference between the idea of 100 thalers and the 100 thalers in my pocket. In such theoretical enterprises 'we cast ourselves out of life . . . into indifferent being, being that is in principle ready and concluded' where 'I . . . am not needed; in which I am, in principle, absent'.[126] Even the attempt by recent philosophy of history to understand life in its process of becoming remains theoretical, abstracted from 'painful' temporality, and the same can be said of modern psychology. Such theoretical truths are always merely possible, unless or until they are made actual by being responsibly affirmed by a living 'I'. When that happens, we experience what Bakhtin calls a 'truly real participating in the individual being-event'[127] and 'communion with the unique unity of being-as-a-whole'.[128] This in turn brings with it an understanding of responsibility, which, Bakhtin states, is fundamental to the possibility of attaining the being-as-a-whole of the being-event; obligation—answerability[129]—is the obverse and concomitant of participation.

But where and how might this being-event of participation and responsibility be found or occur? Bakhtin's answer is twofold: language and historicity. These, however, are (once again) inseparable from the condition of our being responsible (or answerable) for how we live as language-using and historical beings. The most radical expression of this responsibility is the statement that we have 'no alibi in being', i.e., the recognition that we commit ourselves without reserve to how we are in our relation to others. As he would put it in his study of Dostoevsky, 'A person has no internal sovereign territory, he is wholly and always on the boundary; looking into himself, he looks into the eyes of another or with the eyes of another.'[130] Self-affirmation, 'owning' the world that knowledge and cultural inheritance proffer, is possible only as responsibility toward others—and responsibility toward others is possible only for one who 'owns' his own existence.

The relation to the Other, thus conceived, is quite different from a generalized morality that relates to 'people'. 'There is no man-in-general,

---

[126] Ibid. 26.
[127] Ibid. 22. Bakhtin's distinctive Russian expression бытие-событие, which could literally be translated as Being/Being-together, underlines the emphasis on the participative nature of the subject's engagement with reality.
[128] Ibid.
[129] This is the literal translation of Bakhtin's Russian term for 'obligation'.
[130] M. M. Bakhtin, *Problems of Dostoevsky's Poetics*, trans. C. Emerson (Minneapolis: University of Minnesota Press, 1984), 287.

but "I"; there is the limited, concrete Other, my neighbour, my contemporary
... past and future actual people.'[131] Recognizing this leads to a quite different
comportment vis-à-vis the world and others from what is found in a merely
aesthetic attitude. The individual does come to relate to the general, but not as
a relation to 'society' or 'humanity' but in an always concrete relationship
built up of 'I-for-myself', 'the other-for-me', and 'I-for-the other'.[132] Ultimately the only possible point of unity for such a composite society is the unity not
of theory or of the universal but of love: only love allows all to be in their
always concrete and irreducible singularity. But is love achievable?

It is not hard to see in this question a link from *The Philosophy of the Act* to
Bakhtin's later, epochal study of *Problems of Dostoevsky's Poetics,* where he
deals with 'discourse' in Dostoevsky's novels as involving the study of 'language in its concrete living totality, and not language as the specific object of
linguistics, something arrived at through a completely legitimate and necessary abstraction from various aspects of the concrete life of the word'.[133]
Furthermore, the key categories of his exposition of this discourse—dialogue,
double-voiced discourse, polyphony, and unfinalizability—essentially reflect
the understanding of this 'concrete life' as a compound of 'I-for-myself', 'the
other-for-me', and 'I-for-the other'. 'Dialogic relationships', as he says, 'are
reducible neither to logical relationships nor to relationships oriented seman-
tically toward their referential object, relationships *in and of themselves* devoid
of any dialogic element. They must clothe themselves in discourse, become
utterances, become the positions of various subjects expressed in discourse, in
order that dialogic relationships might arise among them.'[134] The most
central of these dialogical relationships is what Bakhtin calls 'double-voiced
discourse', which he calls the 'chief hero' of his investigation, and, in addition
to setting out a taxonomy of the various types of double-voiced discourse, he
also exemplifies it in the world of Dostoevsky's novels. Students of these
novels cannot wisely absolve themselves from a step-by-step study of Bakhtin's commentary. Here, however, it is sufficient only to highlight one or two
points from some of the better-known novels—especially from those that
have played an important role in the history of modern European thought,
Notes from Underground, The Idiot, Demons, and *The Brothers Karamazov.*[135]

---

[131] *K Phiilosophiiii Postupka,* 49.

[132] Ibid. 53.

[133] *Dostoevsky's Poetics,* 181.

[134] Ibid. 183.

[135] It might seem odd not to mention *Crime and Punishment* here. However, as has just been
stated, I am not seeking to give a full summary either of Bakhtin or Dostoevsky, merely to do
enough to bring to the fore the implications for this enquiry of Bakhtin's notion of dialogic
discourse.

Notes from Underground has the form of a confession to the reader by the narrator, the eponymous 'underground man', and, as Bakhtin observes, 'what strikes us first of all is its extreme and acute dialogization: there is literally not a single monologically firm, undissociated word. From the very first sentence the hero's speech has already begun to cringe and break under the influence of the anticipated words of another, with whom the hero, from the very first step, enters into the most intense internal polemic.'[136] But this internalized relation to the other is very far from expressing what would alone give unity to the narrator's world—love. At every point and in every respect, the underground man's relation to others, to himself, and to his world is conflicted, ambivalent, and passive aggressive. His attitude is essentially one of self-hatred: 'The destruction of one's own image in another's eyes, the sullying of that image in another's eyes as an ultimate desperate effort to free oneself from the power of the other's consciousness and to break though to one's self for the self alone—this, in fact, is the orientation of the Underground Man's entire confession . . . He wants to kill in himself any desire to appear the hero in others' eyes (and in his own) . . .'[137]

The Underground Man has understood the impossibility of living in the merely abstract and objective categories of contemporary science and the laws of nature and of history. At the same time he implicitly knows that his life is defined by his utterly individual relation to the equally individual others with whom he has to do and yet his relation to others is profoundly and systematically negative. He cannot find the love that would make it possible for him to accept his limitations and live happily in the world. Thus, whilst the first half of the book sets out his polemical rejection of 'science', the second half climaxes in the story 'Apropos of the Wet Snow' in which he describes his own vile mistreatment of a prostitute, thus illustrating his inability to embrace the possibility of love.

Bakhtin spends little time on *The Idiot*. However, there are several points here that, if we apply Bakhtin's own categories, help deepen the twofold problematization of language and the relation to the other that occurs when meaning is made to depend on the subjective intention of the speaker. For lying, understood precisely as a mode of double-voiced discourse, i.e., as determined by the speaker's conscious or unconscious desire to manipulate, evade, or obstruct the others' access to his intentions, is one of the novel's most pervasive themes. The garrulous Lebedev, a compulsive and buffoon-like liar, is introduced in the opening scene, whilst the basic scenario of part I hinges on a network of deceptions, such as the efforts by General Epanchin and Ganya to conceal their relations to the beautiful but fallen Anastasia

---

[136] *Dostoevsky's Poetics*, 227–8.   [137] Ibid. 232.

Fillipovna, from, respectively, the General's wife and daughter. One of the roles of Prince Myshkin, the eponymous 'idiot', is to expose and complicate these deceptions by naively speaking the truths that others are making great efforts to conceal. But accompanying and flowing from the central web of lies surrounding Anastasia Fillipovna, we also encounter a multiplicity of more or less subordinate lies and liars: Lebedev is constantly at hand to oil the mechanism of the narrative; General Ivolgin's bogus anecdotes about his military career provide comic relief; whilst the young nihilist Ippolit's false lawsuit against the Prince and his subsequent confused confession and attempted suicide reveal a more complex, pathetic, and self-deceiving failure in truthfulness. As for Anastasia herself, her seduction as a child and her subsequent role as a 'kept woman' have made it impossible for her either to know or to live by her true feelings. Entrapped in a network of falsehoods and half-truths she cannot be who she is or who she wants to be and is rendered incapable of loving, a situation that makes the novel's tragic outcome virtually inevitable. Conversely, even though he seems at many points to have insight into the truth and is painstakingly conscientious in his efforts to speak truthfully, Prince Myshkin is repeatedly presented as only partially capable of saying what he means. At crucial moments he stutters, becomes confused, or falls silent. The word of truth that would unite the disparate characters in a communion of love is never spoken.

That such truth-speaking is not simply a matter of being able to state what is objectively the case is particularly marked in the episode of Stavrogin's confession in *Demons*. Here, Dostoevsky's anti-hero approaches the saintly Bishop Tikhon in order (it seems) to confess his many crimes, including the rape of a young girl and his not intervening in her consequent suicide. But, as Bakhtin notes, the whole style of the confession (given to the Bishop in the form of a written document), betrays the ambivalent situation that 'Without recognition, and affirmation by another person Stavrogin is incapable of accepting himself, but, at the same time he does not want to accept the other's judgment of him.'[138] Far from expressing his true thought, the confession becomes another mask behind which Stavrogin withdraws. What he says is correct, but it expresses neither a willingness to accept responsibility for his actions nor a real sense of answerability vis-à-vis others. The text's very matter-of-factness itself betrays this. As Bakhtin describes it:

The style is determined above all by a cynical ignoring of the other person, an ignoring that is pointedly deliberate. Sentences are crudely abrupt and cynically precise...

---

[138] *Dostoevsky's Poetics*, 244. For a good discussion of this scene see also Rowan Williams, *Dostoevsky: Language, Faith and Fiction* (London: Continuum, 2008), 100–10.

Stavrogin attempts to present his word without any evaluative accent, to make it intentionally wooden, to eliminate all human tones in it. He wants everyone to stare at him, but at the same time he repents in an immobile and deathly mask. This is why he rearranges every sentence so that his personal tone does not surface . . . That is why he breaks up his sentences, because a normal sentence is too flexible and subtle in its transmission of the human voice . . . [His sentences] break off, as it were, at just that point where a living human voice begins.[139]

Turning, finally, to *The Brothers Karamazov* it might seem that alongside the many false words that are undoubtedly and pointedly present in the novel, we do nevertheless hear truth being spoken, by the saintly Zosima, by his disciple Alyosha, and, perhaps supremely, in the words of the Gospel of John read over Zosima's body. But is this so?

Again, there is no avoiding the atmosphere of mendacity that permeates the novel. From Fedor Karamazov through the duplicitous Smerdyakov to the smart-arse lawyer, we encounter many different lies and kinds of lies. Where the hard-drinking, hard-loving Dmitri lies almost good-naturedly, on impulse, the self-deceptions of his brother Ivan are more complex and, ultimately, more destructive. Ivan's relation to Smerdyakov and the related question as to who is guilty of the murder of old man Karamazov hinge crucially on what Ivan might have meant with his reported assertion that if God does not exist then everything is permitted and whether he himself understood what he was saying when he indicated to Smerdyakov that he would be away for a couple of days—was this a deliberate hint (as Smerdyakov subsequently claimed) to go ahead and kill the old man, or was it (as Ivan states, before Smerdyakov causes him to doubt it) entirely without any parricidal implications? The whole question of culpability is thus focused on the issue of what these speakers intended with words that, in each case, were open to various interpretations, at various levels of concrete seriousness.[140]

Yet the novel as a whole seems to argue that this miasma of lies, half-truths, and distorted truths is not final and that words of love and forgiveness can be

---

[139] *Dostoevsky's Poetics*, 245. Of course, Stepan Trofimovich Verkhovensky, pseudo-intellectual and aesthete, is another character in this novel in whom the theme of lying is also strongly represented, to the point at which the question has to be asked whether his deathbed conversion and reception of the sacrament might not, after all, be solely or primarily for aesthetic effect. However, in this case, the tragic aspects of the situation have (as with Lebedev) a certain comic colouring.

[140] On the ambiguity of this relationship, see especially V. Kantor, 'Pavel Smerdyakov and Ivan Karamazov: The Problem of Temptation', in G. Pattison and D. Thompson, *Dostoevsky and the Christian Tradition* (Cambridge: Cambridge University Press, 2001), 189–225. See also G. Pattison, 'Unavowed Knowledge', in N.-H. Gregersen and C. Hjøllund (eds.), *Coping with Evil: Perspectives from Science and Theology* (Aarhus: University of Aarhus, 2003), 1–20.

spoken and accepted. In a passage that comments both on Stavrogin's confession and on Zosima, Bakhtin says that the 'culminating points' of Dostoevsky's novels are marked by moments of encounter with the other, especially as represented by the figure of 'a stranger, a man you'll never know', in which there is a 'communion' 'outside the plot and outside [the stranger's] specificity in any plot, as a pure "man in man," a representative of "all others" for the "I." ' Such a communion 'assumes a special character and becomes independent of all real-life, concrete social forms (the forms of family, social or economic class, life's stories)'.[141] Does truth, absolute truth, then break through the fog of deception? Can a Dostoevskian hero—can *we*—speak and hear the word that will give us our pure humanity? Bakhtin seems to suggest it does, and yet it is to be noted that he also emphasizes the momentary and abstract nature of such moments of revelation. They are moments almost outside of the narrative time of the novel, moments of almost eschatological promise. And we note also that, in *The Brothers Karamazov* itself, even Zosima's saintliness is largely denied by his community, and witnessed only in Alyosha's fevered dream, whilst the story of Zosima's life is cast in a hagiographic style that distances it from the concrete, contemporary world shaped by the actions and passions of the other characters. Can such holiness be a reality in a world such as this, in a town not inappropriately named 'beast-pen'? If Alyosha's work in reconciling a gang of quarrelsome boys and his final speech at the grave of Ilyusha, the boy whom they had once bullied, seem to offer a positive answer, we must note that this, nevertheless, does not break the general rule, observed by Bakhtin, of 'unfinalizability'. Alyosha's future life and fate are uncertain, and, in any case, there remain a multiplicity of unreconciled voices. The word 'has far to go', and even the seemingly triumphant conclusion is not without a certain ambiguity.[142] It expresses hope, not accomplishment. But whatever Dostoevsky's or, for that matter, Bakhtin's final view of the matter, both Dostoevsky and Bakhtin testify to the challenges that open up when we begin to regard language in terms of the intentions of those who, in the complex and often violent circumstances of life, are its speakers. In this respect, then, such an emphasis deepens and, it may be, makes yet more intractable the more formal problems of reference that were considered in the previous chapter. At any rate, if language is to become a medium of Being, if it is to become capable of our expressing and communicating to one another who we *are*, then this cannot be without reference to the actual and concrete ways in which we exist in the domain

---

[141] *Dostoevsky's Poetics*, 264.

[142] See the discussion in my *A Short Course in the Philosophy of Religion* (London: SCM Press, 2000), 199–200.

succinctly defined by Bakhtin as that of 'I-for-myself', 'the other-for-me', and 'I-for-the other'. And, as the *Philosophy of the Act* argued and the novels of Dostoevsky had explored in manifold powerful yet nuanced ways, the question then is whether these relationships offer the possibility of genuine mutual understanding, acceptance, and affirmation—whether, that is, we live in a world of love or hate. In this way the rather abstract question of ontology is transformed into a question of real and present human interest. Who we are, our fundamental relation to Being, the kind of beings that we are—all this now depends on how we conceive the 'I-for-myself', 'the other-for-me', and 'I-for-the other'. Thus, the question of language enters into a decisive relation to the question of the other and of the actual common life of human beings. The specific 'distancing' of the self and Being that occurs in language is indissociable from the further distancing that is involved in the situation that the self does not and cannot exist apart from the actual relations to others that constitute its world. It is therefore to the further exploration of this social and relational distance that we now turn.

5

Selves and Others

MASTERS AND SLAVES

Each of the dimensions of the distance to be traversed in the quest for Being—time, space, language, selves and others, and embodiment—relates to, shapes, and is shaped by the others in manifold ways and they can never be absolutely separated out. Thus, in considering time, we were led to see how time itself took on a different profile according as to whether it is experienced as running towards annihilation or as open towards a possible future reconciliation of humans and the divine. This difference can also be phrased as the question: does the temporality of existence mean that we are left to ourselves in the absolutely individualizing confrontation with death, or does it perhaps mean that are we called by and to a new, deeper, broader, and more-inclusive community? Putting it like this shows how the relations of selves and others are already implicated in our time-experience and, in the final section of the discussion of time, we looked at how Edwin Muir's poetic reflections on the mystery of time led him also to explore the possibility of love 'in time's despite' and of a redemption still to come for murderers, victims, and all 'those who hide within the labyrinth of their own loneliness and greatness'.[1] The same connection appears in the case of language. As we have just been seeing, especially when language is considered with regard to the concrete listener and speaker (Bakhtin's 'I-for-myself', 'the other-for-me', and 'I-for-the other'), it becomes impossible to decide whether language can in fact become revelatory of Being without the relations between those who speak it being transformed in such a way as to allow each truthfully to speak love's truth in love to one another. Such revelation would therefore depend on the possibility of mutual openness and transparency in human relations—not in the sense of a causal dependence

---

[1] Muir, 'The Transfiguration'.

but as the mode or 'how' in which the complex interdependence of time, language, selves, and others is effected. Conversely, open and transparent communication would itself be a salient feature of a community that had found peace and understanding.[2] If there were to be a single word that expressed the composite reality in which these dimensions of the distance of human being from Being-Itself came together, it would, perhaps, be *history*— the unfinished and open-ended field in which the relations of selves and others are enacted in the continuing great debate of political, social, cultural, and scientific life. The question then is whether history can be regarded as revealing the true relations of human beings to Being-Itself.

Hegel, amongst the first to face the challenge of uniting the new historical sense and the Platonic-Augustinian view of the relations of time and eternity, well understood that this not only involved seeking an account of how time might enable the transformation and reconciliation of violent human relations. Historical meaning would need to be something more than the quiet interior recollection of a presence of Being that had been or was to come. Or, rather, whilst recollection would certainly be needed by those seeking to understand history, such recollection could only be carried through to a conclusion in the context of the real or actual reconciliation between real and actual human beings.[3] But is it plausible to suppose that such a reconciliation has occurred or even that it is in the process of occurring? At the beginning of philosophy Heraclitus had declared that 'war is the father of

[2] This is the logic of Habermas's linking of the achievement of a just society with communicative action, i.e., with the creation of an 'ideal speech situation' in which all stakeholders in the defining of social and moral norms participate on an equal footing, without their contribution being subverted in advance by the strategic thinking of scientific, technical, or political power-brokers. See, e.g., J. Habermas, *The Theory of Communicative Action*, trans. T. McCarthy (Boston: Beacon Press, 1984).

[3] This is the thrust of the renowned reflection on the Owl of Minerva that takes to the air only at the end of the day. A question which Hegel did not address, however, was that of the retrospective power of such reconciliation. That is, he did not ask the questions that tormented Dostoevsky's Ivan Karamazov: what of the sufferings of those who have gone to their deaths in unrelieved agony, and how can we wish for a future happiness that does not include them? Faith in immortality had been a major feature of Enlightenment theology (namely, Kant) and, precisely because of its apparent absence from Hegelian thought, became a significant focus of philosophical and theological controversy in the period after Hegel's death. See, e.g., L. Feuerbach, *Thoughts on Death and Immortality*, trans. J. A. Massey (Berkeley and Los Angeles: University of California Press, 1980); David Friedrich Strauss, *Die christliche Glaubenslehre* (Tübingen: Osiander, 1841), ii. 697–739. It is no coincidence that, in the *Concluding Unscientific Postscript*, Kierkegaard then chose the question of an eternal happiness as a wedge with which to attack the outcome of speculative thinking. Later in the nineteenth century the sense that historical utopianism also required retrospective action would lead the Russian thinker N. Fedorov to envisage the science of a future society engaging in the project of 'raising the ancestors' which was nevertheless also seen as a Christian task. See the discussion in N. Berdyaev, *The Russian Idea*, trans. R. M. French (London: Geoffrey Bles, 1947), 208 ff.

all things' and, more recently, Hobbes described the basic state of human society as 'the war of all against all'. Hegel himself witnessed the march of opposing armies across Germany and was in a position to understand that if the meaning of human existence was essentially historical, then the philosopher would have to reckon with the fact that 'history is war'.[4] This therefore required an interpretation of conflict that would take entirely seriously the grim realities of human history but would at the same time demonstrate that, like all other historical phenomena, conflict too contained the seeds of its own destruction and that the outcome of conflict would be peace. Augustine had argued long before that the ontological and teleological supremacy of peace was demonstrated by the fact that even those who wage war do so in order to bring about peace,[5] but Hegel hoped to provide an account not only of why we must hope this (as Kant had supposed) but also of the mechanism that would ensure such an outcome.

Central to Hegel's account—and what would become one of the most influential passages of his entire philosophy—was the treatment of 'master and slave' in the *Phenomenology of Spirit*. This discussion hinges on the notion that consciousness cannot be understood simply by the kind of self-analysis of the thinking subject undertaken by Descartes. Rather, as Hegel puts it at the beginning of the section on Master and Slave, 'Self-consciousness is in and for itself in and by virtue of its being in and for itself for another, i.e. it is [or exists] only when it is recognized'.[6] In other words, I can become conscious of myself (as opposed to existing simply in the mode of a non-reflective animal consciousness) only when I know myself to be recognized for what I am by that other. Mutual recognition is therefore fundamental to the possibility of self-consciousness. Moreover, as he emphasizes, this involves a twofold movement such that, first, self-consciousness finds itself facing another self-consciousness that requires it to 'come out of itself' before, secondly, this revelation of otherness or other-being (to translate Hegel's term literally) has to be overcome, a move that involves the transformation both of the other and of itself. And, of course, the same structure holds for the other from whose perspective I myself am 'the other'. The resolution of this situation, therefore, leads to the transformation of both parties, so that neither is at the end what it was at the beginning: each has become

---

[4] I believe this phrase is used somewhere by Geoffrey Studdert-Kennedy. However, the closest analogy I can find in his works is the comment that 'war is and always has been the commonplace of history' (in G. Studdert-Kennedy, *The Hardest Part* (London: Hodder and Stoughton, 1919), 85).

[5] Augustine, *Concerning the City of God against the Pagans*, trans. G. Bettenson (Harmondsworth: Penguin, 1972), Book XIX, ch. 12 (pp. 866 ff.).

[6] G. W. F. Hegel, *Phänomenologie des Geistes*, in *Werke*, iii (Frankfurt am Main: Suhrkamp, 1970), 145.

something other. The history of the relations of self and other is thus embedded in the very basis of self-consciousness itself. Human beings do not exist as the self-conscious beings that they are other than as they have negotiated the passage of the historically concrete encounter with the other.

This seems to involve Hegel in a double claim, reflecting the pervasive and often confusing interplay of structural and historical elements in the *Phenomenology*. On the one hand, it belongs to self-consciousness as such to have undergone the experience of recognition and to know itself to be recognized for what it is by the other.[7] On the other hand, the emergence of a community of mutual recognition has a historically definite form. The separation of these two elements, the structural and the historical, is to some extent artificial, but I shall begin by focusing on the structure of recognition and its role in the dialectic of master and slave, although I shall recur at a later point to the mapping of this structure onto Hegel's historical narrative and the implications that this has for the interpretation of the dialectic as a whole. With regard to this 'structural' dimension, then, it is important to emphasize again that, for Hegel, the dynamics of recognition play a fundamental role in the genesis of self-consciousness. This is not a process that begins when fully formed self-conscious human beings suddenly encounter one another for the first time. Rather, it is only in and through coming to be recognized for what we are by another that we become fully self-conscious.

From the preliminary assertion of the necessity of recognition, Hegel moves to show how this can emerge only in and through a process of conflict. In the first instance, he states, self-consciousness exists only in the mode of being-for-itself, it is a pure 'I' or individual for which the external world has no intrinsic value but is merely what is other than itself, 'inessential' or 'negative', as Hegel puts it. At this level I experience the world as existing solely to serve the satisfaction of my desires, an undifferentiated source of warmth and nourishment. But this relation cannot be sustained when what I encounter is another, opposed ego. For, in this case, the movement of my desire is checked by the counter-movement of an equal and opposite desire. The other will not do what I want unless he or she also wants what I want. I am therefore placed in the situation of needing my desire to be recognized and accepted by the other—as the other is also situated in relation to me. Such a desire for recognition may start by my attempting to subordinate the other's desires to mine, but it will eventually lead me to assert and articulate my own desires in such a way as to make clear to the other, to others, just what it is I am wanting. For Hegel—and we shall come to other ways of understanding this original

---

[7] The term translated here as 'recognition' (*Anerkennung*) is also often translated as 'acknowledgement'.

encounter of self and other—this situation is inherently conflictual. Each can only assert the primacy of its own desires by negating the desire of the other and, Hegel claims, if the other's life obstructs the satisfaction of my desire this raises the question as to whether I value the other's life more than my own desire. The possibility that I might deny the other his right to life in order to satisfy my desire intensifies the need for me to understand this desire and my relation to it. Moreover, any attempt on the other's life might involve risking my own. Thus, to put it crudely, I have to ask: how far am I prepared to go in seeking satisfaction? Am I prepared to risk my own life for the sake of my desire? Or is life more important to me than getting what I want from it? In a passage that (as so often) is opaque in some of its detail but clear in its overall tendency, Hegel writes:

This relationship between the two self-consciousnesses is thus defined in such a way that they prove themselves individually and in their relation to one another through a life and death struggle. They have to engage in such a struggle, since they have to elicit the certainty of being for themselves as their truth, both in the case of the other and of themselves. And it is only when one risks one's life that [one's] freedom is proven, and it is proved that self-consciousness is not simply *being* in the mode of its immediate appearance or its immersion in the encompassing life of the species but that there is nothing in it that cannot be considered as a vanishing moment, that it is only a pure being-for-itself. The individual who has not risked his life may well be recognized as a person, but such a one has not attained the truth of this recognition as a self-sufficient self-consciousness.[8]

In such conflict, human consciousness breaks with its natural life and human relations and human self-consciousness are from here on no longer defined by instinct or spontaneity but by their socially mediated identities. The one who prevails becomes 'master', the one who submits, the 'slave'. But this is by no means the end of the process.

On the one hand, the 'triumph' of the master is mitigated by the fact that once his enemy has been transformed into a slave, the recognition that the latter can offer is devalued. The master who knows himself only in the mirror of his slaves' admiration knows only an empty and worthless image of himself.[9] Perhaps more interesting is the situation of the slave. Although the

---

[8] *Phänomenologie*, 149.

[9] Of course, Hegel does not discuss this here, but alongside the relations of masters and slaves each master is likely to be active in seeking the submission of new enemies, finding other warriors against whom to pit himself and, once again, prove his glory. However, Hegel is implicitly mindful that this process will lead to ever larger social units, in which ever larger groups are subjected to the rule of a single imperial power so that the dialectic of master and slave is worked out not merely in local tribal conflicts but becomes a dynamic force in world history.

fear of death that led him to submit revealed that he preferred the mere continuance of life to the possibility of glory, this fear itself leaves him with an implicit understanding of what Hegel calls the 'simple essence of self-consciousness, absolute negativity, pure being-for-itself'. For the all-encompassing nature of his fear enabled him to experience 'everything fixed being shaken [in] the pure universal movement, the absolute liquefaction of everything stable'.[10] As Hegel also puts it, he has come to know death as an 'absolute Lord', greater than the master to whom, in this life, he must submit himself. Moreover, whilst the master now absolves himself from commerce with mere things (hewing wood, drawing water, serving food, etc.), leaving such material tasks to the slave, this experience of work on the part of the slave instils in him a habit of self-negation that also has a positive outcome in the transformation of the material world into a human product. Through discipline, service, and work, it is in fact the slave who develops what is required for the subsequent development of human civilization, whilst the master remains at an atavistic level in which human life finds fulfilment merely in war, hunting, and similar 'aristocratic' practices.[11]

As has been said, Hegel sees all of this as occurring in a historically specific manner, and its historical 'moment' is indicated by the sub-title of the following chapter of the *Phenomenology*, 'Stoicism, Scepticism, and the Unhappy Consciousness'. This suggests, as proves to be the case, that Hegel sees in the Stoic philosopher the emergence of a 'higher' or more advanced form of consciousness on the part of the slave. This Stoic consciousness is permeated by awareness of the absolute relativity of all phenomenal appearances and of the transience and nothingness of human life. Moreover, this involves the recognition that the master, no less than the slave, is ultimately subject to death and that the whole cosmos is in fact governed by universal laws and principles to which all must submit. 'All things must pass'.

In a footnote in the *Encyclopedia*, Hegel makes quite explicit his view that this particular moment of the dialectic can occur and has occurred only at a quite discrete historical juncture. It is he says, only at the point at which human beings are emerging from a state of nature, i.e., in the archaic societies of the ancient world, that the struggle for recognition takes the form of a life-and-death struggle. Once states and the rule of law have been established then the need for such struggles is eliminated: 'In the State it is the spirit of the

---

[10] *Phänomenologie*, 153.
[11] Hegel's account of the eventual 'triumph' of the slave over the master bears comparison with the very different reading of this same history in Nietzsche's narrative of the 'slave revolt in morality' in *The Genealogy of Morals*.

people, custom, and law that rule. Then the human being is recognized and treated as a reasonable being, as free, as a person, whilst individuals for their part make themselves worthy of such recognition by overcoming the natural inclinations of their self consciousness and obeying a universal will that is in and for itself, namely, the law . . .'[12] This would seem to count against the highly influential interpretation of the master–slave dialectic that was given by Alexandre Kojève.[13] According to Kojève, the 'epoch' of the slave extended through history all the way down to its final resolution in Hegel's own philosophy: the development of modern science and technology and of philosophical knowledge are all outcomes of the subordinates' enforced engagement with the world of matter and their eventual triumph over it. Yet the very terms in which Hegel himself sought to limit the historical scope of the master–slave dialectic invite debate. For these seem precisely to invoke the kind of 'end of history' thesis that would be so generally contested in subsequent philosophical generations. After all, we did not need the erosion of human rights legislation after 9/11 nor even the suspension of the Weimar human rights laws in the Third Reich to know that the achievement of a certain level of law-bound social order could scarcely be regarded as a once-and-for-all achievement such as the invention of the wheel. Precisely because it is a work emerging from the interaction of human wills, such order will need constantly to be re-enacted if it is to gain historical continuity. As an inheritance from our forebears, it only survives if we ourselves affirm its values and make them our own. But this is already to assume that a given social order (in this case the social order of Prussia in the second and third decades of the nineteenth century) has in fact achieved an adequate, just, and equitable balance of powers, rights, and obligations—and this, of course, is to assume rather a lot and certainly more than either Marx or Kierkegaard, from their opposite perspectives, would have conceded. Thus to the extent that recognition or acknowledgement remains only imperfectly achieved or to the extent that, having been achieved, it remains exposed to risks of subversion or neglect—that is, to the extent that even an advanced civilization is at risk of collapsing back into a state of general war (as in the long European civil war of the twentieth century)—the master–slave dialectic might be thought to offer a trans-historical structure of human relationships that is frighteningly persuasive.

---

[12] G. W. F. Hegel, *Enzyklopädie der philosophischen Wissenschaften III*, in *Werke*, x (Frankfurt am Main: Suhrkamp, 1970), 221–2.
[13] See A. Kojève, *Introduction à la lecture de Hegel: Leçons sur la phénoménologie de l'ésprit* (Paris: Gallimard, 1947).

OTHERS: HELL OR LOVE

It is just such a trans-historical and structural application of the dialectic that informs Sartre's account of self and others. We have already seen how Sartre's account of the inherent 'distancing' of consciousness and Being-in-itself problematizes claims to an experience of the immediate presence of Being—indeed, it has been precisely this 'distance' that we have been exploring in the course of the last two chapters and are continuing to explore here. Just as Sartre sees the distancing enacted by consciousness between the for-itself and the in-itself as identical with the annihilation of Being-in-itself, so too do relations between selves and others seem to him to be fated to mutual destruction. He depicts the struggle for recognition as a struggle from which we can never hope to escape and in which we can never achieve either the kind of social recognition that Hegel believed had been secured in modern democratic societies or a more intimate, personal recognition in which individuals become capable of mutual acceptance and affirmation.[14]

In addressing the question of the other, Sartre rejects the view that we infer the existence of other minds from the phenomenal surface of the body and face. Although this is the conventional way in which philosophers approach the topic it is putting the question the wrong way round. For I do not in fact ever have a perception of the other as a mere body from which I then, somehow, have to infer his subjectivity. On the contrary, the other is disclosed to me 'directly' and 'in connection with me' as a subject. Indeed as Sartre sets out to show (and with a strong reliance on Hegel), my being-for-myself as a subject who is also the project of freedom is inseparable from my primordial relation to the other subjectivity. If I am to become, to *be* myself, I must free myself from others and define myself in my own being-for-myself *against* others—although even this 'against' is, of course, still a very definite kind of relationship.

Despite the doubts of some philosophers, the subjectivity of the other is not disclosed in some sort of 'mystic or ineffable experience'. It is in the reality of everyday life that the Other appears to us—but how? Sartre is ready with an example: 'I am in a public park. Not far away there is a lawn and along the edge of that lawn there are benches. A man passes by those benches. I see this man; I apprehend him as an object and at the same time as a man. What does this signify? What do I mean when I assert that this object is *a man?*'[15]

---

[14] As one might see in Buber's account of the I–Thou relationship. See below.

[15] J.-P. Sartre, *Being and Nothingness*, trans. H. Barnes (London: Methuen, 1958), 254.

Although this involves no disruption to the world in which the man is an object among objects, nonetheless, the presence of this human other immediately and totally disorients my perception of the world. The lawn is no longer merely the lawn at which I am looking. It is also the lawn that is seen by the Other. It is no just 'my' lawn. It is also—potentially—'his': 'instead of a grouping *toward me* of the objects, there is now an orientation *which flees from me*':[16]

there is a regrouping in which I take part but which escapes me, a regrouping of all the objects which people my universe. This regrouping does not stop there. The grass is something qualified; it is *this* green grass which exists for the Other; in this sense the very quality of the object, its deep, raw green is in direct relation to this man. This green turns toward the Other a face which escapes me. I apprehend the relation of the green to the Other as an objective relation, but I can not apprehend the green as it appears to the Other. Thus suddenly an object has appeared which has stolen the world from me. Everything is in place; everything still exists for me; but everything is traversed by an invisible flight and fixed in the direction of a new object. The appearance of the Other in the world corresponds therefore to a fixed sliding of the whole universe, to a decentralisation of the world which undermines the centralisation which I am simultaneously effecting.[17]

But this 'decentralisation' is not complete. I do not lose my world altogether despite its flight from me towards the other. After all, the world of objects continues to exist. I continue to see the grass. I continue to see the other man:

the disintegration of my universe is contained within the limits of this same universe; we are not dealing here with a flight of the world toward nothingness or outside itself. Rather it appears that the world has a kind of drain hole in the middle of its being and that it is perpetually flowing off through this hole. The universe, the flow, and the drain hole are all once again recovered, reapprehended, and fixed as an object.[18]

I still have 'my' world, but only to the extent that I resist its disintegration and my being absorbed by the gaze of the Other. But this is not the end of the matter. For it is not just that I am standing there looking at a lawn when another person comes along and also happens to look at the lawn. There is a further possibility: that he might lift his eyes from the lawn and look at me. '[M]y fundamental connection with the Other-as-subject', Sartre writes, 'must be able to be referred back to my permanent possibility of *being seen* by the Other...':[19] 'this relation which I call "being-seen-by-another" far from being merely one of the relations signified by the word *man*, represents an irreducible fact which cannot be deduced either from the essence of the

---

[16] *Being and Nothingness*, 254.   [17] Ibid. 255.
[18] Ibid. 256.   [19] Ibid.

Other-as-object, or from my being-as-subject.'[20] Thus, Sartre states that 'the "Being-seen-by-the-Other" is the *truth* of "seeing-the-other"' and, in short, 'the Other is in principle the *one who looks at me...*'[21] But what does this mean?

Sartre invites his readers to imagine a situation in which they are peering through a keyhole. Whether they are titillated by what they see (or hope to see) or are racked by jealousy and fearful of what will meet their gaze, they are in each case entirely absorbed in what they are doing until, suddenly, footsteps are heard approaching along the hallway. This, Sartre claims, alters the situation entirely and at a stroke. I am now forced to *see myself* precisely because I have become aware of the possibility that someone else will see me. Yet this sudden self-awareness is not the self-awareness of authentic freedom choosing its own project. In the first instance the (potential) presence of the Other identifies me only as a self situated within the domain of unreflective consciousness. In this situation 'I am for myself only as I am a pure reference to the Other.'[22] Nor, Sartre further claims, would the situation be essentially different if the behaviour in which I was discovered was behaviour of which I could be proud—rather than (as in the example given) behaviour of which I am likely to be ashamed. Pride, no less than shame, 'reveal[s] to me the Other's look and myself at the end of that look'.[23] But what are the implications of this revelation of myself at the end of the Other's for my being-for-myself?

First, says Sartre, 'there is a relation of being. I *am* this being,'[24] namely, the being who is seen by the Other within the horizons projected by his freedom. I am how he sees me. The 'me' that is seen is not the self that I choose to be, but the 'one' he chooses to see in me and which is fixed by him in the realm of objects and of things such that I am no longer a centre of freedom but a mere essence, a 'what'. 'The Other as a look is only that—my transcendence transcended.'[25] Or—and note the recourse to a theological motif at this point—'My original fall is the existence of the Other.'[26] This basic conception seems also to be connected at a very basic level with Sartre's atheism, as when he describes how he fell out with God after he had burnt a mat at the age of about 12: 'I was busy covering up my crime when suddenly God saw me. I felt His gaze inside my head and on my hands; I turned round and round in the bathroom, horribly visible, a living target. I was saved by indignation: I grew angry at such a lack of tact, and blasphemed...He never looked at me again.'[27]

---

[20] *Being and Nothingness*, 257.   [21] Ibid.   [22] Ibid. 260.
[23] Ibid. 261.   [24] Ibid.   [25] Ibid. 263.   [26] Ibid.
[27] J.-P. Sartre, *Words*, trans. I. Clephane (Harmondsworth: Penguin, 1967), 65.

In this context Sartre appeals to Kafka and especially to the novels *The Trial* and *The Castle* as exemplifying this situation. Kafka's 'heroes' act in the world, but because their action is in every case potentially see-able by the Other

the *truth* of these acts constantly escapes them; the acts have on principle a meaning which is their *true meaning* and which neither K. nor the Surveyor will ever know. Without doubt Kafka is trying here to express the transcendence of the divine; it is for the divine that the human act is constituted in truth. But God here is only the concept of the Other pushed to the limit . . . That gloomy, evanescent atmosphere of *The Trial*, that ignorance which, however, is lived as ignorance, that total opacity which can only be felt as a presentiment across a total translucency—this is nothing but the description of our being-in-the-midst-of-the-world-for-others.[28]

If, then, I am to become myself and to assert the free transcendence over Being that the original occurrence of consciousness inaugurated, I must contest the limit imposed on me by the 'look' of the 'strange freedom' of the Other. Acknowledging the analogy to Hegel's master–slave dialectic, Sartre concludes that being-for-itself is intrinsically agonistic: it exists in and as the struggle to be itself and to refuse the objectifying projection of the other and its own consequent reduction to mere being in-itself or essence. Yet whereas Hegel envisages the goal of a community of mutually affirming free subjects as a real historical possibility, Sartre offers no eschatological resolution to the state of general violence. For Sartre the process must continue indefinitely as we oscillate between sadism and masochism, between denying the freedom of the other and denying our own freedom. But whichever of these options we choose, we are unlikely to succeed. As was the case with Hegel's 'master', even the sadist must ultimately fail in the task of achieving an immaculate perception of his freedom, since the other whom he reduces to a mere object thereby loses the very quality of humanity that gives the act of recognition its worth.[29]

---

[28] *Being and Nothingness*, 266.

[29] If it is typical of Sartre's account of human relations that he sees violence as rooted in the mutual foreignness of self and other, René Girard's more recent and (in theology at least) highly influential approach to violence sees it as developing out of a blurring of the boundaries of self and other. For Girard the salient feature of human consciousness is its mimetic character. Versus Freud, desire is not to be explained through instinct but is learned. However, the one from whom I learn my desires is typically the obstacle to my being able to fulfil them—because we both now and the same thing. Thus Girard explains the Oedipus complex in terms of the son learning to desire the mother by seeing that she is the supreme object of the father's desire. This situation of mimetic rivalry is clearly fraught with possibilities of violent conflict. Without going further into Girard's development of this idea in terms of the origins and social function of sacrifice, it is tempting to rewrite Sartre's account of the encounter across the lawn in Girardian terms. In this case it would not be a matter of immediate hostility, but of an initial movement of mimesis: the appearance of the other inspires in me for the first time the idea that the lawn might be a desirable possession, precisely because I see the other desiring it; I learn my desire for the lawn from him. If

A further, important development of this scenario—inaugurating one of the most significant of all the cultural events of the late twentieth century—was to be offered by Simon de Beauvoir who, in *The Second Sex*, drew attention to the gendering of this dialectic in historical experience. If the self-assertion of male subjectivity against the indifferent power of nature constantly exposes the man to anxiety and to conflict with those of his fellows who are also engaged in this struggle, woman offers a kind of *tertium quid*:

she is the wished-for intermediary between nature, the stranger to man, and the fellow being who is too closely identical. She opposes him with neither the hostile silence of nature nor the hard requirement of a reciprocal relation; through a unique privilege she is a conscious being and yet it seems possible to possess her in the flesh. Thanks to her, there is a means for escaping that implacable dialectic of master and slave which has its source in the reciprocity that exists between free beings.[30]

Of course, it is only an 'escape' for the man. Woman may allow man to attain the reality that he cannot be by himself, but only by being defined as the Other and subordinated to men in all aspects of social life. 'Woman thus seems to be the inessential who never goes back to being the essential, to be the absolute Other, without reciprocity.'[31] Or, in other words, woman's aspiration towards subjectivity and being-for-herself is forced back in such a way as to keep her perpetually within the limits of the in-itself, as a kind of human incarnation of 'Mother' nature.[32]

We are now close to the philosophical roots of why it is that, in one of his best-known plays, Sartre suggests that all that is necessary to establish the existence of hell is to lock three people up for ever. The fundamental dynamics of such a situation predetermine their interrelationship as the perpetual mutual denial of freedom. Mutual recognition is never secure. In such a

---

we imagine that there is a bench by the side of the lawn, it is only when I see the other appear and look at the bench that I realize it might be a good bench to sit on it, whereupon I immediately want to make sure that I'm going to be the one to sit on it, not him. Of course, the outcome is much the same, although Girard will eventually argue for a possible liberation from such violent mimeticism by means of the Gospels' revelation of the mechanisms that drive it. See, e.g. R. Girard, *The Scapegoat*, trans. Y. Freccero (London: Athlone, 1986). In the light of the discussion of Dostoevsky in the previous chapter, it is relevant to note that key elements in Girard's theory seem to have been worked out in his early studies on the Russian writer. See R. Girard, 'Dosotïevski—du double à l'unité', in *Critique dans un souterrain* (Paris: Grasset, 1976).

[30] Simone de Beauvoir, *The Second Sex*, trans. H. M. Parshley (Harmondsworth: Penguin, 1972), 172.

[31] Ibid. 173.

[32] In addition to de Beauvoir's own extensive unmasking of the 'dreams, fears, and idols' that this way of representing women set in motion, she surely established a paradigm that has remained central to much subsequent feminist thinking. See, e.g., Luce Irigaray, *Speculum of the Other Woman*, trans. G. C. Gill (Ithaca, NY: Cornell University Press, 1985), where it is the representation of woman in psychoanalysis that is taken to task.

situation of radical and unpredictable instability the self can only be itself in the continuing refusal of the objectifying viewpoint of the Other. As existing before the face of the Other I can never entirely be or become myself. Hell is other people.[33]

Sartre's argument is powerful and his illustrations are vivid (though whether we allow them the status of 'phenomenological descriptions' might be debatable)—not least if we have been alerted by, for example, the novels of Dostoevsky, the history of the twentieth century, and the contents of the daily news to the manifold ways in which human beings can fail to become who they are whilst simultaneously frustrating others in their pursuit of freedom and self-commitment. But, at the same time, many readers have felt that there is something almost idiosyncratically negative, pathological even, about his presentation of the self–other relationship. Gabriel Marcel already described Sartre as effecting 'the systematic vilification of man' and to Sartre's vision of an endless alternation of sadism and mechanism opposed a 'fidelity' to those experiences of communion and love in which, he believed, there occurred humanly meaningful revelations of Being.[34] As a counter-example to the mutually annihilating acts of the Sartrean subjects, as exemplified by the eavesdropper at the keyhole (which he described as 'specious'), Marcel offered a picture of a child gathering flowers in a meadow and running up to its mother shouting, 'Look at what *I've* gathered!' In this simple scene Marcel sees both that our sense of self is indeed inseparable from a relation to the other—it is from the other, in this case its mother, that the child seeks recognition of its being and identity—but that this relation is one in which the other is approached as a source of affirmation 'resonating and amplifying', as Marcel puts it, its original pleasure (*jouissance*) in its own being.[35] Similarly, and in pointed opposition to Sartre, Marcel describes my original relation

[33] J.-P. Sartre, *Huis clos* (variously translated into English as *In Camera*, *No Exit*, etc.). In addition to the feminist development of these thoughts, one might also note the radical psychoanalytic application of existential phenomenology made by R. D. Laing. It was central to Laing's anti-psychiatry that the typical psychotic 'problem' was not internal to the individual as a result of that individual's exclusively singular earlier life, but was rather a problem of the whole family context in which the individual became psychotic. As he writes: 'Every relationship implies a definition of self by other and other by self...A person's "own" identity cannot be completely abstracted from his identity-for-others. His identity-for-himself; the identity others ascribe to him; the identities he attributes to them; the identity or identities he thinks they attribute to him; what he thinks they think he thinks they think...' R. D. Laing, *Self and Others* (Harmondsworth: Penguin, 1971), 86. See also idem, *The Divided Self* (Harmondsworth: Penguin, 1965).

[34] See, e.g., his essay 'Existence and Human Freedom' in G. Marcel, *The Philosophy of Existence*, trans. M. Harari (London: Harvill, 1948).

[35] See the essay 'Moi et autrui', in G. Marcel, *Homo viator: Prolégomènes à une métaphysique de l'espérance* (Paris: Aubier, 1944), 15 ff. Marcel's original version of the child's '*C'est moi qui les*

to Being as being *chez soi*, that is, I exist as a being that who is ready 'to receive [the other] in one's own prepared place of reception'.[36]

Before Marcel, the possibility of an original encounter of 'I' and 'Thou', of self and other, in which Being is revealed and each self and each other is caught up in a cycle of mutual affirmation which can appropriately be named 'love', had been paradigmatically stated by Martin Buber in his study *I and Thou*. Buber shared with Hegel, Bakhtin, and Sartre the view that human subjectivity can never be adequately understood by reflection on the internal contents of the individual consciousness. The self is what it is only in and through (or even in and *as*) its relation to the other. Where Kierkegaard emphasized the internal relations of the self ('the self is a relation that relates itself to itself...'), Buber saw the relation to the other as more truly decisive.[37] Indeed, we can never not be in some kind of relation, and the only question is what kind of relation. Essentially, Buber suggests, there are two basic forms of relationship, which he calls I–It and I–Thou.[38] He also refers to these as 'basic words' since, he believes, all relationship is essentially communicative, even when language is not an explicit element in it (so that, for example, I can relate silently to a tree or a cat in the manner of I–Thou, even though neither of us 'speak'[39]).

Buber's account of the encounter with the other as foundational to the existence of the self in a positive sense also makes clear what he—like Marcel—sees as the interconnectedness of the relation to the human and to the divine other. Wherever we are able to say 'Thou', to commit ourselves to the openness in which the other demands our exclusive attention and address, '[t]hrough every single Thou the basic word addresses the eternal Thou'.[40] And, as he further explains, 'In every sphere, in every relational act, through everything that becomes present to us, we gaze towards the eternal Thou; in

---

ai cueillies' emphasizes, as my translation does not, that this is a child who has not yet fully made the passage from the undifferentiated 'me' to the self-conscious subjectivity of the 'I'.

[36] G. Marcel, *The Mystery of Being I: Reflection and Mystery*, trans. G. S. Fraser (London: Harvill Press, 1950), 118.

[37] In this regard, see his influential critique of Kierkegaard, 'The Question to the Single One', in M. Buber, *Between Man and Man* (London: Collins, 1961), 60–108. However, it is now widely acknowledged that Buber's criticism itself misses key elements in Kierkegaard: see the discussion of Kierkegaard's view of love later in this chapter.

[38] M. Buber, *I and Thou*, trans. W. Kaufmann (Edinburgh: T. & T. Clark, 1970), 53. I shall amend Kaufmann's translation by changing 'You' back to the 'Thou' used by Ronald Gregor Smith, Buber's first translator, since Kaufmann's understandable attempt to alter the reception of Buber's idea has, in this respect at least, not succeeded, and the vocabulary of I and Thou persists not only in relation to translations of Buber, but also, e.g., of Feuerbach, Marcel, and in general usage.

[39] Ibid. 57–9, 145.

[40] Ibid. 123.

each we perceive a breath of it; in every Thou we address the eternal Thou, in every sphere, according to its manner . . . Through all of them shines the one presence.'[41] But whilst these spheres include, as he puts it, 'the eloquent muteness of creatures', the form that the 'basic word' I–Thou takes in human society is language, i.e., speech and reply, and that this is also valid for the God-relationship: 'The relation to a human being is the proper metaphor for the relation to God—as genuine address is here accorded a genuine answer. But in God's answer all, the All, reveals itself as language'[42]—confirming again, from yet another angle, the interdependence of self-other relations and language.

For Buber and for Marcel, the relation to the other that is also, implicitly, a relation to God is properly called love. Buber insists (and Marcel would not disagree) that this should not, however, be interpreted in terms merely of 'feelings': 'Feelings accompany the metaphysical and metapsychical fact of love, but they do not constitute it,' a point he illustrates by contrasting Jesus' feeling for the possessed man with his feeling for the beloved disciple: two very different 'feelings', but, Buber says, 'the love is one'.[43] 'Love is responsibility of an I for a Thou,' he adds.[44] But is this love also a revelation of Being? For Marcel, clearly it is—although, as he states many times, what it reveals is precisely the *mystery* of Being. It is not a relation to Being that could ever adequately be transcribed as knowledge. In the case of Buber this is less clear. 'When a man steps before the countenance [of God], the world becomes wholly present to him for the first time in the fullness of presence, illuminated by eternity, and he can say Thou in one word to the being of all beings.'[45] Yet this gives nothing to knowledge:

That before which we live, that in which we live, that out of which and into which we live, the mystery— . . . has become present for us, and through its presence it has made itself known to us as salvation; we have "known" it, but we have no knowledge of it that might diminish or extenuate its mysteriousness. We have come close to God, but no closer to an unriddling of being.[46]

---

[41] M. Buber, *I and Thou*, trans. W. Kaufmann (Edinburgh: T. & T. Clark, 1970), 150.
[42] Ibid. 151.
[43] Ibid. 66.
[44] Ibid. Lévinas, as we shall see, is chary of the word 'love', as of the specific references to Jesus (including a further reference to the crucifixion) with which Buber illustrates his argument. Yet Buber's interpretation of love in the perspective of responsibility is surely also close to what we shall find in Lévinas concerning the ethical responsibility for the neighbour.
[45] Ibid. 157. NB 'to the being of all beings' translates 'zur Wesenheit aller Wesen', which might also be rendered as 'to the essentiality of all essences'.
[46] Ibid. 159–60.

This passage resonates with themes of Being, salvation, and presence with which we are now familiar, and it is certainly not accidental that at this decisive point Buber returns to Exodus 3: 'I do not believe in God's naming himself or in God's defining himself before man,' he writes. 'The word of revelation is: I am there as whoever I am there. That which reveals is that which reveals. That which has being is there, nothing more. The eternal source of strength flows, the eternal touch is waiting, the eternal voice sounds, nothing more.'[47] In other words, the 'name' of God is not to be construed as 'I am that I am' or as Being-Itself, but as an unfathomable presence that cannot be known but can nevertheless be addressed, prayed to, and loved and that grounds the possibility of love in human relations. As Franz Rosenzweig, Buber's collaborator in a new translation of the Scripture, put it, the divine name has a quality of vocativity such that it cannot be separated from contexts of address and calling. When this quality becomes manifest, Rosenzweig says, 'it glances momentarily from the midst of a sentence towards heaven'.[48]

Perhaps, amongst those who learned philosophy through Lévinas and Derrida, it has become customary to belittle 'the I–Thou relationship' as too naive, romantic, or simplistic. Usually, of course, this is only done by those who have not immersed themselves in the enormous hinterland of Buber's thought in which the dimensions of I and Thou are prepared and worked out in textual, historical, theological, and philosophical depth and in which his collaboration with Rosenzweig on the translation of the Hebrew Bible is by no means the least significant part. Lévinas himself was certainly not one to undervalue Buber, yet he was undoubtedly anxious about what he sometimes called the 'orgiastic' aspect of I and Thou and the potential of Buber's formulations to suggest a kind of fusion of self and other in which the distinctiveness and responsibility of each self would be lost.

We shall return to the issues raised by these differences and, especially, to the question as to whether or in what way love might be regarded as the definitive measure of the relationship of self and other. First, however, we turn to Lévinas himself and to the way in which he uses the theme of the other not only to offer a radical alternative to Sartre's vision of history as the incessant and interminable war of all against all but as pointing up some of the central

---

[47] Ibid. 160. As Kaufmann's footnotes indicate, Buber revised the original text to lay greater stress on the 'being *there*' rather than on the simple being of God in the name.

[48] F. Rosenzweig, *Kleinere Schriften* (Berlin: Schocken/Jüdischer Buchverlag, 1937), 190. It is for their lack of sense for this 'undertone' that Rosenzweig reproaches Christian readers of what they call the 'Old Testament': 'The Jewish Bible calls out "Eli! Eli! My God, my God!" and the Old Testament scholars shake their heads and explain: "He's calling for Elias"' (p. 197). It is, of course, not accidental that Rosenzweig makes this point by thus alluding to a central moment in the Christians' own 'New' Testament! See also the discussion of the divine Name in Ch. 1 above.

limiting assumptions of the Western metaphysical tradition. But before doing this, we should pause and take note of the implications of this whole discussion for the development of our enquiry into the relationship of God and Being.

We have been seeking to reflect on the dimensions of the distance that divides the self-conscious subject from the simple enjoyment of a direct sense of the presence of Being and we have, thus far, considered time, space, and language, and are now meditating on the mediation of self-consciousness through the relation to the other. In the course of these reflections I have from time to time suggested that whilst claims to an immediate intuition of Being need to be moderated in the light of these ontological distances, we have not yet encountered anything that decisively and irreversibly signals the impossibility of the relation to Being. We may need to talk of the distancing or weakening of Being in the light of subjectivity, time, space, language, and relationality and we may need to give these terms (distancing and weakening) the greatest force they are able to bear. We may and perhaps must also acknowledge that Being could only ever become present to us as an infinite and unfathomable mystery, but this does not, as yet, require us simply to abandon faithfulness to what we believed were visions of Being once granted or to renounce the hope of a fuller sense of the presence of divine Being to come. Yet if at this point we find that the self is unable to be conceived other than as participant in a history of unending belligerence, if the relation to Being cannot escape from the shadow of violence and the threatened annihilation of one being by another, then it would seem that we must either conclude that the quest for Being is doomed to failure or that its outcome, even if successful, would be so meagre as to make it entirely pointless. Hegel, as we saw, offered one narrative as to how the violence of the historical past can be overcome in the progressive evolution of modern society, but his optimism has largely failed to convince. Sartre's vision of human relations is shaped by scenarios that are often only too recognizable, yet his pessimism seems equally inadequate.[49] Both thinkers, despite their differences, proposed what might be called an ontology of social being, although Sartre's 'ontology' is, of course, consistently negative: as he describes it, it is not 'Being' but the incessant annihilation of Being that determines not only individual consciousness but also the encounters of selves and others.[50] Against this,

---

[49] Of course, Sartre himself rejected the label 'pessimist', despite judging life to be a 'useless passion' and claiming that the future of philosophy would be erected on the foundation of despair. He also alluded to Unamuno's 'tragic sense of life' as offering a leitmotif for existentialist thought, but without endorsing the Spanish philosopher's own avowed hunger for eternal life.

[50] These remarks relate only to Sartre's 'existentialist' writings and not to his subsequent Marxist works.

Marcel and Buber see in the encounter with the other a genuine possibility for expressing and bearing faithful testimony to the mystery of Being. But what would make us decide one way or the other? Does a certain decision regarding Being enable us also to decide about the prospects of human relations? Or does ontology have to wait upon another kind of decision about the nature and destiny of selves and others? And, if that is so, might it not be better at this point simply to abandon the ontological project and to seek another way of interpreting the central issues of how we might live out the search for abiding peace? It is just this abandonment that seems—in opposition both to Sartre's and to Marcel's and Buber's opposed visions of self and other—to be effected in the thought of Emmanuel Lévinas.

BEFORE THE FACE OF GOD

Like 'I–Thou' relationships, 'Dasein', and 'angst', the central tropes of Lévinasian philosophy have become almost commonplace in contemporary theological and philosophical discourse to the point of seeming trite. In the present context, I hope that a brief rehearsal of some of these tropes will help show how Lévinas stakes out a distinctive position vis-à-vis not only Hegel, Sartre, and Buber with regard to the question of the other, but also vis-à-vis Heidegger with regard to the question of Being. Whatever the risks of over-exposure and trivialization, my hope is that Lévinas will in this way help us to move towards what will be a, perhaps the, decisive question of this enquiry.

Like many thinkers before him, Lévinas wonders at the remarkable logic of the verb 'to exist' (*exister*) and the tissue of 'vertiginous' connections that bind Being (*l'Être*) to beings (*étants*), and that make it possible for a being to be an entity (*un être*), a subject, or an existent. In relating to itself as an existent being, the I does not merely tautologously repeat itself (as in the classic formulation of German idealism, A=A), but undergoes 'an event of which the reality and the character, in some manner, surprisingly, announce themselves in the inquietude that accomplishes it'.[51] This might sound Heideggerian, but the inquietude or anxiety of which Lévinas speaks is not anxiety in the face of nothingness or the ecstatic thrownness of the self towards death. If there is an evil that disturbs the self, this does not derive from non-being, nor from its own finitude, but from its actual being: 'It is by

---

[51] E. Lévinas, *De l'existence à l'existant* (Paris: Vrin, 2004), 19.

virtue of itself, not its finitude that existence reveals a tragic scenario that death cannot resolve,' he writes.[52] The starting point is and has to be human life in which we eat, breathe, drink, and kiss in an endlessly alternating sequence of desire and satisfaction that simply is our life in the world. Against Heidegger, but with Marx, he sees no sense in condemning such 'quotidian' reality as inauthentic: hunger and thirst are at least 'sincere', he says.[53] This realm of rather straightforward egoism, this 'place' which the ego occupies and takes possession of, constitutes a totality of experience and life. Within this totality, self and world are intertwined in their very roots and in such a way that the world can become visible to me in a primordial luminosity, lying unveiled before me and so in this way also 'possessed'.

Yet—and here we again note an echo of the Hegelian account of self-consciousness and its necessary passage through the encounter with the other—whilst this world that lies before me can, in principle, be brought into the orbit of my power and, in that sense, is not fundamentally 'other' (the carrot that I eat can be transmuted into my body and become my energy, etc.), 'what is wholly other is others',[54] i.e., other people, since the other self, the other consciousness, is beyond my power and I cannot determine from within myself how that other chooses to be. Yet although this other, unlike the world, cannot be possessed, I am not without a fundamental relation to him (as Lévinas emphasizes, we are speaking of self *and* other), and this relation is already evident in the fact of language.[55] In language 'the same, gathered into its ipseity as I . . . goes outside itself'[56] and the face-to-face of such lived discourse is, for Lévinas, the heart of religion. For religion is or is based on a bond between self and other that, unlike my relation to the world, cannot be absorbed into a totality. Thus, 'It is not I who refuses my consent to the system, as Kierkegaard thought, but the other.'[57] As long as 'I' am alone, as a

---

[52] E. Lévinas, *De l'existence à l'existant* (Paris: Vrin, 2004), 21.

[53] Ibid. 69.

[54] E. Lévinas, *Totalité et infinité: Essai sur l'extériorité* (Paris: Kluwer, 1971), 28.

[55] One might again think of Wittgenstein's insistence—in a very different philosophical context—that there is no private language.

[56] Ibid. 29.

[57] Ibid. 31. We might hesitate before endorsing Lévinas's view as to the difference between his position and that of Kierkegaard, relying as it does on a somewhat standard reading of Kierkegaard that is limited to a small selection of difficult texts that are in key respects opposed by other less widely read but no less 'genuine' works. For example, he comments that although Kierkegaard discussed Abraham's near-sacrifice of Isaac at great length, he never discussed the story of Abraham interceding for Sodom and Gomorrah, yet Kierkegaard did just that in an upbuilding discourse published on the same day as *Fear and Trembling*. For further discussion see Jamie Ferreira, *Love's Grateful Striving: A Commentary on Kierkegaard's Works of Love* (Oxford: Oxford University Press, 2001); Merold Westphal, *Levinas and Kierkegaard in Dialogue* (Bloomington, Ind.: Indiana University Press, 2008); and J. A. Simmons and D. Wood (eds.),

simple, single subjectivity, I can always draw my world into the orbit of my own life and thought or allow myself to be absorbed into my world: when I find myself bound indissolubly to an other with whom I nevertheless cannot thus merge, an other who is always a 'third party' in my relation to the world, totality is no longer possible. And this, for Lévinas, means that ontology is no longer possible. For ontology seeks to reduce beings to 'the same', to 'being', as 'the luminosity in which beings become intelligible'.[58] As examples of this, he cites both the Socratic view of knowledge and Husserlian phenomenology (which latter, he says, thinks existent beings in a horizon that transcends them in such a way that they can have a 'silhouette' but never a 'face'[59]). As an alternative to ontology Lévinas proposes what he, perhaps oddly, calls 'theory', understanding the theoretical stance both as involving respect for the exteriority of the other and as subjecting the egotistical spontaneity of 'the same' to critical reflection. Moreover, and against the grain of much popular 'postmodern' thinking, he accords a certain respect to Descartes, and the latter's emphasis on the infinite, since, as Descartes himself already noted, the infinite, like the other, cannot be encompassed by the 'I': the infinite is not an object amongst objects but is altogether and entirely transcendent. The relation to the infinite is the epitome of the fundamental metaphysical desire for the invisible, for what is 'elsewhere' or 'otherwise', a desire for a u-topia that has never been our fatherland,[60] absolute exteriority. Yet Lévinas speaks of a *relation* to this infinite, a relation that is constituted by the presence of the other, 'the stranger' who, in turning his face expressively towards me calls on me to respond, to accept that I am answerable to him, and am to speak to him.

The issue here is not simply the positing of an other outside the totality of the world that the ego creates around itself or into which it inserts itself. In becoming liberated from the totality of the world through the other, the self is called in a more radical way to become fully individuated. The relation to the other allows it to separate itself from the common time of collective history and from 'the world'. In this new and radical individualism, distinct from that of spontaneous egoism, the participation of self and world is ruptured: the

---

Kierkegaard and Levinas: Ethics, Politics, and Religion (Bloomington, Ind.: Indiana University Press, 2008). Lévinas's two contributions specifically devoted to Kierkegaard are to be found in his *Noms propres* (Paris: Fata Morgana, 1976), 77–92.

[58] *Totalité et infinité*, 33.

[59] Ibid. 36.

[60] Ibid. 22. The allusion is in the first instance probably to Plotinus as well as to the rhetoric of 'fatherland' in National Socialist thought and, in this regard, also Heidegger (as in the latter's lectures on Hölderlin). However, we might also recall Lévinas's use of Bloch, for whom utopia is, after all, not only where we have never been but also a recollection from the childhood of all.

world is disenchanted and the self abandons its earlier gods. This rupture is therefore essentially atheistic—as Lévinas comments, it is 'a great glory for the Creator to have set on his feet a creature capable of atheism'.[61] Such separation of self and world is necessary for the emergence of genuine interiority, truth, and language and thus establishes the preconditions for responsibility. But if responsibility is to become a reality, then the separated self of atheistic autonomy must become capable of attending to the face of the other. Of course, it is only to be expected that not every mention of 'the other' will do justice to all that is actually involved in the claim that the other makes on us. The other is not Heidegger's impersonal 'we', nor the sociologists' 'society', nor even Buber's 'I–Thou', since, Lévinas maintains, this last is premised on a kind of reciprocity—a principle of friendship or, we might say, kinship—that prevents the infinite otherness of the other from appearing. Neither science nor rhetoric (including pedagogy, demagoguery, etc.) treats the other as other, but always presumes upon a certain pre-understanding of the other's identity ('Friends, Romans, countrymen . . .'). The proper relation to the other is and can only be established in and by justice, in attending to the claim that comes to us from the face of the other, in tending to the need of the widow, the orphan, and the stranger.

This, Lévinas insists, is not a matter of 'love', for what is revealed in this claim is, at one and the same time, infinitely elevated (in the form of the Lordship of the One who demands that I act justly) and utterly wretched (in the contrasting form of the widow, alien, and orphan who plead that I act justly *for them*). In both cases, the distance between self and other is too great for 'love' to be an appropriate designation for the relationship. Nor is the claim of justice a revelation of God in the sense that it issues from a vision of a numinous other, which, for Lévinas, would involve a mythologizing of the divine and against which the protest of atheism will always be legitimate. Nevertheless, it is a revelation, not of a God who *shows* himself to human beings (like the gods of paganism) but of a God who *speaks* to them and, in speaking to them, teaches them the law of justice. Only in the practice of justice is the relation to the truly invisible God perfected, and it is as ethics not as theology that this God's teaching is best understood. This, he insists, is the only possible basis for a genuinely *adult* religion.[62]

If there is a simple epitome of this teaching, it is (for Lévinas) the commandment, 'You shall not kill'. Such a commandment does not depend for its

---

[61] *Totalité et infinité*, 52.

[62] Several of these key points clearly involve a differentiation of what Lévinas regards as the distinctively Jewish understanding of revelation not only from paganism but also from Christianity.

authority on the superior power of the one who commands, but on the infinity of the appeal that the face of the other makes to me. This infinity is nothing supernatural, it remains entirely terrestrial and, as such, it is the summons to 'non-violence par excellence'.[63] The same teaching is epitomized in the saying of Dostoevsky's saintly Elder Zosima that 'each of us is guilty before everyone for everyone, and I more than the others', which Lévinas frequently cited.[64] The spontaneous self-assertion of the natural ego and the more radical individualism of the disenchanted, atheistic self are both alike held 'hostage' by their obligation to the other. In this way, the exigency of justice calls to a re-envisioning of history, to an understanding of history as premised on hope, hope 'for the mending of what is irreparable',[65] hope pointing to a future, a time to come that will be an order of liberty, a messianic time that is always future or *à-venir*.

This inevitably too brief résumé of some of the central theses of Lévinasian thinking, whilst showing how Lévinas accepts both the Hegelian and Sartrean challenge to give full weight to the role of the other in the constitution of the self, also shows how he is able to interpret this in such a way as to refuse not only the history of past violence as determinative of historical existence (as Hegel seems to do by claiming that a stable and law-bound social order has subdued humanity's ancient violence) but also the inevitability of violence as a continuing and constitutive element of human relations (as in Sartre). But at what cost? Lévinas is the first to acknowledge that living in the light of the infinite demand of justice is 'difficult'. But sometimes, reading Lévinas, it sounds more than difficult: it sounds impossible. And, if it is really an impossible justice he is asking us to enact, isn't this u-topistic in a too familiarly depressing way, since it points us to a future that is always 'to come' but which never actually comes, a time and a place that is never and nowhere? In the face of such demands, hasn't it become only too evident that the majority response will be to sink back into the comfort zone of spontaneous egoism, cultivating one's own garden and enjoying the world one is at least able to possess? Moreover, by separating ethics from the scientific, social, and humanistic knowledge of human beings' nature and capabilities, doesn't Lévinas make ethics itself somewhat absurd—for what legitimacy can merely societal laws and obligations have in the face of the infinite elevation of the God who commands justice? Isn't Derrida thinking through the tendency of

---

[63] *Totalité et infinité*, 222. However, see the critique by Derrida in J. Derrida, 'Violence and Metaphysics', in idem, *Writing and Difference*, trans. A. Bass (London: Routledge, 2001), 97–192.

[64] For discussion see A. Toumayan, '"I more than the others": Dostoevsky and Levinas', *Yale French Studies*, 104, *Encounters with Levinas* (2004), 55–66. It is important to note that the term translated here as 'guilty' can also bear the sense of 'responsibility', as Toumayan notes.

[65] *Totalité et infinité*, 157.

Lévinasian thought entirely consistently when, in commenting on Kierke-gaard's meditations on the incomprehensibility of the divine command to Abraham to sacrifice Isaac, he states that since 'Every other (one) is every (bit) other,'[66] that is, since every other I encounter is one to whom I owe the duty of absolute responsibility and owe it absolutely, it follows that 'the concepts of responsibility, of decision, or of duty, are condemned a priori to paradox, scandal, and aporia'.[67] 'As soon as I enter into a relation with the gaze, look, request, love, command, or call of the other, I know that I can respond only by sacrificing ethics, that is, by sacrificing whatever obliges me to also respond, in the same way, in the same instant, to all the others.'[68] As Derrida explains, seemingly facetiously, 'How would you ever justify the fact that you sacrifice all the cats in the world to the cat that you feed at home every morning for years, whereas other cats die of hunger at every instant'[69]—or, he asks (and many would think he was now speaking more seriously), how can it be 'ethical' to pursue a career and to enjoy (as well as to fulfil the obligations of) a family life that cannot but require me to turn my face away from the manifold needs that cry out to me from the innumerable multitudes of the world's dispossessed, starving, sick, or otherwise distressed inhabitants? Whatever justification there might be, it would, it seems, have to be (as it was for Abraham) a secret between myself and God, since it is not some-thing I could ever fully or adequately explain at the bar of reason or in terms of the criteria of public accountability.[70] In short, doesn't Lévinas's account need something like a doctrine of love after all, don't we need a reason for wanting to be just, don't we need a motivation for wanting to accept the responsibility of responsibility, don't we need a living bond of mutual communication in order to open the secret of responsibility to a common reflection on what 'we' most need to be doing? To address these questions, we turn now to consider the possibility of understanding the basic relation of self and other as a relation of love.

---

[66] A saying alluding to Lévinas: 'tout autre est tout autre' or 'every other is wholly other', but also to Rudolf Otto's definition of God, in particular the God of biblical revelation, as the 'wholly other'. See R. Otto, *The Idea of the Holy*, trans. J. Harvey (Harmondsworth: Penguin, 1959), 39–44. It had also been one of the catchphrases of early dialectical theology, mirroring Kierkegaard's statement of the 'infinite qualitative difference' between God and human beings.

[67] J. Derrida, *The Gift of Death*, trans. D. Wills (Chicago: University of Chicago Press, 1995), 68.

[68] Ibid.

[69] Ibid. 71.

[70] Ibid. 90ff. where, in addition to the references to (Kierkegaard's) Abraham, Derrida also draws the Sermon on the Mount into the discussion, with especial weight on the injunction to give only ever 'in secret'.

LOVE AND BEING

The question of love has for some time now been haunting this enquiry. In Chapter 1 I noted how Augustinian theology interpreted the restless self's longing for God not only in terms of lack, but also as love, and in Chapter 2 we noted how both Wordsworth and Schleiermacher connect the possibility of retrieving a lost sense of presence with love. The distinction and tension between lack and love can be found both in the Hegelian and Sartrean versions of the encounter with the other and in the various reworkings of this encounter in such thinkers as Marcel, Buber, and Lévinas. Sartre, of course, sees the relationship to the other as determined exclusively in terms of lack and whilst Buber and Marcel offer a vote of confidence in the power of love Lévinas points to a third option, a relation to the other that is not violent but which appeals to the commandment of justice rather than to love. In these terms, whilst Sartre might be characterized as offering a negative ontology, Lévinas's rejection of the primacy of love also requires him to reject ontology. It seems, then, that there is some kind of convergence between the question of love and the question of God and Being. Both questions have long been central to Christian thought (Augustine offers a salient example of this[71]), but if the question of God and Being today strikes us as rather odd, many believers across all main Christian denominations would have no problem with understanding Christian doctrine as the continuing attempt to expound what it means to say 'God is love'. If, as for Lonergan, 'being in love without reserve' completes the movement of which the desire to know and the thirst for Being were preliminary expressions, then how could a Christian reflection on God not move from offering a doctrine of Being to speaking about love? And whilst it is conventional to see Catholic theology as especially emphasizing love and Protestant theology as prioritizing faith, love is by no means absent from the teaching of such key figures of modern Protestant thought as Schleiermacher, Kierkegaard, and Tillich. Moreover, and without yet deciding the relative excellences of love and Being as divine names, it might seem that if we could reach assurance concerning love, then this might also be the best hope there is for reformulating a doctrine of God as Being. For whereas the Sartrean depiction of human relationships as irredeemably violent both confirmed and grounded his conviction as to the impossibility of being-in-and-for-itself, the experience of love would seem to offer a means of crossing the distance that separates self and Being. For if we could know love, and, in

---

[71] And is represented in Christian iconography as holding a flaming heart.

loving, know that this love was true, would we not also then be able to say 'love is' and, in love, find ourselves truly open to Being and made capable of existing in a joyous and abiding experience of the presence of Being?

Even if we limit ourselves in the first instance to love as we know it in human relationships, as an event that is lived in the horizon of our being-in-the-world, this would seem to offer a first and also decisive step. For quite apart from what Scripture itself has to say about the mutual implication of these two loves (love of human beings and love of God), such diverse witnesses as Dante, Schleiermacher, and Kierkegaard (not to mention a great cloud of other known and unknown preachers, poets, and thinkers) all testify to the interrelationship of these two loves. The possibility of a fulfilled and happy love in human relationships would, in this regard, be the surest evidence for and perhaps even an anticipation of fulfilment and joy in the God-relationship. Love may be tongue-tied, incapable of articulating what it really is and wants to say, but, in its dumbness, may it not be the consummation of what articulated speech can never quite say? When we look at one another in love do we not recognize each other as what—or better, as who—we really are? Is love not the resolution of that quest for recognition that Hegel tracked through its distorted and violent forms in the struggles of masters and slaves? And, in Hegel's own thought, was it not precisely the historical revelation of the love of God in the divine humanity of Christ that made possible the ultimate resolution of the dialectics of Being? Is it then the case that we should look to our experiences of human love for assurance as to the reality of our relation to Being? Is it love that will persuade us that beyond or in the depths of our always exploratory, always provisional knowledge of what we encounter in the world it is indeed reality itself, Being, that calls to us?

Many of us know that it is all too easy to be swept off our feet by love and by words of love, and if the statement 'God *is* love' suggests that love is not one attribute amongst others but a definition of the very being of God, we still need to ask whether love could possibly serve as a definition in terms of a 'what' or 'essence'. Even when we know enough of love to know that we are in love, do we ever really know exactly *what* love itself *is*? Dante's vision of God as 'the love that moves the sun and other stars'[72] may give voice to a conviction that the divine love is not merely to be sensed in the affective states of the human soul but is the key to the way God is as creator, i.e., to God's distinct and unique way of being—but can his poetic word be taken as a *definition*, as telling us how things *really are*? Dante's medieval vision grounds

---

[72] *Paradiso*, XXXIII, 145.

love in the divine Being and is envisaged as the means whereby the eternal and immutable divine Being sets the world in motion. But what happens when Being has been unsettled and it is love that is to lead us to the assurance that being really 'is', that is, when Being becomes subordinated to love? Yet if love is what we are seeking, if love is to be our starting point and goal, would it require grounding in anything other than itself? Would a truly pure love need the supplement of Being? Prioritizing love would therefore seem to put Being itself at risk and to raise the question as to whether, if we once have love, ontology is, in the event, needed at all?

Lévinas may or may not have been justified in his anxiety at what he sensed as the 'orgiastic' possibilities of interpreting the I–Thou encounter in terms of love (I think he was not), but Buber himself, whilst accepting and affirming the ecstatic element of love, saw this encounter as also calling for disciplined attentiveness and he interpreted love as inseparable from responsibility. 'Love is responsibility of an I for a Thou', he wrote, adding that this distinguished it from anything that might be reducible to mere feeling.[73] If Buber is right in thus linking responsibility and love, it follows that inscribing love at the heart of the God-relationship need not entail any diminution of the 'adult' quality of that relationship. Nevertheless, precisely if it did prove to be the case that it is love that best reveals who we are, a religious relation centred on love might point us beyond any possible experience of 'Being' in a manner analogous to what Lévinas sees in the ethical relation. For if love is more than—and perhaps even essentially other than—the fusion of self and other, love itself might be what brings about an inner distanciation and differentiation at the heart of the world, pointing us 'beyond Being'. For I can only *love* you if you are indeed another being, whose reality, needs, and sense of self are external to the world of my self-experience.

Lévinas's anxieties about love involving a fusion of self and other in such a way as to preclude the emergence of ethical responsibility were, in this instance, anticipated by Kierkegaard, especially in the latter's collection of fifteen 'upbuilding discourses' on *Works of Love*.[74] Here, Kierkegaard draws attention to the ways in which love, as popularly understood, can all too often be no more than a form of egoism *à deux*, as when the beloved is my 'other self', the one in whom I see myself as I would most like to be. Whether it takes an ethical or a romantic form such love limits itself to 'doing good to those

---

[73] *I and Thou*, 66. A similar link between love and responsibility is drawn by Dostoevsky in *The Brothers Karamazov*—a point that Lévinas passes by, despite his previously noted recourse to the teachings of the Elder Zosima.

[74] Lévinas himself did not recognize this, however. For discussion of his misreading of Kierkegaard see n. 43 above.

who do good to you' (cf. Matt. 5: 46). Kierkegaard develops his critique of the selfishness of this kind of love by means of a twofold distinction. First, he distinguishes between self-regarding and other-regarding forms of love, i.e., between love in which I seek only my own satisfaction and love in which I seek the other's good. Then, he also distinguishes between preferential and commanded love, i.e., between love that arises spontaneously and expresses what I myself want and love that responds to the commandment 'You shall love your neighbour as yourself.' Kierkegaard's argument is that without the external stimulus of the commandment, even such rudiments of other-regarding love that can be found in human relations will always be prone to being reabsorbed, as it were, by the spontaneous egoism of self-regarding love. These distinctions—which Kierkegaard makes in often complex and nuanced ways—were systematized and hardened in Anders Nygren's *Agape and Eros*, a work that had a very significant impact on mid-twentieth-century religious thought. The nub of this distinction is pinpointed when Nygren compares the respective motivations of erotic and agapeistic kinds of love in relation to 'the neighbour': 'Eros does not seek the neighbour for himself; it seeks him insofar as it can utilise him as a means for his own ascent . . . Agape-love is directed to the neighbour himself, with no further thought in mind and no sidelong glances at anything else.'[75] Moreover, although Nygren does not emphasize the role of the commandment in exactly the same way as Kierkegaard, he is no less categorical in insisting that it is precisely the God-relationship that not only explains the difference between these two types of love but makes it possible for agapeistic love to exist at all, since this is the love that is revealed in the self-sacrificing love of God himself, as that is witnessed in the New Testament.[76]

Yet are these distinctions, whether in the form given them by Kierkegaard or by Nygren, as hard and fast as they seem? Of course, life and literature offer innumerable examples of the often highly devious ways in which erotic love very frequently serves a more or less naive self-interest. In this connection, Kierkegaard's hermeneutics of suspicion can reveal many unpleasant truths about what is often called love and call us to a more sober assessment of what is really going on in our relationships.[77] Yet Kierkegaard himself seems to offer at least some examples of how spontaneous and even preferential love can become the basis for or transformed into something approximating a fully

---

[75] A. Nygren, *Agape and Eros*, trans. P. S. Watson (London: SPCK, 1953), 214–15.

[76] Nygren also makes this distinction the key to a reading of church history, in which it is the achievement of the Reformation to have rediscovered the agape principle after it had become synthesized and confused with the eros principle in Patristic and medieval thought.

[77] This is how *Works of Love* is used in Amy Laura Hall, *Kierkegaard and the Treachery of Love* (Cambridge: Cambridge University Press, 2002).

other-regarding love.[78] In *Works of Love* itself he discusses the 'work of love' in remembering the dead, showing how we might allow the memory of someone we love to contribute to ordering and directing our lives. In such remembrance something of the eternal is able to enter into human love, he suggests. But this proposal presupposes that we have, in fact, loved the person who has died and would want them to have the kind of role that we now create for them. Elsewhere, one of the most recurrent figures of Kierkegaard's later authorship is the 'sinful woman' of Luke 7, who, falling at Christ's feet while he is having dinner in the house of Simon the Pharisee, washing them with her tears and wiping them with her hair, receives forgiveness of her 'many' sins 'because she loved much'. Yet, as Kierkegaard's various treatments of her show, this love is not commanded, but comes from a spontaneous sense of needing what she sees in Christ.[79] More generally, if we understand erotic love against the background of the self seeking itself in and through its recognition by the other, this may be interpreted so as to emphasize the egoism of the seeking self, but it also suggests that such a self will not find itself again and achieve its (selfish) end unless it is able to see the other as other and, in some way, to accept at least some elements in the other's view of it that are not reducible to the mere reflection of its own self-projection onto the other. On this view, erotic love would be the motor, the moving force, that projected the self into a situation in which it would be challenged to review its own self-assessment and the legitimacy of its own projects. This would also involve it in having to attend to the needs and interests of the other and perhaps in such a way as to require it to recognize and to wish for the good of the other as the obverse of its desire for the satisfaction of its own good. Against the endless oscillation between sadism and masochism depicted by Sartre, we would then have the possibility of a virtuous circle of love. As Kierkegaard put it, by presupposing love in the other, i.e. by presupposing that the other is motivated in his or her actions (including his or her actions towards me) by love, I do in fact enable the other to love.[80]

Interpreted in this way, Kierkegaard's teaching in *Works of Love* is in significant continuity with the medieval tradition, for which it was customary to distinguish between the love (*amor*) with which the soul sought God for its own benefit and the charity (*caritas*) whereby it began to love God for his own sake, because he is lovable. The transition from the one to the other may be

---

[78] The positive role of erotic or preferential love in *Works of Love* has recently been argued for in Sharon Krishek, *Kierkegaard on Faith and Love* (Cambridge: Cambridge University Press, 2009).

[79] For further discussion see my *Kierkegaard's Upbuilding Discourses* (London: Routledge, 2002), especially 202–10.

[80] See *Works of Love*, especially part II, discourse 1, 'Love Builds Up'.

dramatic. William of Saint-Thierry describes how, as the soul gives itself more and more to its longing for God, it reaches a point in which it is simply overwhelmed by its love. At this point the soul is 'slain' by the 'sweet sword' of love (*amor*) and experiences for itself what Paul meant when he spoke of being crucified with Christ. In the light of this experience, the soul is no longer centred in itself but finds itself in its charity towards God, a transformation that also allows it to become utterly available for the neighbour.[81] More accommodatingly, Francis of Sales describes how even a love that is merely covetous may nevertheless be gradually transformed into a 'holy and well-ordered covetousness', in which one still loves God for love of one's self, i.e., because of one's own neediness, but no longer for love of one's self. Self-love (*amour propre*) is still there, 'but only as a simple motif, and not as the main end'.[82] In this spirit, self-love is ordered through a sequence of loves (of servants, friends, father, Prince) that are marked by a transition from mere utility (servants), through mutual responsibility (friends), to a relation of honour in which the ego has become subordinate to the other—although the relation is still one of spontaneous love (in relation to my father or my Prince, I should not strictly say 'he is my father or Prince', but 'I am his').[83]

The interdependence of eros and agape is illustrated from another side by the remark of Jankélévitch, directed against the view (such as that of Lévinas) that justice requires the suspension of love if it is to be truly just, i.e., truly indifferent to personal bias and truly attentive to objective needs. Jankélévitch writes, 'love is the will of justice, this inspiration of an eloquent and ingenious good-will that is the only sufficient reason for being disinterested, the only permanent guarantee of peace'.[84] In other words, the just person must love justice, if justice is really to be done. Whilst I might grudgingly fulfil the commandment to love (and such a grudging fulfilment might, of course, be better for my neighbour than if I did nothing at all), there must be someone who loves the commandment, someone who wants the commandment to be fulfilled if I am to be persuaded to do it against my own recalcitrant will. Or else, the fact that I do it, even though I do it grudgingly, may actually show that I do, after all, love the commandment, I do love to love, and this love is, in the event, more powerful than whatever it is that makes me not want to do it. Justice therefore points us back, once

---

[81] See William of Saint-Thierry, *De natura et dignitate amoris*, in F. Zambon (ed.), *Trattati d'amore cristiani del XII secolo* (bi-lingual edition), vol. i (Turin: Fondazione Lorenzo Valla, 2007), especially 98–9.

[82] St François de Sales, *Traitté de l'amour de Dieu*, vol. i, in *Œuvres de Saint François de Sales*, vol. iv (Annecy: J. Niérat, 1894), 144.

[83] *Traitté de l'amour*, 145.

[84] V. Jankélévitch, *Les Vertus et l'amour*, vol. ii (Paris: Flammarion, 1986), 138.

more, to love and, as Jankélévitch argues, occasionally referring to another Kierkegaardian text, *Purity of Heart*, to an essentially unconditional intention *to love*. Such a love—and we can certainly feel Lévinas's anxiety levels rising!—will indeed have something 'hyperbolic' about it; it will be passionate, exclusive, motiveless, almost mad, almost messianic, pointing beyond calculation, balance, and order to something 'wholly other', breaking open the order of grace.[85]

Whether the near-delirium of Jankélévitch's prose is a sign that we are approaching the 'orgiastic' confusion of self and other that Lévinas so feared in Buber, it is certainly clear that there is something paradoxical in the account of love he is giving us. For if he sees love as presupposing freedom, choice, and the will to love, he also sees it as a miracle, exceeding the power and control of reason and transcending the ordered world of socially definable freedoms and obligations. Even when it is expressive of a will to love, love is not simply a matter of 'will', least of all of the rational will of Kant, Fichte, and Hegel. Rather, it is the disposition of the heart, a kind of intentionality that is not so much chosen by its subject as constitutive of the very being of that same subject. If I am truly to love, I must be in love or must be loving: it is *I* that must love and not a part of me, my mind, my body, or my will—and it is just this totality of involvement that is meant by 'the heart'. But, as in the doctrines of Francis of Sales and Fénelon (to whom Jankélévitch frequently refers for illustration), the total focusing of intention in the loving heart is far from being a simple heightening of the ego. On the contrary, it seems to catapult the self beyond all the possible motivations and calculations of self-seeking, and, at the same time and in the same degree, beyond its habitual sense of self-identity. The 'self' that loves is a self radically stripped of self-indulgence and self-satisfaction. As Jeanne de Chantal, reflecting the teaching of Francis of Sales, wrote: 'There are souls amongst those whom God conducts along this path of simplicity, whom the divine bounty denudes of all satisfaction, desire, and sentiment in such an extraordinary way, that they can scarcely support or express themselves, because what is going on in their inner self is so thin, so delicate and imperceptible—so that they can be at the extreme point of the spirit—that they do not know how to talk about it.'[86] Such love, as Jankélévitch understands it, loves the other simply because the other is there to be loved and does so not because of any virtue in the other

---

[85] Ibid. 230–45.

[86] Quoted in H. Brémond, *Histoire littéraire du sentiment religieux en France depuis la fin des guerres de religion jusqu'à nos jours*, vol. ii (Paris: Blou and Gay, 1923), 556. It is not implausible to see Simone Weil as a modern representative of the kind of inner experience being described by Jeanne de Chantal, especially in the light of her writing on detachment, self-effacement, and decreation (see, e.g., the treatment of these topics in Simone Weil, *Gravity and Grace*, trans. E. Craufurd (London: Routledge and Kegan Paul, 1963).

nor because of any reason in oneself such that one *should*—and still less because of any advantage one might see for oneself in doing so. It is just what happens. It is the pure intention of love.

But, to repeat an earlier question, doesn't such a prioritizing of love dissolve the need for any supplementary ontology? Would a really pure love, a love perhaps purer than any we can conceive, need to say anything about 'being' at all? Isn't an 'ontology of love' maybe a contradiction in terms? If the movement of love might be capable of traversing the distance that separates the self from its true Being, would it want to? Wouldn't that be a distraction from—love itself?

In support of the view that love might be happy just to let go of 'Being', we might note the following points. First, even in the minimal form reported by Jeanne de Chantal, there remains a dimension of freedom and of choice, i.e., of self-conscious subjectivity, in the loving self and therefore (on the basis of the preceding analyses) a certain distancing of the self from Being.[87] In the second place, when directed towards human beings, love seems no longer to be determined by the nature of its 'objects'. In contrast to love understood as the fulfilment of the dialectics of recognition, this love is no longer a matter of seeing each other for what we truly are. Instead, the love that we are now describing seems to forget what it might have learned in such moments of recognition. This love does not love the other for what or who he or she is. Even if the other is 'really' unworthy of being loved, this 'extreme' love loves anyway. It is for this reason that Jankélévitch affirms the excess of love over equity, arguing that even if love moves me to give to a beggar who is, in fact, deceiving me as to his poverty, love is nevertheless justified since it gives to the man and not to what the man presents himself as.[88] Yet, thirdly (though Jankélévitch does not himself discuss this), this example also shows that love itself, its meaning and its truth, will always be 'in play' in the relations of selves and others. Even if its truth is guaranteed by the intention of the heart, the total meaning of an act of love does not finally escape the general configuration of relationships of which it is a part. I love not just in order to satisfy my need to love, but in the hope of contributing to the transformation of human relationships in the light of and to the end of love's final triumph in human affairs. That this triumph remains, perhaps, distant does not invalidate present, provisional acts of love, but it does mean that they lack a certain

---

[87] Similarly, even though Weil's emphasis on decreation seems to involve the annihilation of subjective agency, she equally insists that we must freely consent to it, i.e., we must *obey* necessity and are not merely compelled by it. Only so can the divine–human relationship be figured as love—a point which is central to her spiritual vision.

[88] *Les Vertus et l'amour*, 258.

completeness, that they are never, as yet, all they could or might be. Each act of love is a kind of appeal to a future consummation, an 'End' still to come. And this, fourthly, indicates that love too has an intimate relation to time. 'Love is not love that alters when it alteration finds,' but there is scarcely an experience of love in which its 'truth' is not, however implicitly, to be tested by time. Whether it is the spontaneous pledge on the part of two lovers that they will belong to one another 'forever' or whether it is the plea of the injured man to his helper to 'stay with me', love cannot be abstracted from time—which, in most human scenarios, means from the struggle with time, a struggle to vindicate 'love in time's despite', as the title of a poem by Edwin Muir puts it.

With regard to the role of self-conscious intentionality, the excess of love over the nature of its object, the involvement of love in the relations of selves and others, and love's voluntary or involuntary exposure to the test of time, it therefore seems that love by no means escapes the tensions and ambiguities of the distancing of self and Being that we have been exploring in the last few chapters. If we believe that, in love, we truly become who we are and 'find' our true Being—a revelation, perhaps, 'beyond' anything that mere knowledge could tell us—such a discovery will itself have to submit to the humbling rubric of distance: the self that is revealed in love will never simply be the self that I am but the self that I could possibly be or become, if I were to stay true to that revelation. And, finally, what this revelation reveals will, in all likelihood, be something that I can only speak of in fumbling, misleading, or, at any rate, inadequate terms. Souls who love, as Mme de Chantal put it, 'do not know what to say'. If Shakespeare's Cordelia was arguably mistaken in believing that love had to be silent, many of his other heroines (Viola, Rosalind, etc.) knew that being true to love often meant having to say just the opposite of what they might have wanted to say—or that all they were able to say was far from being all that was in their hearts to say. And other writers multiply the tale. If love is what most naturally and spontaneously calls forth poetry, nothing is harder to write about than love—and as for the poets themselves, their testimony is not always to be trusted, as Kierkegaard is assiduous in pointing out. For, as he argued, what is decisive in love is not what we are able to say about it: love is born in the hidden depths of the heart, but insofar as it is knowable it all, it is by its fruits and not by the words with which we present those fruits. As we have already heard him say, there is not a word that cannot become a word of love, and not a word that incorrigibly demonstrates that love is present. Sometimes even the harshest word may be uttered for the good of the hearer, whilst, conversely, the Grand Inquisitor of Dostoevsky's tale tells us that he 'corrected' Christ's teaching out of love for human beings, a comment that suggests that the language of love can even be used to justify the greatest of crimes. Love—if we are to speak of it at all—cannot be disentangled from the dialectics of language and representation that distance our human experience from the presence and plenitude of Being and cannot be appealed to as resolving these dialectics apart from the actual experience of love and the acceptance of the responsibility that such experience brings with it.

In the last chapter, I sought to show how language is bound up with the relations of selves and others in such a way that the struggle to speak truly of love, to speak love's truth, points us back, once more and from another angle, to the world of human relations so that it is only in the light of loving human relationships that it becomes truly possible to speak truly of love. The preceding paragraphs suggest something of the challenges that such an undertaking must face even with regard to what we call personal relationships. Can it, then, be possible to do even more, to expand our faith in love beyond the personal sphere until it grows into a hope that society as a whole might be transformed in the name and image of love? Could love ever become the foundation of a human community in such a way that we might look to the advent of 'one great fellowship of love throughout the whole wide earth', a 'family of man' that would embrace and include all within its loving arms? That, it might be said, is the hope invested in the Church itself, a communion of saints characterized by the love they show to one another, but it is also a hope that even in Christian theology (and, perhaps, already in Hebrew prophecy) looks beyond ecclesiastical or faith-community forms to a political order in which power and justice might become subordinated to love or in which love, power, and justice would be integrated in the fullness of God's Kingdom.[89] Were that to come about, would we not then know who we really were, would we not have entered into an adequate and joyous relation to our own being, would we not have become, at last, fully human, perhaps (recalling Marx's designation of history this side of the classless society as mere *prehistory*), fully human for the first time? If charity is sometimes 'cold', relations in such a fully humanized community would have the warmth of love and friendship.

Perhaps it is for this reason that Pavel Florensky insisted that 'The greatest agapic love is realizable only in relation to friends, not in relation to all people, not "in general".' And, he adds, this 'greatest agapic love consists in the laying down of one's soul for one's friends', not just in the sense of being ready to die for them, but in being ready for 'the sacrifice of one's entire organization,

---

[89] On the relations of love, power, justice, and Being see P. Tillich, *Love, Power and Justice* (London: Oxford University Press, 1954).

one's freedom and calling. He who wishes to save his soul must lay it all down for his friends, and his soul will not live again if it does not die.'[90]

An analogous hope that the final goal of human community is more than justice would seem also to be reflected in the inclusion of 'fraternity' in the revolutionary slogan of 'liberty, equality, and fraternity'—as if to acknowledge that the formal principles of liberty and equality could only truly work and could only be sustained if they were infused with a spirit of brotherly love. Noting (as does Derrida) but not dwelling on the gender limitations of this slogan, we might glimpse here a multiplying network of associations, in which love becomes interpretable not only in terms of eros and agape, or passion and charity, but as friendship, fraternity, sorority, and amity. But can there be what Derrida called a 'politics of friendship'?[91] Where, in a world that certainly does not exemplify the universal rule of love, are the friends to be found who might enact such a politics? Derrida conducts his enquiry into the possibility of such a politics in the light of a saying attributed to Aristotle, 'O my friends, there is no friend.' As he shows, this teasing saying can be taken many ways, but it nicely epitomizes the challenge: how might we—could we ever—proceed from a world in which there are no friends or in which friendship exists only in unstable, ambiguous, or distorted forms to a world of genuine and universal fraternity? We might not wish to endorse the politics of the Nazi jurist Carl Schmitt, but, as Derrida acknowledges, Schmitt's definition of the political as hinging on the power of the sovereign to define the common enemy is a chillingly persuasive epitome of politics as we know it. If we are in a world defined by such a politics of enmity, how might it be transformed into a politics of friendship? Certainly not by a politics that substituted the class enemy for the national enemy, nor yet the substitution of the ideological enemy by the religious or civilizational enemy. Derrida notes also how Nietzsche's Zarathustra addresses himself to the task of creating a community of friends and does so as an intentional parody of Christ's creation of a community of disciples—yet even if Nietzsche's intention is parodic, Zarathustra's own aim seems to have been anticipated by Christ's statement in John 15: 5 that the disciples are 'disciples' no longer, but friends. But whether in an anti-Christian or a Christian form, Derrida believes that a politics of friendship is, for now, still 'to come', still a messianism awaiting its time. But as long as such a politics is still awaiting its time, the testimony of love to Being must remain distant, weak, and ambiguous. However, this does not so much amount to a call for reasserting the priority of Being over love

---

[90] P. Florensky, *The Pillar and Ground of the Truth*, trans. B. Jakim (Princeton: Princeton University Press, 1997), 326.

[91] See J. Derrida, *Politics of Friendship*, trans. G. Collins (London: Verso, 1997).

but rather weakens the claim of Being still further, since the coming of the Kingdom of Being is now dependent on what, in itself, is only weak and ambiguous.

But is Derrida right in insisting that such a community of friendship and love can only ever be 'still to come'? Take the model of community associated with the term *sobornost*, one of the key ideas of the Russian religious philosophy of the early twentieth century.[92] Whatever the authentic basis for the idea in the life and theology of the Eastern Church, *sobornost'* was taken by these Russian religious philosophers to be a kind of community in which the personality of the individual was subordinated neither to hierarchical nor to other objective or external constraints. Whilst the future is not necessarily absent from the vision of *sobornost'*, this is not where its centre truly lies. Rather, it was envisaged as a community in which, as articulated by, e.g., Berdyaev,[93] the free encounter of 'I' and 'Thou' was spontaneously deepened and expressed in the 'We', each preserving their distinctive individuality (as, perhaps, in Bakhtin's view of concrete relationships as built up of 'I-for-myself', 'the other-for-me', and 'I-for-the other'). Against the modern Western conception of the self as an isolated ego, Berdyaev asserts that 'Love and friendship are man's only hope of triumphing over solitude' and only love and friendship offer the hope of a community that is not merely a society but a communion.[94] Such a community may be symbolized in eschatological terms, but it is better conceived of in terms of a kind of super-history, a history of human beings' spiritual existence that is always related to but never arrives in any given moment of historical time. As such it is a past and present as well as a future reality and can therefore be expressed as tradition—although, for Berdyaev, tradition of this kind never comes with the weight of authority but can only ever exist as a memory of and an appeal to freedom. 'Tradition is a supra-personal and *soborny* experience, the creative spiritual life transmitted from generation to generation, uniting the living and the dead and thereby overcoming death... tradition is the memory which brings resurrection, the victory over corruption, the affirmation of eternal life.'[95]

---

[92] Both *sobornost'* and friendship are also used to interpret the meaning of a community of love by Jankélévitch. See *Les Vertus et l'amour*, 286–7.

[93] For a brief statement of what Berdyaev means by *sobornost'* and its historical background see, e.g., N. Berdyaev, *The Russian Idea*, trans. R. M. French (London: Geoffrey Bles, 1947), 163–6;

[94] N. Berdyaev, *Solitude and Society*, trans. G. Reavey (London: G. Bles, 1938), 89. NB, it is not accidental that Bakhtin uses the same liturgically charged terms for participation and communion in his account of language in *The Philosophy of the Act* as Berdyaev uses here (see previous chapter).

[95] N. Berdyaev, *Freedom and the Spirit*, trans. O. F. Clarke (London: Geoffrey Bles, 1944), 331. *Soborny* is an adjective related to *sobornost'* and is the term used in the Eastern Churches' creed translated in the Western tradition as 'Catholic'.

Such memory, he says in many places, is 'creative', it 'is not a conserving but a creatively transfiguring memory. It wishes to carry forward into eternal life not that which is dead in the past but what is alive' and, as such, it is a pledge that 'the last word belongs not to death but to resurrection'.[96] In a manner that might bear some comparison with Heidegger's view of the poetic word as conveying what is essential in the past into the present in such a way as to direct us to what is also essential in the present, Berdyaev states that 'The past which lives on in the memory of the present is . . . a transfigured past, which our creative acts have helped to reintegrate into our present. Memory is not merely the conservation of the resurrection of the past; it implies creative innovation and the creative transfiguration of the past.'[97] In contrast to Heidegger, however, Berdyaev emphasizes that receiving and understanding what has been delivered from the past is more a matter of freedom and creative transformation than of simply attending or listening to the truth of Being to which the poetic (or, in this case, prophetic) word testifies. Such a *sobornost'*-community is eschatological and, to that extent, *à-venir*, but by virtue of the creative and transfiguring power of memory it is also a community in which I am able to participate now, in the present, and to do so as 'in communion' with all those who have similarly participated in it in the past.

Yet, not unlike Derrida, Berdyaev sees no need to ground such a community in any specific ontology and he typically presents his thought as a philosophy of freedom in opposition to any possible ontology. Being, he argues, is a mental construction devoid of reality: 'Being,' as he puts it, 'does not exist.'[98] Worse still, 'Slavery to being is indeed the primary slavery of man.'[99] The reason for this is precisely because of the inadequacy of Being in relation to understanding the meaning of personal, subjective existence and life. 'The being of ontology,' he says, 'is a naturalistically conceived being, it is nature, it is substance, but not an entity, not personality, not spirit, not freedom.'[100] Aware of the difficulties of stripping language of apparently ontological claims, he adds that 'Being as a subject means something entirely different [from being as an object] and ought to have another name. Being as subject is personal existence, freedom, spirit.'[101] Elsewhere he distinguishes two types of philosophy, in one of which freedom takes priority over Being whilst in the other Being takes precedence over freedom, to which he comments that 'I, personally, have made my choice:

[96] N. Berdyaev, *Slavery and Freedom*, trans. R. M. French (London: Geoffrey Bles, 1943), 111.
[97] *Solitude and Society*, 100.
[98] *Slavery and Freedom*, 78.
[99] Ibid.
[100] Ibid. 80.
[101] Ibid.

I have resolutely chosen . . . the primacy of freedom over Being.'[102] On this basis the communion of 'I's and 'Thous' in the 'We' of *sobornost'* would be neither describable nor explicable in terms of nature, history, or ontology. Love's fulfilment and love's true meaning would lie outside of and beyond Being.[103] Whether it is because it is always still 'to come' (Derrida), or whether because it exists only as a creative yet commemorative transfiguration of what is given in time (Berdyaev), the ideal of a community of friendship and love seems not primarily interested in making or keeping ontological promises.

Of course, it might be objected that without ontological grounding a doctrine of love will evaporate in a mist of good intentions. To which we might respond with Jankélévitch by asking what love could possibly be if it was once dissociated from good intentions. Deciding for love cannot wait on the revelation of Being nor is love a proof or demonstration of Being as such. Therefore, if we continue to speak of the coming of such a community as fulfilling or revealing who we really are, then we do so in, with, and under all the limitations that inhere in the distance of every hope, every articulated word, and every human relation from Being-Itself. But if we then think of love as revealing what is more properly basic than Being, such that Being-Itself only comes to be by the grace of love, does it follow that Being—no matter how weakened by the loss of its foundational status—has no role in the economy of love? But how might love ground Being? What would—what could—this mean? And what kind of Being might such love bestow or allow?

One way of answering this question would be to have recourse to the kind of mythologizing of metaphysical reflection that we find in Jakob Boehme and to speak of the *Ungrund* or abyss prior to Being in which the divine life itself is born as love. Via Schelling and Soloviev this was an important element in

---

[102] *Solitude and Society*, 18. Another example is the critique of 'ontological philosophy' (under which he includes both Hegel and Heidegger) in his *The Beginning and the End*, trans. R. M. French (London: Geoffrey Bles, 1952), 104–17, a critique largely based on Jakob Boehme's theory of the Ungrund.

[103] An analogous view to that of Berdyaev, but less polemically phrased, is John Zizioulas's distinction between an ontology of substance and an ontology of personal freedom. See J. Zizioulas, *Being as Communion* (London: Darton, Longman and Todd, 1985). Here, for example, Zizioulas states that 'The manner in which God exercises His ontological freedom, that precisely which makes Him ontologically free, is the way in which he transcends and abolishes the ontological necessity of the substance . . .' (*Being as Communion*, 44). In this regard we may say that Berdyaev is true to the Platonizing tendency of Eastern Christian thought, which here follows Plotinus in locating the decisive *Seinsdifferenz* not in the distinction of created or uncreated Being, nor even of finite and infinite Being, but of noetic and sensuous Being (*ousia*), i.e., between Being endowed with self-consciousness and Being that simply (and, we might say, 'merely') *is*. Self-conscious Being—personal Being in Berdyaev and Zizioulas's sense—is therefore spoken of as 'Being' only in an analogous or homologous sense. See Plotinus, *Ennead* VI, 1.

Berdyaev's account of the primacy of freedom over Being. Drawing on both Boehme and Berdyaev, Luigi Pareyson made the essential point in somewhat cooler terms when he pointed out that whilst Heidegger spoke of how speech brings the world of mortals into being he did not speak of this as involving the choice between good and evil or the call to love the neighbour in their unique singularity.[104] But that kind of answer—which can be read as providing a bridge between classical metaphysics and more recent post-metaphysical thought[105]—gives only the most abstract of formulas, even if it also has a certain poetic or mythic expressiveness. To put it in the terminology of *Being and Time*, such claims still require an adequate phenomenological account of how they might be revealed or how they might work out in the thick detail of human existence. Once we come down from the metaphysical heights, where in such existence might we look to find or to vindicate the triumph of love? Are mortals who are characterizable in terms of finitude, ignorance, and errancy capable of knowing such love? Can a love that is always *à-venir* also become incarnate?

These questions remind us that the human beings whose consciousness opens up an ever-expanding network of distances marked by time, space, language, and relationality are also—and perhaps most basically—corporeal or bodily beings. It is therefore to an examination of embodiment and the implications of embodiment for our relation to Being that we now turn.

---

[104] See the discussion in L. Pareyson, *Ontologia della libertà* (Turin: Einaudi, 1995), 463 ff.

[105] In this regard I note the importance of Pareyson in the development of Vattimo's weak thought.

6

Embodiment

THE PRIMACY OF THE BODY

The meaning of the distance that separates the self from the truth of its being has been shown to be indissociable from the kind and quality of its relations to others in such a way that the possibility of interpreting existence in terms of a relation to Being-Itself becomes dependent on the utopian possibility of a fully realized community of love, friendship, or *sobornost'*. In the phrase of Emmanuel Mounier, 'the kingdom of Being is amongst us'.[1] But we have had reason to question whether such a community of love is appropriately described as a kingdom of *Being*. If, as Berdyaev maintained—and Derrida's politics of friendship also seems to imply—its advent is dependent on the free mutual choice of all who participate in it (the kingdom will come only when prayed for from the hearts of all), then it would seem no longer to be a kingdom of Being but a kingdom founded on a more original non- or pre-ontological freedom. However, whilst the role of freedom might indeed signal a significant distancing or weakening of the direct relation to Being to which advocates of Romantic presence aspired it might still be possible to understand this as refiguring rather than straightforwardly denying that relation. Even Berdyaev seems to acknowledge something like this when, in *Solitude and Society*, he describes the personality as 'immersed' in Being. Here, it seems, 'the depths of existence' are effectively identified with 'immersion in Being' and religion is said to be 'man's revealed life, his life in the depths of Being'.[2] 'We must affirm the primacy of integral man,' he asserts, 'of man rooted in the very heart of Being, as against the consciousness of the confrontation of subject and being'.[3] Yet although Berdyaev now seems to subscribe to

---

[1] E. Mounier, *Introduction aux existentialismes*, in *Œuvres*, iii: *1944–50* (Paris: Éditions du Seuil, 1962), 165 ff.

[2] N. A. Berdyaev, *Solitude and Society*, trans. G. Reavey (London: G. Bles, 1938), 7.

[3] Ibid. 31.

the possibility of there being some kind of intuition of Being, this is still an intuition that cannot find any single adequate objective form. The existential subject participates in Being, but precisely this presence of the subject within Being shows Being itself to be internally differentiated, as when Berdyaev speaks of 'a transcendence of being operative in the heart of Being'.[4]

In the preceding chapter I questioned how it might be if Being were to be only by the grace of love and asked what kind of Being love might bestow or allow? Quite concretely, *where* and *how* might such Being be made manifest to us? One answer, which might be said to be so obvious as to be constantly overlooked (as it is constantly overlooked by philosophers, theologians, and other thinkers), is, simply, the body. For where else might love become manifest if not in the life of the body? And who is the being whose restless questioning of existence was the starting point of this whole enquiry if not an embodied being, whose existence, life, and whole sensibility is inconceivable other than as a bodily life-form?[5]

Certainly this was not forgotten by such personalist thinkers as Berdyaev, Mounier, and Marcel. Even if Berdyaev is not consistent as to whether the affirmation of Spirit involves the denial of Being he is consistent in emphasizing that the affirmation of Spirit does not require us to reject or denigrate the body. He is clear that the 'flesh' to which the New Testament opposes the life of the Spirit is not to be equated with the physical body but with sin, a point that he sees as especially clearly stated in the assertion that the only unforgivable sin is the sin against the Spirit.[6] Spirit is not only divine, 'it is also divinely human, divinely worldly',[7] and the process of theogony is inseparable from the concrete existence in the world of divine humanity. As will Lévinas, he

---

[4] Ibid. 43.

[5] The term 'embodied' could seem to imply some sort of spiritual substance that became embodied only at a certain moment in time. Clearly there have been both philosophical and theological views of the human being that have found the centre of our identity in some timeless or sempiternal 'soul' that has only a more or less accidental relation to the body. On such views my real self or soul is not determined by my action or suffering in the world, by the experiences of beauty and pain that sensuous existence alone makes possible. This soul is ultimately separable from my body, and whether in one life or through many loses nothing essential when it passes out of the body. Such a view can, for example, be found in sources as diverse as Plato and the *Bhagavad Gīta*. See, e.g., *Phaedo*, 79B–80E; *Bhagavad Gīta*, II, 11–30. And, as we have already seen, a classical Christianized version of this view is found in Thomas's eschatological vision of the soul that, having sloughed off the earthly body, rests eternally in unchanging contemplation of the divine glory (see Ch. 1 above). As such teachings fully acknowledge—indeed, it is central to their view of what it is to be a self—such a 'soul' has little or nothing in common with the kind of empirical self that many people might spontaneously identify as their real 'me', i.e., the self that enjoys this or that kind of work, leisure, entertainment, or pursuits (as when we say of someone 'He enjoys good wine' or 'She loves riding').

[6] N. A. Berdyaev, *Spirit and Reality*, trans. G. Reavey (London: G. Bles, 1939), 21.

[7] Ibid. 33.

follows Max Picard in seeing the face of the other and the light in the eyes of the other as the primary locus of the call to assume spiritual responsibility toward that face and that light and it is in our acceptance of the responsibility that this vision entails that we pre-eminently discover what it means to exist as freedom and as Spirit.[8] Mounier makes the point with special clarity and force when, at the outset of his study *Personalism*, he writes that 'The human being is a body in the same way [*au même titre*] that he is spirit: entirely "body" and entirely "spirit",' going on to comment that 'Out of his most basic instincts—eating and reproduction—man has made such subtle arts as cuisine and the arts of love.'[9] Personalism is not spiritualism or idealism, but 'I am a person from the most elementary basis of my being upward, and far from bringing about a depersonalization my existence as incarnate is an essential factor in my personal identity.' Or, as Mounier also puts it, ' "I exist subjectively", "I exist bodily" are one and the same experience'—and he is so far from seeing this as a departure from Christianity that he can say 'The indissoluble union of soul and body is the axis of Christian thought.'[10] In Marcel's terminology it is only in being bodily present with or to the other that the exigency of Being can be experienced, and it is only within the horizon of such bodily presence that we can properly understand Marcel's nice comment that my primary relation to Being is not in being-for-myself but being *chez soi*.[11] For Marcel it is further axiomatic that this ontological exigency of a basic openness to the other—of self-transcendence—is, at its deepest, properly experienced also as the exigency of God. 'The exigency of God', he says, is 'simply the exigency of transcendence disclosing its true face.'[12] As in many respects, this personalist convergence on the body as the site of a free encounter with the other in which freedom occurs as the acceptance of mutual responsibility is anticipated by Buber, for whom the bodily encounter with the other is a superlative instance of the I–Thou relationship. This is, for example, especially clear in his description of the various ways in which it is possible to encounter a tree—as a picture, as a movement, as the object of scientific enquiry, as a mathematical construct— culminating, 'if will and grace are joined', in a relation in which the tree ceases to be an It and claims my attention with the exclusiveness characteristic of the Thou. In this moment, Buber says, 'it confronts me bodily': *es leibt mir gegenüber*—'it bodies over against me'.[13]

[8] See, e.g., *Solitude and Society*, 126.
[9] E. Mounier, *Le Personnalisme*, in *Œuvres*, iii. 441.
[10] Ibid.
[11] G. Marcel, *The Mystery of Being*, i: *Reflection and Mystery*, trans. G. S. Fraser (London: Harvill Press, 1950), 118. See discussion in preceding chapter.
[12] Ibid., ii. 3.
[13] M. Buber, *I and Thou*, trans. W. Kaufmann (Edinburgh: T. & T. Clark, 1970), 58.

Such affirmations of embodiment are characteristic of a broad swath of modern thought, and it would be possible to find a similar emphasis in thinkers who are otherwise far apart. Yet exorcizing the 'ghost in the machine' is by no means easy. Arguably, there is a kind of idealism in language itself that constantly lures us back to attributing more independence to the 'subject' than the reality of the case allows. Take the case of Feuerbach, who resolutely proclaimed his commitment to a thorough-going materialism, calling on philosophy to abandon its seemingly innate idealism and instead to reflect on the human condition within the boundaries of bodily experience. In this spirit he exhorted his philosophical contemporaries to 'think in existence', telling them:

Desire not to be a philosopher, as distinct from a man; be nothing else than a thinking man. Do not think as a thinker, that is, with a faculty torn from the totality of the real human being and isolated for itself; think as a real and living being, as one exposed to the vivifying and refreshing waves of the world's oceans. Think in existence, in the world as a member of it, not in the vacuum of abstraction as a solitary monad...[14]

Human beings, he insisted, are entirely defined by their sensuous life: 'The heart does not want abstract, metaphysical or theological objects; it wants real and sensuous objects and beings.'[15] Yet he was almost immediately ridiculed by Max Stirner for populating his own philosophy with what Stirner called ghosts or phantoms, abstractions such as 'Man', 'Love', 'the Heart', that had no real, sensuous existence.[16] Following Stirner, Marx and Engels pointed to the ahistorical nature of Feuerbach's materialism and its failure to engage the real, concrete circumstances in which human beings had to struggle for the satisfaction of even their most basic bodily needs.[17] Language, it seemed, had misled Feuerbach into believing that it was enough to replace the timeless categories of idealism with a rhetoric of materialism.

Really to reflect on human existence from within the limits of embodied life, Feuerbach's critics argued, would call for a very different kind of thinking. Marx offered one such version. But whatever their differences, Feuerbach, Marx, and other nineteenth-century materialists typically sought to show how the complex phenomena of mental life could be explained by simple,

---

[14] L. Feuerbach, *Principles of the Philosophy of the Future*, trans. M. Vogel (Indianapolis: Hackett, 1986), 67. For an interesting comment on the significance of the *Principles* for theology, see 'An Introductory Essay', by Karl Barth, in L. Feuerbach, *The Essence of Christianity*, trans. M. Evans (New York: Harper, 1957).

[15] *Principles*, 54.

[16] See Max Stirner, *The Ego and its Own*, ed. D. Leopold (Cambridge: Cambridge University Press, 1995).

[17] See Karl Marx, 'Concerning Feuerbach', in idem, *Early Writings*, trans. R. Livingstone and G. Benton (Harmondsworth: Penguin, 1975), 421–3.

general laws of a material nature. At the same time, the mechanistic physiology inherited from the French Enlightenment and further developed by English utilitarians enforced a widespread expectation that ultimately the whole range of human thought and sensibility would be reduced to data that would then in turn be explicable through the application of statistical laws—precisely the kind of materialism lampooned by Dostoevsky in *Notes from Underground*. Dostoevsky's 'underground man', obsessed with his liver, the Petersburg weather, and smells, rails against those who try to explain human behaviour and human freedom in terms of universal laws of nature.[18]

'For pity's sake,' they'll shout at you, 'you can't rebel: it's two times two is four! Nature doesn't ask your permission; it doesn't care about your wishes, or whether you like its laws or not. You're obliged to accept it as it is, and consequently all its results as well. And so a wall is indeed a wall . . . etc., etc.,' My God, but what do I care about the laws of nature and arithmetic if for some reason these laws and two times two is four is not to my liking?[19]

A radical and new approach would be offered by Nietzsche, although it seems that he did occasionally subscribe to some kind of physiological reductionism. However, the very thoroughness of Nietzsche's refusal to countenance anything like an immaterial thinking substance paradoxically allowed him to reinstate the kind of mental phenomena that a more scientific materialism regarded as mere epiphenomena. Precisely because mind is nothing but the thinking body, everything that is manifested in mind, in self-conscious life, is, in its own terms, legitimate. The body celebrated by Nietzsche is not a machine but an expressive, living organism. His aim was not simply to explain 'mind' in terms of 'matter' but to get out of the dualism that supposed mind and matter to be two distinct spheres connected by a relationship of cause and effect. Nietzsche sees the joy, the passion, and the desire of the body as being themselves constitutive of reality in such a way that their being expressed in image, metaphor, and poetry does not have to be explained in terms of some higher or more basic order of Being: they are themselves the expressive explanation of what human being is. Or, more precisely, they are themselves the primary revelation of what human life is in the process of

---

[18] I am aware of the important mid-twentieth-century debate about Marx's own 'humanism' and the attempt to separate Marx out from the more mechanistic versions of dialectical materialism promulgated in his name. However, in Russia, and probably elsewhere, the mid- and late nineteenth century saw a broad convergence between the kind of materialism promoted by Feuerbach and a particularly hard-nosed version of empiricism, a combination generally referred to as nihilism (especially when further coupled with revolutionary political activism). See, e.g., A. Walicki, *A History of Russian Thought from the Enlightenment to Marxism*, trans. H. Andrews-Rusiecka (Oxford: Clarendon Press, 1988), especially ch. 11.

[19] F. M. Dostoevsky, *Notes from Underground*, trans. R. Pevear and L. Volokhonsky (London: Vintage, 1993), 13.

becoming, since because there really is only the body, and the body is only a flow of temporal energy, there is no 'Being', no trans-temporal essence that tells us what human life 'is'; there 'is' only the incessant self-expression of life in consciousness. It is in this sense that we might read passages such as the following (from Zarathustra's speech 'On the Despisers of the Body'):

'I am body and soul'—this is how the child speaks. And why should one not speak like children?

But the awakened person, the one who knows, says, 'I am entirely body and nothing beyond that, and soul is only a word for a something connected to the body.

The body is a great reason, a multiplicity with one meaning, a war and a peace, a herd and a herdsman.

Your little reason too is an instrument of your body, my brother: what you call 'Spirit' is a little tool and toy for your great reason.

You say 'I' and are proud of this word. But what is greater—what you don't want to believe in—is your body and its great reason that do not say 'I' but enact 'I'.[20]

On this view, it is not science that is most true to life, but art, and living artistically is the best expression of what is really going on in life. If it was Freud who inherited Nietzsche's method of suspicion in its application to the self-deceptions of morality and religion, it was perhaps Jung who was ultimately the truer Nietzschean by virtue of his openness to the whole range of psychic life and his consequent acceptance of religious and mythological symbols as no less primary than the biological urgings of sexuality. For a consistent Nietzscheanism there is no primary or secondary, there is only the struggle for primacy amongst multiple symbolic transformations of life and the only issue is which is the stronger.[21] Whatever standpoint we occupy or develop, it is only another form of the self-expression of bodily life.

Nietzsche, of course, understood what he was saying as intrinsically destructive not only of religion but also of the philosophical quest for a

---

[20] F. Nietzsche, *Also Sprach Zarathustra*, in F. Nietzsche, *Werke*, ii, ed. K. Schlechta (Frankfurt am Main: Ullstein, 1969), 574.

[21] It is fairly obvious that Nietzsche's representation of this situation in terms of struggle and the conflicts engendered by the will to power is already highly interpretative. But even if this view has a long philosophical lineage (we recall again Heraclitus' dictum that 'war is the father of all things'), as well as deriving considerable plausibility from the facts of history and from a certain Darwinianism, we are also able to consider alternative views, such as those of Jung, for whom psychic life is not fundamentally constituted as adversarial but as tending towards balance, integration, or a dynamic homeostasis. Of course, everything said in Ch. 5 about the uncertainty as to whether it is love or enmity that is ultimately dominant in human life might be repeated here: the Nietzschean 'will to power' must itself survive the challenge of the 'will to concord'. This is all the more pertinent if we understand 'will to power' as intended not in terms of crude physical conflict but as a conflict between different views or expressions of life, such as 'living artistically' versus 'living ascetically'. We should also note that in the quoted passage Nietzsche himself hails the body not only as 'war' but also as 'peace'.

'Being' above, beyond, or behind the phenomenal life of embodied beings. The implication of this position is that the more we understand human life from the perspective of embodiment the less we will want or need to appeal to the idea of Being as the necessary ground or telos of existence. A truly rigorous adhesion to the reality of life would give us no more than what occurs in the 'free play' of becoming, but 'becoming aims at nothing and achieves nothing', Nietzsche wrote.[22] 'Being' is not simply a residue of a supposed 'real world' beyond this world of ephemeral illusion (as he argues in *Twilight of the Idols*[23]), but Being is itself merely a generalized expression for becoming[24]—which, as we have just heard, aims at nothing and achieves nothing and is therefore incapable of giving meaning to anything. In terms of the metaphor of distance that has been a constant point of reference in this enquiry: if self-consciousness, time, language, and relatedness mediate the Being that is sought by actual human subjects in such a way as to put a virtually infinite distance between self and Being, then a perspective originating from within the onward flow of embodied life would seem to demand that we finally let Being go—as Nietzsche himself assumed. All that is left is a chaos that, as the meditation on the death of God puts it, leaves a world unchained from its sun, its centre, and moving simultaneously 'backwards, sideways, forwards, in all directions', with no above or below.[25] Bodily existence is simply the outpouring of sheer becoming, entirely inexplicable in terms of any kind of transcendent Being, divine or merely impersonally absolute.[26]

Although this vision leads Nietzsche to reject both philosophical idealism and Christianity, he seems basically to agree with Plato and Aristotle, Augustine, and Aquinas that the materiality of bodily life is not compatible with a clear and distinct intuition of Being. Indeed, even at the point at which Christian doctrine insists on the resurrection of the body in opposition to Platonic thinking regarding the immortality of the soul, the accounts of the resurrection body in pre-modern theology typically represented it in ways that precisely minimized its 'bodily' character. As we have seen in Chapter 1,

---

[22] F. Nietzsche, *The Will to Power*, trans. W. Kaufmann (New York: Vintage, 1967), 12.

[23] F. Nietzsche, *Twilight of the Idols*, trans. R. J. Hollingdale (Harmondsworth: Penguin, 1968), 40–1 (see also F. Nietzsche, *Götzen-Dämmerung*, in *Werke*, iii, ed. K. Schlechta (Munich: Carl Hanser, 1969)).

[24] F. Nietzsche, *Aus dem Nachlass der Achtzigerjahre*, in *Werke*, iv, ed. K. Schlechta (Munich: Carl Hanser, 1969), 548.

[25] F. Nietzsche, *Die fröhliche Wissenschaft*, in *Werke*, ii, ed. K. Schlechta (Munich: Carl Hanser, 1969), 127.

[26] A religious rewriting of this Nietzschean vision is found in the 'new religion of life' promoted by Don Cupitt in a sequence of books published over the last decade. *Life, Life* (Santa Rosa, Calif.: Polebridge, 2003) and *Above us only Sky* (Santa Rosa, Calif.: Polebridge, 2008) provide effective summaries of this *Lebensreligion*.

classical Christian accounts of the resurrection body depict it as a body no longer subject to change, no longer moved by the promptings of the senses, but focused solely and exclusively on the selfsame unchanging presence of the divine Being. But is such a body still a 'body' in any sense that we can recognize? In the same vein Christian asceticism has mostly denied that the body is as such evil but also has characteristically regarded the body as the seat of temptation: as often, Augustine's *Confessions* provide a classic statement of the case, as, in Book X, he lists sexual desire, eating and drinking, smelling, hearing, and seeing as salient occasions for sin.[27] Nevertheless, despite the general assumption that embodiment and true Being are mutually exclusive, it will be the argument of this chapter that, contra Nietzsche, it is in fact in embodied life-experience that God draws near in such a way as to be name-able as a God who 'is'. This may—we shall see that it does—call for a significant reinterpretation of what we mean by Being and, in connection with that, by speaking of God as Being. At the same time, in the spirit of Berdyaev's invocation of a creative transformation of the past, it also establishes a perspective from within which many dead voices from the religious tradition can once more speak to us and become a part of our present and future thinking about God.

Despite Nietzsche's own application of the principle of embodiment, he may be taken as importantly contributing to breaking the deadlock between idealist and materialist accounts of the body and opening the way to a more phenomenologically attentive approach. Such an approach does not presuppose the dogmatic materialism associated with certain models of reductive science (e.g. Feuerbach, Marx, Freud, and such contemporary reductionists as Dennett[28]). Such models may be valid and applicable within certain limits and their scope and detail are currently expanding with extraordinary rapidity, but their explanations and the interventions based on them (whether for healing or enhancement) do not exhaust all that is given to us in the living self's own self-experience. Whilst each of us is capable of understanding that a given physical state—hunger, sexual excitement, sickness, or disease—will have its specific aetiology and is susceptible of being altered through the application of chemical or other interventions, this physical dimension does not 'explain' what that state *means;* whether, for example, it is experienced as challenging, thwarting, or affirming our sense of self and our life possibilities.

---

[27] *Confessions*, X, 28–35—not that these exclude what Augustine called 'spiritual sins' such as pride. The medieval English spiritual writer Walter Hilton is likewise attentive to the problems of spiritual ills, but this does not prevent him from spending considerable time expounding the image of the five senses as the windows through which temptation enters the soul. See Walter Hilton, *The Ladder of Perfection*, trans. L. Sherley-Price (Harmondsworth: Penguin, 1957).

[28] See, e.g., Daniel Dennett, *Freedom Evolves* (New York: Viking, 2003).

Even though extreme states such as are experienced in the advanced stages of sickness will limit our human options in radical and measurably painful ways, it is clear that the wide range of responses to such states and the possibility of transforming our responses to them indicate that there is something more in play than a simple chain of physiological causes-and-effects. For one person the advent of sickness is a mere restriction of physical powers, to be dealt with by strictly medical means and, for the rest, by trying to get on with life 'as normal'. For another, this may be primarily experienced as an opportunity to reconsider one's aims, values, and relationships, perhaps even (though maybe only after much struggle) to be welcomed.[29] The body that is at issue here is the lived body, the body which I *am*, which I experience myself *as*: not so much the body *in* which as the body *as* which I live and move and have my being in the world.

In order to explore further what this might mean, I shall draw on the development of phenomenology found in Maurice Merleau-Ponty. Merleau-Ponty was neither the first nor the only thinker of the phenomenological tradition to note the centrality of the body. We have, for example, seen how Heidegger's early lectures on *The History of the Concept of Time* identified the moment of being bodily face to face with the intentional object of intuition as the paradigmatic instance of fulfilled intentionality, as when I just stand there looking at the bridge or the tree in my garden. However, this insistence on the embodiedness of existence is rarely thematized in an explicit way in Heidegger's subsequent work. Similarly, the examples we considered in Chapter 2 of claims to an immediate experience of the presence of Being all located that experience in the sphere of bodily encounters with the material presence of the natural world. This did not, however, prove enough to halt the distancing of self and world brought about through reflection and recollection. More steadily focused on the involvement of the body in every moment of

---

[29] The 'Order for the Visitation of the Sick' in the Book of Common Prayer instructs ministers to tell the sick to know 'certainly' that 'for what cause soever this sickness is sent unto you . . . that if you truly repent you of your sins and bear your sickness patiently . . . it shall turn to your profit, and help you forward in the right way that leadeth to everlasting life'. One might think also of St Paul, glorying in his weakness (2 Cor. 11: 30) or of the sickness that enabled Julian of Norwich to 'know more of the physical suffering of our Saviour, and the compassion of our lady and of those who were there and then were loving him truly and watching his pains' (Julian of Norwich, *Revelations of Divine Love*, trans. C. Wolters (Harmondsworth: Penguin, 1966)). Examples could easily be multiplied. In a different context we might think of the large divergences in prospective parents' responses to prenatal screening indicating, e.g., the possibility of the child to be born having Down's syndrome or the debates about what it means to suffer 'disability', i.e., whether these are simply and straightforwardly disadvantages or opportunities for other kinds of experience than what is presumed to be normality.

self-conscious life is Lévinas, for whom work, sexuality,[30] and tending to the bodily needs of the widow, the orphan, and the stranger are integral to the just life required of us by God: it is not the categorical imperative that calls us to the work of justice, but the face of the stranger pleading for our attention.[31] However, the most thorough and most effective phenomenological analysis of the self from the perspective of the lived body was probably that of Maurice Merleau-Ponty and it is therefore to some of the relevant points of his thought that we now turn in order to help us think further about what has been called 'the body's recollection of being'.[32]

A PHENOMENOLOGY OF THE LIVED BODY

If Heidegger judged the essential contribution of Husserlian phenomenology to have been the idea of intentionality, Merleau-Ponty gave greater prominence to the phenomenological 'reduction', the process by which the data of philosophy were 'reduced' to what was simply given in the lived experience of life. But although Husserl developed this reduction in such a way as to focus on knowledge of essences, this was not, according to Merleau-Ponty, in order to consider such knowledge in abstraction from life. Rather, as he put it, 'Husserl's essences are destined to bring back all the relationships of

---

[30] Sexuality was not a particular focus of the discussion of Lévinas in the previous chapter, but see, e.g., *Totalité et infinité*, 162–89 for a discussion of the interrelated themes of habitation, work, and relations between the sexes.

[31] See, e.g., Lévinas's objection to Buber that the latter's account of the relation to the other is too idealistic: 'That saying Thou will always from the beginning and already have passed through my body (right down to the hands that give); that it consequently presupposes my body (qua my own body), things (qua objects of pleasure) and the hunger of others; that the act of saying is thus incarnated, i.e., by means of the speech organs or song or artistic activity; that others are always qua others the poor and bare (at the same time as being my Lord); that the relationship is consequently essentially asymmetrical—these as the positive ideas that guide "my objection".' E. Lévinas, *Noms propres* (Paris: Fata Morgana, 1976), 46. Whether there is really any opposition between Lévinas and Buber on this point is another matter; see above and n. 13.

[32] The phrase is the title of a study by David Levin that uses Heidegger, Jung, and Merleau-Ponty to develop a genial and interesting programme of psycho-social therapy for those suffering the afflictions of modern nihilism. The 'stake' Levin places on his proposal is nothing less than 'our relation to Being as such', which he glosses as ('among other things') 'Our groundedness, our rootedness, our autochthony, our balance and upright stature, our bearing and carriage, our steadiness of gait, our path, and the goals on this path' (D. M. Levin, *The Body's Recollection of Being: Phenomenological Psychology and the Deconstruction of Nihilism* (London: Routledge and Kegan Paul, 1985), 94). Levin's study focuses on concrete therapeutic proposals, but he has some interesting comments on how, despite a great many insightful 'analyses of perceptual and gestural capacities', Heidegger never really incorporates the body into his account of Dasein's Being (ibid. 41ff.).

experience, as the fisherman's net draws up from the ocean quivering fish and seaweed.'[33] In this way phenomenology undercuts the age-old divisions between empiricists and idealists, between those who interpret mental life on the basis of sensation and those who insist on the priority of judgement. It is no longer a matter of seeking the conditions that make experience possible, as in transcendental philosophy, but 'of uncovering the operation which brings [experience] *into reality*, or whereby it is constituted'.[34] In fact, it is impossible entirely to abstract from experience. We do not start from mind and then lead it through reflection towards nature, as in Cartesian doubt, and, according to Merleau-Ponty, Cartesian doubt itself is better understood as 'nature rising to the concept' on the basis of an experience springing up 'without knowing whence it springs'.[35] Much conventional philosophy seems to regard the world as a spectacle and the body as a kind of mechanism used by an impartial and detached mind to view and explain the world, but this opens the way to the reduction of the living body to its physico-chemical properties; moreover, it seems to bear little relation to how we actually do experience the world. Experience is not a compilation of subject, object, and the mechanism of perception but a spontaneous whole: 'In ordinary perception we find a fittingness and meaningful relationship between the gesture, the smile and the tone of a speaker. But this reciprocal relationship of expression which presents the human body as the outward manifestation of a certain manner of being-in-the-world, had, for mechanistic physiology, to be resolved into a series of causal relations.'[36] In other words, if I meet my friend on the street and he smiles at me, I do not infer that he is well-disposed towards me—I simply see a friendly greeting. In order to understand the relationship of self and world, then, we do not need to construct a system of transcendental conditions or to determine the physiological causes of behavioural acts, nor do we need to try to get behind the appearances by rigorous introspection to see what's 'really' going on. We simply need 'to rediscover phenomena, the layer of living experience through which other people and things are first given us'[37] and given in experience as 'a whole charged with immanent meaning'.[38] These programmatic claims recall those of the lectures on *The History of the Concept of Time*, only it is striking that whereas Heidegger's examples concern chalk, bridges, and trees, Merleau-Ponty draws more from the sphere of human relationships. Of course, the point is

---

[33] M. Merleau-Ponty, *Phenomenology of Perception*, trans. C. Smith (London: Routledge, 1962), p. xv.

[34] Ibid. 38.

[35] Ibid. 42. That is, it is 'better' understood like this than when it is portrayed as a consciously and freely adopted method.

[36] Ibid. 55.   [37] Ibid. 57.   [38] Ibid. 58.

not the mere claim, but the adequacy and inherent persuasiveness of the phenomenological description that is to vindicate it. How, then, does Merleau-Ponty see the phenomena, 'the living experience through which other people and things are first given to us'?

First, he directs our attention back to the body. 'The body is the vehicle of being in the world, and having a body is, for a living creature, to be intervolved in a definite environment, to identify oneself with certain projects and to be continually committed to them,' he writes.[39] This is the primary reality from which subject and object, for-itself and in-itself, psychic and physiological are abstracted. The body is not itself to be construed as an object amongst objects, and although it is possible to look at it in that way, as when it is laid out on the dissecting table, this is not the primary form in which we ourselves experience our embodiment. The body is the way in which I communicate with my world, it is 'an attitude directed towards a certain existing or possible task', or 'it is the darkness needed in the theatre to show up the performance'[40]—a striking image, and one to which we shall return. If the body can be represented as an object in objective space, this is only because that space has itself been produced out of the body's own 'ferment'.

Crucial to the concept of the body being developed here is that the body is not simply an inert entity. Rather, it exists in a kind of perpetual motion as a 'centre of potential actions' and oriented towards 'the possible'.[41] This is what Merleau-Ponty calls the 'motor intentionality' of the body, or the body as 'project'. Comparable to what we have already heard both from Heidegger and from Lévinas about the future orientation of the self, Merleau-Ponty too sees the bodily self as intrinsically futural and therefore as not susceptible to being analysed or defined exclusively in terms of its present state or past history. Once this is recognized, psychology will no longer limit itself to seeking the past causes or the present physiological state of the subject's behaviour, but will look for the '*reason* or intelligible condition of possibility for the state of affairs'.[42] As in phenomenology generally, the interpretation of the self is guided by the intentionality that binds the self to its intentional objects; however, Merleau-Ponty especially emphasizes that this is not just a matter of a certain 'mental' attitude but is fundamentally constituted by a bodily movement towards that object. Actual subjects are always already in a world that they engage through their action, 'consciousness is in the first

---

[39] Ibid. 82.   [40] Ibid. 100.   [41] Ibid. 109.

[42] Ibid. 120. This is also related to Merleau-Ponty's view of psychoanalysis, namely, that insofar as it sought to reduce psychology to biology by explaining mental life in terms of sexuality, it missed the true merit of Freud's findings, i.e., that even biology—sexuality—is humanly meaningful (see ibid. 158).

place not a matter of "I think" but of "I can".[43] Expressing the body's intentional involvement with its world, consciousness is not 'in' space or 'in' time, but 'it inhabits space and time'.[44] As such it is the lived 'union of essence and existence'.[45]

In this regard, the basic structure of bodily existence already anticipates the essential project of metaphysics. For, as Merleau-Ponty sees it, metaphysics—understood implicitly as the question of Being—'is not localized at the level of knowledge' (i.e., it does not begin with second-order reflection on problems of knowledge): 'it begins with the opening out upon "another", and is to be found everywhere.'[46] Although the body lives the union of essence and existence, it does so as intentional movement, as projecting itself towards what, in one sense, it has already intuitively apprehended but which it has not yet fully taken up into consciousness. Thinking back to the kinds of examples used by Heidegger, this seems to mean simply that in seeing an object such as a tree, my initial act of seeing it as a tree ('Oh, look—a tree!') already involves in a more or less undifferentiated way what I then distinguish as its defining attributes ('What beautiful flowers it has', 'What interestingly patterned bark', or 'Listen to the nightingale in its branches'). This is a situation in which the subject's bodily involvement (or, as Merleau-Ponty puts it 'intervolvement') in its world means both that we are always already in the midst of the things and relationships that constitute this world whilst, at the same time, we are always extending ourselves beyond them and, thereby, drawing the world itself back into this extended space. Revealed to me only in my forward movement toward, into, and beyond it, the world I experience is always and necessarily incomplete: 'Though I may say that I am enclosed in my present . . . the transcendence of remote experiences encroaches upon my present and brings a suspicion of unreality even into those [experiences] which I believe to be coincident with my present self. Though I am here and now, yet I am not here and now.'[47]

Reminding ourselves that, at this point, Merleau-Ponty is simply discussing the dynamics of perception, we can nevertheless see something of the metaphysical implications to which his argument is pointing. These emerge perhaps even more clearly in his further comment that 'It is thus of the essence of the thing and of the world to present themselves as "open", to send us beyond their determinate manifestations, to promise us always "something else to see". This is what is sometimes expressed in saying that

---

[43] M. Merleau-Ponty, *Phenomenology of Perception*, trans. C. Smith (London: Routledge, 1962), 137.

[44] Ibid. 138.   [45] Ibid. 147.   [46] Ibid. 168.   [47] Ibid. 331.

the thing and the world are mysteries.'[48] Can we interpret this as meaning that even in the most ordinary everyday acts of perception we—we bodily, embodied seeing entities—are already oriented in some inarticulate way towards a certain mystery of Being?

That this might be an appropriate way of reformulating Merleau-Ponty's position seems to be confirmed by his remarks on what he appears to have regarded as a kind of pre-eminent instance of perception: painting. This is because what we see in painting is the outcome of just that movement of immersion-in and transcendence-of, of presence and incompleteness, of here-and-now and not-here-and-now, that is occurring in every actual perception. As he writes, 'painting celebrates no other enigma but that of visibility'.[49] He continues,

The painter's world is a visible world, nothing but visible: a world almost demented because it is complete when it is as yet only partial. Painting awakens and carries to its highest pitch a delirium which is vision itself, for to see is *to have at a distance*; painting spreads this strange possession to all aspects of Being, which must in some fashion become visible in order to enter into the work of art . . . It gives visible existence to what the profane vision believes to be invisible . . . reaching beyond the 'visual givens' [it] opens up a texture of Being of which the discrete sensorial messages are only the punctuations or the caesurae. The eye lives in this texture as a man lives in his house . . . [W]hile he is painting [the painter] practices a magical theory of vision. He is obliged to admit that objects before him pass into him or else that . . . the mind goes out through the eyes to wander among objects . . . the same thing is both out there in the world and here in the heart of vision—the same or, if one prefers, a similar thing, but according to an efficacious similarity which is the parent, the genesis, the metamorphosis of Being in his vision. It is the mountain itself which from out there makes itself seen by the painter; it is the mountain which he interrogates with his gaze.[50]

This process of ceaseless change and transmutation of forms in an endless traffic between self and world, as enacted in painting and understood in just these terms by such modern artists as Klee and Cézanne, provides an effective and, for Merleau-Ponty, decisive critique of the Cartesian psychology of space and vision. Descartes had sought to explain vision in terms of thought and to understand space as a kind of abstract container that is neutral with regard to its contents, exceeding all possible partial and fragmentary points of view. Modern painting reverses this project and, in words of Cézanne quoted by

---

[48] Ibid. 333.

[49] M. Merleau-Ponty, 'Eye and Mind', trans. C. Dallery, in idem, *The Primacy of Perception*, ed. J. E. Edie (Evanston, Ill.: Northwestern University Press, 1964), 166. See also the essay 'Cézanne's Doubt' in M. Merleau-Ponty, *Sense and Non-Sense*, trans. H. L. Dreyfus and P. A. Dreyfus (Evanston, Ill.: Northwestern University Press, 1964).

[50] *The Primacy of Perception*, 166.

Merleau-Ponty, the modern painter 'thinks in painting'.[51] This, he adds, indicates that it has 'metaphysical significance'. What modern painting reveals is the dimension of depth that is visible only from the point of view of a particular, localized orientation towards the world. But this is not depth in the sense of the third dimension of which perspectival drawing creates the illusion. It is rather a kind of first or even primordial dimension from which height, depth, and width are abstracted. It is, Merleau-Ponty says, 'a voluminosity we express in a word when we say that a thing is *there*', and which he goes on also to call a 'deflagration', a 'dehiscence', or a 'fission' of Being, which 'comes "I know not whence"' as an inside view of things; it is a kind of nothing, or 'primordial ground', an 'internal animation' or 'radiation of the visible', from within which things seem to form themselves and in the power of which the painter's line 'no longer imitates the visible; it "renders visible"; it is the blueprint of a genesis of things'.[52] It is, Merleau-Ponty sums up, 'mute Being which itself comes to show forth its own meaning'—which, he comments, applies as equally to figurative as to abstract painting, since 'no painting, no matter how abstract, can get away from Being . . . even Caravaggio's grape is the grape itself'.[53]

It is by virtue of this constant reference to Being that, even and precisely when it is solely engaged in visually interpreting the visible world, painting is always oriented towards a certain transcendence, a point Merleau-Ponty makes somewhat indirectly, by quoting words of Paul Klee used as the painter's epitaph: 'I cannot be caught in immanence'—words that the philosopher calls 'the ontological formula of painting'.[54] This is clearly not 'transcendence' in the sense of classical metaphysics. It is not a reference to a sphere or dimension of Being external to or outside the world. It is the transcendence of the depth, in which and out of which the world comes to meet the eye that looks deeply into it. As such it is not Being that ever achieves a final form, and, seen with Cézanne's eye, a bowl of fruit is as good an approach to it as any metaphysical argument—but Klee will see it otherwise again. If it is the ground on which our world takes shape, it is a ground that is itself constantly moving or shifting,[55] and Merleau-Ponty acknowledges that some will regard it as a misnomer 'to call "Being" that which never

---

[51] *The Primacy of Perception*, 178.

[52] The references in this sentence are (in sequence) to ibid. 180, 180, 187, 188, 181, 181, 182, 182, 181, and 183.

[53] Ibid. 188.

[54] Ibid.

[55] That each painter will experience and represent this ground in accordance with his or her own distinctive vision reinforces the basic principle of the foundation of our experience of the world in the bodily *movement* that unites and founds self and world, essence and existence.

fully *is*.[56] But—and perhaps this is an implicit rebuke to Sartre's assumption that any deficiency at all in Being, any gap, fissure, or distance between consciousness and Being renders any positive account of Being impossible[57]—this will only disappoint those who suffer from the 'groundless regret' of 'not being everything'. 'If creations are not a possession, it is not only that, like all things, they pass away; it is also that they have almost all their life still before them.'[58]

Although these reflections concern the act of painting, their application is not limited to the special situation of the painter but extends to perception in general, for which the painter (that is, the painter when painting) offers the philosopher a paradigmatic case. It is certainly in keeping with such a more general application that although life never comes to an end as long as we are living it and therefore 'I cannot be known to myself in advance of experience' (and consequently also have to accept a degree of ambiguity in my self-knowledge[59]), if it is actually the case that I do will, love, or believe then it will be possible for me to know that this is how I am. Thinking can assure me as to my being how I experience myself as being if it allows itself to be guided by the actual content of my bodily intentional movement towards my world.[60] Such an experience of truth may not yield 'a genuine eternity and participation in the One' but through 'concrete acts of taking up and carrying forward' the meaning that we encounter in our temporal dealings with ourselves, our world, and others,[61] we may also experience that eternity which is 'not another order of time, but the atmosphere of time'.[62]

We might especially note here how Merleau-Ponty's use of the term 'Being' inverts some of the key assumptions underlying classical theistic ontology. For when Merleau-Ponty speaks of Being, it is clear that he is not speaking about *a* Being that is most true to itself when it is known in abstraction from the manifold of sense-experience but the Being that becomes present to us in the most concrete, most densely layered, most intensely radiant moments of our lives (perhaps akin to Hopkins's instress, perhaps akin to Marion's saturated phenomenon[63]). It is 'Being' to which only the thickest of descriptions could

---

[56] *The Primacy of Perception*, 190.
[57] Or possibly to Bataille, or even to a certain kind of theological ontology!
[58] *The Primacy of Perception*, 190.
[59] *Phenomenology of Perception*, 381.
[60] Ibid. 382.
[61] Ibid. 394–5.
[62] Ibid. 393.
[63] It is striking that Marion too uses Cézanne's conversations to illustrate what he means by the 'saturated phenomenon'. See J.-L. Marion, *Being Given: Towards a Phenomenology of Givenness*, trans. J. C. Kosky (Stanford, Calif.: Stanford University Press, 2002), 46 ff. Marcel already

ever do justice, 'Being' that is neither a thing nor transcendent to the world of things, but what, in experience, presses upon us, encompasses us, and overwhelms us with assurance as to the reality of what we are experiencing.

Spatiality is a salient feature of Merleau-Ponty's account of voluminous depth and therefore also integral to his understanding of our experience of Being. It is, in fact, fundamental to his account of perception in general that the embodied self is not only a temporal but also a spatial being, not in the sense of existing 'in' space but as grounding our experience of space through the manner of its intentional comportment. In these terms it founds what he calls 'a spatiality of situation'.[64] Spatiality is, of course, not absent from the other phenomenological readings of the human situation we have been considering.[65] It is not accidental that much of this enquiry has been guided by the partly spatial metaphor of the 'distance' separating consciousness and Being, the scope of which we have explored in terms of time, space, language, and relationships.[66] But perhaps, reflecting on Merleau-Ponty's account of embodiment as intentional motility, we might think of this metaphor more literally: to learn to recognize the nearness of Being is not then to learn to follow a philosophical argument, but to learn how to draw near to what is already near to us in our being in the world. Let us think again about an example we considered at an earlier stage in this enquiry. In Chapter 2 we noted how Wordsworth emphasizes the role of memory and anticipation in 'Lines composed above Tintern Abbey', thereby generating a sense of distance at the heart of the reader's experience of the 'presence' that the poet has felt and of which he now wishes to speak. However, as was also noted in Chapter 3, Wordsworth's poem is no less attentive to the role of spatial distance, to the alternation in the poet's life of absence and presence from just this particular place and of the relationship between this and the other places in which his life has been, is, and will be lived. In this regard it is important to note how the poem's title already draws our attention to the place of its composition, and

---

spoke of the saturation of experience by an intelligibility that is revelatory of Being and which resists being made into an object of empirical investigation (see *The Mystery of Being*, i. 155–6).

[64] *Phenomenology of Perception*, 100. Lakoff and Johnson show in some detail how bodily motility generates a wide-ranging set of what they call 'orientational metaphors' that are typically spatial in character, and that mould our understanding of many emotional and social situations. Thus the basic pairing of up/down can be used to map moods, health, power relations, etc. Whilst their metaphorical nature means that they can generate new meanings that can become quite remote from their original bodily source, the meanings that come to adhere to these terms are, they say, 'not randomly assigned' since 'no metaphor can ever be comprehended or even adequately represented independently of its experiential basis'. See G. Lakoff and M. Johnson, *Metaphors We Live By* (Chicago: Chicago University Press, 1980), 18–19.

[65] See Ch. 3 'Space, Place, and Time'.

[66] It is also, of course, a partly temporal metaphor.

its genesis in the actual presence of the place about which it is written. In the light of this title the poem seems to offer itself to us as writing *en plein air*, just as Cézanne would paint in the actual presence of Mont Saint-Victoire. In this perspective the way in which a certain place calls to us is not just a matter of maintaining a memory of its presence in the past or the hope of a return in the future, but it is first and foremost a call *from* that place that we might come *to* it, it is an invitation to *draw near*, that we might *be there*. In this sense, then, Wordsworth's poem might be read as epitomizing the task to be undertaken in an enquiry into God and Being that wants to do more than compare, contrast, and evaluate the views of a selection of modern thinkers and writers, but actively seeks to arrive at that place where, if anywhere, it might be possible to speak of God as giver of every good and perfect gift. This is not to say that we must all go on a pilgrimage to Tintern Abbey if we are to understand the poem. Rather, what is evoked in us is a reordering and redirection of our lived sense of spatial movement that neither involves us in going to Tintern Abbey nor is reducible to a purely 'spiritual' sense, as if the movement at issue was 'only' a symbol or 'merely' a metaphor.[67] In the next chapter we shall consider the possibility that the place towards which that movement leads us is, in the end, characterizable only as no place, emptiness, nihility, or *khôra*, but however else we might interpret those elusive words, Merleau-Ponty reminds and forewarns us that it cannot be anywhere other than the place where we already are, the place from which we always begin, the place that is enacted by our own bodily presence in the world.

Merleau-Ponty himself does not speak of either the field of nihility or of *khôra*, but he does speak of 'Being' and of eternity. Undoubtedly, his is not the 'Being' nor yet the 'eternity' of Neo-Thomist thought, since it is not a possible object of knowledge. Yet it seems not to be so far from the revelation of Being as *mystery* that Marcel—writing specifically as a Christian, Catholic thinker— also finds in our day-to-day dealings with our world and, especially, with others. This is not so much a revelation of a world or a reality beyond our experience, but of that dimension of our experience that calls on us to be faithful, charitable, and generous witnesses to the truth of Being we have been enabled to see.[68] But if Marcel's mystery of Being points and calls us to the

---

[67] In one sense, then, this means rejecting Augustine's comment on references to pilgrimage in Psalm 120 as to be taken in a spiritual and not a corporeal sense. At the same time, as so often in Augustine, what is said serves to, as it were, corporealize the spiritual: 'Pilgrimage is not to be understood in a corporeal sense, but the soul is said to go on pilgrimage' (see also the discussion of Augustine's use of bodily imagery later in this chapter).

[68] More generally, Merleau-Ponty's argument seems to be in significant continuity with Marcel's understanding of the relationship between body and Being, albeit developed with greater phenomenological rigour.

possibility of religious existence, can we say the same of the 'Being' of which Merleau-Ponty writes here? It would seem that, despite speaking of the metaphysical significance of what is revealed in painting, Merleau-Ponty does not invite us in any way to suppose that the voluminous ground of perception requires further grounding in a transcendent order of Being. But does a religious point of view actually require such an onward reference? Merleau-Ponty himself seems to think not, at least not in the case of Christianity. Elsewhere, for example, he expressed his opinion that the Christian God is not a God of transcendent height 'above' the world of bodily experience but a 'mysterious' sense of 'another self in ourselves which dwells in and authenticates our darkness'.[69] What this gives us is, perhaps, an 'I-do-not-know-what' or an 'almost nothing', to borrow Jankélévitch's expressions.[70] But it is not quite nothing. Though unstable, unfinalized, and always open to creative re-invention and transformation it is, after all, the possibility of a revelation of Being. As a revelation from the very depths of embodied existence it is, from the point of view of classical Christian theology, a revelation grounded in what is weakest, most fallible, and most distant from the plenitude of divine Being. It is the truth that is revealed in the vision of humanity, 'the thing itself', as a 'bare, forked animal', nothing more. But perhaps here too it is true that the best we can hope for are the crumbs that fall from the tables of the metaphysically rich, which, so long as we are not afflicted with the 'groundless regret' of not being invited to the best metaphysical seats, may nevertheless be enough to satisfy—for a while (which is in any case enough, since, honestly, we don't have very long)—our metaphysical hunger.

BODY, BEING, GOD (I)

One way of developing the 'metaphysical' potential of a view of the human person focused resolutely on the primacy of embodiment is found in the work of Lakoff and Johnson, who, in their study of what they call 'the Embodied Mind and its Challenge to Western Thought', argue more explicitly than does Merleau-Ponty for understanding spiritual life from the perspective of embodiment. They describe such an 'embodied spirituality' as 'an ethical

---

[69] M. Merleau-Ponty, *The Prose of the World*, trans. J. O'Neill (Evanston, Ill.: Northwestern University Press, 1973), 84. Elsewhere, he also relates this to Augustine's sense of God as being closer to me than I am to myself (see *Sense and Non-Sense*, 173–4).

[70] This is the theme of his trilogy *Le Je-ne-sais-quoi et le presque-rien* (Paris: Éditions du Seuil, 1980).

relation to the physical world' which, through 'imaginative empathetic projection', brings about 'a form of "transcendence," a form of *being in the other*'.[71] The 'Being' and the 'God' of such a spirituality can be figured only in the language of metaphors that are themselves generated by our bodily life in the world, but whilst they can sometimes seem dismissive of such ideas ('Metaphysics . . . is a fancy name for our concern with what is real'), they also argue that it is not inappropriate to allow metaphor to invest our self-projection towards the ineffable God with a degree of passion, such that God can 'not only . . . be imagined but . . . approached, exhorted, evaded, confronted, struggled with, and loved. Through metaphor, the vividness, intensity, and meaningfulness of ordinary experience becomes the basis of a passionate spirituality'.[72]

Their proposals resonate with a broad current of contemporary theology in which, over the last thirty or so years, 'the body' has emerged as a major topic. Often, this has been in the context of feminist approaches and has involved sharp criticisms of traditional Christian doctrines as well as of the philosophical assumptions informing both classical and modern theological reflection. Writing of the marginalization of the flesh in Christianity, Margaret R. Miles sums up the critical—and creative—thrust of this 'rehabilitation of the flesh':[73]

In Christianity the body scorned, the naked body, is a female body. Ironically, the contemporary feminist concern for recovering the female body lies at the heart of the ancient Christian project. To represent the female body, not as erotic—as 'erotic' has been culturally constructed—not as the object of fascination and scorn, but as revelation and subjectivity is to correct and complete the Christian affirmation of body. It is to present the flesh, not made word, but given voice to sing its own song.[74]

---

[71] G. Lakoff and M. Johnson, *Philosophy in the Flesh: The Embodied Mind and its Challenge to Western Thought* (New York: Basic Books, 1999), 565–6.

[72] Ibid. 569. Although Lakoff and Johnson do not refer to Merleau-Ponty's work very frequently and also tend towards a reductionist approach to mental phenomena, the central role they give to the grounding of our conceptual system via metaphor in the 'sensimotor system of our brains', i.e., the organ of the body's being-in-the-world as a mobile, intentional centre of activity ('the body in the mind,' as they call it), invites comparison with Merleau-Ponty's insistence on the centrality of the body's motility in the genesis of consciousness.

[73] The expression 'rehabilitation of the flesh' was already a rallying cry amongst some radical thinkers of the early 1830s, who also claimed Schleiermacher's early Romantic theology as an inspirational source.

[74] Margaret R. Miles, *Carnal Knowing: Female Nakedness and Religious Meaning in the Christian West* (London: Burns and Oates, 1992), 185. Of course, it would be misleading to suggest that this was exclusively a feminist preoccupation. If feminism played an especially important role in galvanizing theologians (as also scholars in other disciplines) into looking again at the body, this has now led to the (re-)discovery and reappraisal of large swaths of historical and textual material in contexts and for purposes that are as varied as the field itself. A further extension of this rehabilitation of the flesh—developed in a perspective drawing on process thought—is to see the world itself as embodying God. From a large range of literature see also David Brown's almost encyclopaedic treatment of embodiment and religion in his *God*

Many of those who have most emphasized the centrality of the body have adopted or been influenced by phenomenological approaches in which the body is not approached as an object in the world but as a lived body of meaning, in which—as in Merleau-Ponty's account of painting—the 'how' of our bodily experience involves a constant movement between 'inside' and 'outside'. It is from this perspective of the lived body that the following remarks seek to illustrate—and to do more would require a whole new study—what it might mean to traverse the distance that separates the world presented in and to self-consciousness from the presence of Being. In doing so, I hope to indicate what it might mean for embodied beings such as we are to 'draw near' to Being or to experience the 'nearness' of Being, and, more particularly, to consider how such nearness might be registered in thinking that addresses the question of God and Being in dialogue with the classical sources of Christian theology and modern European thought.

Recent theological discussions of 'the body' have, very often, focused almost exclusively on issues of sex and gender. In a broad cultural perspective the reasons for this are somewhat obvious since the suppression of sexual activity and desire had been a salient feature of much traditional Christian and pagan ascesis. Yet one might also say that it reflects the alienated conditions under which many Western academics now work, such that 'sexuality' is experienced as the main focus of basic bodily needs and desires in an artificial and 'cerebral' environment. But, of course, eating,[75] weeping,[76] seeing,[77] walking,[78] and urges that drive us to seek silence and solitude,[79] to kneel,[80] and to dance[81] are no less integral to our experience of embodiment. A complete phenomenology

---

and Grace of Body: Sacrament in Ordinary (Oxford: Oxford University Press, 2007), which suggests something of the range of possibilities this new attention to the body opens up.

[75] See, e.g. A. Schmemann, *The World as Sacrament* (London: Darton, Longman, and Todd, 1966). Schmemann inverts Feuerbach's materialistically intended dictum 'You are what you eat' into a sacramental category.

[76] See below.

[77] Merleau-Ponty's interpretation of Cézanne significantly emphasizes the bodily nature of vision. See also my *Art, Modernity and Faith* (London: SCM Press, 1998), 134–54.

[78] See, e.g., Richard Long, *Walking the Line* (London: Thames and Hudson, 2005).

[79] See, e.g., Max Picard, *The World of Silence*, trans. S. Godman (London: Harvill Press, 1948); Sara Maitland, *A Book of Silence* (London: Granta, 2008).

[80] Etty Hillesum several times remarks on the urge to kneel as part of her religious awakening in the period leading up to her deportation to Auschwitz. See E. Hillesum, *Etty: A Diary 1941–43*, trans. A. J. Pomerans (London: Jonathan Cape, 1983). Hillesum's diary is one of the key reference points of Oliver Davies's study *A Theology of Compassion*. Her letter of 24 August 1943 merits being used as a compulsory preface to any work in modern theology.

[81] See David Brown, *God and Grace of Body*, especially ch. 2, 'The Dancer's Leap', 61–119. Also the editors' 'Introduction' to Ann Loades and D. Brown, *The Sense of the Sacramental* (London: SPCK, 1995).

of the religious body which would do justice to all of these and to the vast number of other relevant experiences would be a task for a theological generation and I shall not even attempt such a thing here. I shall, however, briefly offer some general comments on the relationship between texts and bodies, before considering two examples, trembling and weeping, of how modes of bodily existence attest the divine–human relationship; I shall then conclude this chapter by considering how our understanding of this relationship, thus embodied, is affected by the way in which the concrete encounter with the other is, for us embodied beings, its pre-eminent and normal site.

For most of this enquiry we have been engaged in reading and interpreting texts. As such, and not least in the light of Derridean grammatology, it might seem that we are limited to sources that presuppose the suspension of bodily presence. Yet if we have in fact no other ground of being than the dynamic forward movement of living bodily life, even writing will and must bear the traces of this movement, no matter how thinly or abstractly. In their *Metaphors We Live By* Lakoff and Johnson offer one model of how the living body might be present in language, and in written as well as in spoken language.[82] Another might be developed from Gadamer's understanding of language as bringing to expression the human being's relation to the world, where the world is not understood as an ensemble of objects to which the individual words of language point but in the sense that language raises what is otherwise a mere environment to the level of a lived world and, in doing so, reveals something of its Being.[83] And although the power of texts to evoke the lived somatic reality of religious existence has rarely if ever been used as a formal criterion for constructing a reading-list for the theological curriculum (and also despite the fact that many works of systematic theology generate a stifling air of abstraction remote from anything corporeal) it is striking that a significant number of what might be called religious classics are strongly marked by the presence of the lived body. Augustine, Kierkegaard, and Dostoevsky—to name only three—could not have had anything like the impact they have in fact had and they could not speak to us in the way they do if it was not for what we might call the bodily intelligence of their writing. Even when the explicit or intended content of what they write no longer commands our assent, even when (as is certainly the case with both Augustine

---

[82] See n. 64 above.

[83] See H.-G. Gadamer, *Wahrheit und Methode* (Tübingen: Mohr, 1975), especially 415 ff. In connection with this Gadamer somewhere points out that even silent reading is accompanied by bodily changes wrought as we re-perform the text in reading (our pulse quickens, the hairs on the back of the neck bristle, or we let forth a gentle sigh . . .)—a comment that may be taken as also drawing attention to the inherently bodily nature both of our being-in-the-world and of the language in which that being is brought to expression.

and Kierkegaard) they view the body itself in a theoretical framework very different from that which is being embraced here, the power and clarity with which they give voice to the body's own involvement in what they are saying nevertheless enables them still to direct us towards what is most crucial in the religious relationship.[84] Arguably, then, our bodily response to texts is already in some measure silently effective in the way in which religious tradition sifts and brings to prominence those texts that best figure a distinctive religious experience and understanding. Far from being a matter for reproach (as it is from the point of view of the kind of philosopher who accepts only clear, distinct, and unambiguous ideas and univocal propositions as the currency of philosophical exchange), it would seem to be intrinsic to the merit of most classic religious texts that they are strongly marked by traces of the lived body. So, when Augustine speaks of the 'unquiet heart' seeking its rest in God, he is not merely speaking metaphorically—or rather, in speaking metaphorically he is also speaking the language of the body, such that we seem, almost, to hear the (literal) pounding of his heart, beating against his rib-cage.[85] If the longing for rest in the immutable Being of God is—as Augustine himself insists—a 'spiritual' and not a corporeal longing, if hungering and thirsting or being on fire for God are to be understood metaphorically, as inward and not outward states, Augustine nevertheless has no other way of talking about them than with the language of the body and, in the event, he was effective in exploiting this language with a vividness and a force that few writers have matched.[86] Perhaps it is precisely because Augustine felt so keenly the entanglement of his immutable and eternal soul in the mutable, time-bound turbulence of bodily life that that same bodily life could become so ubiquitous in his work. In any case, it is not accidental that it was the meditations on

---

[84] This does not necessarily mean that literature (and perhaps painting) should replace work now classified as philosophy or theology, since, as in the texts under discussion, even formally 'theological' or 'philosophical' texts may offer eloquent testimony to 'the body in the mind'. To take a fairly random sample: Luther, Calvin, Francis of Sales, Newman, Buber, Barth, and Simone Weil would all, in their different ways, illustrate the same point—and the list could easily be extended. Perhaps the game begins to be lost when theological education is conducted primarily through the study of texts that were themselves produced exclusively or primarily for an academic environment (which became especially marked from the nineteenth century). The moral of the tale would then be that academic work in theology should not feed upon itself, i.e., by writing monographs and articles about other theologians' work, but rather seek to engage with and to clarify the world outside the academy, in this case the world of human beings' religious (or, for theology, specifically confessional) lives and experiences.

[85] Rather than metaphor, it might in such instances be more appropriate to think of 'images', in the specific sense we encountered in Bachelard, i.e., as direct phenomenologically accessible revelations of the kind of relation to Being that they bring to expression (see Ch. 3 'Space, Place and Time' above).

[86] In some of his sermons he even draws his listeners' attention to how much he is sweating!

temptation in Book X of the *Confessions* that provided Heidegger with a text through which to work out the concept of care that would provide him with one of the decisive features of his account of being-in-the-world since the structure of care is precisely that of a self who does not and cannot exist other than in and through its involvement in its world.[87]

The same is true of many of the key figures of the medieval spiritual tradition, and even if the invocations of tears, sighs, shudderings, hot flushes, and other bodily manifestations of intense devotion sometimes became mere conventions, the power of the images in which the language of the spiritual life expresses the bodily involvement of the soul in the search for God is repeatedly renewed in its more original exponents. This is underwritten by the kind of theological claim made, for example, by William of Saint-Thierry, when he argues that the Latin *sapientia*, the divine wisdom sought by the restless heart, is etymologically derived from *sapor*, meaning taste, and in his treatise *On the Nature and Dignity of Love* he goes on to show how this connection is manifested in the traces of the innate 'taste' for divine wisdom that are discernible in the workings of the five senses, effectively reversing the Augustinian hermeneutics of suspicion in this regard.[88]

In what might at first seem like a very different religious situation, Kierkegaard too portrays the religious individual in terms that self-consciously deploy bodily images to an exceptionally high degree.[89] We noted Merleau-Ponty's comparison of the body to 'the darkness needed in the theatre to show up the performance', and remembering also his further comments about Being (and maybe even God) as discoverable in the depths of embodiment, it is striking that, on several occasions, Kierkegaard too uses the image of God as the spectator concealed in the darkness of the auditorium before whom the conscious self enacts the drama of its life in fear and trembling.[90] Reading this metaphor from a phenomenological point of view would then suggest that

---

[87] See my 'Heidegger, Augustine, and Kierkegaard: Care, Time and Love', in Craig de Paulo (ed.), *The Influence of Augustine on Heidegger: The Emergence of an Augustinian Phenomenology* (Lewiston, NY: Edwin Mellen Press, 2006).

[88] William of Saint-Thierry, *De natura et dignitate amoris* (ch. 28) in F. Zambon (ed.), *Trattati d'amore cristiani del XII secolo*, vol. i (Turin: Fondazione Lorenzo Valla, 2007), 111.

[89] This aspect of Kierkegaard's work is been especially sharply noted in, e.g., Helle Møller Jensen, 'Freeze! Hold it Right There', in N.-J. Cappelørn, H. Deuser, and J. Stewart (eds.), *Kierkegaard Studies Yearbook 2000* (Berlin: de Gruyter, 2000), 223–9, which applies Lakoff and Johnson's notion of metaphors of orientation to the interpretation of the discourse 'Preserving One's Soul in Patience'. G. Heath King's *Existence: Thought: Style: Perspectives of a Primary Relation* (Milwaukee: Marquette University Press, 1996) is a perhaps somewhat disorganized attempt to draw attention to something similar, occasionally successfully. A more systematic and literary approach is found in Isak Winkel Holm, *Tanken i Billedet: Søren Kierkegaards Poetik* (Thinking in images: SK's poetics) (Copenhagen: Gyldendal, 1998).

[90] See my *Kierkegaard: The Aesthetic and the Religious* (London: SCM Press, 1998), 170–4.

the most telling terms of religious language will be precisely those that are generated when what is said in the luminous space of discourse and action becomes aware of and responsive to the infinitely mysterious darkness of embodied life out of which and for the sake of which our words are spoken.

One example amongst many is found in Kierkegaard's short work *Repetition*. Formally dedicated to the problem of movement in philosophy, *Repetition* accomplishes its task by telling us about a thinker pacing up and down his room and undertaking journeys that attempt to repeat past experiences and about a lover who disappears into hiding to flee experiences of insomnia, nausea, numbness, and lack of purpose that he likens to pointlessly drifting clouds. The tone is set in the opening line, when the pseudonymous author, Constantin Constantius (whose very name evokes the stasis that 'repetition' is to banish), comments that 'When the Eleatics denied motion, Diogenes, as everyone knows, came forward as an opponent. He literally did come forward, because he did not say a word but merely paced back and forth a few times, thereby assuming that he had sufficiently refuted them.'[91] Humorous, parodic, slightly absurd—*Repetition* operates with a very different tonality from its companion work (*Fear and Trembling*), but, like that, it does not merely deploy bodily metaphors as striking illustrations of its philosophical message but reconceives the problems of philosophy in the language of an embodied imagination. The same might be said of *The Concept of Anxiety*, in which this 'concept' is expounded with reference to vertigo and to the 'glance of an eye' that reveals the eternal in time more directly than even a sigh or a word.[92] Later, especially in *Concluding Unscientific Postscript*, Kierkegaard will reproach the speculative thinkers of German idealism for forgetting their bodies, whilst his own exposition of the religious life in a sequence of upbuilding discourses will express the task of becoming Spirit in images of looking, wrestling, weeping, crawling, walking, running, labouring, swimming, sailing, and ageing—performing 'the body's recollection of being' that the speculative philosophers have forgotten. However, perhaps the most striking example is that which is advertised in the title of perhaps his best-known work, *Fear and Trembling*, and it is to a brief 'phenomenological' meditation on the religious meaning of such 'trembling' that we now turn. This will be followed and complemented by a further meditation on the closely related theme of 'weeping'.

---

[91] S. Kierkegaard, *Fear and Trembling/Repetition*, trans. E. H. and H. V. Hong, SKS 4 (Princeton: Princeton University Press, 1983), 131. Kierkegaard's own passion for walking is also not irrelevant here.

[92] S. Kierkegaard, *The Concept of Anxiety*, trans. R. Thomte, SKS 4 (Princeton: Princeton University Press, 1980), 87.

EXCURSUS: TREMBLING AND WEEPING

Although Derrida's distinctive prioritization of writing over speaking might superficially seem to place his thought at the furthest possible remove from the lived bodily reality of the speaking voice and the listening ear, he was acutely sensitive to the trace of the living body in the written texts on which he commented. Thus, in the discussion of Kierkegaard's *Fear and Trembling* in *The Gift of Death* and before going on to such 'concepts' as 'faith', 'sacrifice' or 'the leap' that preoccupy most of Kierkegaard's philosophical and theological commentators, Derrida pauses at the title and invites us to hear in it a point of departure that is unmistakably bodily. Distinguishing trembling from a mere 'quiver or shiver' (of which he says that it may be a merely transitory moment, like water quivering before it boils, 'a preliminary and visible agitation'[93]), he describes the former as an 'irrepressible shaking', a sign of a traumatism about to be repeated—

As different as dread, fear, anxiety, terror, panic, or anguish remain from one another, they have already begun in the trembling, and what has provoked them continues, or threatens to continue, to make us tremble...We tremble in that strange repetition that ties an irrefutable past (a shock that has been felt, a traumatism that has already affected us) to a future that cannot be anticipated; anticipated, but unpredictable... approached and unapproachable...and we tremble from not knowing...whether [the shock] is going to continue, start again, insist, be repeated...I tremble at what exceeds my seeing and my knowing although it concerns the innermost parts of me, right down to the soul, down to the bone, as we say.[94]

As Derrida's own text continues, it is clear that, following Kierkegaard (and St Paul, from whom the expression derives), he recognizes that 'fear and trembling' is being taken here precisely as characterizing the most intimate moment of the God-relationship, the moment when God and Abraham draw near in an exchange (a demand, an act of obedience) that tests both their identities, putting the kind of being that each of them is on the line. But this moment of complicity that binds God and Patriarch is first known and experienced in the trembling itself, a trembling that continues and accompanies whatever else is to be said by way of conceptualizing and interpreting what passes between them. Fear and trembling—and this is surely the thrust of Kierkegaard's own text as well as of Derrida's commentary—is not a passing moment (like the 'quiver' of which Derrida spoke) but the

---

[93] J. Derrida, *The Gift of Death*, trans. D. Wills (Chicago: University of Chicago Press, 1995), 53.
[94] Ibid. 54.

atmosphere, the condition of speaking about God at all. If we were to master it, to calm down, or to control ourselves—we would no longer be speaking of God. Trembling is the way the lived body draws near to God or apprehends the possibility of a God's advent.

One aspect of this was highlighted in Rudolph Otto's phenomenological description of the experience of the 'holy' (or what he calls the 'numinous') as an experience of a 'Mysterium Tremendum', a phrase that leads him to an extended analysis of the 'tremendum'. In this analysis Otto identifies 'tremor' as a specific emotional response that is related both to fear and to 'awe' (he uses the English word). The shudder in which it manifests itself may, at its crudest level, be the kind of thing we experience when listening to a ghost story but it also 'reappears in a form ennobled beyond measure where the soul, held speechless [at the presence of the holy], trembles inwardly to the farthest fibre of its being'.[95] But 'trembling' is not only a phenomenon of the kind of negative states that Kierkegaard's and Otto's descriptions of the fear-and-trembling-inducing mystery of holiness might seem to emphasize. Trembling is also, after all, the movement of the leaf at the first touch of vivifying rain, it is the response of the body to the approach of the beloved, perhaps experienced by Solomon's beloved 'faint with love' (Song of Songs 5: 8), but perhaps also when we have yet to consciously recognize that such and such a one has become the beloved. It is often the body's testimony to love before love is known. Nor does this only apply to erotic love, for we are also shaken by the sight of suffering or the spectacle of injustice and we tremble with anger at wrongdoing—and all before we come to reflect on how we might respond, how we should judge, or what we are to do. Then again, we tremble with excitement on the eve of a journey or adventure. The religious significance of trembling has been most explicitly acknowledged in such movements as the Quakers and Shakers of early modern Britain and America, but already in the first millennium of Christianity Isaac of Nineveh could write that 'Everything that takes place with reverence and trembling . . . is seen by God as a choice offering.'[96] Yet often we ourselves scarcely know what our trembling means: whether it is a manifestation of fear or whether, like a certain degree of stage-fright, it is a way of anticipating the fulfilment of an active or passive desire. In this sense, 'trembling' seems to be beyond or prior to good and evil or ethical valuation, pointing us directly to something more basic than the construction of experience as 'positive' or 'negative'. What is this?

[95] R. Otto, *The Idea of the Holy*, trans. J. W. Harvey (Oxford: Oxford University Press, 1923), 31.
[96] Isaac of Nineveh, *'The Second Part': Chapters IV–XLI*, trans. S. Brock (Leuven: Peeters, 1995), 71.

In all its forms 'trembling' seems to mark the loss or slippage of autonomy, the moment when the self loses control of its somatic boundaries and becomes unable to prevent the involuntary movements of the muscle and skin that are the site of its concrete presence in and to its world. As an ontological image, then, 'trembling' reveals very precisely how the self-contained ego must be disrupted if it is to be opened up to the other—physical or personal, human or divine. Such loss of ego may well issue in a negative outcome—sickness or death or one or other destructive psychic response (becoming overwhelmed by fear, or adopting a slavish attitude to another person or to God). But if 'trembling' may be a prelude to hell, the rupture in the continuity of ego and body that it manifests can also be an early signal that we are being made ready for heaven. And recalling too the intercalation of body and language, we may say that it is also a very precise somatic correlate of the 'reverberation' or 'vibration' of which Heidegger and Bachelard respectively speak in describing how Being becomes manifest in language: not as simple presence or as a stable, static object to which language somehow points us, but as reverberating or vibrating in the spoken word. The hesitation and trembling in which such a word is spoken are an effective acknowledgement that neither now nor in time to come will this word ever be adequate either to its object or to its own thinking of that object, neither to the *res* nor to the *intellectus* and therefore never finalizable—yet there is no other way, no other manner in which we can say what is in the heart and on the tongue. It is not the commanding word of the orator, not the decisive word of the judge, nor even the deliberate word of the expert. It is the word of those who stand before what can never be spoken, but which ever and again calls upon them to speak.

An especially perceptive account of trembling as manifesting the crisis of autonomy and the birth-pangs of the religious self can be seen in the role played by Raskolnikov's various fits of trembling and shaking in Dostoevsky's *Crime and Punishment*. The first time we are alerted to this recurrent feature of his comportment is when, in the opening chapter, he arrives at the house of the pawnbroker he is planning to kill ('With a sinking heart and nervous trembling he came up to a most enormous house . . .'[97]), the next is when he receives a letter from his mother which, as R. D. Laing has explained, sets out the double-bind that is generative of Raskolnikov's 'impossible' psychological predicament.[98] As the novel progresses, Raskolnikov falls into a kind of mental and bodily fever, frequently marked by fits of trembling and shaking.

---

[97] F. M. Dostoevsky, *Crime and Punishment*, trans. R. Pevear and L. Volokhonsky (London: Vintage, 1993), 5.
[98] Ibid. 30. R. D. Laing, *Self and Others* (Harmondsworth: Penguin, 1961), 165–73.

These stand in a clear tension with his ambition of making himself an 'exceptional man' who, by taking complete control of his own destiny, is able to override the conventions of social morality. The connection is made explicit in the crucial scene between Raskolnikov and Sonya Marmeladova, the prostitute whose pure heart will, in the end, prove his salvation. Having expounded to her the impossibility of her situation in the world of St Petersburg's vice-ridden slums, he continues

What can be done? Smash what needs to be smashed, once and for all, and that's it—and take the suffering upon ourselves! What? You don't understand? You'll understand later ... Freedom and power, but above all, power! Over all trembling creatures, over the whole ant-heap ... That is the goal! Remember it![99]

Yet Raskolnikov cannot even control the trembling of his own body, a trembling that discloses the limits of the self he is vainly attempting to become and that, had he attended to it, would have revealed the impossibility of his fantasies of becoming a kind of superman beyond good and evil.[100]

In the same scene with Sonya we are also told of another kind of trembling, occasioned by Raskolnikov's demand that Sonya should read to him from the Gospel.

Sonya opened the book and found the place. Her hands were trembling; she did not have voice enough. She tried twice to begin, but kept failing to get the first syllable out.[101]

As the scene continues, attention is repeatedly drawn to the hesitations, pauses, and tremblings that interrupt Sonya's reading, phenomena which, we are told, Raskolnikov—perhaps unsurprisingly—understands.

He understood only too well how hard it was for her now to betray and expose all that was *hers*. He understood that these feelings might indeed constitute her *secret*, as it were ... But at the same time he now knew, and knew for certain, that even though she was anguished and terribly afraid of something as she was starting to read, she also had a tormenting desire to read, in spite of all her anguish and apprehension, and precisely *for him*, so that he would hear it, and precisely *now*...[102]

---

[99] *Crime and Punishment*, 329–30.

[100] It could be argued that Dostoevsky uses the phenomenon of physical trembling to symbolize or illustrate the fevered state of Raskolnikov's mind, as if the external action of the novel was merely an allegory of an inner, spiritual drama. But this kind of distinction doesn't exist for this novelist. The fevered thoughts (about which we hear a great deal in the course of the novel) and the physical trembling are equally basic phenomena of Raskolnikov's personal mode of being. The body may be the picture of the soul, but the soul, in turn, is the picture of the body.

[101] *Crime and Punishment*, 325–6.   [102] Ibid. 326.

In Sonya's case too, it seems, trembling is occasioned by the ontological instability of the relationship between self and world and the threat that her situation poses to the inner integrity of her ego. Yet there is a sense in which her trembling is more the mirror-image than the analogue of his. For whilst his project is aimed at separating himself out from and elevating himself above others, hers is precisely to bear witness to divine love in a situation of brutalized social relationships, epitomized in the alcoholism, child abuse, and prostitution that pervade the lower strata of St Petersburg life. Her 'secret' is a surrender, a self-abandonment to God, that cannot be enacted or find form in the world, and so her trembling marks the constantly disputed boundary between who she inwardly knows herself to be and the identity that society imposes on her.

The phenomenon of weeping seems naturally to complement that of trembling. Weeping has been an important and attested feature of Christian existence from its beginnings. Against the background of a strong biblical attestation, Catholic theology has long spoken of the 'gift of tears',[103] and the role of tears is vividly illustrated in the lives of many saints—the entries in Ignatius of Loyola's private journal often comment only on whether a particular day was or was not marked by tears.[104] In Eastern Christianity the theme of tears is closely associated with the experience of compunction, as in the writings of Isaac of Nineveh.[105] Whilst there are special gifts that are not relevant to the needs of all Christians, all should have tears, according to Gregory of Nazianzus. Tears are a 'fifth Baptism' (after the crossing of the Red Sea, the baptism of John, Christ's baptism in the Spirit, and the baptism in blood of the martyrs).[106] But, as is more emphasized in the Western tradition, tears also have the positive meaning of weeping for heavenly goods, which, in a writer such as Augustine, comprises a fuller relation to Being-Itself. Watered by the tears of his anxious mother (which prompted him to speak of himself as a 'child of tears'[107]) Augustine's own spiritual journey towards God is

---

[103] According to the article on 'Larmes' in the *Dictionnaire de spiritualité*, the expression 'gift of tears' is first encountered in Athanasius' treatise *De virginitate*. See *Dictionnaire de spiritualité*, vol. ix (Paris: Beauchesne, 1976), 292. As the article makes clear, Athanasius is formulating what is already widely known in Christian living.

[104] See the translation in Antonio T. De Nicolas, *Ignatius of Loyola, Powers of Imagining: A Philosophical Hermeneutic of Imagining through the Collected Works of Ignatius of Loyola* (Albany, NY: State University of New York Press, 1986). See also E. M. Cioran, *Tears and Saints*, trans. I. Zarifopol-Johnston (Chicago: Chicago University Press, 1995).

[105] On the theme of compunction in general see Irénée Hausherr SJ, *Penthos in the Christian East* (Kalamazoo, Mich.: Cistercian Publications, 1982). Hausherr comments that 'compunction, mourning and tears go together so much that they are, through metonymy, virtual equivalents' (*Penthos*, 9). On Isaac, see Hilarion Alfeyev, *The Spiritual World of Isaac the Syrian* (Kalamazoo, Mich.: Cistercian Publications, 2000), ch. 5 'Tears', 129–42.

[106] On both points see 'Larmes', 293.

[107] *Confessions*, III, 12.

marked by moments of intense weeping. Immediately before he hears the voice telling him to take and read the text that will occasion his conversion, he describes himself lying under a fig tree and giving himself up to tears.[108] Centuries later, and after the innumerable weepings of medieval saints and sinners, but still in essential continuity with Isaac and Augustine, Francis of Sales explains that when God puts the fire of his love into our hearts this melts them in such a way as to produce tears that, in turn, become an 'eau de vie', a fire-water, that increases the ardour of the heart's longing for the unique source of life.[109] A similar image is found in the Protestant world in one of Kierkegaard's later discourses, 'One Who Is Forgiven Little Loves Little', and Kierkegaard several times depicts the quintessential moment of the religious life by referring to the image of the woman described in Luke chapter 7 as falling at the feet of Christ and washing them with her tears.[110]

John Caputo takes Augustine's tears as a way of bringing together Augustine and Derrida, seeing tears as expressive of the two North African thinkers' passion for, respectively, the eternal and the impossible. Thus, when Derrida speaks of his 'whole life' as 'inviting calling promising, hoping sighing dreaming, convoking invoking provoking, constituting engendering producing, naming assigning demanding, prescribing commanding sacrificing,' Caputo speaks of this as 'eighteen ways to pray and weep'.[111] In Christian spirituality, tears are, inevitably, provoked not only by reflection on one's own sins, but also by the spectacle of Christ's sufferings in the Passion. Indeed, these two are intimately connected in that the tortures suffered by Christ are seen by the penitent as the result of his or her own sin, whilst sorrow at Christ's sufferings is itself the most urgent motive of repentance—a complex of relationships that pervades the piety of the medieval and early modern periods. The great altarpieces that so dramatically depict the sufferings of Mary and the disciples at the foot of the cross are, in this respect, a visual

---

[108] *Confessions*, VIII, 12.

[109] François de Sales, *Traitté de l'amour de Dieu*, in *Œuvres*, vol. iv/1 (Annecy: Niérat, 1894), 154.

[110] S. Kierkegaard, *Without Authority*, trans. H. V. and E. H. Hong, SKS 11 (Princeton: Princeton University Press, 1997), 174. Kierkegaard's extensive reading in Pietistic literature provided a conduit to the medieval spiritual traditions that also lie behind de Sales's writings. On the tears of the sinful woman see Søren Landkildehus, 'Through a Veil of Tears: The Image of Christ in Kierkegaard's Discourses on The Woman who was a Sinner', in R. Kralik et al. (eds.), *Kierkegaard and Christianity: Acta Kierkegaardiana*, vol. iii (Toronto: Kierkegaard Circle and Kierkegaard Society, 2008), 132–41. Even if there is no question of a direct borrowing, it is at the very least striking that the Danish term *Sorg*, customarily translated as 'sorrow' or grief (as in 'sorrow for sin'), is cognate with the German *Sorge* that, via Heidegger, comes to be the 'Care' that is distinctive of Dasein's way of being.

[111] See *The Prayers and Tears of Jacques Derrida*, pp. xviii–xix. The theme of tears is further developed at various points in Caputo's study, especially 291–9.

instruction to the faithful in how and why to weep, whilst the words of Bach's Passion chorales and arias repeatedly make the link between sorrow at Christ's sufferings and recognition of one's own sin.

As in the case of trembling, tears also feature at crucial moments of Dostoevsky's novels. When Raskolnikov finally goes to the crossroads to confess his crime, he is said to have experienced a fire that softened him throughout as he did so, filling him with delight and happiness, 'and the tears flowed'.[112] Of course, Dostoevsky is a nineteenth-century novelist (and a Russian!), and we might assume that weeping and tears are merely part of the furniture of the kind of novels he wrote. How could one deal with stories of drunkenness, domestic violence, the deaths of children, murder, and unhappy love without tears? Nevertheless, it is clear that, at several points, the novelist gives a special weight to them. The Elder Zosima (whose teachings were in part shaped by Dostoevsky's own reading of Isaac of Nineveh) exhorts his listeners to 'Kiss the earth and love it, tirelessly, insatiably, love all men, love all things, seek this rapture and ecstasy. Water the earth with the tears of your joy, and love those tears.'[113] Alyosha, Zosima's disciple, puts this into practice when, exhausted from sitting beside the corpse of his recently deceased mentor and overwhelmed by a dream in which Zosima himself has appeared to him as a guest at the wedding in Cana of Galilee, he rushes out and throws himself to the ground.

He did not know why he was embracing it, he did not try to understand why he longs so irresistibly to kiss it, to kiss all of it, but he was kissing it, weeping, sobbing, and watering it with his tears, and he vowed ecstatically to love it, to love it unto ages of ages. 'Water the earth with the tears of your joy, and love those tears...,' rang in his soul. What was he weeping for? Oh, in his rapture he wept even for the stars that shone on him from the abyss, and 'he was not ashamed of this ecstasy'.[114]

Alyosha's tears are not to be interpreted simply as expressing a kind of overheated Slavic emotionalism but they 'perform' Alyosha's being reunited with the world, with himself, and with God. As the narrator comments, 'He fell to the earth a weak youth and rose up a fighter... "Someone visited my soul in that hour," he would say afterwards with firm belief in his words...'[115] Tears of this kind not only manifest but also effect the crossing of the distance

---

[112] *Crime and Punishment*, 525. It is also perhaps significant that although we are not told that he now no longer trembles, he is described as having become calm and walking straight towards the police station to acknowledge his crime 'quite briskly'.

[113] F. M. Dostoevsky, *The Brothers Karamazov*, trans. R. Pevear and L. Volokhonsky (London: Vintage, 1992), 322.

[114] Ibid. 362.

[115] Ibid. 363.

that divides us from ourselves, from our depths, and from the (divine?) Being concealed in those depths.

Tears, like trembling, make manifest the breakdown of the controlling ego in its relation to the body: when the sight is blurred by tears, we no longer see the boundaries between self and world with our accustomed clarity. There is undoubtedly a significant overlap both in the occurrence and in the ontological meanings of trembling and tears but, in a way that goes beyond the rupturing of the ego that is manifest in trembling, tears bespeak our involvement with the personal other and testify that we are not, cannot, and should not be alone in the world.[116] In weeping for each other I and Thou come together in one. Tears are the beginning of charity. In the moment of his tearful ecstasy, Alyosha 'wanted to forgive everyone and for everything, and to ask forgiveness, oh, not for himself! but for all and for everything, "as others are asking for me," rang again in his soul'.[117] And it was from pity for Jerusalem, we are told, that 'Jesus wept' (Luke 19: 41). The connection between tears and charity is also marked at several points in the Western tradition, as when Bernard makes a threefold division between tears wept for oneself, for one's neighbour, and for the Lord.[118]

It might seem as if the identification of trembling and weeping as instances of the body's involvement in the spiritual life is somewhat arbitrary, but not only are these phenomena widely attested in the Christian tradition, they seem also to be intimately related to the basic moods of fear (*phobos*) and pity (*eleos*) that Aristotle saw as central to the experience of tragedy and which the dramatic presentation of tragic events sought to purge through catharsis.[119] In face of the horror of existence and a universal history of war, the trembling and weeping that mark the religious life might therefore seem appropriate means of transforming a tragic view of life and bringing about acceptance, peace, and joy—and doing so in a manner that is not merely 'aesthetic' in a Kierkegaardian sense.

In any case, they provide two eminent and well-attested instances of how it is only with, and never without, the lived body that we are able to cross the

---

[116] For an extended discussion of the phenomenological meaning of tears see D. Levin, 'Crying for a Vision', in his *The Opening of Vision: Nihilism and the Postmodern Situation* (London: Routledge, 1988), 167–340. Levin too sees tears as involuntarily effecting the breaking down of the ego's attempt to control the self but also thereby providing a basis for the practice of care, understood in a sense derived from *Being and Time* but involving a set of specific ontic commitments (particularly with regard both to justice and to mysticism) that go beyond anything we find in Heidegger.

[117] *The Brothers Karamazov*, 362.

[118] 'Larmes', 297.

[119] *Poetics*, 1452b–1453a.

distance that separates us from the depths in which our existence is folded into the world in such a way that our own existence and the being of the world become real to us. Not even the purest religious love seems possible without such bodily enactments of religious meaning as the beating heart, a kind of trembling, and tears of contrition, joy, and compassion. But this is not to be understood in such a way that the body is merely the instrument for the expression of religious ideas or aspirations. Rather, the kind of bodily events we have been considering simply are the way in which our being religious occurs. But, if a verbally articulated religious view of life is in this way an interpretation of what, in the first instance, is a bodily event, this also means that religious existence belongs on the common ground of human existence in which we all continuously participate by virtue of our embodiment. The hand that is stretched out toward the wounded person may not be understood by the person reaching out as religious (and perhaps it is best, as we have heard argued, if it is 'in secret' and so secret that the other hand doesn't even know what is being done[120]), but it may, according to Matthew 25: 31–46 (the parable of the sheep and the goats), in the end, be interpreted, and rightly, in a religious sense.

BODY, BEING, GOD (II)

In a sense we now return to the point at which this enquiry began in earnest, when we reflected on how, especially in the Latin tradition of the West, the desire for God is articulated in terms that assimilate it to the longing for a fuller, deeper, more abiding Being in such a way that the God of the Patriarchs and the God who is Being-Itself become one. We have now seen something of how this longing is not only comprehensible in terms of the lived body but is pre-eminently so—and there is perhaps no one in whom both the power and the paradox of this conjunction is more evident than Augustine. Few, if any, are more eloquent than Augustine in describing the agitations, distractions, and sufferings with which life in the body afflicts the human heart, plunging us into a state of restlessness and unease, disturbing the social and ideological constructions of reality that we have erected around our fragile, vulnerable bodies to keep us from collapsing into the vertiginous abyss that threatens to

---

[120] Adnès interestingly reflects on the disappearance of 'tears' from modern Christianity in connection with what he regards as their essential secrecy: the gift of tears, he writes, 'perhaps conceals itself and surrounds itself with silence. This secrecy and this modesty will always be the guarantors of its truth' (in 'Larmes', 303).

open beneath our every step. And if Augustine's heart cries out for a kind of Being that is ultimately unattainable by human beings—unless it were at the price of surrendering everything that makes us human—it is only because he is to such an extraordinary degree conscious of the power of the body over every facet of his thinking, feeling mind. Yet perhaps it is in just such experiences of the unquiet heart, in the sensed need of God that they awaken, that we find not only the beginning but also the end of religion, so that we could pray for nothing greater than 'to know our need of God'. However, to say that *what* our unquiet hearts need *is God* is to say what cannot or can only uncertainly, hesitantly, ambiguously, equivocally, and indirectly be said. If the depths of embodiment reveal a space in which we seem to find ourselves given to ourselves, as if from another realm of Being, as if our own lives were and were to be lived as gifted,[121] then naming the giver of this gift as 'God' is, in the end, to say that we do not know *what* it is. But even when they do not yet know what it is they seek, even if all they have to go on is an 'I-do-not-know-what' and an 'almost nothing', and even if their first steps are accompanied by fear and trembling and tears of contrition, those who know their need of God and who find the freedom and the courage to follow the promptings of their hearts are free to commit themselves to trusting the reality of those promptings and to interpreting them as pointing out the path that leads to God. Their fear and trembling and their tears persuade them in a degree and in a manner that no 'ontology' can do. Yet it is precisely this sense of something real—their own reality!—being at issue that also makes it possible, perhaps even natural, for them to speak of what they are seeking or of what draws them forward as, in some sense, 'Being'.

If the religious—Augustinian!—soul might be all too eager to see the turmoil of bodily life as the first stirring of the love of God, we must also remember that, according to the argument of this enquiry, there is no shortcut from the concrete specificity of embodied existence to some other realm of Being. The reality of God may resonate in the immediate experience of embodied existence but this is not to say that God is the immediate object of a specifically religious kind of intuition or perception. With the mainstream of Christian tradition it seems best to say that we never get to 'see' God in this world. But, in any case, we must remind ourselves at this point that we are considering the question of God only with regard to the issue of God's way of Being and our way of relating to that Being. The question is not whether or how we might be justified in speaking of God in terms of fatherhood or providence or goodness, but is simply a question of how God can or could *be*

---

[121] For further discussion of the theme of gift see the section 'The Possibility of the Gift' in the following chapter.

at all for us. In this sense, whatever this enquiry might in the end encourage us to say about God over and above giving a sense to speaking of divine Being is and will remain minimal.

Over the previous chapters we have seen how the apprehension of Being ultimately dovetails with the desire for a community of friendship and love, but this is something different from making God himself the mirror-image of human emptiness and thereby exposing God to the kind of reductionist argument that sees religious belief as mere wish-fulfilment.[122] Yet precisely with regard to the convergence of ontological desire and the longing for a kingdom of love on earth, naming God as the proper goal of what the unquiet heart desires has consequences for life in the world and can be seen to serve the fulfilment of that desire and that longing. For naming the goal of all our striving as 'God' is to take a small but decisive step towards liberation from the kind of cyclical violence endemic to human relations so brilliantly yet disturbingly portrayed by Sartre. For Sartre's unhappy universe is in part the outcome of individuals who, because they are no longer able to direct their ultimate passion to God, direct it instead toward other human individuals. Yet—as, in a sense, Sartre rightly sees—such passion is too excessive to be lavished on any other human individual. None of us can bear it. We are not suited to being each other's gods or each other's worshippers and when individuals project their desire for absolute Being into their relationships with others the outcomes are predictably disastrous. In such a universe we are repeatedly condemned to be dominators or dominated, annihilators or annihilated. When, however, God is identified as the proper focus of our ultimate desire for fullness of Being, human beings are immediately liberated from having to fulfil such impossible roles. When we set our hearts on God we are absolved both from having to be the foundation of our own being and from justifying our own existence in and though our alternately tyrannical and submissive comportment towards others. Simply in the aspect of being, God already gives effect to a love that frees us to be ourselves, to escape the relentless cycle of sadism and masochism, and to be together in new and more creative ways.

The saving element in the encounter with the human other, I therefore suggest, is not a permutation of each being the other's impossible object of

---

[122] This is an argument perhaps best condensed in Marx's statement that 'Religion is the sigh of the oppressed creature, the heart of a heartless world and the soul of soulless conditions. It is the opium of the people.' See K. Marx, *Early Writings*, trans. R. Livingstone and G. Benton (Harmondsworth: Penguin, 1975), 244. See also, e.g., L. Feuerbach, *The Essence of Faith According to Martin Luther*, trans. M. Cherno (New York: Harper and Row, 1967); F. Nietzsche, *Also Sprach Zarathustra*, 571–4 (one example amongst many); S. Freud, *The Future of an Illusion*, trans. W. D. Robson-Scott (London: Hogarth Press, 1961).

desire. Rather, it is a moment of friendship, of togetherness in being, in which the one neither overwhelms nor is absorbed into the other, but the two draw near to one another and are established in a nearness that allows each to be who they are. The conversations that unfold in such a place of meeting will tend not so much towards an ecstatic moment of illumination as to an exchange of words or silences that, for a certain time and in a certain place, holds open a space of being together that allows the depth of darkness encompassing our conscious lives to be sensed and acknowledged. This darkness may be viewed reductively as no more than the darkness of bodily life (what Kierkegaard at one point calls our 'cryptogamous' life), but it may, as we have heard both Merleau-Ponty and Kierkegaard—from very different points of view—suggest, also be a mode of God's being present 'as another self in ourselves which dwells in and authenticates our darkness'.[123] And when that is so, then we will be less likely to think of the 'darkness' with which our conscious life is encompassed on every side as the threatening darkness of an all-devouring vortex and more able to accept it as the deep peace of an oceanic abyss. The friendship that takes shape in such a place will no longer be the love of an alter ego but a way of being together in which each gives to each time and space to work out how to make something better out of the ruins of what might have been, ruins that lie everywhere in our private lives and our common social reality; where it is no longer a question of demanding, accusing, judging, seducing, or adoring but of enabling each to find the space of freedom in which to become who they believe themselves to be capable of being. It is no longer the struggle of master and slave, but of Zosima's teaching of all-encompassing love and responsibility. The spiritual community is neither an expression of erotic desire nor of cold charity nor even of utopistic yearning, but rather comes to pass as the kind of life together that is possible only to friends capable of sharing the space and acknowledging the distance that belong to all embodied being.[124]

This is not a programme for placid self-contentment, since where we are and where we are striving to be do not coincide. As Merleau-Ponty forcefully argued, the body is not a site of stasis but of a dynamic movement, always projecting itself beyond its present towards new objects, new encounters, new possibilities

---

[123] The phrase, we recall, is Merleau-Ponty's (*The Prose of the World*, 84). See n. 69 above.

[124] It is, of course, entirely open to question as to whether or how far the realization of such a spiritual community coincides with the social vision of any actual ecclesiastical community. However, I would hope that these remarks both reflect and might prove fruitful both for the development of pastoral theology and for noting the role of pastoral practice for the overall development of theology. As Luther long ago argued, theology is a practical and not a speculative science and it is the concrete forms of our life together that will decide the truth or expose the falsehood of any more purely theoretical claims.

of experience. We are not yet all we shall be. For now, and other than in transient moments of epiphany, we still experience presence as a place we have yet to find or to which we have yet to return; we still experience ourselves as what we have yet to become; we still experience time as awaiting all that is yet to arrive; and we still experience language as caught in a struggle to say what hasn't yet been said. If embodiment means that our relation to God can in one aspect be said to be 'always already' it does not absolve us from the tension of this 'not yet'.

The point at which we have now arrived in this chapter opens a perspective from which to re-read the course of this enquiry up to this point and to reinterpret all that has previously been said about presence, the for-itself, time, space, language, and the relation to the other in their implied or explicit reference to bodily life. It is only in the body's way of registering a certain presence and a certain longing that we are drawn to understand—to *live*—our relation to Being as more than an intellectual construct, an ideal focus, or a metaphysical principle. Embodied being is, simply, the kind of Being that best corresponds to the exigency of love, the kind of Being that love bestows, and the kind of Being in which love is proved—whether it is a matter of *eros* or of *agape*. It is only when our words resound with the depths of embodiment that Being itself becomes meaningful. More precisely, embodiment is not so much a mode of the presence of Being as the measure of the nearness and distance of our relation to Being and, therefore, of the God who is Being-Itself. When we say 'God is', whether in a predicative ('God is good') or an existential ('God exists') sense, the purchase of what is said rests upon such movement towards God and such rest in God as can be testified by the immediacy of bodily life. We ourselves, in the fullness and in the penury of our embodiment, are the stake in whatever ontological claims we make concerning God. There is nothing behind or beyond that to which we can appeal—which is why speaking of God is always, potentially, witness and martyrdom and even self-martyrdom, if it turns out that we have, in fact, wasted our lives by staking them on what turns out to be error and delusion. What could be more 'real' than such a choice? What could be more a matter of 'to be or not to be'?

At the start of this section I suggested that this now lengthy enquiry seemed to be in the process of returning to its beginning, but this remark could also be taken in a hostile sense. For the time and place of embodied being-with-others that has been identified as the condition of articulating the God-relationship in terms of Being is precisely what Augustine and a great cloud of religious witnesses have experienced as fearfully exposing the self to mutability, decay, and death. And who can deny that we who share an embodied life together on earth must each of us—all of us—pass out of existence into 'we know not what, we know not where' (Dryden)? Isn't this precisely what the great tradition of Christian thought said we needed to be redeemed from? Drawing the understanding of divine Being into the ebb and flow of embodied life is precisely to strip it of what makes it 'Being', even if it allows for a certain residual, but non-absolute 'divinity'—so isn't this another case of reductionism, of collapsing the infinite qualitative difference separating human and divine into the closed circuit of immanence? Isn't it, after all, what some theologians would call 'nihilism'?

Perhaps it is not really fruitful in what hopes to be a serious enquiry to pay too much attention to that kind of charge, since it smacks more of sloganizing than of thoughtful reflection. Nevertheless, it is clear that there is a question to be addressed, and that more must be done to make clear the kind of Being or the kind of relation to Being that is still possible if we accept without reserve the reality of embodiment as the condition of all religious existence. In terms of classical philosophical terminology the maximum that might be arrived at on these terms would be to speak of a certain mingling of Being and non-being, or what that terminology has also called possibility or potentiality. In the next chapter I shall therefore seek to reflect on what it might mean to think and speak of God under the rubric of possibility and whether doing so still allows us to use the word 'God' in any significant sense at all.

7

Possibility, Nothingness, and the Gift of Being

POSSIBILITY, EXISTENCE, AND THEOLOGY

When the question of Being is made dependent on the possibility of a future community of love (Chapter 5) and on the lived reality of a fragile bodily life that, in an Augustinian perspective, is shot through with non-being (Chapter 6), it might seem that the possibility of an assured knowledge of transcendent immutable Being has become no more than—a possibility. The theme of possibility has in fact haunted this enquiry for some time. It is, for example, implicit in the basic phenomenon of the distancing of consciousness and Being, which Sartre also described in terms of possibility. However, it is a peculiar kind of possibility that he described as 'lack'. Why? Because since the possibility of becoming present to myself—coinciding in presence with the being that I am—is impossible, 'possibility' signifies that which I can never be. As Sartre sums up: 'The possible is *the something* which the For-itself lacks in order to be itself . . . The possible . . . has the being of a lack and as lack, it lacks being. The Possible is not, the possible is possibilized to the exact degree that the For-itself makes itself be . . . [it] determines in schematic outline a location in the nothingness which the For-itself is beyond itself.'[1]

Heidegger too conceives the question of existence as a question of possibility: 'Dasein', he writes, 'always understands itself in terms of its existence—in terms of a possibility of itself: to be itself or not itself.'[2] As he later explains: 'In each case Dasein is its possibility, and it "has" this possibility, but not just as a property, as something present-at-hand would. And because Dasein is in each case essentially its own possibility, it can, in its very Being, "choose" itself and win itself; it can also lose itself and never "win" itself; or only "seem" to do so.'[3] In other words, Dasein—ontically the human subject—cannot be

---

[1] *Being and Nothingness*, 102.
[2] *Being and Time*, 41/19. [3] Ibid. 68/43.

understood in conventional philosophical terms as a certain kind of substance defined by a particular set of attributes, such as a capacity for language or moral decision-making. In the Heideggerian perspective, language is not an attribute that I 'have', but a possibility to be realized in speaking and listening. Similarly, a 'moral sense' exists only to the extent that and in the way that I enact the peculiar kind of reflection and decision-making that we call being moral.

Of course, unlike Sartre, Heidegger does speak about the possibility that I might choose *and win myself*—which, for Sartre, would be to effect what he regards as the impossible return to a kind of self-presence that, from the standpoint of consciousness, is always already lost.[4] But although Dasein (at least in its 'average everyday' mode of fallenness) always 'lags behind' its own possibilities and never achieves the being-a-whole towards which it strives, it does relate to this being-a-whole as a real possibility and not a simple impossibility. Being-a-whole is a future that I anticipate for myself and by means of which I define myself: it is a future that, when I resolutely lay hold of it (as in authentic being-towards-death), reveals who I *am*. In these terms, then, I *am* my possibility.[5] However, even when Heidegger seems most confident as to the possibility of such a possibility, he also acknowledged that resolutely laying hold of it would engender a certain reticence, since to speak of it would be to expose it to the entropic flow of 'idle talk'. It is perhaps for similar reasons that, in his later 'history of Being', even the poetic word that speaks forth truth is inherently enigmatic and its fulfilment constantly deferred.

These last remarks also remind us that once we have abandoned the view that language directly and unambiguously intends its object and is capable of disclosing the unity of being and essence of that object and therefore capable of showing us 'what' it *is*, then everything that we say, in language, will essentially culminate in an appeal to possibility. For every statement must then be considered in principle corrigible, 'a raid on the inarticulate' that reveals one possibility of understanding what it is we are dealing with—but this one possibility will only ever be understandable by being related or opposed to other possibilities, leaving 'the inarticulate' itself to withdraw into its own pre-verbal silence. And when what we say about the world enters

---

[4] 'A horizon of possibility that is always already lost' is the gloss Michael Theunissen gives to Kierkegaard's concept of despair. See M. Theunissen, *Der Begriff Verzweiflung: Korrekturen an Kierkegaard* (Frankfurt am Main: Suhrkamp, 1993), especially 102–4.

[5] These rather sketchy comments and selective quotations would, of course, need considerable refining in order to do justice to Heidegger's position. For example, one would need to distinguish between the level of the *existentiell* resoluteness that you or I might (or might not) show in relation to our deaths and the possibility of an authentic existential reflection on the meaning of Being. However, at the same time, these two levels are importantly connected, such that the ontological possibility of a truthful revelation of being requires the attestation of such individual acts of *existentiell* resoluteness.

into the skein of our human relations, and especially when we communicate with one another about our human feelings, thoughts, and motivations, then, as we have seen, the uncertainty as to whether the other is or isn't 'in' what she or he is saying spreads an atmosphere of supposition around even the most acutely articulated insights and analyses. In human relationships, every statement becomes a question, a hypothesis, a possibility. Do you, can you, could you mean it?

Is it then possible for us to emerge from this miasma of possibilities? Is it possible that (one day!) the half-light and often discordant polyphony that Dostoevsky's novels so painstakingly narrate might be dispelled by the light of a universal experience of amity? Might love (one day, sometime!) bring us to a place in which we could speak the truth without the fear, and see and affirm what each is saying to each? Can we, may we, hope for that moment, that time (one day, sometime, in the end!), when we might freely enter into a common and open space of truth in which our words tell us what we really think and who we really *are*? And if the continuing history of injustice and violence testifies that we are not there yet, then it would seem that a fulfilled relation to Being, really being able both to know and to say who we ourselves are, becomes in an emphatic sense a matter of hope. But is real hope possible— or is it plainly, and in the worst sense, utopistic? Is possibility itself possible—or is it (as Sartre's view suggests) self-defeating, such that understanding ourselves in and through our possibilities (above all the possibility of a coming age of truth) is *ipso facto* to deny ourselves the foothold in reality that alone might give leverage to our relation to history? Won't preoccupation with possibility always end in disappointment, since possibility inherently volatilizes the real? But even if we still hope in hope in the face of such counsels of despair, isn't it nevertheless clear that if the day, the time, and the end in which all our hopes are fulfilled has not, as yet, arrived, then we cannot really *know* what it is we are hoping for? And if we have never known it, who knows what fulfilment would really be like? Who knows what it would really *be*? Doesn't the content of our hope then become 'possibility' in yet another sense, i.e., that it might possibly be this or might possibly be that? Doesn't the not-yet of fulfilment mean that the content of possibility is itself up for discussion, such that it comes back to us to consider and choose just those possibilities in which we believe our fulfilment might best be accomplished? Even on the premises of hope, doesn't our human being then dissolve into the being of possibility?

These questions are answered in the Aristotelian-Thomist tradition by an insistence on the primacy of actuality over possibility (or potentiality) and from the Aristotelian-Thomist point of view the barrage of questions fired off in the preceding paragraph could be read as using a purely logical sense of possibility in order to subvert a more adequate metaphysical reflection on the dependence of possibility on actuality. Thus, the reflection that a Kingdom of Love might or might not come on earth could be seen as a case of the kind of possibility in play when we say of any proposition that it could be true or not, as in 'It could rain tomorrow or not' or 'This might be a piece of amber or it might not.' In such cases, the fact that the truth of what is being said is dependent on a future state of affairs that cannot as yet be verified makes no essential difference. However, this is something rather different from saying that a given entity exists merely in a state of possibility.[6] If I say 'This is an oak tree,' what I am saying is possibly true and possibly false. If I am referring to what is in fact a beech tree it is false, whilst if I am referring to the venerable oak that has stood on the village green since the sixteenth century, it is true. If, however, I am referring to an acorn the situation is slightly more complex. In this case, we may say, the acorn is an oak tree—potentially: that is, it has the potential or capacity to become an oak tree or that it has the possibility of becoming an oak tree.[7] When it has fully grown and become the magnificent oak it has the potential to be, then it will actually be an oak. Thus, actuality is ontologically prior to potentiality. What actually *is* is not a merely chance outcome of a configuration of possibilities but potential is determined by act: only what is hot can cause an entity that has the potential to become hot (e.g., a piece of wood) to do so. In Aquinas' 'Five Ways' of demonstrating the existence of God, a Being that is fully in act—a Being that is pure act—is deemed to be necessary in order for anything to be at all: 'Being' cannot emerge from potential unless it is brought to be by something that actually is. On this view, the conundrum of the chicken and egg will always be answered in favour of the chicken.[8] Possibility or potentiality is a deficient mode of

---

[6] It is in this connection that Brentano argued that there is a basic difference between Aristotle's 'potential' and modern 'possibility'. See F. Brentano, *On the Several Senses of Being in Aristotle*, trans. R. George (Berkeley and Los Angeles: University of California Press, 1975), 27–8.

[7] 'Possibility', 'Potentiality', and 'Capacity' are only some standard ways of translating the Aristotelian *dynamis*. In his lectures on Aristotle's *Metaphysics θ*, Heidegger notes also what his English translators render as force, art, talent, capability, competence, aptitude, skill, violent force, and power (thus the English translation is itself sub-titled 'On the Essence and Actuality of Force'). See M. Heidegger, *Aristotle's Metaphysics θ: On the Essence and Actuality of Force*, trans. W. Brogan and P. Warnek (*Gesamtausgabe*, vol. xxxiii) (Bloomington, Ind.: Indiana University Press, 1995), 59–61.

[8] This position is, of course, effectively diametrically opposed to that of Darwin, for whom the emergence of new species is indeed the result of random mutations amongst an assembly of beings that have the potential to become all manner of different beings. In a sense, the inversion of the Aristotelian/Thomist 'ranking' of Actuality and Possibility that will be proposed in this chapter can be considered as taking the Darwinian revolution seriously as metaphysics.

being, such that a thing that is merely possible is less than what really is or what has fully actualized its being.

Now it might seem that *Being and Time* could be read in an Aristotelian-Thomist sense on this point, since it bespeaks a concern with realizing or actualizing what, for now, is only the possibility of living as a whole and therefore, to put it in scholastic terms, to pass from a state of potentiality to one of actuality—to become what we *are*. So too in the case of hope for a utopian future of love and understanding, since, as the New Testament already understood, hope that is fulfilled is no longer hope but quietly yields to love. As in the case of Augustine's often quoted comment that war always aims at peace, doesn't hope too always aim at its own cessation? Doesn't hope somehow already have to know the power of God as sufficient to ensure the triumph of love over all that is evil? Authenticity, love, and peace would thus, in their different ways, seem to be the ultimate reason why it is possible for us to seek self-realization, to hope, and to strive to overcome war. The logical possibility that a Kingdom of Love might (one day) arrive one earth will remain a purely logical possibility unless human beings really do have the potential or capacity for living authentically together in love and peace. If possibility is not to remain a purely empty and self-defeating category (as in the Sartrean account), and no matter how eloquently it speaks to us about possibilities that exceed biological and social necessity, mustn't it point beyond itself towards the reality that, for now, it merely anticipates?

If, then, we can only understand human existence when we understand it in the light of the full actualization of all its possibilities, i.e., when we see it for what it really is, mustn't this apply all the more to God? For if God is understood in terms of Being or Being-Itself, then a God who was merely 'possible' would seem incapable of explaining himself, let alone of providing a basis for understanding anything else. Surely God has to be what and as God is, if God is to be anything at all? For, if God does not fully realize all his possibilities, then either God must in turn be less than Being-Itself (which must, by definition be what and as it truly is), or else there is neither God nor Being but only the endless chaos of nihilistic relativity. As Aquinas puts it, if God is eternal, it is necessary that there is no potency in him—a statement for which in, e.g., the *Summa contra Gentiles*, he offers the six following reasons. First, because a being that has an element of potency can be or can not-be, but God cannot not-be, therefore there is no potency in God's being. Secondly, because act precedes potency since potency cannot raise itself to act without the agency of what is already actual. As God is first Being and first Cause there can therefore be no potency prior to God's being actually God. Thirdly, because a necessary Being is in no way a possible Being, since it has no cause external to itself, as a possible Being has; therefore, since God is a necessary being, he is 'in no way a possible Being, and so no potency is found in his substance'. Fourthly, an agent that is not wholly in act cannot be the first agent, since it would then only come to be in act through participation in something. 'The first agent, therefore, namely God, has no admixture of potency but is pure act.' Fifthly, since motion (i.e., 'being moved' or moving from one state to another) is the act of that which exists in potency and God is absolutely impassible and immutable, God has 'no part of potency'. Sixthly, for a being to move from potency to act, there must be a prior Being already in act; there can be no infinite regress, and therefore there must be a being 'that is only in act and in no wise in potency. This being we call God.'[9]

Must we, then, reaffirm the medieval view that it is by being *actus purus*, the pure Act, that God is thereby also suited to be the sole ground of all that exists and the only assurance of 'things hoped for'?[10]

But if we can only ever speak of the divine Being in the dialectic of analogy and negation and since the content of all our analogies is derived from our own creaturely experiences of Being (i.e. of Being-in-beings), then whatever it means for God to be the pure actuality in whom all possibilities are fulfilled is something that will only be meaningful to us in terms of our experiences of the nearness and the distance of Being. That is to say, the meaning of a pure Act is, for us, conceivable only on the basis of and in the language of experiences that are a mixture of possibility and actuality—and even when we speak of an *actus purus*, the very dynamics of representation mean that this *actus purus* 'exists' for us only as possibility, a transcendent possibility beyond our horizon of experience. It is not and cannot be fully actual here and now in our actual experience, which, as I have many times noted, cannot but be 'distanced' from Being-Itself.

Such a radical reordering of the relationship between possibility and actuality seems, in fact, to be one of the salient outcomes of *Being and*

---

[9] Thomas Aquinas, *On the Truth of the Catholic Faith* (*Summa contra Gentiles*), trans. V. J. O'Bourke (New York: Image Books, 1956), Book I, Q. 16 (pp. 100–1). Commenting on Thomas's text *Quaestiones disputatae de potentia*, Edith Stein argues that Thomas allows for a certain potency in God. However, since this is then said to be neither passive nor 'opposed to' actuality but is a kind of 'active potency' that 'does not exist aside from or outside his act' it is hard to see what new element this introduces other than the purely formal point that the *actus purus* of God enacts the actualizing of everything that has the potentiality to be. But that is merely tautologous. See E. Stein, *Finite and Eternal Being: An Attempt at an Ascent to the Meaning of Being*, trans. K. F. Reinhardt (Washington, DC: ICS Publications, 2002), 2.

[10] Ernst Bloch suggested that there was a very different way of reading Aristotle that he called 'Left-Aristotelianism' and that he saw represented in medieval philosophy itself by Avicenna. On this view, the possibilities contained in matter had the power to realize themselves without the prior existence of a fully actualized form. See E. Bloch, *Avicenna und die Aristotelische Linke* (Berlin: Rütten and Loening, 1952).

Time. For Heidegger insists there that Dasein *is* its possibilities, and it is precisely in having to be its possibilities, in having to choose itself from amongst its possibilities, that Dasein can exist at all.[11] Nor is this diminished by his conviction—at least in *Being and Time*—that these possibilities can be grasped and lived in a primordial and authentic manner. Whilst it may be the case that a certain natural endowment may be essential if I am to have the potential to become an Olympic athlete, this is not the case when it is a matter of simply being who I am, as I am. Here, it is not the fact of an 'actual' capacity that matters, i.e., a potential defined by its relation to a given actuality, but simply a relation to what exists only as possibility.

From the Thomist standpoint, this will seem like covert humanism, an attempt to measure God by the standards of such finite, temporal, changeable beings as we are, beings who are always in a mixed state of act and potency, striving towards but never (in this life) achieving our true being. But even in a properly theological perspective—perhaps especially in a properly theological perspective—the question needs to be asked whether the pre-eminence of actuality is as indisputable as Thomas thinks. One might even ask whether the concern with what is actual does not signal a basic confusion of genres. This is a point recently proposed by Ingolf Dalferth, who suggests that whilst science is properly concerned with what is the case and philosophy with what might be the case (i.e., determining the conditions under which statements might be meaningful or true), theology addresses what is the case strictly in the horizon of eschatology, i.e., of what is absolutely future. As Dalferth also puts it, the language of science is in the indicative, philosophy in the subjunctive, and theology in the eschatological indicative.[12] In a theological perspective, to say that God is creator is to say that he is the one who brings about both

---

[11] In the lectures on *Metaphysics θ*, Heidegger in fact offers a reading of Aristotle that finds a distinction between Being considered as *ousia* (the scholastic substance) and Being considered in terms of possibility/actuality, thus subverting the simple identification of substantial and actual Being or of 'what' an entity is and 'how' it is. This allows him to imply an affinity between his own philosophy and that of Aristotle, whilst continuing to keep his distance from the 'ossified' tradition of scholasticism. Nevertheless, Catriona Hanley seems correct in concluding her discussion of these lectures with the comment that, for Heidegger (and as opposed to Aristotle), 'Human being as living into finite possibility, and as aware of its own possibility, precedes actuality in the order of understanding. Between Aristotle and Heidegger, there is then a shift from the priority of the eternal to the priority of the finite' (C. Hanley, *Being and God in Aristotle and Heidegger: The Role of Method in Thinking the Infinite* (Lanham, Md.: Rowman and Littlefield, 2000), 163).

[12] I. Dalferth, *Die Wirklichkeit des Möglichen* (Tübingen: Mohr Siebeck, 2003), 121–3. In a different key, Caputo questions whether the vocabulary of act and potency really helps Thomas in articulating his own theological project since it cannot do justice to his 'higher metaphysical purposes' that presuppose a Christian conception of the divine *esse* that transcends all other entities (see *Heidegger and Aquinas*, 137–9).

actuality and possibility. God, in other words—and no matter what problems this statement makes for developing a meaningful theological discourse—is prior to both actuality and possibility: each reflects only an aspect of the absolute, eschatological reality that God is, which, being eschatological, is not (yet) available to us as an object of knowledge. If the world determines the horizon of actuality within which alone human life can be lived, i.e., if it is the ground of everything that is or that can be, then the actuality of the world cannot itself be determinative for the absolute actuality of God which, in this sense, is a kind of actuality beyond actuality, an actuality that is no longer a principle of explanation as to why what is the case is so or why what there is exists.[13] But, then, is 'actuality' still the term that best articulates what is being sought here? Is an 'eschatological indicative' still an 'indicative' in any recognizable sense? Doesn't it too acquire a certain subjunctive quality as a statement about what might or may be?[14]

Perhaps, then, we might do well to reconsider what another age might have called the 'excellence' of possibility as a legitimate and even decisive feature of our God-relationship. In doing so, it is of course acknowledged that a reflection on possibility will never yield a statement as to what is the case but only what might be so. But if our question concerns the possibility of hope (and, specifically, hope for a transformation of human relationships that would enable us finally to speak truth, fearlessly, in love), do we actually need more than an assurance that it *might* be so, and that hope is therefore possible? Might it not be that the mere possibility of hope is enough, since, once hope has been released into the world, it is itself a power capable of effecting the advent of what is hoped for? In this sense the question is not determined by whether human beings have an innate potential for realizing the pure form of humanity in a community of love but whether their ability to hope that it might be so can be effective in transforming existence in the light of a freely endorsed commitment to love. In this spirit, we might think that hope is enough to make us believe that truth might be spoken and that we might presume on the good will of those to whom we speak and listen—a presumption that would seem basic to any kind of genuine communication. 'I hope I may say this . . . I hope you are telling me the truth . . . I hope that you are listening, really listening to what I'm saying'—these phrases indicate how hope might engender and nourish the virtuous circle of love, how love itself

---

[13] See especially 139 ff.

[14] Or, if not, doesn't it fall back into a case of what Derrida referred to as the 'hyperessentiality' that characterizes standard forms of negative theology? See also (again) R. Kearney, *The God who May Be: A Hermeneutics of Religion* (Bloomington, Ind.: Indiana University Press, 2001), especially 80–100.

requires us to be hopeful, hoping for the best for the other, hoping that the other can become better than he or she appears to be. In the face of everything that might persuade us otherwise, then, is hope possible? What might we hope for? What is possible? Is God possible?

THE EXCELLENCE OF POSSIBILITY

As a way of focusing this question I turn to Kierkegaard's programmatic statement in *The Sickness unto Death* that 'God is: that all things are possible or that all things are possible is God.'[15] Kierkegaard's statement deliberately plays upon several passages of the Gospels, as when Jesus tells the disciples about the inversion of values in the coming Kingdom of God and how the poor will take precedence over the rich, and comments that whilst this may be impossible for human beings 'for God all things are possible' (Mark 10: 27 and parallels), or in the prayer in Gethsemane, when Jesus prays for himself 'Abba, Father, for you all things are possible; remove this cup from me; yet not what I want, but what you want' (Mark 14: 35 and parallels).[16] Kierkegaard's statement does not simply repeat these formulations, however, but intensifies them. It is not just that God has the capability to do all things, but this capability is itself made to serve as a definition of who God is: 'God *is* that all things are possible.'

The context of this statement is a discussion of the way in which the polarities of finite/infinite and possibility/necessity shape the specific forms of human despair. As Kierkegaard argues the case, these polarities are intrinsic to all human life and each has its proper part to play in the constitution of the self, so that no one can be eliminated or downgraded without this resulting in a pathology of the self, i.e., despair.[17] In these terms, an inappropriate indulgence in possibility is a dangerous sign, typical, Kierkegaard thinks, of Romantic fantasists and dreamers and all those who refuse to take seriously

---

[15] S. Kierkegaard, *The Sickness unto Death*, trans. E. H. And H. V. Hong, SKS 11 (Princeton: Princeton University Press, 1980), 40 (amended). Theunissen notes that this is an 'unorthodox' definition—see *Der Begriff Verzweiflung*, 112.

[16] See also Luke 1: 37 where an analogous phrase is used by the angel in responding to Mary's hesitancy as to the possibility of her conceiving the divine child—'for nothing will be impossible with God'.

[17] A similar account of how the polarities of Being become distorted into 'structures of destruction' can be found in Paul Tillich, *Systematic Theology* (Welwyn: Nisbet, 1968), vol. i/2, ch. VII and vol. ii/2, ch. XV.

the necessary demands of life on earth.[18] However, he pays greater attention to the despair of necessity, which he defines in terms of its lack of possibility. This, to paraphrase, is the kind of despair in which a person is locked into a meaningless routine or surrenders their freedom, willingly or unwillingly, to external social or material forces. Noting that the kind of hope with which a young person starts out in life ('youthful idealism') is typically unable to sustain itself in the face of work and responsibility, Kierkegaard suggests it is just at the point at which such natural and spontaneous hope for a humanly fulfilled and meaningful life collapses that the real question of hope—and therefore of possibility—kicks in. What Kierkegaard calls the 'battle of faith' (which, he says, is also a battle for possibility) begins precisely at the point at which, 'humanly speaking', salvation has become an empty phrase and life has revealed itself to be one damned thing after another:[19] 'When someone faints, we call for water, eau de Cologne, smelling salts; but when someone wants to despair, then the word is: Get possibility, get possibility, possibility is the only salvation . . . when it depends upon *faith*—then only this helps: that for God all things are possible.'[20] Whether with regard to oneself or to others, when a person's project for their life collapses in ruins, provoking them to cry out (or, as Kierkegaard also sometimes envisaged, silently to brood over what they perceive as the fact) that everything is meaningless or hopeless, that there's no point to it all, or that they can't do anything about it, then salvation is believing that 'all things are possible for God', since 'God is, that all things are possible'.[21]

Note that, from its opening pages on, *The Sickness unto Death* was not concerned to address the self's relations to the external world—where it is clearly true that, no matter how audacious one's hope, not everyone can, for example, become President of the United States but only those born in America can do so. Instead, the thrust of the text was established by the opening definition of the self as a relation that relates itself to itself, a definition that, whatever other questions it raised, clearly identified the

---

[18] This thought lies at the heart of Kierkegaard's use of possibility in his critique of aesthetic existence. See, e.g., my *Kierkegaard: The Aesthetic and the Religious* (London: SCM Press, 1999), 145–6 and idem, *The Philosophy of Kierkegaard* (Chesham: Acumen, 2005), 40–2.

[19] Kierkegaard seems primarily to be thinking about the kind of despair that lies behind the façade of bourgeois existence, but, as his other writings suggest, the same logic could also be applied to cases of despair arising from more extreme situations of persecution, abuse, or suffering (somatic or social).

[20] *Sickness unto Death*, 38–9, slightly amended.

[21] Or, as he puts it in *The Concept of Anxiety*, 'Whoever is educated by anxiety is educated by possibility, and only those who are educated by possibility are educated according to their infinity' (S. Kierkegaard, *The Concept of Anxiety*, trans. R. Thomte, SKS 4 (Princeton: Princeton University Press, 1980), 156 (adapted)).

matter at issue as the inner orientation or condition of the self and the way in which it feels about itself and its life—not whether it is equipped for succeeding in one or other external undertaking. In other words, it is not an analysis of the self in terms of such varied projects as becoming a painter, a soldier, a parent, priest, or President of the United States, but of how I relate myself to my own particular life-project, whatever that may be. In these terms the metaphysical question of possibility is a question that potentially does and arguably should concern each of us, even if the concrete content of what is possible will differ from individual to individual. The fact that I have to focus my life on one or other undertaking or task in order to give content to my life does not preclude my understanding these particular projects in relation to a more ultimate or encompassing horizon of possibility that shapes *how* I go about relating myself to the particular choices I make. Believing that God is that all things are possible does not help me decide whether I want to be an artist or a CEO, but it may nevertheless affect my attempts to live out my choice. If my project is to become a painter but I get thrown out of art school, does this mean that all things are not, after all, possible? Not necessarily, since if I truly believe that all things are possible I may simply seek other means to realize this ambition. As long as I believe there is still possibility—and always will be—I will never entirely succumb to despair and it will never be 'the end of the road'; faith in possibility, then, not as faith in the possibility of achieving this or that, but as faith in the openness of life, faith in the possibility of there always being a way ahead—'tomorrow is another day'.[22]

In his idiosyncratic yet influential study of *Kierkegaard and Existential Philosophy*, Lev Shestov seized on the definition of God as being 'that all things are possible' as a kind of leitmotif for Kierkegaard's thought. The phrase seemed well suited to illustrate Shestov's own critique of Western philosophy as having been overwhelmingly determined by a kind of rationality that subordinated the freedom of individual thinking and willing to universal and exceptionless laws, whether these were conceived naturalistically or theologically.[23] Socrates, Plato, Aristotle, Stoicism, medieval philosophy, Spinoza, Hegel, and Husserl are amongst those who serve Shestov as defining representatives of this tendency. In the Kierkegaard book and elsewhere, he frequently epitomizes this view by citing Epictetus' suggestion that even

---

[22] Something of this seems to be captured in Jonathan Lear's account of what he calls 'radical hope'. See J. Lear, *Radical Hope: Ethics in the Face of Cultural Devastation* (Cambridge, Mass.: Harvard University Press, 2008). One thinks also of Camus's assertion that 'One must imagine Sisyphus happy' (see Albert Camus, *The Myth of Sisyphus*, trans. J. O'Brien (Harmondsworth: Penguin, 1955), 111).

[23] Shestov's characteristic way of 'Shestovizing' his supposed sources was already noted by contemporaries, but this does not mean that his interpretations are without interest!

Zeus would have to submit to the laws of necessity. Only occasionally, in such varied figures as Plotinus, Pascal, Kierkegaard, Dostoevsky, and Nietzsche, has an alternative point of view surfaced, although, as Shestov sees it, this is rarely carried through with complete consistency. Not even the most radical of exceptional thinkers are capable of enduring the abyssal terror that opens up for thinking and willing when the realm of universal laws has once been abandoned—a failure of nerve that (according to Shestov) also befell Kierkegaard. Only the Bible is truly consistent in the emphasis it places on human beings' capacity to think all things, will all things, and believe all things—if only one freely chooses to do so.

Unsurprisingly, Shestov sees Kierkegaard's exploration of Abraham's readiness to sacrifice Isaac as importantly challenging the near-universal faith in the universal laws of ethics. Abraham's faith that even if he should kill Isaac he would nevertheless get Isaac back and see God's promise fulfilled in the world exemplifies what it might mean to believe that 'God is that all things are possible.' He finds something similar in the case of the young man of *Repetition* who finds consolation in Job's refusal to explain his sufferings in terms of some religious, cosmic, or moral law. In pitting Job against Hegel, Kierkegaard 'reverses the course of time, returning to an epoch thousands of years in the past, when people didn't even dream of any of the things that our knowledge and our science have brought us'.[24] Yet Shestov asserts that even Kierkegaard, who went so far in challenging the universal laws of necessity and reason, doesn't—*daren't*—go all the way. In support of this claim he notes that whilst Kierkegaard said that if he had had faith he would have got Regine back and married her after all, he was nevertheless unable to make the necessary act of faith and, faced with Abraham, confessed his own incapacity to understand or to emulate the latter's suspension of the ethical. More seriously, he finds evidence, especially in Kierkegaard's later religious writings, that this is not just a matter of Kierkegaard reflecting on his own private lack of faith. On the contrary, he depicts Kierkegaard as subjecting the Christian God to the same external necessity as Epictetus subjected Zeus. Shestov sees a paradigmatic illustration of this in Kierkegaard's reflections on Christ's cry of abandonment from the cross: 'My God, my God, why have you forsaken me?' Kierkegaard comments on this that although the emphasis is usually placed on what Christ is suffering in this moment, the sufferings of God must have been even more terrible. As Shestov quotes Kierkegaard, 'It seems to me that it must have been even more frightful for God to hear this cry. To be immutable at this point! Frightful! But no—that is not what is most frightful: what is

---

[24] L. Chestov, *Kierkegaard et la philosophie existentielle: Vox clamantis in deserto* (Paris: Vrin, 1972), 39–40.

most frightful is to be immutable and yet at the same time to be love: Oh! infinite, profound, unfathomable suffering!'[25] As opposed to the biblical Job, even Christ and even God must in the end submit, and the best we can do is therefore, like them, submit 'to the horrors that are visited upon us and therein find our blessedness'.[26] The hope that Kierkegaard offers, that things might be otherwise, is strangled at birth. But is this criticism justified?[27]

In *The Sickness unto Death* itself it is clear that the question of salvation is focused specifically on the possibility of forgiveness. Salvation is not simply a matter of being rescued from change and decay but also, crucially, a matter of being saved from our own complicity in the factors that caused our subjection to time, change, and chance in the first place. In other words, it is a matter of repentance and forgiveness. Shestov understands this and from the opening pages positions his study of Kierkegaard as relating to the doctrine of the Fall and the question of its possible reversal.[28] However, it seems as if he himself missed both a nuance in Kierkegaard and a certain implication of his own thought.

Let us go back to Christ's cry of abandonment. Now, whilst Kierkegaard does indeed appear to depict God as powerless, this powerlessness is not absolute. God, as Kierkegaard describes him, is unchangeable *and* he is love. Yet, even if, with regard to the laws of nature that he has himself decreed, God must be true to his own decree and is therefore powerless to change them, this is not the case with regard to love. God's love, as Kierkegaard understands it, expresses the divine choice to be love or, more simply still, *to love*. God could have dealt with his distress in the face of Christ's sufferings by, as it were, retreating into indifference—as, in an earlier part of his authorship, Kierkegaard had unmasked the bored indifference of Romantic aestheticism as a means of anaesthetizing life's sufferings.[29] That God suffered in the face of Christ's death on the cross is precisely a result of God's having chosen to be love: that is, the extent to which God suffered in the face of the cross was in direct proportion to the extent to which he continued freely to love not only the Son whom he had sent into the world but also the world that was putting

[25] Ibid. 229.

[26] Ibid. 230.

[27] In two essays on *Fear and Trembling* and *Repetition* in a book dedicated to Shestov Rachel Bespaloff implicitly argues that Shestov has sold Kierkegaard short. See Rachel Bespaloff, *Cheminements et carrefours* (Paris: Vrin, 1938), 100–88 and especially 144.

[28] Shestov read *Being and Time* as an attempt simultaneously to force Kierkegaard's treatment of the Fall and original sin into the framework of Husserlian phenomenology and to do the same to the topics of the Fall and original sin. See N. Baranova-Shestova, *Jiizn' L'va Shestova* (Paris: La Presse Libre, 1983), ii. 17.

[29] See especially *Either/Or*, part 1.

the Son to death. Something analogous holds good also of human beings. If the issue is not about how we might live righteous lives but whether we might find it possible to go on hoping and believing in ourselves and our future in the face of our own culpability for the mess we find ourselves in—if, that is, it is a matter of repentance and forgiveness—then we can indeed freely repent and freely receive forgiveness, even if we have no means available for altering the external circumstances brought about by our previous wrong choices. To take Shestov's example: if it was a lack of faith on Kierkegaard's part that he broke with Regine, it does not follow that in the moment when he realized this he should have rushed to her and tried to pick up the threads, perhaps imploring her to leave her new husband for him. That sort of behaviour does, of course, happen in some novels—*Eugene Onegin* for example—and doubt-less in some lives. But the case of *Eugene Onegin* itself illustrates why the attempt to re-establish a lost love might be so far from being an act of faith as to reveal the hero's depth of despair. And even if we regard Onegin's 'discovery' of his love for Tatiana as true (which is eminently debatable), it is hard to commend his subsequent love-making to her. On the contrary, he would have been truer to this new-found or newly rediscovered love had he had the courage to be faithful to it in what Kierkegaard might have called 'hidden inwardness'. Yet if the logic of 'what is done is done and cannot be undone' may be unassailable on its own terms (remember that lack of a proper relation to necessity is also a mark of despair according to *Sickness unto Death*), this does not of itself determine the attitude we take to what has been done and how we carry forward into the future our memory and our responsibility for our deeds. 'What's done is done and cannot be undone'—but this does not preclude our being free either to persist in guilt and self-hatred and to allow our future to be immobilized by the past or, conversely, to accept ourselves in spite of being unacceptable and, in the power of this acceptance, find our-selves on a path into a radically new future.

We are free to ... but are we? Isn't it precisely the problem of the person crying out for possibility that they experience themselves as crushed by the weight of necessity, that they are not able to be themselves or do what they want to do? Isn't asking them to believe in possibility asking the impossible? Shestov concedes that it is, but that is just what the Bible asks of us:

God means that all things are possible. God means that that knowledge to which our reason so avidly aspires and towards which it draws us irresistibly does not exist. God means that neither does evil exist. All that exist are the original *fiat* and the paradisal *valde bonum*, in the face of which all the truths based on the principle of non-contradiction and on that of sufficient reason, as well as many other laws, collapse and turn into phantoms. It is impossible for human beings to tear themselves away from the seducer who shows them [their] nothingness and suggests to them something of the indestructible anguish of this nothingness. It is impossible for human beings to stretch their hands towards the tree of life, and they are obliged to find nourishment from the fruits of the tree of knowledge, even when they are convinced that these serve only to make them powerless and to bring about their death. But is this human 'impossibility' the truth? Wouldn't it rather be solely a testimony to human impotence, a testimony that makes sense only to the extent that we continue in that impotence?[30]

In his study of forgiveness, Vladimir Jankélévitch—who acknowledged a certain inspiration from Shestov—emphasized that the impossibility of locating forgiveness in any calculus of rationality is integral to its really being forgiveness. Forgiveness is not just a matter of time healing or of coming to understand the reasons why the person who wronged me did what he did,[31] nor is it sufficiently motivated by the thought that perhaps, after all, the person concerned is not as guilty as they might seem or that my generous act of forgiveness might itself bring about their amelioration;[32] still less is it the same as resigning myself to the impossibility of vengeance or to the fact that justice requires me to hold my hate in check. The moment I set out my reasons for forgiving someone, it is no longer forgiveness I am talking about but a calculative act, an economic exchange in which forgiveness is the price paid for bringing about a desired outcome. In these terms, it might even seem best to keep quiet about it, and to register it as a pre-eminent subject of apophatic discourse.[33] For forgiveness exceeds all possible calculations. It is offered without anticipation of any measurable outcomes and is incommensurable with anything I might say about it, yet if 'forgiveness forgives in the night as remorse suffers in the night . . . this night presages a dawn . . . [it] is never the black night of despair'.[34] Little as we are able to say about it, Jankélévitch assures us that there nevertheless is 'a hyperbolic forgiveness, that forgives without reasons';[35] a forgiveness that does not forgive the guilty because they are really innocent or despite their being guilty but because—if there is any 'because' at all—they are guilty: a pardon that is not merited by the one forgiven and not planned by the one who forgives, and, also without being reducible to an emotional surge of compassion, forgives 'at a stroke, for everything, for always'.[36] Such a pardon does not stop at welcoming back the lost son but shows its excessive quality by dressing him in the best robe, killing the fatted calf, and holding a feast in his honour. That, says Jankélévitch in a

---

[30] *Kierkegaard*, 359–60.
[31] V. Jankélévitch, *Le Pardon* (Paris: Aubier, 1967), 12.
[32] Ibid. 140–9.   [33] Ibid. 149–56.   [34] Ibid. 159.
[35] Ibid. 156.   [36] Ibid. 201.

final characteristic flourish, 'is the inexplicable, unjust, mysterious great feast of forgiveness'.[37] Forgiveness occurs and can only occur as an 'event', a new thing, an act of grace, and a gift occurring in the context of a personal relation of forgiver and forgiven.[38] From the perspective of rationality—including the rationality that finds expression in justice—forgiveness is impossible: but we are nevertheless to believe in the possibility of such an impossibility.

The excessive, mysterious, and 'event' character of forgiveness means that there cannot be a general law of forgiveness such that I *must* forgive or am *obliged* to forgive, as in the cynical remark that God will always forgive because that's his métier. Forgiveness is neither God's nor anyone else's métier. Forgiveness, when it happens, is always a miracle—and, Christian theology might add, a new creation. It is, as a play on the French *pardon* (forgiveness) and *don* (gift) allows Jankélévitch to insinuate, only possible as a gift, free and entire. But this means that 'forgiveness' cannot be required of us. The social wisdom that advises us to forgive and forget may have its place, but it is often used in such a way as to make clear that it is not really forgiveness that is being talked about. It was therefore far from inconsistent on Jankélévitch's part to oppose the introduction of a statute of limitations regarding the crimes committed during the Nazi occupation. Although he declares that 'Forgiveness died in the death camps', the context of this remark makes it clear that it is not what happened in the past that rules out the possibility of forgiveness but the relations of those whom it concerns in the present. In the sentences preceding the assertion that 'Forgiveness died in the camps' he asks, 'But have they ever asked us to forgive them?' To which he adds, 'It is only the distress and the dereliction of the guilty that give meaning and reason to forgiveness. When the guilty are fat, well-fed, prosperous, enriched by the "economic miracle", forgiveness is a sinister joke.'[39] The issue is not the past itself, but the bad faith manifest in the present demands for amnesty and reconciliation, demands that subordinate the sufferings of the innocent to social convenience. In this context, he sees it as entirely appropriate to protest against

---

[37] Ibid. 201. As in the case of Shestov, it should be emphasized that Jankélévitch's use of the New Testament and of other theological texts is not to be taken as a sign that he is operating under anything other than secular philosophical premisses.

[38] Ibid. 12.

[39] V. Jankélévitch, *L'Imprescriptible* (Paris: Éditions du Seuil, 1986), 50. For a respectful but critical discussion of Jankélévitch's refusal to forgive, see J. Derrida, *Pardonner: L'Impardonnable et l'imprescriptible* (Paris: L'Herne, 2005). Amongst other questions that he raises, Derrida asks whether, in fact, there might not be a forgiveness that precedes the plea of the guilty and, if there is such a thing as an absolute forgiveness, whether it might not be a matter for God rather than human beings. At such points, we might say, Derrida begins to sound surprisingly evangelical.

a moral amnesty that is nothing but a shameful amnesia...In this case, to forget would be a grave insult to those who died in the camps and whose ashes are mixed in its earth forever, it would betray a lack of dignity and seriousness, a shameful frivolousness. Indeed, the memory of what happened is indelible for us, as indelible as the tattoos that former prisoners have on their arms...When the sophists of today counsel us to forget, we shall all the more register our silent and powerless horror in face of the dogs of hatred, we will think all the more of the agony of those deported and without graves and of the little children who never returned. Because this agony will endure until the end of the world.[40]

Does this mean forgiveness is impossible? Of course. Does it mean forgiveness cannot and will never occur? No—because forgiveness does not happen as the outcome of a set of calculable possibilities but only ever as a free event that is even more miraculous than the original freedom of paradise, since it is the upsurge of freedom in the context of a fallen humanity for whom the original freedom itself has become an impossible memory. Forgiveness, as the title of the book containing Jankélévitch's essay against the statute of limitations puts it, cannot be prescribed, it is not and cannot be a matter that could ever be legislated into existence. If it happens it will always and forever be as a miracle, and only in the light of such a miracle could we say that the impossible would, after all, be possible. Jankélévitch's determination to keep alive the memory of the dead—even if this leads him to refuse forgiveness—is one, paradoxical, way of registering such a possibility, for it refuses the despair that would conclude that those dead lives were, because dead and because killed in the way in which they were killed, therefore meaningless. If, in Kierkegaard's terms, the choice is between despair and faith, we might then say that when refusing forgiveness is intended as a way of remembering and affirming the humanity of the murdered rather than horror at the act of the murderer then—even if faith in the forgiveness of sins is lacking—such refusal will nevertheless be closer to faith than it is to despair. Conversely, accepting the logic of 'forgive and forget' might indicate no more than despairing of the possibility of justice ever being done.[41]

In this connection we might note the importance of the passage headed 'Interlude' in Kierkegaard's *Philosophical Fragments*. Here Kierkegaard addresses the question whether the past is more necessary than the future or, as he puts it, 'has the possible, by having become actual, become more

---

[40] *L'Imprescriptible*, 63.

[41] For a discussion of the relationship between the positions of Jankélévitch, Derrida, and Kierkegaard on forgiveness see Hugh Pyper, 'Forgiving the Unforgivable: Kierkegaard, Derrida and the Scandal of Forgiveness', *Kierkegaardiana*, 22 (2002), 7–23.

necessary than it was?'[42] Against the grain of contemporary idealist thinking, he argues that with regard to the event of incarnation—the paradoxical occurrence in historical time of God's self-giving as the condition of forgiveness—the past never does become necessary and that the possibility of human beings entering into a saving relation to this event is not dependent on any historical knowledge they may have concerning it. For the possibility of divine forgiveness has no date, no cause, and cannot become actual apart from its being freely accepted by those who need it. But just as, for Christians, the memory of the cross is the memory of that common human need, so too (we might say), the remembrance of the murdered must be kept alive until those who need forgiveness come to know that need. Within historical experience, marked as it is by the continuity of war and terror, the possibility of divine forgiveness will therefore paradoxically involve keeping alive the remembrance of what only God can forget.

These reflections on what Jankélévitch referred to as the *indicible*, 'the unspeakable', do not merely illustrate one case amongst many of what might be required for us truly to believe in a triumph of love and reconciliation that would enable the human community to speak the truth of its being in a common discourse of peace. Rather, and with regard to a pre-eminent instance of what is at stake, they indicate the magnitude of what that might require, since such a peace would require the impossible to become possible.

BECOMING NOTHING

Already in Aristotle, being, substance, form, and actuality are grouped together in opposition to non-being, matter, and potentiality. For if a thing merely has the potential to become a certain something (as the seed has the potential to become a tree), it by no means follows that it will necessarily realize that potential (as Jesus pointed out, the seed may be eaten by a bird or fall on unsuitable ground). To the degree that it is the mere possibility of realizing its form, an entity is therefore not what it is or all that it could be: in other words, its being is in some degree vitiated by non-being. Aquinas underlines this point when he states that if God is eternal then there can be nothing merely potential in him, since, to the degree that a substance has any admixture of possibility it is possible also for it not to be what it is. The Being that necessarily exists will therefore be without any trace of

---

[42] S. Kierkegaard, *Philosophical Fragments*, trans. H. V. and E. H. Hong, SKS 4 (Princeton: Princeton University Press, 1985), 72.

possibility.[43] Possibility is therefore a kind of trace of non-being within Being, the index of a given entity's mutability and corruptibility and, since possibility is a feature of the sublunary world in general, a marker of the world's falling-short of true Being. Not only is possibility, as it were, downgraded in terms of its relation to actuality (as the more excellent), it is also declared suspect in terms of its affinity to non-being.

A further testimony to this complex of ideas—which, precisely in the way that it reverses the Aristotelian-Thomist understanding also, in its way, confirms its importance—is that of Hegel. The point may be centred on the question of movement. In the Aristotelian scheme this is defined precisely in terms of the transition from possibility to actuality: motion is an entity's coming to be what it is when it is moved from a state of possibility by the presence of what is already in act. To take the familiar example from Aquinas's argument for the existence of God from the fact of motion: a piece of wood, that has the potential to burn, catches fire when it is exposed to what is already at its burning point. On a grander scale, the prime mover is constantly bringing the whole universe into Being by virtue of being the Pure Act in which all possibilities are realized and which is thus able to move all entities that are still only in a state of potential towards full realization of their being. Hegel—whose concept of causality is, of course, very different from that of the medieval thinker—deals with movement at the very beginning of his logic, where he accounts for it in terms of the necessary interrelation of Being and Non-Being. Movement, in fact, is this interrelation: the continual passing of Being into Non-Being and of Non-Being into Being. Wherever there is movement, including the movement from potentiality to actuality, Non-Being is, in some measure, in play. More emphatically, it is precisely the power of the negative that generates movement in Hegel's system.[44]

Against the background of this long-standing association of the ideas of nothingness and possibility, we turn again to Heidegger, whose discussion would once more be decisive for the shape of the twentieth-century understanding of nothingness. *Being and Time* portrayed Dasein as striving to become the whole that it never can be except by taking into itself the extreme possibility of its own impossibility, i.e., by resolutely anticipating its own death. This is also described by Heidegger in terms of Dasein taking

---

[43] *Summa contra Gentiles*, I, 16 (cf. n. 9 above).

[44] See G. W. F. Hegel, *Wissenschaft der Logik I*, in *Werke*, v (Frankfurt am Main: Suhrkamp, 1969), 82–115. Amongst other reasons, this is why Kierkegaard rejects Hegel's view that such a transition might come about by necessity and argues that it will always have the character of a leap. For further discussion of Hegel's treatment of becoming and Kierkegaard's critique see Clare Carlisle, *Kierkegaard's Philosophy of Becoming* (Albany, NY: State University of New York Press, 2005).

responsibility—or 'becoming guilty'—for the 'nullity' (*Nichtigkeit*) of its existence. Why is its existence 'null'? Because, as we have seen, the existence of Dasein continually transcends its essence: always lagging behind its possibilities, it is never (existentially) what it is (essentially). But even if this situation issues in an act of authentic resoluteness in which Dasein confronts and takes upon itself the prospect of its own death, this nullity becomes all the more salient since Dasein's identity is then defined precisely in terms of its ceasing to be. Whether with regard to the incompleteness of life in the world or the annihilation of that life in death, the 'thrown project' as which Dasein exists is permeated by nothingness. Insofar as it exists only as lagging behind its own possibilities—it is nothing; insofar as it realizes the one possibility that would enable it to be a whole (death) it ceases to be—and it is nothing.

In *Being and Time* itself, Dasein's awareness of the nothingness of its being occurs in the mood that, following Kierkegaard, Heidegger calls anxiety. We have already outlined how Kierkegaard envisaged anxiety as the way in which the self becomes aware of its own freedom. In an image also used by Sartre,[45] he portrays the infinite possibilities which are revealed in this awareness as inducing a kind of vertigo in which the anxious self 'grasps at finitude', i.e., retreats into what Sartre would call the 'bad faith' of purely finite roles and tasks that the self deludes itself into believing are prescribed by metaphysical, natural, social, or psychological laws. Kierkegaard's view of the interrelationship of anxiety and nothingness is clearly illustrated in his retelling of the story of the Fall and, especially, of the prelapsarian state of Adam and Eve. As opposed to some traditional theological accounts that emphasized Adam's perfection, Kierkegaard describes the first humans as simple, child-like creatures, lacking the qualities of self-consciousness and freedom by which we define our humanity. Yet, he notes, even in this primitive state, they were humans. 'In innocence', he writes, 'man is not qualified as spirit but is psychically qualified in immediate unity with his natural condition. The spirit in man is dreaming'[46]—where, for Kierkegaard, 'spirit' means precisely existing as a centre of self-conscious freedom. In this state, spirit is not absent, it is, in humanity's most primitive forms, our destiny to become spirit—but it is 'dreaming', that is, it is a possibility that we have not yet made our own. As such it both belongs to us, as our dream, yet, in another sense, it is something we lack, a nothing. 'In this state [of innocence] there is peace and repose, but there is simultaneously something else that is not contention and strife, for there is indeed nothing against which to strive. What then is it? Nothing. But

---

[45] *Being and Nothingness*, 30.
[46] *The Concept of Anxiety*, 41.

what effect does nothing have? It begets anxiety.'[47] As he will later say, 'Anxiety and nothing always correspond to each other.'[48]

In its Heideggerian reworking in *Being and Time* anxiety becomes the basic mood in which the self becomes aware of the nothingness that is revealed both in the way in which Dasein lags behind its essential possibilities and in its mortality. Two years on from *Being and Time*, in his inaugural lecture at Freiburg University, *What is Metaphysics?*, Heidegger returned to the theme of nothingness. As in *Being and Time*, anxiety is once more given a crucial role. In anxiety, Heidegger claims, we experience the slipping away of the world we customarily rely on and, in this slipping away, are confronted with the 'nothing' that constantly hovers in and around human existence. Yet, at the same time, this 'nothing' makes it all the more astonishing that there are beings at all: 'In the clear night of the nothing of anxiety the original openness of beings as such arises: that they are beings—and not nothing,' Heidegger says.[49] 'Da-sein' means 'being held out into the nothing',[50] yet in this 'nothing' the world of beings presents itself to me *as a whole*. However, in approaching this point, Heidegger has woven another theme into the discussion: boredom. For boredom too is a mood in which I become aware that underlying my preoccupation with this and that, with each particular role or task, I am always tacitly oriented towards being-as-a-whole. Even and precisely then when we are not actually busy with things or ourselves this 'as a whole' overcomes us—for example in genuine boredom. Such boredom is still distant when it is only this book or that play, that business or this idleness, that drags on. It irrupts when 'one is bored'. 'Profound boredom, drifting here and there in the abysses of our existence like a muffling fog, removes all things and human beings and oneself along with them into a remarkable indifference. This boredom manifests beings as a whole.'[51]

Anxiety and boredom thus constitute a state of mind that is at one and the same time a kind of calmness and a kind of uneasiness that 'leaves us hanging, because it induces the slipping away of beings as a whole',[52] or it is a 'parting

---

[47] Ibid.

[48] Ibid. 96.

[49] M. Heidegger, 'What is Metaphysics', trans. D. F. Krell, in M. Heidegger, *Pathmarks*, ed. W. McNeill (Cambridge: Cambridge University Press, 1998), 90 (*Wegmarken* (*Gesamtausgabe*, vol. ix), Frankfurt am Main: Klostermann, 2003).

[50] Ibid. 91.

[51] Ibid. 87.

[52] Ibid. 88. Alongside boredom and anxiety, Heidegger also mentions another possibility by which the presence of beings as a whole might be awakened in us, namely, 'our joy in the presence of the Dasein—and not simply of the person—of a human being whom we love' (p. 88). However, he does not develop this possibility to the same extent, and it seems legitimate to wonder what implications this might have had for his later 'path of thinking' as a whole had

gesture toward beings that are submerging as a whole'.[53] However, this 'slipping away of beings as a whole' is not a simple annihilation of the world that would leave merely an empty void. Dasein, after all, continues to exist, in a way; it continues to be in the world, in a way—only it is never quite connecting either with its existence or its world.

In lectures from the same period, Heidegger offers a more extended treatment of boredom. He starts by noting the prevalence of contemporary forms of cultural analysis, of which Oswald Spengler is perhaps the best-known example. Such analyses, Heidegger says, talk about culture in general terms—the spirit of the West, scientific rationality, Enlightenment values (one is tempted to add 'postmodern mistrust of meta-narratives', 'the new world-order', 'the clash of civilizations', and such like)—but, if we are honest, such generalizations don't really tell us anything significant about what's going on and that is why, in the end, they bore us. However, the boringness of the present age is susceptible to being turned around. Really to experience profound boredom would be to become attuned to the possibility of being-as-a-whole. How so?

In answering this question, Heidegger distinguishes three levels of bore-dom. Each is seen to have an intrinsic connection to our experience of time (Heidegger's German term is *Langeweile*, literally translatable into English as a 'long while'), which, as *Being and Time* argued, is the basic horizon within which we experience the meaning of Being. This is most obvious in the case of the first, a four-hour wait at a provincial railway station. There may be many things we can do in this situation—go for a walk, count the trees, look at our watch, sit in the waiting room—but none of them arises out of the projects that define our being-in-the-world, they have nothing to do with the rest of my life. Such boredom leaves us with the impossibility of being-as-a-whole, of fulfilling the free acts that could allow us to experience our life as a whole. Even the railway station, which might serve our project by functioning as a place for boarding the train, denies itself to us as a railway station and offers itself only as a place to wait, train-less. Instead of being able to get on with living I'm left in a kind of limbo as time drags by.[54]

This points towards what Heidegger calls a 'more original form of bore-dom'. Here boredom is no longer merely something occasioned by external

---

he done so—we can at the very least imagine a very different 'later Heidegger' from the one we know.

[53] Ibid. 90.

[54] M. Heidegger, *The Fundamental Concepts of Metaphysics: World, Finitude, Solitude*, trans. W. McNeill and N. Walker (Bloomington, Ind.: Indiana University Press, 1995), 78–105 (*Grundbegriffe der Metaphysik: Welt-Endlichkeit-Einsamkeit* (*Gesamtausgabe*, vols. xix/xxx), Frankfurt am Main: Klostermann, 1983).

things denying themselves to our projects; rather, the role of our own comportment comes all the more clearly into view. In this case, I go out for an evening with friends. We have what is generally regarded as a good time but, on returning home, I suddenly realize that I have been bored all evening. This seems strange since, after all, time didn't drag during the evening, I didn't once (maybe) look at my watch. How could we talk about being held in limbo by time dragging?

Maybe we have to look more deeply in this case and, if we do, a certain relationship between the self and its projects and its orientation towards being-as-a-whole seems once again to be in play. Perhaps the very fact that I went out just for a bit of relaxation 'seeking nothing more' is a sign that I lack or have lost the capacity to take an essential interest in my self and have become ready to go along with whatever goes on, and in this abandonment 'an emptiness can form'.[55] 'Becoming bored or being bored is determined by this emptiness forming itself in our apparently satisfied going along with whatever is going on. Thus here too, in this form of boredom, we find a being left empty, and indeed an essentially more profound form thereof in contrast to the previous one.'[56] 'This emptiness is a being left behind of our proper self.'[57]

And here too time is involved. After all, we gave ourselves the time to go out, we had time for going out . . . yet, having taken the time, nothing happens with it, and, in relation to time, we are therefore once again held in limbo by it and, Heidegger says, 'in a more profound way'. We have left ourselves time, but time has, as it were, withdrawn, it has abandoned us, it shows itself only as if it wasn't there. In the relaxing, pleasant company of our friends, we have lost time that might have been turned towards the possibility of becoming a whole.

The clue to the third and most profound level of boredom is found in such expressions as 'It bores me.'[58] 'What is this "it"?,' Heidegger asks.[59] Now, however, the issue is not the external passage of time: it is Dasein itself, and its 'innermost freedom', i.e., the fundamental attitude it takes with regard to itself. In this case no particular thing makes me bored, but everything is indifferent. Nevertheless, albeit in negative mode (by refusing them), this situation points to the 'very possibilities of its doing and acting' that

---

[55] Ibid. 119.

[56] Ibid. 119–20.

[57] Ibid. 120.

[58] This literally translates Heidegger's German. Perhaps it would be sufficient to think of the English 'It's boring', although that lacks the self-reflexive dimension of the German expression (found also in French).

[59] *Fundamental Concepts*, 134–5.

make Dasein what it is.[60] In this indifference the fundamental relation of Dasein to its basic possibilities (the basic demand on Dasein 'that it is given to him—to be there'[61]) is brought into question. In this situation of the most profound boredom, Dasein is therefore attuned to what concerns it most fundamentally, experiencing a moment of vision in which 'the most extreme demand' is announced to man, namely, the demand to be-there.[62]

This, then, restates the teaching of the inaugural lecture: that the mood constituted by anxiety and boredom and the nothingness that they reveal is itself a preliminary to the revelation of beings-as-a-whole, disclosing 'the original openness of beings as such: that they are beings—and not nothing'.[63] And this generates a further insight and question: 'Only on the ground of wonder—the revelation of the nothing—does the question "why?" loom before us'[64]—and this, Heidegger adds, is the metaphysical question, the question of Being, in the form 'Why are there beings at all, and why not rather nothing.'[65] To paraphrase: nothing is not simply the kind of being attributed to the for-itself; nothing is the mode in which the for-itself gains access to being, or the mode in which Being itself is revealed to the for-itself or, in Heidegger's formulation, Being calls to us. Nothingness is no longer something to flee, but the ground on which we might first come into relation to being-as-a-whole. Yet we cannot bring ourselves into relation to the nothing through our own decision or will: our transcendence in relation to beings-as-a-whole is not the transcendence of unlimited freedom but of the being that is a 'place-holder for the nothing'.[66] We must let the nothing reveal itself to us and then, in the nothing, become ready to hear the call of Being.

Heidegger's procedure at this point has been insightfully challenged by Jean-Luc Marion. Far from boredom being a state in which we might be open to the 'ultimate demand'[67] of Being, Marion suggests that it is far more plausible to see it as a state in which Being would be prevented from saying or meaning anything at all. Someone who is profoundly bored is no less bored

---

[60] *Fundamental Concepts*, 140.

[61] Ibid. 165.

[62] Ibid.

[63] Ibid. 90.

[64] Ibid. 95.

[65] Ibid. 96.

[66] It is also striking that in this lecture Heidegger does not once mention death in connection with this 'nothing'—whereas in *Being and Time* it was precisely death that had played the central role in disclosing to Dasein the nullity of its thrown being and thereby brought about Dasein's confrontation with the question as to its own possibilities for being-as-a-whole.

[67] *Fundamental Concepts*, 171.

by the claim of Being than by anything else: 'boredom', Marion says, 'does not evaluate, does not affirm, does not love.'[68] Boredom disqualifies every call and every claim, and even the call or claim of Being would expose itself to being judged boring, were it to occur in the life of someone profoundly bored. Boredom may well free Dasein from having to be what it is in the manner of everyday conformism and it may even make it open to some new call or occurrence in its existence, but it does so in such a way as to remove the ground for privileging Being and the call or claim of Being: 'The pure form of the call plays before any specification, even of Being . . . The claim calls *me*,' Marion states. Perhaps one could say that the bored person eventually realizes, 'I've got to do something'—but this 'doing something' is, as such, entirely lacking in specificity and, for Marion at least, it requires a predetermined interpretative move to see in this a call of Being. It is not Being that calls, but 'the pure form of the call', before or beyond Being.[69]

This is not the point at which to take further the particular reasons that lie behind Marion's objection, and I merely note it as unsettling the apparent Heideggerian assumption that the kind of being held out in nothingness that Dasein undergoes in boredom might be experienceable as a preliminary form of openness to Being. Nothingness, the implication is, says nothing and leads nowhere. But is that the end of the matter?

[68] J.-L. Marion, *Reduction and Givenness*, trans. T. A. Carlson (Evanston, Ill.: Northwestern University Press, 1998), 190. For further discussion see J. Schrijvers, '"And there shall be no more boredom": Problems with Overcoming Metaphysics in Heidegger, Levinas and Marion', in P. M. Candler and C. Cunningham (eds.), *Veritas: Transcendence and Phenomenology* (London: SCM Press, 2007). Another argument against Heidegger is simply that boredom is one of those things we have to live with and there's nothing deep about it at all. See Lars Svendsen, *A Philosophy of Boredom*, trans. J. Irons (London: Reaktion, 2005).

[69] Marion does not, however, discuss the further development of Heidegger's thought in the years following the inaugural lecture when the 'call of Being' comes to be mediated through the poet and the poetic word that calls to mortals in the power of the holy. If we were to take this into account then an *existentiell* narrative of the progression from *Being and Time* through the inaugural lecture and the lectures on boredom and on to the meditations on this poetic word might run something like this: *A young philosopher grapples with the meaning of life in face of the all-encompassing prospect of an ineluctable death. However, time goes on and there seems to be no resolution to the anxiety with which these questions fill him. Eventually, even the most impassioned of young philosophers gets rather bored with it all. Nothing really interests him anymore. Finally, however, he opens a book of poetry by Hölderlin and, all of a sudden, the poetic word seems to grip him and open the real possibility of a new way of Being . . .* Of course, this leaves open the question as to the call of the poet himself, i.e., what enables the poet, also a mortal, to speak such a word? What is the divine fire that marks him out, how do we recognize it, and what does it mean for the poet's own life? For a discussion of some of these points see my *Routledge Guidebook to the Later Heidegger*, 171–5.

ON THE FIELD OF NIHILITY (*KHÔRA*?)

The theme of nothingness has long been associated with Buddhist metaphysics, sometimes leading to the depiction of Buddhism as a 'nihilistic' religion (by Nietzsche, for one[70]). In the twentieth century, traditional Buddhist ideas of nirvana as a state of nothingness or emptiness were reinterpreted in dialogue with existential philosophy in the thinkers of the Kyoto School. Undoubtedly their views have been controversial—both as an interpretation of Buddhism and as an interpretation of Western thought—but they can provide us with a preliminary orientation (and there will not be scope to achieve more than this here) towards the 'excellence' of nothingness.

A founding figure of the school was Nishida Kitarō whose last work, 'The Logic of *Topos* and the Religious Worldview', effectively condenses his key teachings. Naturally there are certain basic assumptions that distinguish Nishida as a religious thinker from the religious thinkers of the West. Although he affirms God as 'the fundamental concept of religion',[71] Nishida's interpretation of God seems to be limited to the horizons established by the interplay of self and world, i.e., to be conceived as essentially immanent. God is not the transcendent creator of the world but is experienced and known only in and through the self's life in the world. Yet Nishida's concept of the world is also somewhat different from that of classical Western metaphysics. He defines the world as 'the contradictory self-identity of the many and the one', it 'exists and moves of itself' such that it constantly negates itself in the production of new forms, as time and space continually affirm and negate each other: the world is what it is in a synchronic spatial totality, at this moment, now—yet, in this very moment, it negates itself and is transformed into something new. The same logic extends to the relations between particular entities and the world as a whole and to self-conscious life, in which the contradictory self-identity of self and world is brought to the highest level of intensity as the self both focuses the reality of the world as a whole (it does not and cannot exist apart from the world) yet also determines itself 'self-expressively'.[72] On this basis, it is as impossible for Nishida to accept the

---

[70] Nietzsche's view of Buddhism was essentially shaped by Schopenhauer. On the latter's role as an interpreter of Buddhism see C. D. J. Ryan, *Schopenhauer's Philosophy of Religion* (Leuven: Peeters, 2009).

[71] K. Nishida, 'The Logic of *Topos* and the Religious World View: Part I', *Eastern Buddhist*, 18/2 (1986), 2. For a fuller discussion see my *Agnosis: Theology in the Void* (Basingstoke: Macmillan, 1996), 108–37. A more recent exponent of the kind of dialogue of Buddhist thought and Western philosophy exemplified by the Kyoto School is Masao Abe.

[72] 'The Logic of *Topos* I', 2–6.

determination of reality in terms of the constructions of subjective consciousness as it is for him to endorse the reduction of consciousness to the ebb and flow of a material substratum or of historical forces. Each is what it is only in and through its other. He therefore utilizes the notion of *topos* (place, site, or field) to envisage the self's way of being in the world. The reality of the world, he suggests, is not so much to be thought of as the underlying ground of consciousness but as the place of consciousness, 'the self-forming historical world, which is immediate to our self'.[73] And, since the world is in every respect contradictorily self-identical, we ourselves, in our conscious life, are the place where the world happens.

But how does this help us understand religious life? The question of religion, according to Nishida, rises from a realization of the inner contradictions of the self, above all the realization that I exist as a being determined by the ineluctable reality of death in which I will cease to be. We must, Nishida says, think this thought through to its ultimate conclusion, to the point at which, as he puts it, 'To know our eternal death is the fundamental reason of our existence. For only one who knows his own eternal death truly knows that he is an individual.'[74] Such knowledge of our eternal death may also be conceived as an encounter of the relative and the absolute, i.e., of the relative reality of my individual life with the absolute reality of my death or nothingness.[75] 'To know one's own death means that one is nothing and being at the same time.'[76] It is in the heightened sense of this contradictory encounter of life and death, absolute and relative, being and nothingness, in my own self-conscious life that religious existence finds its source and term. But becoming conscious of the existential simultaneity of being and nothingness is not the final step in the development of the religious consciousness. This occurs when the self in its entirety, as the being that vis-à-vis its death is also nothing, finds itself on the absolute *topos* where being and nothing coexist in what might be called a more objective way. At this point the coexistence of being and nothingness is no longer a more or less accidental feature of the individual's anguished consciousness of mortality, but is revealed as a feature of existence as such. Starting from the position of the self that is assured of its

---

[73] Ibid. 13.

[74] Ibid. 18. The resonances with Heidegger's account of being-towards-death are by no means accidental. On the relations between Heidegger and the Kyoto School thinkers, see, e.g., the articles by Nishitani, Yuasa, Takeichi, and Mizoguchi in G. Parkes (ed.), *Heidegger and Asian Thought* (Honolulu: University of Hawaii Press, 1987); also H. Buchner (ed.), *Japan und Heidegger: Gedenkschrift der Stadt Meßkirch zum hundersten Geburtstag Martin Heidegger* (Simaringen: Jan Thorbecke, 1989).

[75] 'The Logic of *Topos* I', 19–20.

[76] Ibid. 27.

own existence in an 'average everyday' sort of way, we pass through what Nishida calls the Great Death or Great Doubt to find ourselves on an infinite field of being-and-nothing. To know ourselves as we truly are and to be what we truly are requires not merely reflection on the absolute future annihilation of the self that I am, but the experience of my absolute nothingness.

Nishida's thought was further developed by his pupil Nishitani Keiji in terms of what the latter called the field of nihility or emptiness (*śūnyatā*) and brought into critical dialogue with Sartrean existentialism. As Nishitani glossed Nishida's teaching, this field of nihility undercuts the kind of distinctions between inner and outer, within and without, subjective and objective that have characterized many Western discussions of consciousness and the relations of self and world. Therefore, although 'this opening up of nihility is one of the elemental realizations of subjectivity', 'it is not "subjective" in the narrow sense of the field of consciousness that confronts the "objective" world as phenomena . . . The self-presentation of nihility is rather a real presentation of what is actually concealed at the ground of the self and of everything in the world.'[77] And, Nishitani adds, 'It is an awareness that lies on the *far side* of everything that psychology can apprehend precisely by virtue of being all the more on the *near side* of the subject.'[78] When these reflections are brought to bear on Sartre's view of the relations of being and nothingness, this latter appears rather thin. Essentially, Sartre's identification of nothingness with the self-transcendence of consciousness restricts nothingness to a purely subjective or egoistic perspective. As Nishitani reads him, Sartre 'presents [nothingness] like a wall at the bottom of the ego or like a springboard underfoot of the ego. This turns his nothingness into a basic principle that shuts the ego up within itself . . . as long as this nothingness is still set up as something called nothingness-at-the-bottom-of-the-self, it remains what Buddhism repudiates as "the emptiness perversely clung to".'[79] For, as Nishida had emphasized, the absolutely contradictory self-identity of reality means that whilst the world itself could not *be* without nothingness, nothingness in turn manifests itself in the being of the world. In experiencing my own nothingness, the absolute 'near side' of my existence already opens my access to the 'far side' of the world beyond me. Sartre paradoxically—from Nishitani's point of view one might almost say pig-headedly—turns the self's experience of its own nothingness into a kind of ground or principle, 'like a stake driven into the ground for the self to be tied to', but, Nishitani comments, 'Only absolute emptiness is

---

[77] K. Nishitani, *Religion and Nothingness*, trans. J. Van Bragt (Berkeley and Los Angeles: University of California Press, 1982), 17.

[78] Ibid.

[79] Ibid. 33.

the true no-ground [*Ungrund*]. Here all things—from a flower or a stone to stellar nebulae and galactic systems, and even life and death themselves—become present as bottomless realities.'[80] This also leads him to criticize Sartre's focus on self-conscious action and self-conscious choices as the means by which we become what we are, as in the slogan, 'You are the sum of your actions.' By fixating on subjective self-consciousness, Sartre has no perspective in which to allow for the reality of the simple occurrence of things as a manifestation of the field of absolute nihility beyond the dualities of subject and object, conscious and unconscious. On this field the simple being of the world is already an expression of emptiness merely by being what and as it is. As in Suzuki's discussion of the visibility of suchness in the simple being of the *nazuna* flower,[81] it is sufficient to become aware of a 'mode of being where the pine tree is the pine tree itself, and the bamboo is the bamboo itself' since doing so is itself possible only when we take our stand on the field of nihility that allows all things to be what and as they are.[82]

As always when we are dealing with a fundamental encounter that is not just a matter of opposed arguments but of basic world-views, there are many detailed points that would need to be teased out really to do justice to how the Kyoto School thinkers used Japanese religious experience to interpret fundamental questions of Western philosophy. Here, I wish only to emphasize how they allow us to reappraise the respective excellences of actuality and possibility in the light of the designation of possibility as the locus of 'non-being' or nothingness. For in relation to absolute emptiness, actuality itself becomes relative to and 'contradictorily self-identical' with what is merely possible, with what has not yet become what it is or is ceasing to be what it is. Self, world, and God all exist as what and how they are by virtue of a constant interplay of Being and nothingness such that nothingness cannot be considered as a mere

---

[80] Ibid. 34. Nishitani's allusion to Jacob Boehme's concept of *Ungrund* also invites a wider comparison of that concept to the idea of the field of nihility. The theme of the *Ungrund*, sometimes referred to as the 'abyss of Being', but, in any case, understood as somehow prior to Being, was especially influential in Schelling's philosophy and, from there, was also taken up by Tillich and by some of the Russian religious philosophers. It is not coincidental that, in relation to the larger discussion in this chapter, Schelling also came to understand the history of primordial being as a history of three potencies or possibilities in the life of God. But, although this is fruitful in terms of imagining how one might conceive of personality as not dependent on substance ontology, doing justice to the idiosyncratic complexity of Schelling's thought would require an excessive detour from the main line of this enquiry. See also the themes broached in the conclusion to Ch. 5.

[81] See Ch. 2 above.

[82] *Religion and Nothingness*, 128. Another example Nishitani gives is an extract from Dostoevsky's largely autobiographical *The House of the Dead* where the narrator describes looking up from his labour detail at a distant Kirghiz settlement, forgetting the wretchedness of his situation in a vision of 'God's world, a pure and bright horizon, the free desert steppes' (ibid. 8).

privation of Being but is itself integral to Being. On this view, were Being to shake itself loose from the encumbrance of nothingness it would itself collapse into nothingness.

We can refine this point a little further by distinguishing between two levels (or two senses) of nothingness in play here. The first is the level at which actuality and possibility relate as dialectical polarities of Being. At this level the non-being that inheres in possibility is a part of the process whereby particular entities emerge, take shape, and pass away and, by their collective interaction, constitute the world we live in and know. Already here, an element of nothingness is inseparable from there being a world at all. This, of course, would not be news to Augustine, since he would see in it the reason why the world as we know it is a world of anguish and pain. On the Zen Buddhist view, however, Being cannot be separated out from its entanglement with nothingness without the whole system that we call the world (inclusive of the human selves that inhabit it) collapsing. In the life of the total cosmos, Being and nothingness are never anything other than relative, but such relative being and relative nothingness find their ground at a second level of nothingness, and it is this that Nishitani calls the field of nihility. This is not a 'ground' external to the phenomenal world but is the *topos*, place, site, or field within or as which beings occur. We may therefore describe this field in the terms that Dalferth used of God: that it is the possibility of both possibility and actuality. Is the field of nihility, then, effectively a name for God?

I wish to approach this question somewhat indirectly, via another term that, thanks to Derrida,[83] has recently re-entered the vocabulary of the philosophy of religion. It is a term derived from Plato's *Timaeus*, namely, the *khôra* or, as it is often translated, the 'receptacle' that is the condition of both intelligible forms and their sensible copies coming into being.[84] The retention of Plato's Greek term in the title of Derrida's own essay on the subject is indicative of his characteristic attentiveness to the problems of translation and how, from within the perspective of conventional logic, it is hard rightly to name something that 'seems to be neither this nor that yet at the same time being this and that'.[85] Variously spoken of as 'place', 'location', 'region', 'country', 'mother', 'nurse', 'receptacle', etc., all translations and

---

[83] Especially in his essay *Khôra* (Paris: Galilée, 1993) but also in the earlier lecture 'Comment ne pas parler: Dénégations', in J. Derrida, *Psyché: inventions de l'autre*, ii (Paris: Galilée, 1987–2003), 173 ff.

[84] Jan Van Bragt, Nishitani's translator, suggests that *khôra* is, in fact, identifiable with the field of nihility. See *Religion and Nothingness*, pp. xxx–xxxi. He also mentions Aristotle's idea of *hypokeimenon*, Einstein's notion of a force-field, and Jaspers's concept of 'the encompassing' as further parallels. For the 'receptacle', see *Timaeus* 48E–53D.

[85] Derrida, *Khôra*, 16.

interpretations are bound by 'retrospective projections which may always be suspected of being anachronistic'.[86] All will fail to say exactly 'what' *khôra* is, since *khôra* isn't actually anything, it has no essence and stands outside the realm of the nameable (which leads Derrida also to refrain from referring to it as '*the khôra*'); at one point Plato speaks of it in terms of myth, at another in terms of logos, but it is really neither: rather, it is the point of indifference of both, it is what precedes or what is the condition or possibility of both myth and logos. In words that could have been found on a page of Kyoto School philosophy, Derrida writes that that as the opening up of what is 'a seemingly empty space' 'between the sensible and the intelligible, belonging neither to the one nor to the other' and although it is not 'the void' *khôra* is a 'a gaping opening, an abyss or a chasm' that makes a 'place' for the 'cleft between the sensible and the intelligible, between the body and the soul' to emerge.[87]

Derrida himself will, with customary caution, focus his interpretation on the implications for philosophy of supposing such a beginning prior to the beginning of philosophy in the philosopher's concern to distinguish logos from myth and the intelligible from the sensible and he will, perhaps predictably, bring it also into connection with the possibility of writing. But, like the field of nihility of the Kyoto thinkers, might *khôra* also be interpretable in religious terms? Isn't *khôra*, like the field of nihility, aptly describable as the possibility of both possibility and actuality and, as such, a potential name of God ('God as khôra, perhaps,' Derrida himself muses[88])? Might *khôra* be a way of naming the divine matrix of the origin of beings, that which, prior to Being, 'gives' being to beings?[89]

In order to address these questions adequately we need also to examine the links between what Derrida has to say about *khôra* and two other central themes in his writings: negative theology and 'the gift'.

With regard to negative theology, the question of naming has already been broached, when it was asked whether *khôra* is a name of God. But the question is even more difficult than it might at first appear, since how do

---

[86] Ibid. 24.

[87] Ibid. 45.

[88] J. Derrida, *Sauf le nom* (Paris: Galilée, 1993), 112. See also John D. Caputo, *The Prayers and Tears of Jacques Derrida: Religion without Religion* (Bloomington, Ind.: Indiana University Press, 1997), 37: 'What takes place in this discourse about a desert ... an empty place? God or *khôra*? What is the wholly other ... God or *khôra*? What do I love when I love my God, God or *khôra*? How are we to decide? Do we have to choose?' Later (p. 137), Caputo suggests that although there can be no question of 'ousiological reassurances' there can, nevertheless, be some sense in which *khôra* does, after all, 'give', 'like a strange mother who gives without engendering'. I should add that, in conversation, Caputo has expressed his scepticism as to the convergence of what Derrida has to say about *khôra* and Buddhist discussions of nihility.

[89] *Khôra*, 30.

we know what *khôra* names anyway, if we are not Greek speakers? What, then, would we be saying if we said that *khôra* 'really' means *God*? What would we be saying about *khôra*? What assumptions would we be making about reality? And what would we be saying about God? Derrida's retention of the Greek term (albeit in Latin script) has, as we have seen, highlighted the problem of saying what it is that is at issue here concerning this ground that is not a ground, this possibility before possibility, this 'third genre'. How might such a problematic term help us name God? We seem in some sense to be back at the point at which Heidegger's account of a kind of negative revelation of Being in the mode of boredom left us: what, in this situation, what, at the point of absolute nothingness, what, on the field of nihility, what, in the neutral balance of possibility and actuality, might move us to speak of Being or God? And, were we to do so, what could we say that would say more than what is said in speaking of nothingness, empty possibility, *khôra*?

We shall return to the question of negative theology shortly, but first turn to the question of the gift. Why does this question arise at just this point?

Think about what happens when we follow the reduction of beings back to their location in or on a field of nihility/*khôra*. This reduction seems to issue in a situation of absolute indifference, sheer facticity, or Heideggerian 'thrownness', extended in a kind of flat generality. All we can say about our life in the world, it seems, is that this is how it is: there is no further ground or reason for it being so, there is nothing beyond the simple 'thisness' or 'suchness' of existence. The world and we ourselves are just there. That's all there is. 'This is it.' Both in this chapter and in considering Suzuki's exposition of the Zen experience of presence[90] we have seen how this situation may be interpreted in a manner that might be called religious or, at least, mystical. [91] However, from the point of view of Jewish, Christian, or Islamic theology such an empty affirmation or such an affirmation of emptiness would seem to fall short of what needs to be said if we are to speak of God. The believer can scarcely be satisfied with the reduction of 'God' to the neutral featureless field of nihility. Isn't all of this to subordinate God, He Who Is, to a pre-divine but sub-personal vacuum? Isn't it to place something before God and therefore to make God less than God, less than the creator who made all things out of nothing, who is the giver of every good and perfect gift—Being itself, life, goods, joys, and sorrows? Where, in the face of *khôra*, is there a possibility for Eucharistic living, for a life lived as thanksgiving? On the field of nihility or in

---

[90] See Ch. 2 above.

[91] That such an experience is one of the tropes of contemporary religious life has been argued by Don Cupitt in his study *The Meaning of It All in Everyday Speech* (London: SCM Press, 1999).

relation to *khôra* is there anything to be grateful for, or any*one* there to be grateful *to*? How, then, might we speak here of Being or life as a 'gift'?

THE POSSIBILITY OF THE GIFT

Over the last decade or so, 'the Gift' has become a key topic in philosophy of religion and theology. There are several strands to this discussion. The first takes its cue from Marcel Mauss's anthropological research into gift-giving and his demonstration of how this often functions as a means of establishing and enforcing power relationships within societies. On this basis there is no such thing as a free gift, since giving is always determined by more or less conscious social or interpersonal strategies.[92] Another strand derives from Heidegger's reflections in the late lecture *Time and Being* where he interpreted the expression *es gibt* (normally translated and understood in German simply as 'there is') in terms of its literal meaning 'it gives'. Applying this to Being, as in the statement 'es gibt Sein', he advanced the possibility of an act of giving more original than the relation to Being itself, thereby also underwriting his reinterpretation (or perhaps we should say, deepening his interpretation) of thinking as thanking. In the light of this the task of the philosopher is transformed from thinking upon Being to giving thanks for what gives Being. But what does give Being? What is the 'it' in 'it gives'? In *On Time and Being* he says that it is the event of understanding, *Ereignis*, itself.[93] 'It' is not any*thing* or any*one*. And although Heidegger elsewhere associates the event of understanding with 'the holy', it is consistent with the a-theistic character of his thought from *Being and Time* onwards that he declines to

---

[92] For a useful anthology of relevant sources see Alan D. Schrift, *The Logic of the Gift: Toward an Ethic of Generosity* (London: Routledge, 1997).Two good introductions to and overviews of the theological debate are Robyn Horner, *Rethinking God as Gift: Marion, Derrida, and the Limits of Phenomenology* (New York: Fordham University Press, 2001),which especially stresses the philosophical context; and Risto Saarinen, *God and the Gift: An Ecumenical Theology of Giving* (Minnesota: Liturgical Press, 2004), which is more narrowly theological. A useful summary of Derrida's possible contribution to theological reflection on the gift is found in Steven Shakespeare, *Derrida and Theology* (London: T. & T. Clark, 2009), 149–74. See also John D. Caputo and Michael J. Scanlon (eds.), *God, the Gift and Postmodernism* (Bloomington, Ind.: Indiana University Press, 1999), where key participants in the debate about the gift, including both Derrida and Marion, are brought into conversation.

[93] M. Heidegger, *Zur Sache des Denkens* (*Gesamtausgabe*, vol. xiv) (Tübingen: Niemeyer, 1969), 20 (M. Heidegger, *On Time and Being*, trans. J. Stambaugh (New York: Harper Colophon, 1976)).

identify this with the Christian (or Jewish) God. There is a 'giving', yet no one who gives, it seems.

The possibilities for Christian theology to find in this a 'point of contact' for a renewed dialogue with philosophy are self-evident, since gift is a long-standing (if not always fully acknowledged or thematized) trope of theology and, for that matter, ordinary religious life and worship, whether the focus is on the original gift of creation, the gift of divine grace in Christ, or the repetition of that gift in Eucharistic life.[94]

But are gifts at all possible? Is it appropriate—at the point of absolute nothingness or of the possibility of possibility and actuality—to speak of a gift?

Derrida, who comments that the question of the gift had been involved in all his works after 1977–8, seems to argue that the gift is impossible. Why? Because if Mauss is correct about the social exchange of gifts as a means of mediating power relationships, and if giving is always a matter of A (the giver) giving B (the gift) to C (the recipient), then the very possibility of a pure gift is undermined from the beginning. Social giving is always inscribed within an economy of circulating objects and values such that 'the gift' imposes a debt and an obligation that cannot be refused. It is an exercise of sovereignty and power, which will often provoke the recipient who does not wish to be in a merely subordinate position to repay in excess of the original gift—a dynamic that, in Mauss's observation, led to the massive wastefulness of much gift-giving in pre-modern societies, where what was given would be consumed, burned, or sacrificed. A pure gift, by way of contrast, would require that the giver should not give so as to impose on the recipient: the giver would have to conceal himself; similarly, the gift would have to appear as other than a gift in order not to become an obligation or debt; and, finally, the recipient would

---

[94] Catholicism also speaks of the 'gift of authority', a concept which Saarinen somewhat critically discusses. An influential theological response to the philosophical debate about the gift is also found in the work of John Milbank. However, whilst the motive for developing a theology of the gift is clear, it is far from obvious that Milbank achieves what he sets out to do when he describes his study *Being Reconciled: An Ontology of Pardon* (London: Routledge, 2003) as an account of the Christian doctrine of reconciliation from the perspective of the gift. Milbank sets up a false antithesis between the evil of modern nihilism and a life lived in the light of the gift that largely vitiates what he sets out to do. I say a false antithesis because the account of evil's distinctly modern, nihilistic form, which effectively blames Kantian ethics for the Holocaust, is so utterly shallow as to allow only a rather empty and abstract view of the gift itself to emerge (not to mention the fact that it also trivializes both philosophy and the Holocaust). That being said, I am not unsympathetic to Milbank's attempt to relate Arendt's category of the 'banality of evil' to the Augustinian tradition of thinking of evil as non-being. See my *A Short Course in the Philosophy of Religion* (London: SCM Press, 2001), 181–3.

need absolutely to forget the gift.[95] Derrida does not conclude from this that 'the gift' is impossible in an absolute sense, but merely that, were there to be a gift, it would be an event accomplished in a paradoxical moment tangential to the reciprocity of economic circulation, a gift given in secret and given in such a way that the left hand wouldn't know what the right was doing.[96]

This can be illustrated by the example of the connection drawn by Janké-lévitch between the possibility of forgiveness (*pardon*) and the possibility of gift (*don*), where the giving of forgiveness acquired a certain apophatic quality. For the act of forgiveness that presents itself as such will always be open to the suspicion that it is a ploy within a system of power relationships that has a certain advantage in view. What more effective system of social control has there been than the penitential system of the Middle Ages, a system founded precisely on the Church's monopoly of forgiveness? When forgiveness becomes explicit it enters the realm of power and thereby subverts the free, irrational, and excessive character of true, unmotivated forgiveness, forgiveness that forgives simply because it forgives. Only forgiveness of this latter kind would be what Derrida calls forgiveness 'without sovereignty', i.e., without the act of forgiveness becoming a means of the forgiver exercising power over the one forgiven.[97] A similar insight, it seems, underlay Kierke-gaard's commitment to indirect communication as the only truly liberative form of religious communication between human beings, since otherwise the recipient of the communication is made dependent on the communicator. This concern not only manifested itself in his frequent use of pseudonyms, but also in the often rather beautiful disclaimers with which he prefaced his directly religious writings, as, e.g., in the preface to the *Four Upbuilding Discourses* of 1844, where he addresses to himself to 'that single individual whom I in joy and gratitude call *my* reader, that favourably disposed person

---

[95] See J. Derrida, *Donner le temps*, i: *La Fausse Monnaie* (Paris: Galilée, 1991), especially 17–32.

[96] See, e.g., *The Gift of Death*, 82–112. The allusion to the left hand, etc., is, of course, to the Sermon on the Mount (as Derrida makes explicit).

[97] See J. Derrida, 'Le Siècle et le pardon', in idem, *Foi et savoir* (Paris: Éditions du Seuil, 1996). This too accords with the demands of the Sermon on the Mount that our acts of religion should not become a means of securing social recognition and status. The terms are somewhat different, but the logic corresponds to Lévinas's insistence that whilst we may understand our lives as lived before the face of God, we can have no direct vision of God's own face, which is infinitely elevated above everything worldly. Only on such conditions might our gratitude and our good works be undertaken as freely chosen responsible acts and not the merely reflexive working of a causal reciprocity between giving and receiving. Not as the direct imparting of Being to beings, nor yet as the cause who causes Being to impart itself to beings, but only as the possibility of possibility and actuality, only as the possibility of the possibility of forgiveness surpassing the actuality of the closed system of the fallen world might God, on this account, give Being.

who receives the book and gives it a good home ... [who] by accepting it does for it ... what the temple box did for the widow's mite, sanctifying the gift, giving it meaning and transforming it into much'.[98] The author of such meditations, he insists, only ever approaches the reader as one who has come to bid farewell, because he only ever wants the reader to think of him 'as one who has gone away'.[99]

But leaving aside for a moment the question as to whether the gift is possible or not, the question of the gift also, in its way, returns us to the question about Being and about God as Being/Being-Itself. This is because, as Heidegger's formulation 'Es gibt Sein' brings to a head, it is a question about whether it is basically Being that sets the horizon for all that is—including giving—or whether Being itself may not be given to us by something more fundamental. But then, as was asked with reference to the field of nihility/ *khôra*, what would then allow us to say of such a more fundamental ground that it *gives* the possibility of Being—of there being anything at all, and not nothing? Why 'gives'? Why not just content ourselves with the sheer facticity of the world's being there—'there is', 'il y a': why complicate matters further? Keeping such questions open, I want to turn now to the attempt made by Jean-Luc Marion to argue for the legitimacy—indeed, the necessity—of the notion of the gift by means of what he claims to be a strictly phenomenological analysis of the notion of givenness.

Going back to Husserl, Marion argues that it is a basic and defining aim of Husserlian phenomenology to treat what is given to consciousness solely in terms of its givenness and so to know things just as they are given and not otherwise. Phenomenology seeks to free 'the givenness in presence of each thing' from all conditions and restrictions, he states.[100] But how is this givenness given? One answer we seem to find in Husserl is that it is given in intuition. We have seen how Heidegger understands this in terms of the categorial intuition of Being and how this provides him with a path from Husserlian phenomenology towards the question of Being. However, Marion doubts whether this is the sole way of understanding Husserl. Another way (which he sees as that taken by Derrida) would be to understand categorial intuition as disclosing an a priori ideality of meaning that does not in any way

---

[98] S. Kierkegaard, *Eighteen Upbuilding Discourses*, trans. H. V. and E. H. Hong, SKS 5 (Princeton: Princeton University Press, 1990), 107 (translation adapted).

[99] Ibid. 295, 179. It is striking in the context of the present discussion that Kierkegaard distinguishes between the pseudonymous works as the works of his left hand and the upbuilding writings as those of his right. See my article 'Kierkegaard's Hands', in Robert L. Perkins (ed.), *International Kierkegaard Commentary: The Point of View* (Macon, Ga.: Mercer University Press, 2010).

[100] *Reduction and Givenness*, 1.

refer to Being and that does not require an intuitive accompaniment or means of presencing.[101] For Derrida himself (according to Marion) this separation of the ideality of meaning from the kind of presence given in intuition also means abandoning the will-o'-the-wisp of presence itself. Meaning is now released into an infinite play of possibilities where signification is no longer dependent on being validated by intuition or reference to the presence of the signified. A third possibility is that of Husserl himself, who limits himself to what Marion calls the 'objectness' of the appearances of consciousness, i.e., knowing them only to the extent that they can be formalized in terms of objectifiable cognition and specified in terms of definable attributes.

Against all of these interpretations, Marion seeks to understand the phenomenological reduction to the 'pure givens' that we find in consciousness as revealing a givenness that neither refers to Being, nor dissolves into a free play of significations, nor—importantly—is limited to what is knowable. Of course, we do not have an intuition of 'givenness': givenness itself is not a thing or an entity, but, as Marion puts it, 'givenness can only appear indirectly, in the fold of the given'.[102] Lived experience is itself the medium in which such appearing occurs, although not in the sense that what is given is explicable in terms of experience. Rather, when we focus on what is truly, actually given, we find that it is neither a subjective meaning nor a reference to an entity beyond or behind what we see. What we see in a painting, for example, is not a configuration of lines and colours, nor the intention of the artist, nor the object that it is a painting of. What we see, what is given us to see, is what Cézanne called 'the effect',[103] something that is not itself visible in the narrow sense, but 'super-visible', something that allows Baudelaire to speak of 'melody' in a painting.[104]

Anticipating the charge that he is covertly introducing theological or metaphysical assumptions into his analysis, Marion insists that he is holding fast to the phenomenological reduction and that if this reduction is carried through to the end what we find are not the abstract forms of mathematics or logic (as in Husserlian phenomenology) but what he calls 'the saturated phenomenon'.[105] Such a phenomenon is given not otherwise than as exceeding all possible horizons of generalizable understanding, including that of Being. It is an intuition that 'gives too intensely for the gaze to have enough heart to truly see what it cannot conceive, only barely receive, or sometimes

---

[101] Ibid. 5.
[102] J.-L. Marion, *Being Given: Towards a Phenomenology of Givenness*, trans. J. C. Kosky (Stanford, Calif.: Stanford University Press 2002), 39.
[103] Ibid. 49.
[104] Ibid. 48.
[105] See the reference to Marcel's use of this term in Ch. 6 n. 63 above.

even confront'.[106] The given is not the most abstract, but the most excessive of phenomena.

In these terms, then, it is possible for Marion to argue that givenness itself is properly describable not as a mere datum, a neutral facticity of occurrence, but as gift. What Mauss and Derrida reject in rejecting the possibility of the gift was never worthy of being called a 'gift',[107] for 'The gift arises from itself without being inserted in the economic circle where exchange would in advance orient it, prompt it, and consume it. The singular appearing of the gift must therefore be described such as it shows itself of itself insofar as it gives (itself).'[108] Ultimately, he will say, the gift is most fully manifest in what philosophy calls the subject and Heidegger calls Dasein, namely, the one who becomes a self by receiving his self as a gift of what gives itself, called into being by the paradoxical call of givenness that calls the self forth into being. This self is further—and decisively—revealed as gifted with the possibility of love, of loving and being loved.[109]

Without further following the details of Marion's exposition of the gift, two points need special (re-)emphasis. The first is that Marion claims throughout to be operating exclusively on the basis of phenomenological analysis, owing nothing to anthropological, sociological, or, for that matter, to theological models of the gift (even if, finally, what he says of the gift comes to coincide rather closely with what Christian theology also says on the subject).[110] The second is that givenness is not determined by Being, but comes from outside or from beyond Being and, therefore, if theology (or for that matter philosophy itself) were to find in the topic of the gift a possibility for naming the giver of the gift as God then whatever would be said about God in that respect would also have to be said without reference to being, outside of, beyond, or simply without Being—as Marion argued in his *God without Being*.[111]

---

[106] *Being Given*, 203.

[107] Although, as we have seen, Derrida does not, strictly speaking, reject the possibility of the gift in all senses—even if he says that it is 'impossible'. However, this impossibility is not obviously different in kind from the utter paradoxicality that Marion will also conclude is an essential feature of the gift.

[108] *Being Given*, 83.

[109] See ibid., Book V.

[110] Whether this claim is in fact sustainable has been challenged by, e.g. D. Janicaud in *Le Tournant théologique de la phénoménologie française* (Combas: Éditions de l'Éclat), 1991, 39 ff. Janicaud's concern is to resist the intrusion of theology into philosophy, but theology might, from its own point of view, have grounds for questioning the smoothness with which Marion passes from phenomenological investigations to Christian conclusions.

[111] See J.-L. Marion, *God without Being: Hors texte*, trans. T. A. Carlson (Chicago: University of Chicago Press, 1991). The French title is *Dieu sans l'être*.

This brings us back to the question of negative theology, especially as formulated by Derrida. For even if we follow Marion's argument to the point at which givenness transmutes into 'gift' (which is actually conceding quite a lot), it would seem that something more would be needed before we could confidently name the giver as 'God'. And, even were we to name the source of the gift as God, it might, on such terms, prove a self-destructive move on the part of any theology that was committed to naming God as 'He Who Is'. Throughout this enquiry we have spoken of the 'distance' that the event of human subjectivity opens up between the self and the presence of Being, but the spacing-out of divine–human relationships effected in the structure giver–gift–recipient might seem to introduce a separation between our lived experience of life as gifted and Being as complete—even if differently articulated—as that which Sartre thought to establish. But without suggesting that Marion is merely redescribing the situation of the Being-less self of Sartrean existentialism, what might such a God without Being have to do with us, who, however far we lag behind our possibilities, feel ourselves *to be* in some way—and at the very least in the way that embodied beings cannot doubt the testimony of their own bodily being? And what actually differentiates this God who gives from beyond Being from nothingness or from the field of nihility/*khôra*? For such a God can never appear within the horizon of Being, i.e., within every possible reflection on what is or might be the case or on what is or might come to pass, and is therefore surely tantamount to nothing. And if Being itself is a gift, even the first or most original of all gifts, to whom might we be thankful and how might we give thanks? If the basic possibility of our being here at all is gifted, what does this possibility mean? Doesn't being gifted meaning having possibilities amongst which to choose or possibilities we are required to cultivate if they are to come to fulfilment? If I in my existence—or if you and I in our love for one another[112]—are the primary instance of 'the gifted', doesn't this once more return the question to a question of possibilities, to our responsibility for deciding which of our possibilities to affirm, whether freely to commit ourselves to the possibility of love that is gifted us or to isolate ourselves in the emptiness of hatred and self-hatred. And what would this mean in the context of actual, lived human relationships?

---

[112] It is basic to Marion's whole account that the consummate form of the gift is love: that my most basic, most important possibility concerns loving and being loved. See J.-L. Marion, *The Erotic Phenomenon*, trans. S. E. Lewis (Chicago: University of Chicago Press, 2007). However the theme is already present in his *Prolegomenon to Charity*, trans. S. E. Lewis and J. L. Kosky (New York: Fordham University Press, 1991) and is affirmed also in *Being Given*.

It is precisely in relation to such questions that we get to see why phenomenology itself cannot finally decide the issue for us. For what reflection on
possibility ultimately yields is, simply—possibilities. And what these possibilities mean is determinable only through dialogue and action. Whether life is
ultimately a play of sheer facticity, an event within an indifferent field of
nihility, whether it is a gift of God, and whether that gift comes to us as a gift
of Being or, somehow, from beyond Being—these are questions for which
there are no ready-made answers, as if we could simply straightforwardly say
which of these possibilities was 'true'. In fact, there are not even agreed
methods for deciding what criteria of truth might be applicable.

Imagine, by way of a parable, that a believer in God, a Buddhist, and a
scientific reductionist had each arrived by a path proper to their belief and
discipline on the field of nihility and that they encountered one another there.
What might they have to say to each other that would convert the others to
the speaker's point of view? What might the believer say that would prove that
the place and the possibility of this meeting was a gift of God? What might the
scientist say to prove that it simply was reality and that this is all that should
be said? What might the Buddhist say to communicate the 'wondrous Being'
that emanated from the abyss of emptiness (although, being a Buddhist, he or
she—unlike the believer and the scientist—might not feel the need to say
anything at all)? In each case it is a matter of a basic way of envisaging the
world and of human life in the world and, as such, it is also a kind of
understanding that can only be communicated and accepted in freedom, as
a view I freely and gladly embrace without having been forced or coerced into
it in any way. It is simply how *I* see the world, and to want me to see it some
other way would be to want me to cease to be who and as I am, which would
be to want me to cease to be. On that basis the three travellers would soon find
themselves—even in this infinitely open space—in a situation analogous to
that of the three characters in Sartre's *Huis clos*: all would experience the
others as obstructing their ability just to be as and who they are. Instead of
trying to convert each other, they might therefore do better to begin by
welcoming each other and accepting the legitimacy of their respective basic
responses to what all agree is something of great wonder.[113] This would not
preclude the possibility that in their subsequent conversations a luminous
word from one or other of the companions (as they had now become) would

---

[113] And note: the viewpoint that each represents and offers to the other conversants is not an
arbitrarily adopted theoretical position, but reflects a freely accepted responsibility that has
already been assumed in their respective forms of life, namely, the believer's responsibility for
living by faith, the Buddhist's responsibility for following the eightfold path, and the scientist's
responsibility for rigorous research.

suddenly bring about a change of view or even heart. Conversions couldn't be ruled out, but they could properly occur only on the ground of charity, as an event within the unfolding story of their friendship, and as a free and heartfelt decision on the part of the one converted. What each would give to each would be a possibility of understanding, but whether that possibility was accepted would be down to each to decide.

For the questions that present themselves at this level are not about states of affairs but about possibilities of self-understanding (inclusive of mutual understanding) that—returning to our actual world—cannot be decided outside the all-encompassing dialogue of all with all, a dialogue that runs all the way through political, academic, and media discussions of our contemporary human condition, but that is also endlessly discussed in the intimacy of friendship and in the confidential words we share with our pastors and counsellors.[114] Ultimately, there are no final reasons outside the developing course of dialogue itself that require us to decide for Being or gift, Being or personality. This would be so even if we had a closer or fuller knowledge of Being than we actually do. But, distanced as we are from an immediate presence to Being by the structures of self-consciousness, time, space, language, relationships, and embodiment, how we speak of Being is always going to come back to particular configurations of just these structures. In other words, it will always be a question of how, now, in this context, speaking with just these interlocutors, in just this language, we are to decide what it is best to say, to affirm, or to deny of Being, nihility, or the gift.[115] This does not mean that all we can do is to say whatever comes into our heads to say. For our language itself is answerable to the exigencies of its history and context and to the relationships of its speakers and this already gives to speaking and thinking a certain orientation, a certain content, and a certain structure. We are always already in the midst of a conversation, and if this prevents us from constructing an overarching logos of Being this same conversation will already have given our thinking a certain direction and have drawn our attention to what, here and now, we are saying. Essentially, then, the question concerns how the whole community of language-users at this time (and, in the case of the English language, this potentially means the whole human community) understands itself, its words, its history, and its responsibilities. Once more, the question as to how we understand the meaning of our relation to Being and the further relationship of that meaning to the question

---

[114] This process of transformative reception seems close to what Derrida means by bringing a question—such as the question of negative theology—into universal discourse in the spirit of friendship (see, e.g., *Sauf le nom*, 71).

[115] Think of the issues around interpreting the *indicible* in the language of the perpetrators.

of God can only be resolved in the light of and to the degree that we come close to a politics of friendship, a rule of amity in which truth may be spoken without threat or fear. Whether we refine this question in terms of a political philosophy à la Habermas, whether we preach the claim of this kingdom in the present, or, trembling and weeping, pray in silence that it may come (or, perhaps, combine these or other strategies), are options we must decide with an eye to where we are coming from and an eye to where we are going and want to go, as well as a judgement about where we are now. But in, with, and under these contextual considerations, we nevertheless do not lose sight of the fact that what we are asking about is what is most worth remembering, what is most worth hoping for, and what is most worthy of being praised, and nor do we forget that if Being is founded upon love and if love cannot be itself unless it is freely willed and chosen we are always free to affirm the possibility that our life really is God's good and perfect gift and that, as the giver of this good and perfect gift, God *is*.

There is, then, nothing in the sheer facticity of the human condition that renders it impossible for us to experience our existence as God's gift and to interpret such experience as fundamental to the possibility of naming God as 'Being-Itself' or 'He Who Is'. Evidently, 'experience' does not in this case mean the purely passive imprint of a pre-existing state of affairs but an event of understanding in which we ourselves are freely and creatively active. More-over, since what is at issue is how to name God, this event of understanding is also an event of language. But it has been one of the hallmarks of the modern (and, for that, matter, of the so-called postmodern) world that the name of God has become deeply problematic—psychologically, politically, and, not least, metaphysically. The apophatic moment inherent in every theology seems to have found its historic moment and to have drained the way of affirmation of much of its ancient power. There are many reasons for this situation, some of which we have explored in this book. Metaphysically, they include a recognition of what I have a number of times called the 'weakening' of the sense of Being and of how our knowledge of God is inseparable from the complex historical, linguistic, social, and even bodily forms in which human life is lived. This may indicate a certain dislocation of the identifica-tion of God in terms of Being from its former central and defining place in Christian theology, but this is not the same as a simple denial of divine Being.

And there is more. Take these lines from Hölderlin's poem 'Homecoming':

> When we bless the meal, whom may I name, and when we
> Rest from the livelong day, tell me, how should I give thanks?
> Do I name the exalted one then? A god does not love what's unfitting.
> To grasp him, our joy is almost too small.

> We must often keep silent; holy names fail,
> Hearts are beating but speech yet holds back?[116]

The question of naming God is not only a matter of metaphysical reflection or of rhetorical aptitude: it is also a matter of joy, and if the preceding chapter suggested that trembling and weeping were characteristic bodily expressions of religious longing, neither should be taken solely as figures of negative psychological states. Joy too trembles and joy too weeps. Nor can joy be confined to the closed circle of obligation and enforced gratitude: joy simply is what and as it is, freely itself, and, when it speaks, it is as likely to speak in song as in propositions.

Such reflections seem to lie at the root of tendencies in recent theology to emphasize the doxological character of theology, reminding us that the original office of the theologian was not to pursue *Wissenschaft* but to articulate the community's offering of praise.[117] But how far does such an approach really take us?

Derrida, as we have seen, could allow for a certain kind of Messianic prayer: prayer as prayer of longing for the unknown God, the God to whom, in fear and trembling, we turn with tear-drenched faces, the God whom we seek in solitude, in silence, on our knees, knowing only the love and the longing, with sighs and groans too deep for words (Romans 8: 26). But when joy finds expression in the language of praise and thanksgiving, it seems to cross a line that the philosopher found himself unable to cross, as when he voiced his suspicion that, even when it is not 'an act of constative predication', the hymn of praise 'qualifies God and determines prayer, determines the other, Him to whom it addresses itself, refers, invoking Him even as the source of prayer'.[118] Whether what is said in such songs of praise speaks of God in the Trinitarian vocabulary of the persons of Father, Son, and Spirit, of *ousia*, essence, substance, Being, generation and procession, immanent and economic relations, *perichorēsis* and the passing-into-one-another of the divine persons in movement, dance, and play, or whether it speaks only of God as good, loving, gracious, sheltering, merciful, and constant in loving-kindness, even the purest doxological theology seems to want to say *what God is* in a way that goes beyond the movement of longing experienced in prayer. And once that

---

[116] Translated from the text in M. Hamburger, *Friedrich Hölderlin: Poems and Fragments* (London: Anvil Press, 2004), 337.

[117] See, e.g. Catherine Pickstock, *After Writing: On the Liturgical Consummation of Philosophy* (Oxford: Basil Blackwell, 1998). However, despite the great difference in rhetorical style, this is already essentially the position of J. N. D. Kelly in his *Early Christian Doctrines* (London: A. & C. Black, 1958). In both cases, however, there seems to me to be an equivocation as to the precise status of the discourse thus grounded.

[118] *Derrida and Negative Theology*, 111.

happens, we seem no longer to be in the domain of pure prayer or pure praise. Once we enter the realm of articulated speech, we are in a domain where the ontological claim implicit in each 'what' will bear the stress of distance and nearness and must be interpreted and accounted for if it is to carry us with it.[119] In an ecclesiastical context, that will mean doctrinal exposition, but such exposition cannot simply suspend the complex network of distances that map our being in the world or, if it does, it is hard to see what there is to stop it from degenerating into mere dogmatism. Yet if we see only distance, what do we have to add to Sartrean nihilism?

According to whichever brand of suspicion they practise, theologians of suspicion will find dogmatism or subjectivism, metaphysics or nihilism, wherever they choose to look. If, however, the primary task of theology is not to speak about other theologians but to find words most suited to praising the excellencies of God and if, as Hölderlin has reminded us, joy is the essential medium of praise, then apophasis and ontology, the silence of the Buddha and the wonder of the scientist, might each, according to time and circumstance, serve the free movement of human spirit in which and in which alone religion can flourish. What truly matters, then, is to set that movement in motion, to awaken the longing that, whether it figures itself as lack or as love, looks to God as the one in whom all our human possibilities find their beginning and their end. It is in this spirit that Augustine opens his sermon on Psalm 42 by speaking of his longing to speak of the longing for God to those who long for God. Here, as so often, Augustine is the most eloquent opponent of his own theology, for the truth of our God-relation is not to be found in the satisfaction of such longing and the transformation of the religious individual into an image of the selfsame immutability of divine Being, as Augustine supposed: rather, our human perfection is precisely to know our need of God, and this need is too great to be finalized in any theology capable of answering the demands of what society and the academy today understand as 'knowledge'. The greatest of gifts is not our capacity for knowledge, but the freedom to seek one whom we might thank for the immeasurable joy of being in a world inhabited by creatures whom it gladdens our hearts to love. And if this sounds sermonical, then we might also remember—as Augustine has just reminded us—that the task of the sermon is not so much to instil dogmatic truths or issue moral imperatives but more fundamentally to move its auditors to recognize how and how much they want God. To this end it will not naturally find expression in indicatives or imperatives. Instead, as it poses questions, offers hypotheses, and opens new ways of looking at its subject

---

[119] This would, after all, seem to limit the scope of the kind of appeal to the immediate experience of the slave chorus made by Westphal. See Introduction, p. 9.

matter, it will speak in a mode that is better described as subjunctive or optative. Only so can it both preserve the speaker's awe at the possibility of God's nearness and the freedom of the listener in relation to what is being said.

Another way of putting this is to say that univocal statements regarding existent states of affairs and non-cognitive intuitions of unmediated presence do not exhaust the possibilities of our being able to be aware of and to speak about Being. 'It may be so' need not be taken as a state of suspension awaiting the resolution of what is being spoken about in a judgement as to whether or not it is in fact the case. It may, equally, express an original mental comportment that involves a particular and distinctive way of relating to, apprehending, and speaking about Being. It may, for example, be the comportment that especially and uniquely enables us to discern what Jankélévitch has referred to as the charm, the enchantment, or the melody of Being-in-beings,[120] an openness to being in which levity plays no less a role than earnestness and resoluteness. Nevertheless, if we thus seem to be allowing for a certain re-admission of speaking of God 'as' Being, this is not forgetful of everything said in the previous chapter about the role of bodily life as the sole milieu in which and through which Being can become meaningful to embodied beings such as we are, living on earth, thinking of heaven.

CONCLUDING QUESTIONS: PROSTHESIS AND METANOIA

I should like to conclude by looking very briefly at just one example of how the way in which we formulate the meaning of the Being of God will be shaped by the exigencies of the world in which we actually live and by the human possibilities that such a world reveals. More specifically, I should like to look at how the very question of human possibilities and their limits has become one of the fundamental issues of our time. What provokes this question is, quite simply, the constantly growing power of contemporary technology to determine the scope of human possibilities and the widespread doubt as to whether those who manage and implement the development of technology are to be allowed to decide which possibilities of human flourishing are to be

---

[120] See V. Jankélévitch, *Le Je-ne-sais-quoi et le presque rien*, vol. i (Paris: Éditions du Seuil, 1980), especially 94 ff.

pursued and which are to be neglected or rejected. The question also—and increasingly—relates to the very nature of human embodiment itself.[121]

From its beginnings in the early modern period, what we now know as science has aimed not merely at knowledge but at extending human possibilities to the point of transforming human being itself. Already in Bacon's *New Atlantis*, in which a group of travellers discover a lost civilization in which science and science-based technology are pursued under the tutelage of the order of Salomon's House (a kind of prototype for the Royal Society), a representative of the order describes their aims as follows: 'The End of our Foundation is the knowledge of Causes, and secret motions of things; and the enlarging of the bounds of Human Empire, to the effecting of all things possible.'[122] And, in an appendix to the *New Atlantis*, Bacon lists some of these possibilities, including:

The prolongation of life. The restitution of youth in some degree. The retardation of age. The curing of diseases counted incurable. The mitigation of pain. More easy and less loathsome purgings. The increasing of strength and activity. The increasing of ability to suffer torture or pain. The altering of complexions, and fatness and leanness. The altering of statures. The altering of features. The increasing and exalting of the intellectual parts. Versions of bodies into other bodies. Making of new species. Transplanting of one species into another. Instruments of destruction, as of war and poison.[123]

Much of this programme is, of course, recognizable in the continuing achievements of medicine and bio-engineering and what cannot as yet be done is enthusiastically advocated by proponents of transhumanism. The confluence of bio-engineering and the electronically generated virtual world promises (or threatens) a future in which human being will become a play of simulacra, of entities that both are and are-not, that are infinitely malleable and plastic, that can transmute or morph into other forms, other entities, 'versions of bodies into other bodies', as Bacon put it. In cyber-space, all things will be possible, I can be the hero I never have been in life, I may become male, female, wise, silly, fragmented, here and not here, I can die and behold I live! How far this transhumanist vision is still science fiction and how far it indicates the next step in the history of applied science may be open to debate (it surely is), but even as a vision of which human possibilities are most worth realizing it is already controversial—not least because it would seem to be predicated on the abandonment of all that has been true of human beings in the past.

---

[121] The background of this section is found in my book *Thinking about God in an Age of Technology* (Oxford: Oxford University Press, 2005).

[122] Francis Bacon, *The Major Works*, ed. B. Vickers (Oxford: Oxford University Press, 1996), 480.

[123] Ibid. 488–9.

It may well be the harbinger of a new order of being in which the reality of those entities that will inhabit it will find full and adequate expression for their life-choices, but will it be a human order and will it answer the human question as to the human meaning of Being? Recalling Jankélévitch's insistence on holding fast the memory of the Holocaust, is there something in the long history of suffering humanity and in the reality of contemporary suffering that the prophets of a technocratic future are overlooking? What is the value of being a perfect cyber-being, if becoming one means cutting all the threads that join me to the history of humanity hitherto? Why should I be ashamed of dying as all my forebears have died and as many, many morally better human beings than me have died? And does any technology yet devised do anything at all to free us from our freedom freely to love or to withhold ourselves from loving? Could any possible technology do that without emptying the words 'love' and 'freedom' of all content? On the contrary, don't we already see a kind of atrophy of compassion amongst those most able to access technologies of life-enhancement? These are a lot of questions to pose at the end of an enquiry such as this, pointing as they do to the possibility of a basic conflict between the kind of future that might emerge from visions of technological perfectibility and a future lived from the memory of suffering,[124] between a future that can be brought about through planning and calculation and a future that can only be received as a gift. But if, holding fast to the memory of suffering, the future nevertheless does lie before us as a gift, and if that gift comprises within itself technically enhanced possibilities of self-direction, could we claim that gift without *metanoia* (repentance) and without forgiveness? Which of these possible futures is the possibility we most need to lay hold of and realize? How might we decide? Or how might we remain open to both? In such questions the question as to our most basic and most urgent possibilities forces itself upon us: *prosthesis*—maybe; *metanoia*—maybe; gift—maybe; God—maybe.

In theology, questions of technology are often treated as specialist questions within the sub-discipline of Christian Ethics, but the scope of the challenge they pose goes far beyond anything which such a sub-discipline might adequately address. That is why Heidegger saw in *the* question concerning technology the primary form that the question of Being is taking in our time. In the accelerating impacts of technology across the whole of human life, the nature of human being is itself being put in question—and therefore also the way in which our experiences of human being might provide us with an analogy or sign of divine Being. If Bacon's 'versions' of

---

[124] The reference is of course to J. B. Metz's seminal essay 'The Future Ex Memoria Passionis', in E. H. Cousins (ed.), *Hope and the Future of Man* (Philadelphia: Fortress Press, 1972), 117–31.

human bodies into other kinds of bodies are becoming a real possibility for contemporary or future science, what does that mean for the embodied experience of a dynamically relational and conversational inner space that provides us with the best measure we have of 'reality' and, therewith, of the 'real presence' and real Being of God? These questions are asked—as I believe they were asked by Heidegger—as genuine questions. How we collectively answer them will show what or who we really take God to be and what we take ourselves, God's creatures, really to be.

Bibliography

Ancient and Medieval Philosophy (1) Primary Sources

Anselm, *Anselm of Canterbury*, ed. and trans. J. Hopkins and H. Richardson, vol. i (London: SCM Press, 1974).

Aristotle, *The Metaphysics*, trans. H. Tredennick (Cambridge, Mass.: Harvard University Press, 1961–2).

Augustine, *Concerning the City of God against the Pagans*, trans. H. Bettenson (Harmondsworth: Penguin, 1972).

——, *Confessions*, trans. W. Watts (Cambridge, Mass.: Harvard University Press, 1912).

——, *Expositions on the Book of Psalms*, vol. ii (Oxford: Parker, 1848).

——, *The Trinity*, trans. E. Hill (Brooklyn, NY: New City Press, 1991).

Bonaventure, *Works of St Bonaventure: Itinerarium Mentis in Deum* (The progress of the mind towards God), ed. and trans. P. Boehner and Z. Hayes (Saint Bonaventure, NY: Saint Bonaventure University Press, 2002).

Dionysius (Pseudo-), 'The Divine Names', in *The Complete Works*, trans. C. Luibheid (New York: Paulist Press, 1987).

Plato, *Republic*, trans. P. Shorey (Cambridge, Mass.: Harvard University Press, 1937).

Plotinus, *Enneads*, trans. A. H. Armstrong (Cambridge, Mass.: Harvard University Press, 1966).

Thomas Aquinas, *On Being and Essence*, trans. A. Maurer (Toronto: Pontifical Institute of Medieval Studies, 1971).

——, *On the Truth of the Catholic Faith* (*Summa contra Gentiles*), trans. V. J. Bourke (New York: Image Books, 1956).

——, *Summa theologiae*, trans. T. McDermott OP (London: Eyre and Spottiswode, 1964).

William of Saint-Thierry, *De natura et dignitate amoris* in *Trattati d'amore cristiani del XII secolo* (bilingual edition), ed. F. Zambon, vol. i (Turin: Fondazione Lorenzo Valla, 2007).

Ancient and Medieval Philosophy (2) Secondary Literature

Brunn, E. zum, *St. Augustine: Being and Nothingness* (New York: Paragon House, 1986).

Caputo, John D., *Heidegger and Aquinas: An Essay in Overcoming Metaphysics* (New York, Fordham University Press, 1982).

Dauphinais, M., David, B., and Levering, M. (eds.), *Aquinas the Augustinian* (Washington, DC: Catholic Universities of America Press, 2007).

Davies, B., *The Thought of Thomas Aquinas* (Oxford: Oxford University Press, 1992).

Floucat, Y., 'Étienne Gilson et la métaphysique de l'acte de l'être', *Revue Thomiste*, 102/3 (July–September 1994).

Gilson, E., *Being and Some Philosophers* (Toronto: Pontifical Institute of Mediaeval Studies, 1952).

——, *The Spirit of Mediaeval Philosophy*, trans. A. H. C. Downes (London: Sheed and Ward, 1936).

Kenny, A., *Aquinas on Being* (Oxford: Oxford University Press, 2002).

Kerr, F., *After Aquinas: Versions of Thomism* (Oxford: Blackwell, 2002).

Lubac, H. de, *The Mystery of the Supernatural*, trans. R. Sheed (London: Geoffrey Chapman, 1967).

Marenbon, J., 'Aquinas, Radical Orthodoxy and Truth', in W. J. Hankey and D. Hedley (eds.), *Deconstructing Radical Orthodoxy: Postmodern Theology, Rhetoric and Truth* (Aldershot: Ashgate, 2005).

Maritain, J., *The Degrees of Knowledge*, trans. B. Wall and M. R. Adamson (London: G. Bles, 1937).

——, *Existence and the Existent* (New York: Image Books, 1948).

Mascall, E., *He Who Is: A Study in Traditional Theism* (London: Longman, Green and Co., 1943).

——, *Existence and Analogy: A Sequel to 'He Who Is'* (London: Longman, Green and Co., 1949).

——, *The Opennness of Being: Natural Theology Today* (London: Darton, Longman and Todd, 1971).

Owens, J., *The Doctrine of Being in the Aristotelian 'Metaphysics': A Study in the Greek Background of Mediaeval Thought* (Toronto: Pontifical Institute of Mediaeval Studies, 1963).

Prouvost, G., 'Étienne Gilson–Jacques Maritain', *Revue Thomiste*, 102/3 (July–September 1994).

Stein, E., *Endliches und Ewiges Sein* (*Gesamtausgabe*, vols. xi/xii) (Freiburg: Herder, 2006). English translation by K. F. Reinhardt, *Finite and Eternal Being: An Attempt at an Ascent to the Meaning of Being* (Washington, DC: ICS Publications, 2002).

Stump, E., *Aquinas* (London: Routledge, 2003).

Wippel, J. F., 'Metaphysics', in N. Kretzmann and E. Stump (eds.), *The Cambridge Companion to Aquinas* (Cambridge: Cambridge University Press, 1993).

Heidegger

(1) Works by Heidegger in German

Beiträge zur Philosophie (vom Ereignis) (*Gesamtausgabe*, vol. lxiii) (Frankfurt am Main: Klostermann, 1989).

Einführung in die Phänomenologische Forschung (*Gesamtausgabe*, vol. xvii) (Frankfurt am Main: Klostermann, 1994).

Erläuterungen zu Hölderlins Dichtung (*Gesamtausgabe*, vol. iv) (Frankfurt am Main: Klostermann, 1996).

Frühe Schriften (*Gesamtausgabe*, vol. i) (Frankfurt am Main: Klostermann, 1978).

Geschichte der Philosophie von Thomas von Aquin bis Kant (*Gesamtausgabe*, vol. xxiii) (Frankfurt am Main: Klostermann, 2006).

Grundbegriffe der Aristotelischen Philosophie (*Gesamtausgabe*, vol. xviii) (Frankfurt am Main: Klostermann, 2002).

Hölderlins Hymne 'Andenken' (*Gesamtausgabe*, vol. lii) (Frankfurt am Main: Klostermann, 1982).

Hölderlins Hymne 'Der Ister' (*Gesamtausgabe*, vol. liii) (Frankfurt am Main: Klostermann, 1984).

Hölderlins Hymnen 'Germanien' und 'Der Rhein' (*Gesamtausgabe*, vol. xxxix) (Frankfurt am Main: Klostermann, 1989).

Holzwege (*Gesamtausgabe*, vol. v) (Frankfurt am Main: Klostermann, 1950).

Logik: Die Frage nach der Wahrheit (*Gesamtausgabe*, vol. xxi) (Frankfurt am Main: Klostermann, 1995).

Metaphysik und Nihilismus (*Gesamtausgabe*, vol. lxvii) (Frankfurt am Main: Klostermann, 1999).

Phänomenologie des Religiösen Lebens (*Gesamtausgabe*, vol. lx) (Frankfurt am Main: Klostermann, 1993).

Phänomenologische Interpretationen ausgewählter Abhandlungen des Aristoteles zur Ontologie und Logik (*Gesamtausgabe*, vol. lxii) (Frankfurt am Main: Klostermann, 2005).

Prolegomena zur Geschichte des Zeitbegriffs (*Gesamtausgabe*, vol. xx) (Frankfurt am Main: Klostermann, 1979).

Seminare (*Gesamtausgabe*, vol. xv) (Frankfurt am Main: Klostermann, 2005).

Vorträge und Aufsätze (Stuttgart: Neske, 1954) (also *Gesamtausgabe*).

Was Heißt Denken (*Gesamtausgabe*, vol. viii) (Frankfurt am Main: Klostermann, 2002).

Was ist Metaphysik? (*Gesamtausgabe*, vol. ix) (Frankfurt am Main: Klostermann, 2003).

Zur Sache des Denkens (*Gesamtausgabe*, vol. xiv) (Tübingen: Niemeyer, 1969).

(2) Works by Heidegger in English

Aristotle's Metaphysics θ: On the Essence and Actuality of Force, trans. W. Brogan and P. Warnek (*Gesamtausgabe*, vol. xxxiii) (Bloomington, Ind.: Indiana University Press, 1995).

Being and Time, trans. J. Macquarrie and E. Robinson (*Gesamtausgabe*, vol. ii) (Oxford: Blackwell, 1962).

Contributions to Philosophy (From Enowning), trans. P. Emad and K. Maly (*Gesamtausgabe*, vol. lxiii) (Bloomington, Ind.: Indiana University Press, 2000).

The Fundamental Concepts of Metaphysics: World, Finitude, Solitude, trans. W. McNeill and N. Walker (Bloomington, Ind.: Indiana University Press, 1995).

History of the Concept of Time, trans. T. Kisiel (*Gesamtausgabe*, vol. xx) (Bloomington, Ind.: Indiana University Press, 1985).

Hölderlin's Hymn 'The Ister', trans. W. McNeill and J. Davis (*Gesamtausgabe,* vol. liii) (Bloomington, Ind.: Indiana University Press, 1996).

Identity and Difference, trans. J. Stambaugh (*Gesamtausgabe,* vol. xi) (New York: Harper and Row, 1969).

'Introduction to "What is Metaphysics?"', trans. W. Kaufmann, in W. McNeil (ed.), *Pathmarks* (*Gesamtausgabe,* vol. ix) (Cambridge: Cambridge University Press, 1998).

'On the Essence of Truth', trans. John Sallis, in W. McNeill (ed.), *Pathmarks* (*Gesamtausgabe,* vol. ix) (Cambridge: Cambridge University Press, 1998).

Plato's Sophist, trans. R. Rojcewicz and A. Schuwer (*Gesamtausgabe,* vol. xix) (Bloomington, Ind.: Indiana University Press, 1997).

Poetry, Language, Thought, trans. A. Hofstadter (New York: Harper and Row, 1971).

What is Called Thinking?, trans. J. Gray and F. Wieck (*Gesamtausgabe,* vol. ix) (New York: Harper, 1968).

(3) **Secondary Literature on Heidegger**

Buchner, H. (ed.), *Japan und Heidegger: Gedenkschrift der Stadt Meßkirch zum hundersten Geburtstag Martin Heidegger* (Sigmaringen: Jan Thorbecke, 1989).

Caputo, John D., *Demythologizing Heidegger* (Bloomington, Ind.: Indiana University Press, 1993).

Edwards, P., *Heidegger's Confusions* (New York: Prometheus Books, 2004).

El-Bizri, Nader, *The Phenomenological Quest between Avicenna and Heidegger* (Binghamton, NY, State University of New York Press, 2000).

Faye, E., *Heidegger, L'introduction du nazisme dans la philosophie* (Paris: Albin Michel, 2005).

Hanley, C., *Being and God in Aristotle and Heidegger: The Role of Method in Thinking the Infinite* (Lanham, Md.: Rowman and Littlefield, 2000).

Kisiel, T., *The Genesis of Heidegger's Being and Time* (Berkeley and Los Angeles: University of California Press, 1993).

——, and Sheehan, T., *Becoming Heidegger: On the Trail of his Early Occasional Writings, 1910–1927* (Evanston, Ill.: Northwestern University Press, 2007).

Malpas, J., *Heidegger's Topology: Being, Place, World* (Boston: MIT Press, 2006).

Mattéi, J.-F., 'Emmanuel Faye, l'introduction du fantasme dans la philosophie', in *Heidegger: La Pensée à l'ère de la technique et de la mondialisation* (Strasbourg: Éditions Portique, 2006), 53–81.

Parkes, G. (ed.), *Heidegger and Asian Thought* (Honolulu: University of Hawaii Press, 1987).

Pattison, G., 'Heidegger's Hölderlin and Kierkegaard's Christ', in S. Mulhall (ed.), *Martin Heidegger* (Aldershot: Ashgate, 2006).

——, 'Heidegger, Augustine and Kierkegaard: Care, Time and Love', in C. De Paulo (ed.), *The Influence of Augustine on Heidegger: The Emergence of an Augustinian Phenomenology* (Lewiston, NY: Edwin Mellen Press, 2007).

——, *The Routledge Guidebook to the Later Heidegger* (London: Routledge, 2000).

Rudd, A., *Expressing the World: Skepticism, Wittgenstein, and Heidegger* (Chicago: Open Court, 2003).
Westphal, M., 'Overcoming Onto-theology', in John D. Caputo and Michael J. Scanlon (eds.), *God, the Gift and Postmodernism* (Bloomington, Ind.: Indiana University Press, 1999).

Kierkegaard (Primary and Secondary)

Bespaloff, R., *Cheminements et Carrefours* (Paris: Vrin, 1938).
Cappelørn, N.-J., and Deuser, H. (eds.), *Kierkegaard Studies Yearbook 1996* (Berlin: de Gruyter, 1996).
——, (eds.), *Kierkegaard Studies Yearbook 1997* (Berlin: de Gruyter, 1997).
Carlisle, C., *Kierkegaard's Philosophy of Becoming* (Albany, NY: State University of New York Press, 2005).
Chestov, L., *Kierkegaard et la philosophie existentielle: Vox clamantis in deserto* (Paris: Vrin, 1972).
Eriksen, E. E., *Kierkegaard's Category of Repetition: A Reconstruction*, Kierkegaard Monograph series 5 (Berlin: de Gruyter, 2000).
Fenves, P., *'Chatter': Language and History in Kierkegaard* (Stanford, Calif.: Stanford University Press, 1993).
Ferreira, M. J., *Love's Grateful Striving: A Commentary on Kierkegaard's Works of Love* (Oxford: Oxford University Press, 2001).
Grimsley, R., *Kierkegaard and French Literature* (Cardiff: University of Wales Press, 1966).
Hall, A. L., *Kierkegaard and the Treachery of Love* (Cambridge: Cambridge University Press, 2002).
Holm, I. W., *Tanken i Billedet: Søren Kierkegaards Poetik (Thinking in Images; SK's Poetics)* (Copenhagen: Gyldendal, 1998).
Kierkegaard, S., *Søren Kierkegaards Skrifter*, ed. N.-J. Cappelørn et al. (Copenhagen: Gad, 1997 continuing).
——, *The Concept of Anxiety*, trans. R. Thomte, SKS 4 (Princeton: Princeton University Press, 1980).
——, *Concluding Unscientific Postscript*, SKS 7 (Princeton: Princeton University Press, 1992).
——, *Eighteen Upbuilding Discourses*, SKS5 (Princeton: Princeton University Press, 1990).
——, *Fear and Trembling/Repetition*, SKS 4 (Princeton: Princeton University Press, 1983).
——, *Philosophical Fragments*, SKS 4 (Princeton: Princeton University Press, 1985).
——, *The Sickness unto Death*, SKS 11 (Princeton: Princeton University Press, 1980).
——, *Two Ages*, SKS 8 (Princeton: Princeton University Press, 1978).
——, *Without Authority*, SKS 11 (Princeton: Princeton University Press, 1997).
——, *Works of Love*, SKS 9 (Princeton: Princeton University Press, 1995).
King, G. Heath, *Existence: Thought: Style: Perspectives of a Primary Relation* (Milwaukee: Marquette University Press, 1996).

Krishek, S., *Kierkegaard on Faith and Love* (Cambridge: Cambridge University Press, 2009).

Landkildehus, S., 'Through a Veil of Tears: The Image of Christ in Kierkegaard's Discourses on the Woman who was a Sinner', in R. Kralik et al. (eds.), *Kierkegaard and Christianity: Acta Kierkegaardiana*, vol. iii (Toronto: Kierkegaard Circle and Kierkegaard Society, 2008).

Lippitt, J., *Humour and Irony in Kierkegaard's Thought* (Basingstoke: Macmillan, 2000).

Møller Jensen, H., 'Freeze! Hold it Right There', in N.-J. Cappelørn, H. Deuser, and J. Stewart (eds.), *Kierkegaard Studies Yearbook 2000* (Berlin: de Gruyter, 2000), 223–9.

Pattison, G., *Kierkegaard: The Aesthetic and the Religious* (London: SCM Press, 1998).

——, 'Kierkegaard's Left Hand', in Robert L. Perkins (ed.), *International Kierkegaard Commentary: The Point of View* (Macon, Ga.: Mercer University Press, 2010).

——, *Kierkegaard's Upbuilding Discourses: Philosophy, Literature and Theology* (London: Routledge, 2002).

——, *The Philosophy of Kierkegaard* (Aldershot: Ashgate, 2005).

——, 'Representing Love: From Poetry to Martyrdom or Language and Transcendence in Kierkegaard's Works of Love', *Kierkegaardiana*, 22 (2002), 139–54.

Perkins, Robert L. (ed.), *International Kierkegaard Commentary*, xix: *The Sickness unto Death* (Macon, Ga.: Mercer University Press, 1987).

Pyper, H., 'Forgiving the Unforgivable: Kierkegaard, Derrida and the Scandal of Forgiveness', *Kierkegaardiana*, 22 (2002).

Simmons, J. A., and Wood, D. (eds.), *Kierkegaard and Levinas: Ethics, Politics, and Religion* (Bloomington, Ind.: Indiana University Press, 2008).

Theunissen, M., *Der Begriff Verzweiflung: Korrekturen an Kierkegaard* (Frankfurt am Main: Suhrkamp, 1993).

——, 'The Upbuilding in the Thought of Death: Traditional Elements, Innovative ideas, and Unexhausted Possibilities', trans. G. Pattison, in Robert L. Perkins (ed.), *International Kierkegaard Commentary: Prefaces and Writing Sampler and Three Discourses on Imagined Occasions* (Macon, Ga.: Mercer University Press, 2006).

Modern French Philosophy

Bachelard, G., *The Poetics of Space*, trans. M. Jolas (Boston: Beacon Press, 1994).

Beauvoir, S. de., *The Second Sex*, trans. H. M. Parshley (Harmondsworth: Penguin, 1972).

Camus, A., *The Myth of Sisyphus*, trans. J. O'Brien (Harmondsworth: Penguin, 1955).

Caputo, John, D., *The Prayers and Tears of Jacques Derrida: Religion without Religion* (Bloomington, Ind.: Indiana University Press, 1997).

Derrida, J., *De la grammatologie* (Paris: Éditions de Minuit, 1967).

——, *Donner le temps*, i: *La Fausse Monnaie* (Paris: Galilée, 1991).

——, *Foi et savoir* (Paris: Éditions du Seuil, 1996).

——, *Khôra* (Paris: Galilée, 1993).

——, *Pardonner: L'Impardonnable et l'imprescriptible* (Paris: L'Herne, 2005).

——, *Psyché: L'Invention de l'autre*, ii (Paris: Galilée, 1987/2003).

——, *Sauf le nom* (Paris: Galilée, 1993).

——, *La Voix et le phénomène: Introduction au problème du signe dans la phénoménologie de Husserl* (Paris: Presses Universitaires de France, 1967).

——, *The Gift of Death*, trans. D. Wills (Chicago: University of Chicago Press, 1995).

——, 'How to Avoid Speaking: Denials', trans. K. Frieden, in H. Coward and T. Foshay (eds.), *Derrida and Negative Theology* (Albany, NY: State University of New York Press, 1992).

——, *The Monoligualism of the Other or the Prosthesis of Origin*, trans. P. Mensah (Stanford, Calif.: Stanford University Press, 1998).

——, *Politics of Friendship*, trans. G. Collins (London: Verso, 1997).

——, *Writing and Difference*, trans. A. Bass (London: Routledge, 2001).

Howells, C., 'Conclusion: Sartre and the Deconstruction of the Subject', in idem (ed.), *The Cambridge Companion to Sartre* (Cambridge: Cambridge University Press, 1992).

Girard, R., 'Dostoïevski—du double à l'unité', in *Critique dans un souterrain* (Paris: Grasset, 1976).

——, *The Scapegoat*, trans. Y. Freccero (London: Athlone, 1986).

Irigaray, L., *Speculum of the Other Woman*, trans. G. C. Gill (Ithaca, NY: Cornell University Press, 1985).

Janicaud, D., *Le Tournant théologique de la phénoménologie française* (Combas: Éditions de l'Éclat, 1991).

Jankélévitch, V., *L'Imprescriptible* (Paris: Éditions du Seuil, 1986).

——, *Le Je-ne-sais-quoi et le presque-rien*, 3 vols. (Paris: Éditions du Seuil, 1980).

——, *Le Pardon* (Paris: Aubier, 1967).

——, *Les Vertus et l'amour*, vol. ii (Paris: Flammarion, 1986).

Kojève, A., *Introduction à la lecture de Hegel: Leçons sur la phénoménologie de l'ésprit* (Paris: Gallimard, 1947).

Lévinas, E., *De l'existence à l'existant* (Paris: Vrin, 2004).

——, *Dieu, la mort et le temps* (Paris: Grasset, 1993).

——, *Discovering Existence with Husserl*, trans. Richard A. Cohen and Michael B. Smith (Evanston, Ill.: Northwestern University Press, 1998).

——, *Noms propres* (Paris: Fata Morgana, 1976).

——, *Totalité et infinité: Essai sur l'extériorité* (Paris: Kluwer, 1971).

Marcel, G., *Homo viator: Prolégomènes à une métaphysique de l'espérance* (Paris: Aubier, 1944).

——, *The Mystery of Being*, vol. i, trans. G. S. Fraser (London: Harvill Press, 1950); vol. ii trans. R. Hague (London: Harvill Press, 1951).

——, *The Philosophy of Existence*, trans. M. Harari (London: Harvill, 1948).

Marion, J.-L. *Dieu sans l'être* (Paris: Presses Universitaires de France, 1991).

——, *Being Given: Towards a Phenomenology of Givenness*, trans. J. C. Kosky (Stanford, Calif.: Stanford University Press, 2002).

Marion, J.-L. *The Erotic Phenomenon*, trans. S. E. Lewis (Chicago: University of Chicago Press, 2007).

——, *God without Being: Hors texte*, trans. T. A. Carlson (Chicago: University of Chicago Press, 1991).

——, *Prolegomenon to Charity*, trans. S. E. Lewis and J. L. Kosky (New York: Fordham University Press, 1991).

——, *Reduction and Givenness*, trans. T. A. Carlson (Evanston, Ill.: Northwestern University Press, 1998).

Merleau-Ponty, M., *Phenomenology of Perception*, trans. C. Smith (London: Routledge, 1962).

——, *The Primacy of Perception*, trans. J. M. Edie (Evanston, Ill.: Northwestern University Press, 1964).

——, *The Prose of the World*, trans. J. O'Neill (Evanston, Ill.: Northwestern University Press, 1973).

——, *Sense and Non-Sense*, trans. H. L. Dreyfus and P. A. Dreyfus (Evanston, Ill.: Northwestern University Press, 1964).

——, *The Visible and the Invisible*, trans. A. Lingis (Evanston, Ill.: Northwestern University Press, 1968).

Mounier, E., *Introduction aux existentialismes*, in *Œuvres*, iii: *1944–50* (Paris: Éditions du Seuil, 1962).

——, *Le Personnalisme*, in *Œuvres*, iii: *1944–50* (Paris: Éditions du Seuil, 1962).

Ricœur, P., *Time and Narrative*, vol. i, trans. K. McLaughlin and D. Pellauer (Chicago: Chicago University Press, 1984).

Sartre, J.-P., *Being and Nothingness*, trans. H. Barnes (London: Methuen, 1958).

——, *L'Existentialisme est un humanisme* (Paris: Nagel, 1970).

——, *Words*, trans. I. Clephane (Harmondsworth: Penguin, 1967).

Todorov, T., *Théories du symbole* (Paris: Éditions du Seuil, 1977).

Toumayan, A., '"I more than the others": Dostoevsky and Levinas', in *Yale French Studies*, 104, *Encounters with Levinas* (2004), 55–66.

Westphal, M., *Levinas and Kierkegaard in Dialogue* (Bloomington, Ind.: Indiana University Press, 2008).

Russian Philosophy and Literature

Bakhtin, M. M., *K Phiilosophiiii Postupka* (Towards a philosophy of the act), in idem, *Chelovek b Miire Slova* (Man in the world of discourse) (Moscow: The Russian Open University, 1995).

——, *Problems of Dostoevsky's Poetics*, trans. C. Emerson (Minneapolis: University of Minnesota Press, 1984).

Baranova-Shestova, N., *Jiizn' L'va Shestova* (The life of Lev Shestov) (Paris: La Presse Libre, 1983).

Berdyaev, N. A., *The Beginning and the End*, trans. R. M. French (London: Geoffrey Bles, 1952).

——, *Freedom and the Spirit*, trans. O. F. Clarke (London: Geoffrey Bles, 1944).

——, *Slavery and Freedom*, trans. R. M. French (London: Geoffrey Bles, 1943).

——, *Solitude and Society*, trans. G. Reavey (London: G. Bles, 1938).

——, *Spirit and Reality*, trans. G. Reavey (London: G. Bles, 1939).

Dostoevsky, F. M., *The Brothers Karamazov*, trans. R. Pevear and L. Volokhonsky (London: Vintage, 1992).

——, *Crime and Punishment*, trans. R. Pevear and L. Volokhonsky (London: Vintage, 1993).

——, *Notes from Underground*, trans. R. Pevear and L. Volokhonsky (London: Vintage, 1993).

Fedorov, N., *What was Man Created For? The Philosophy of the Common Task*, trans. E. Koutaisoff and M. Minto (London: Honeyglen, 2008).

Florensky, P., *The Pillar and Ground of the Truth*, trans. B. Jakim (Princeton: Princeton University Press, 1997).

Jones, J., *Dostoevsky* (Oxford: Clarendon Press, 1983).

Kantor, V., 'Pavel Smerdyakov and Ivan Karamazov: The Problem of Temptation', in G. Pattison and D. Thompson, *Dostoevsky and the Christian Tradition* (Cambridge: Cambridge University Press, 2001).

Pattison, G., 'Unavowed Knowledge', in N.-H. Gregersen and C. Hjøllund (eds.), *Coping with Evil: Perspectives from Science and Theology* (Aarhus: University of Aarhus, 2003).

Tolstoy, L., *The Death of Ivan Ilych and Other Stories*, trans. A. Maude (New York: New American Library, 1960).

Walicki, A., *A History of Russian Thought from the Enlightenment to Marxism*, trans. H. Andrews-Rusiecka (Oxford: Clarendon Press, 1988).

Williams, R., *Dostoevsky: Language, Faith and Fiction* (London: Continuum, 2008).

Other

Alfeyev, H., *The Spiritual World of Isaac the Syrian* (Kalamazoo, Mich.: Cistercian Publications, 2000).

Arendt, H., *The Life of the Mind*, 1-volume edn. (San Diego: Harcourt, 1977, 1978).

Bacon, F., *The Major Works*, ed. B. Vickers (Oxford: Oxford University Press, 1996).

Baillie, J., *The Sense of the Presence of God* (London: Oxford University Press, 1962).

Balthasar, Hans Urs von, *The Glory of the Lord*, vol. iii: *Lay Styles*, ed. J. Riches et al., trans. A Louth et al. (Edinburgh: T. & T. Clark, 1986).

Barth, K., *Church Dogmatics*, i/1, trans. G. Bromiley (London: T. & T. Clark, 2004).

——, *Church Dogmatics*, ii/1: *The Doctrine of God*, ed. G. Bromiley and T. F. Torrance (London: T. & T. Clark, 2004).

——, 'Introductory Essay', in L. Feuerbach, *The Essence of Christianity*, trans. M. Evans (New York: Harper, 1957).

Brémond, H., *Histoire littéraire du sentiment religieux en France depuis la fin des guerres de religion jusqu'à nos jours*, vol. ii (Paris: Blou and Gay, 1923).

Brentano, F., *On the Several Senses of Being in Aristotle*, trans. R. George (Berkeley and Los Angeles: University of California Press, 1975).

Brown, D., *God and Enchantment of Place: Reclaiming Human Experience* (Oxford: Oxford University Press, 2004).

——, *God and Grace of Body: Sacrament in Ordinary* (Oxford: Oxford University Press, 2007).

Brown, P., *The Coming of the Saints* (Chicago: Chicago University Press, 1981).

Brueggemann, W., *The Land: Place as Gift, Promise and Challenge in Biblical Faith* (Philadelphia: Fortress Press, 1982).

Brunner, E., and Barth, K., *Natural Theology*, trans. P. Fraenkel (London: Geoffrey Bles, 1946).

Buber, M., *Between Man and Man* (London: Collins, 1961).

——, *I and Thou*, trans. W. Kaufmann (Edinburgh: T. & T. Clark, 1970).

Bultmann, R., *History and Eschatology* (Edinburgh: Edinburgh University Press, 1975).

Burns, R. M., and Rayment-Pickard, H., *Philosophies of History: From Enlightenment to Postmodernity* (Oxford: Blackwell, 2000).

Bychkov, O., and Fodor, J. (eds.), *Theological Aesthetics after von Balthasar* (Aldershot: Ashgate, 2008).

Candler, P. M., and Cunningham, C. (eds.), *Veritas: Transcendence and Phenomenology* (London: SCM Press, 2007).

Caputo, John D., and Scanlon, M. J. (eds.), *God, the Gift and Postmodernism* (Bloomington, Ind.: Indiana University Press, 1999).

Childs, B. S., *Book of Exodus: A Critical Theological Commentary* (Louisville, Ky.: Westminster John Knox Press, 2004).

Cioran, E. M., *Tears and Saints*, trans. I. Zarifopol-Johnston (Chicago: Chicago University Press, 1995).

Coreth, E., 'Immediacy and the Mediation of Being: An Attempt to Answer Bernard Lonergan', in P. McShane (ed.), *Language, Truth and Meaning: Papers from the International Lonergan Conference 1970* (Dublin: Gill and Macmillan, 1971).

Cupitt, Don, *Above us only Sky* (Santa Rosa, Calif.: Polebridge, 2008).

——, *Life! Life!* (Santa Rosa, Calif.: Polebridge Press, 2003).

——, *The Meaning of It All in Everyday Speech* (London: SCM Press, 1999).

——, *The New Religion of Life in Everyday Speech* (London: SCM Press, 1999).

——, *The Religion of Being* (London: SCM Press, 1998).

——, *Taking Leave of God* (London: SCM Press, 1980).

Dalferth, I., *Becoming Present: An Inquiry into the Christian Sense of the Presence of God* (Leuven: Peeters, 2006).

Davies, O., *A Theology of Compassion: Metaphysics of Difference and the Renewal of Tradition* (London: SCM Press, 2001).

De Nicolas, A. T., *Ignatius of Loyola, Powers of Imagining; A Philosophical Hermeneutic of Imagining through the Collected Works of Ignatius of Loyola* (Albany, NY: State University of New York Press, 1986).

Dennett, D., *Freedom Evolves* (New York: Viking, 2003).

Dreyfus, H., *On the Internet* (London: Routledge, 2001).

Eaton, J. H., *Vision in Worship: The Relation of Prophecy and Liturgy in the Old Testament* (London: SPCK, 1981).

Ebeling, G., *Introduction to a Theological Theory of Language*, trans. R. A. Wilson (London: Collins, 1973).

Eliade, M., *The Myth of the Eternal Return, or Cosmos and History*, trans. W. R. Trask (Princeton: Princeton University Press, 1954).

——, *The Sacred and the Profane: The Nature of Religion*, trans. W. R. Trask (New York: Harcourt, Brace and World, 1959).

——, *Symbolism, the Sacred, and the Arts*, ed. D. Apostolos-Cappadona (New York: Crossroad, 1986).

Eliot, T. S., *Four Quartets* (London: Faber and Faber, 1944).

Elkins, J., and Morgan, D. (eds.), *Re-enchantment* (London: Routledge, 2008).

Feuerbach, L., *The Essence of Faith According to Martin Luther*, trans. M. Cherno (New York: Harper and Row, 1967).

——, *Principles of the Philosophy of the Future*, trans. M. Vogel (Indianapolis: Hackett, 1986).

Feyerabend, P., *Against Method* (London: Verso, 1988).

Freud, S., *The Future of an Illusion*, trans. W. D. Robson-Scott (London: Hogarth Press, 1961).

Gablik, S., *The Reenchantment of Art* (London: Thames and Hudson, 1992).

Gadamer, H.-G., *Wahrheit und Methode* (Tübingen: Mohr, 1975).

Gasquet, J., *Joachim Gasquet's Cézanne: A Memoir with Conversations*, trans. C. Pemberton (London: Thames and Hudson, 1991).

Graham, G., *The Re-enchantment of the World: Art versus Religion* (Oxford: Oxford University Press, 2007).

Grenz, Stanley J., *The Named God and the Philosophy of Being: A Trinitarian Theo-Ontology* (Louisville, Ky.: Westminster John Knox Press, 2005).

Gunton, C., *Becoming and Being* (London: SCM Press, 2001).

Habermas, J., *The Theory of Communicative Action*, trans. T. McCarthy (Boston: Beacon Press, 1984).

——, *Die Zukunft der menschlichen Natur* (Frankfurt am Main: Suhrkamp, 2001).

Hadot, P. *Exercices spirituels et philosophie antique* (Paris: Albin Michel, 2002).

Harsthorne, C., and Reese, William L., *Philosophers Speak of God* (Chicago: Chicago University Press, 1953).

Hausherr, I., SJ, *Penthos in the Christian East* (Kalamazoo, Mich.: Cistercian Publications, 1982).

Hegel, G. W. F., *Enzyklopädie der philosophischen Wissenschaften III*, in *Werke*, x (Frankfurt am Main: Suhrkamp, 1970).

——, *Phänomenologie des Geistes*, in *Werke*, iii (Frankfurt am Main: Suhrkamp, 1970).

——, *Phenomenology of Spirit*, trans. A. V. Miller (Oxford: Clarendon Press, 1977).

——, *Wissenschaft der Logik I*, in *Werke*, v (Frankfurt-am-Rhein: Suhrkamp, 1969).

——, *Wissenschaft der Logik II*, in *Werke*, vi (Frankfurt am Main: Suhrkamp, 1969).

Hick, J., *Death and Eternal Life* (London: Collins, 1976).

Hillesum, E., *Etty: A Diary 1941–43*, trans. A. J. Pomerans (London: Jonathan Cape, 1983).

Hilton, W., *The Ladder of Perfection*, trans. L. Sherley-Price (Harmondsworth: Penguin, 1957).

Hölderlin, F., *Friedrich Hölderlin: Poems and Fragments*, ed. and trans. M. Hamburger (London: Anvil Press, 2004).

Hook, S., *The Quest for Being and Other Studies in Naturalism and Humanism* (New York: Delta, 1963).

Hopkins, G. M., *Poems and Prose of Gerard Manley Hopkins*, ed. W. H. Gardner (Harmondsworth: Penguin, 1953).

Horner, R., *Rethinking God as Gift: Marion, Derrida, and the Limits of Phenomenology* (New York: Fordham University Press, 2001).

Husserl, E., *Zur Phänomenologie des inneren Zeitbewußtseins* (*Husserliana: Edmund Husserls Gesamte Werke*, vol. x), ed. R. Boehm (The Hague: Marinus Nijhoff, 1966).

Hyman, G., *The Predicament of Postmodern Theology: Radical Orthodoxy or Nihilist Textualism?* (Louisville, Ky.: Westminster John Knox Press, 2001).

Isaac of Nineveh, *'The Second Part': Chapters IV–XLI*, trans. S. Brock (Leuven: Peeters, 1995).

James, W., *Varieties of Religious Experience* (London: Collins, 1960).

Julian of Norwich, *Revelations of Divine Love*, trans. C. Wolters (Harmondsworth: Penguin, 1966).

Jüngel, E., *God's Being is in Becoming: The Trinitarian Being of God in the Theology of Karl Barth* (Edinburgh: T. & T. Clark, 2001).

Kant, I., *Critique of Pure Reason*, trans. Norman Kemp Smith (London: Macmillan, 1933).

Kearney, R., *The God Who May Be: A Hermeneutics of Religion* (Bloomington, Ind.: Indiana University Press, 2001).

Keller, H., *The Story of my Life* (New York: Doubleday, 1903).

Kelly, J. N. D., *Early Christian Doctrines* (London: A. & C. Black, 1958).

LaCocque, A., and Ricœur, P., *Thinking Biblically: Exegetical and Hermeneutical Studies* (Chicago: Chicago University Press, 2003).

Laing, R. D., *The Divided Self* (Harmondsworth: Penguin, 1965).

——, *Self and Others* (Harmondsworth: Penguin, 1971).

Lakoff, G., and Johnson, M., *Metaphors We Live By* (Chicago: Chicago University Press, 1980).

——, ——, *Philosophy in the Flesh: The Embodied Mind and its Challenge to Western Thought* (New York: Basic Books, 1999).

Lear, J., *Radical Hope: Ethics in the Face of Cultural Devastation* (Cambridge, Mass.: Harvard University Press, 2008).

Levin, D. M., *The Body's Recollection of Being: Phenomenological Psychology and the Deconstruction of Nihilism* (London: Routledge and Kegan Paul, 1985).

——, *The Opening of Vision: Nihilism and the Postmodern Situation* (London: Routledge, 1988).

Loades, A., and Brown, D. (eds.), *The Sense of the Sacramental* (London: SPCK, 1995).

Lonergan, B. J. F., *Insight* (New York: Philosophical Library, 1970).

——, 'Metaphysics as Horizon', in *A Lonergan Collection*, ed. F. Crowe (Montreal: Palm, 1967).

Long, R., *Walking the Line* (London: Thames and Hudson, 2005).

Maitland, S., *A Book of Silence* (London: Granta, 2008).

Marx, K., *Early Writings*, trans. R. Livingstone and G. Benton (Harmondsworth: Penguin, 1975).

Metz, J.-B., 'The Future Ex Memoria Passionis', in E. H. Cousins (ed.), *Hope and the Future of Man* (Philadelphia: Fortress Press, 1972).

Milbank, J., *Being Reconciled: An Ontology of Pardon* (London: Routledge, 2003).

——, *The Word Made Strange* (Oxford: Blackwell, 1997).

Miles, M. R., *Carnal Knowing: Female Nakedness and Religious Meaning in the Christian West* (London: Burns and Oates, 1992).

Moltmann, J., *The Trinity and the Kingdom of God* (London: SCM Press, 1981).

Muir, E., *Collected Poems* (London: Faber and Faber, 1984).

——, *Essays on Literature and Society* (London: Hogarth Press, 1965).

Nietzsche, F., *Also Sprach Zarathustra*, in *Werke*, ii, ed. K. Schlechta (Frankfurt am Main: Ullstein, 1972).

——, *Aus dem Nachlass der Achtzigerjahre*, in *Werke*, iv, ed. K. Schlechta (Munich: Carl Hanser, 1969).

——, *Die fröhliche Wissenschaft*, in *Werke*, ii, ed. K. Schlechta (Frankfurt am Main: Ullstein, 1969).

——, *Twilight of the Idols*, trans. R. J. Hollingdale (Harmondsworth: Penguin, 1968).

——, *The Will to Power*, trans. W. Kaufmann (New York: Vintage, 1967).

Nishida, K., 'The Logic of *Topos* and the Religious World View: Part I', *Eastern Buddhist*, 18/2 (1986).

Nishitani, K., *Religion and Nothingness*, trans. J. Van Bragt (Berkeley and Los Angeles: University of California Press, 1982).

Nygren, A., trans. P. S. Watson, *Agape and Eros* (London: SPCK, 1953).

O'Meara, T., and Weisser, C. D., *Paul Tillich in Catholic Thought* (London: Darton, Longman and Todd, 1965).

Otto, R., *The Idea of the Holy*, trans. J. W. Harvey (Oxford: Oxford University Press, 1923).

Panofsky, E., *Studies in Iconology* (New York: Harper and Row, 1962).

Pascal, B., *Pensées*, trans. A. J. Krailsheimer (Harmondsworth: Penguin, 1966).

Pattison, G., *A Short Course in the Philosophy of Religion* (London: SCM Press, 2000).

——, *Agnosis: Theology in the Void* (Basingstoke: Macmillan, 1996).

——, *Art, Modernity and Faith* (London: SCM Press, 1998).

——, *Thinking about God in an Age of Technology* (Oxford: Oxford University Press, 2005).

Picard, M., *The World of Silence*, trans. S. Godman (London: Harvill Press, 1948).

Pickstock, C., *After Writing: On the Liturgical Consummation of Philosophy* (Oxford: Basil Blackwell, 1998).

Rahner, K., *Foundations of Christian Faith*, trans. W. V. Dych (London: Darton, Longman and Todd, 1978).

Rosenzweig, F., 'Der Ewige', in *Kleinere Schriften* (Berlin: Schocken/Jüdischer Buchverlag, 1937).

——, *The Star of Redemption*, trans. W. H. Hallo (Notre Dame, Ind.: Notre Dame Press, 1970).

Ryan, C. D. J., *Schopenhauer's Philosophy of Religion* (Leuven: Peeters, 2009).

Saarinen, R., *God and the Gift: An Ecumenical Theology of Giving* (Minnesota: Liturgical Press, 2004).

Sales, François de, *Traité de l'amour de Dieu*, in *Œuvres de St. François de Sales*, vol. iv (Annecy: Niérat, 1894).

Schleiermacher, F. D. E., *On Religion: Speeches to its Cultured Despisers*, trans. R. Crouter (Cambridge: Cambridge University Press, 1988).

Schmemann, A., *The World as Sacrament* (London: Darton, Longman, and Todd, 1966).

Scholem, G., *Major Trends in Jewish Mysticism* (Jerusalem: Schocken, 1941).

Schrift, A. D., *The Logic of the Gift: Toward an Ethic of Generosity* (London: Routledge, 1997).

Sheldrake, P., *Spaces for the Sacred* (London: SCM Press, 2001).

Smith, R. G., *The Doctrine of God* (London: Collins, 1970).

Steiner, G., *Real Presences* (London: Faber, 1989).

Stirner, M., *The Ego and its Own*, ed. D. Leopold (Cambridge: Cambridge University Press, 1995).

Studdert-Kennedy, G., *The Hardest Part* (London: Hodder and Stoughton, 1919).

Surin, K., *Christ, Ethics, and Tragedy: Essays in Honour of Donald Mackinnon* (Cambridge: Cambridge University Press, 1989).

Suzuki, D. T., *Mysticism: Christian and Buddhist* (London: George Allen and Unwin, 1957).

——, *Zen and Japanese Culture* (New York: Bollingen, 1969).

——, *Studies in Zen Buddhism (First Series)* (London: Ryder, 1958).

——, *Studies in Zen Buddhism (Second Series)* (London: Ryder, 1985).

Svendsen, L., *A Philosophy of Boredom*, trans. J. Irons (London: Reaktion, 2005).

Tennyson, Alfred Lord, *A Collection of Poems*, ed. C. Ricks (New York: Doubleday, 1972).

Theunissen, M., *Negative Theologie der Zeit* (Frankfurt am Main: Suhrkamp, 1991).

Tillich, P., *The Boundaries of our Being* (London: Collins, 1973).

——, *The Courage to Be* (London: Fontana, 1962).

——, *A History of Christian Thought* (London: SCM Press, 1968).

——, *Love, Power and Justice* (London: Oxford University Press, 1954).

——, *The New Being* (New York: Scribner, 1955).

——, *The Shaking of the Foundations* (London: SCM Press, 1949).

——, *Systematic Theology*, 3 vols. in one, separately paginated (Welwyn Garden City: Nisbet, 1968).

——, *Theology of Culture* (London: Oxford University Press, 1959).

Turner, D., *Faith, Reason and the Existence of God* (Cambridge: Cambridge University Press, 2004).

Unamuno, M. de, *Tragic Sense of Life*, trans. J. E. C. Flitch (London: Macmillan, 1921).

Urmson, J. O., *The Greek Philosophical Vocabulary* (London: Duckworth, 1990).

Vattimo, G., *After Christianity*, trans. L. D'Isanto (New York: Columbia University Press, 2002).

——, *Belief*, trans. L. D'Isanto and D. Webb (Cambridge: Polity Press, 1998).

——, with Caputo, J. D., *After the Death of God* (New York: Columbia University Press, 2007).

——, and Rovatti, P. A. (eds.), *Il pensiero debole* (Milan: Feltrinelli, 1983).

Viller, M. (ed.), *Dictionnaire de spiritualité*, vol. ix (Paris: Beauchesne, 1976).

Weil, S., *Gravity and Grace*, trans. E. Craufurd (London: Routledge and Kegan Paul, 1963).

Westphal, M., *Overcoming Onto-theology: Toward a Postmodern Christian Faith* (New York: Fordham University Press, 2001).

Whitehead, A. N., *Process and Reality* (New York: Harper and Row, 1960).

Wilkins, J., *An Essay towards a real Character and a Philosophical Language* (London: The Royal Society, 1668).

Wittgenstein, L., *Philosophical Investigations*, trans. G. E. M. Anscombe (Oxford: Basil Blackwell, 1972).

Wordsworth, W., *Poems* (London: Dent, 1955).

Yannaras, C., *On the Absence and Unknowability of God: Heidegger and the Areopagite* (London: T. & T. Clark, 2005).

Zabala, S. (ed.), *Weakening Philosophy: Essays in Honour of Gianni Vattimo* (Montreal: McGill-Queen's University Press, 2007).

Zizioulas, J., *Being as Communion* (London: Darton, Longman and Todd, 1985).

Index

Abe, M. 302n71
Abraham 18, 19, 178, 218n57, 222, 263, 288
absolute 303
abyss 29, 271, 305n80, 307
accidents 21, 42, 43
act, actuality 42, 44–5, 47, 48, 71, 279–84, 294–5, 306, 308
acknowledgement *see* recognition
Adam 178, 190–1, 296
agape 226–8, 232–3, 275
alētheia see Truth as unconcealment
Alfeyev, H. 267n105
amity *see* friendship
amor 35n56, 227, 228
analogy 53–5, 107, 158n23, 186
Angelus Silesius 187
anguish *see* anxiety
Anna the prophetess 119
Anselm of Canterbury 2, 24–5, 30
anticipation 77, 122, 123, 126–7, 254, 263, 264, 278
anxiety 23, 93, 97, 100, 116–17, 147, 217, 262, 263, 286n21, 296–7, 306
apophantic discourse 166–8
Apophaticism/ apophatic theology 50–5, 99, 185, 311, 318, 320
Aquinas, Thomas, *see* Thomas
Arendt, H. 3, 310n94
Aristotle, Aristotelianism 6, 10, 10n19, 20, 33n50, 36–50, 71, 80, 84, 149, 157, 164, 167–72, 180, 244, 270, 279–82, 283n11, 294–5, 306n84
Arnold, M. 65n27
art 243
associationism 160
Athanasius 267n103
atheism 29, 209, 220, 309–10
Aufhebung 161, 162–3
Augustine, Augustinianism 10, 19, 21–36 *passim*, 44, 50–86n96, 99, 103, 106n4, 108, 109–13, 117, 119, 139, 146–7, 148, 149, 154n16, 156, 202, 223, 244, 245, 255 n67, 256n69, 259–61, 267–8, 271–2, 275, 306, 20
authenticity 94, 122, 124, 175
autonomy 75, 265

Averroes 40, 42, 43
Avicenna 40, 43, 47, 282n10

Bach, J. S. 269
Bacon, F. 322, 323
Bachelard, G. 147–8, 260n85, 265
Baillie, J. 56n3
Bakhtin, M. M. 157, 192–9, 200, 213, 234, 234n94
Balthasar, H. U. von 61n19
Barth, K. 12, 14, 48n84/n85, 51, 107n7, 179, 179n87, 241n14, 260n84
Bashō 66–7
Baudelaire, C. 313
beatific vision *see* vision of God
Beauvoir, S. de 211
becoming 113–6, 120, 124, 139, 193, 244, 295n44
Being / being
Being is at issue throughout the book: the
    following offer only a selection of key
    aspects discussed. See also under God.
as-a-whole 101, 122, 192, 193, 278, 297–300
beyond Being 51, 185, 314
essential being 29
eternal Being 20, 29, 225
exigency of 240
existential being 29
existential use of 275
fidelity to 156
for-itself 77, 83–4, 96, 97, 102, 104, 114, 156, 158, 204, 205, 207, 249, 275, 277
forgetfulness of 129
ground of 29, 30
immutable 225
in-itself 77, 96, 97, 102, 158, 207, 249
in-and-for-itself 223
-in-the-world 86, 87, 148, 224, 261, 303
-Itself 39 *see also* God as Being-Itself
Kingdom of 238
necessary Being 20, 24, 281–2, 294
New Being, the 31–2
predicative ascription of 275
simplicity of 47, 305
'reverberating' Being 148, 176, 265

Being is at issue throughout the book: the
  following offer only a selection of key
  aspects discussed. (cont.)
  towards death 100, 174, 278, 303n74
  unchanging Being 29
  under erasure 16, 177, 182, 183
  weakening of 102, 108, 216, 318
  withdrawal of 182
Berdyaev, N. 107n7, 201n3, 234–7, 238,
  239–40
Bergson, H. 83
Bernard of Clairvaux 270
Bespaloff, R. 289n27
Bhagavad Gīta 105, 239n5
Bible *see also* Vulgate, King James Bible, New
  Testament 18–21, 22n18, 33, 40, 108n11,
  140, 178–9, 215, 224, 288, 290
Bloch, E. 127, 219n60, 282n10
body *see also* embodiment 26, 60, 70, 80, 105,
  172, 191, 191n122, 239–40
Boehme, J. 107n7, 236–7, 305n80
Bonaventure 26n26
book, the 180–1, 184
Book of Common Prayer 246n29
boredom 297–301, 308
Bragt, J. van 306n84
Brémond, H. 229n86
Brentano, F. 280n6
Brock, W. 90
Bronzino, A. 109n12
Brown, D. 142n91, 257–8n74, 258n81
Brown, P. 56n2
Brueggemann, W. 141n86
Brunn, E. zum 22n17
Brunner, E. 179n87
Buber, M. 14, 19–20, 187n114, 207n15,
  213–15, 217, 220, 223, 225, 229, 240,
  247n31, 260n84
Buchner, H. 303n74
Buddhism 65–7, 302–9, 316–17, 320
Bultmann, R. 14n26, 103n1
Burns, R. M. 104n1
Bychkov, O. 61n19

Cajetan, T. 48
call 129–30, 132, 186, 255, 300–1
Calvin, J. 19, 260n84
Camus, A. 287n22
Candler, P. M. 301n68
Cappelørn, N.-J. 76n65, 261n89
Caputo, J. D. 6n.8, 102n138, 132n75, 141n86,
  188n118, 268, 283n12, 307n88, 309n92
Caravaggio, M. M. da 252

care (*Sorge*) 100–1, 123, 261, 268n110,
  270n116
caritas see also agape *and* charity 35n56, 227
Carlisle, C. 295n44
categorial intuition 63, 67–73, 312
categories 42, 63n22, 70, 83, 85
Cézanne, P. 61, 74, 142, 251–2, 253n63, 255,
  258n77, 313
Chalcedon, Council of 47
change *see also* motion 21–7, 29, 289
Chantal, J. de 229, 230, 231
charity 270, 317
Chestov, L. *see* Shestov, L.
Childs, B. S. 19n8
choice 76, 113, 116–17, 121, 122, 229,
  277–8, 288
Christ, Christology 14, 62, 134, 224, 231, 233,
  267, 268–9, 288–9, 310
Church, the 232
Cioran, E. M. 267n104
Cloud of Unknowing, The 52
Coleridge, S. T. 59n9, 78
commandment 220–1
communion 234, 234n94
concern 119
conflict 203–6
conscience 174
consciousness 70, 75, 79, 96–7, 100, 101,
  114, 202–6, 207, 218, 249–50, 277, 303,
  304, 317
contemplation *see* vision of God
contingency 43, 97
Coreth, E. 38n61
courage (to be) 28, 32, 117, 272
creation (*see also* God as creator) 23, 32–6,
  40, 43, 75–6, 109–13, 136, 310
  out of nothing 23, 43
creativity 235
Cross, R. 63n20
Crowe, F. 38n61
Cunningham, C. 301n68
Cupitt, D. 89n98, 99, 107n10, 158n23,
  244n26, 308n91
Curtius, E. R. 181

Dalferth, I. 56n3, 283–4, 306
dance, dancing 6, 129–30, 134, 137, 258
Dante Alighieri 35, 224–5
Darwin, C./ Darwinianism 28, 243n21,
  280n8
Dauphinais, M. 21n14
David, B. 21n14
Davies, O. 15n27, 258n80

Da Vinci, L. 64
Davis, J. 143
death 22, 24, 24n22, 30–1, 92–3, 100, 103,
    115, 122–9, 133–5, 139, 174, 200, 205,
    217–18, 265, 275, 295–6, 300n66, 301
    n69, 303
deconstruction 3, 12, 52n104, 102n140, 184
Dennett, D. 245
depth 65, 252
Derrida, J. 1, 3, 8, 10, 12, 52n104, 96n116,
    102n139, 141n86, 149n3, 150, 157, 158,
    163, 177, 178, 180–8, 215, 221–2, 221
    n63, 222n70, 233–5, 238, 259, 263–4,
    268, 284n14, 292n39, 306–9, 309n92,
    310–11, 311n96, 311n97, 312–14, 317
    n114
Descartes, R. 2, 83, 84, 181, 202, 219, 251
desire 98, 195, 203–4, 218, 242, 264, 273–4
despair 78–9, 94, 134, 279, 285–6
destiny 30
Deuser, H. 76n65, 261n89
dialogue 194, 317
différance 183
Diogenes 262
disenchantment of the world 56–7, 220
distance (between being and
    consciousness) 11, 55, 56–102, 156, 216,
    223, 230–2, 238, 254, 258, 270–1, 277,
    282, 315, 317, 320
distention 111, 112
Doré, G. 64
Dostoevsky, F. M. 12, 13, 61n18, 74, 96,
    126n61, 155–6n20, 157, 193, 194–9,
    201n3, 211n29, 212, 221, 225n73, 231,
    242, 259, 265–7, 269–70, 279, 288,
    305n81
double-voiced discourse 194, 195
doxology 319
Dreyfus, H. 153n14
Dryden, J. 275
dualism 28, 192, 242
Duns Scotus 40, 43, 47, 62–3, 63n22, 68n41,
    81n77
dynamics 30

eating 66, 240, 258
Eaton, J. H. 76
Ebeling, G. 18, 151n6
Edwards, P. 12n21
Eckhart, Meister 67, 185, 187n115
Einstein, A. 28, 143, 306n84
El-Bizri, N. 11n20
Eleatic philosophy 262

Eliade, M. 129n68, 141–2
Eliezer, Rabbi 181
Eliot, T. S. 108, 132, 133–6, 139, 142, 150,
    151, 155, 157, 182
Elkins, J. 57n4, 142n91
embodiment 15, 16n29, 26, 137, 200, 238–76,
    317, 322
empirical knowing/ empiricism 115, 248
emptiness 79n72, 255, 299, 304–5
Engels, F. 241
enlightenment (Buddhist) see also *satori* 66
ens 42
Epictetus 287–8
epiphany 108n11, 122, 132, 135, 275
Ereignis 175–7, 182, 309
Eriksen, N. N. 118n32
eros see also *amor and* desire *and* longing 26,
    226–8, 233, 264, 275
eschatology 25–7, 112–13, 183, 189, 198, 210,
    231, 234–5, 239n5, 283–4
esse 38n64, 48
essence 21, 29, 34n54, 38–49 *passim*, 52, 60,
    63, 72, 73, 80–6 *passim*, 90–9 *passim*, 113,
    114, 115, 123, 129, 130, 166, 184, 214
    n45, 224, 247, 296, 307, 319
    as *das Gewesene* 130–1
essentia 38n64, 80, 84–5, 89, 101
estrangement 30, 34n54
Eternal, the 19–20, 22, 92, 110, 116, 118–22,
    124, 139, 213, 227, 283n11
eternal life 26, 91, 234–5
eternal recurrence 136
Eternity *see also* the Eternal *and* eternal
    life 23, 25–6, 43, 110, 117, 120, 128, 201,
    253, 255
ethics 225
Eucharist 56, 308, 310
Eugene Onegin 290
Eve 296
event (of appropriation, of language, or of
    understanding) see *Ereignis*
evil 34–5, 116, 217, 237, 266, 290,
    310n94
existence 2, 29–30, 34n54, 41–50, 73, 81,
    82, 85–6, 89–102, 123, 193, 238,
    277–8, 296
existentia 81, 84–5, 89–90
existential use of 'to be' 46
existentialia 85
Existenz 85, 90, 99
Exodus, Book of 18–20, 77n68, 215
experience 56–61, 73, 77, 80, 123n44, 162–3,
    191n122, 207, 248, 253, 275, 318

face, the 219, 240, 247, 311n97
faith 6, 12, 75, 94, 95, 99, 117, 134, 139, 286,
   288, 290
Fall, the/ fallenness 24, 30, 34, 137–8, 139,
   142, 190–1, 278, 289, 289n28, 296
falsehood 42, 169, 172
fantasy 160–1, 163
Faye, E. 131n74
fear and pity 270
Fedorov, N. 201n3
feeling 59
feminism 156n23, 211, 257
Fénélon, F. 229
Ferreira, J. 218
festival 23–4, 25, 129, 174
Feuerbach, L. 130, 201n3, 213n38, 241, 245,
   258n75, 273n122
Feyerabend, P. 12
Fichte, J. G. 229
finitude, the finite 28, 30, 217, 283n11, 285,
   296
first cause 2, 5
Florensky, P. 232–3
Floucat, Y. 8, 19n7
Fodor, J. 61n19
Fondane, B. 93n110
forgiveness 270, 289–94, 310n94, 311, 323
form 30, 39n64, 41, 42, 44, 45, 47, 294
freedom 30, 43, 96–7, 126, 142, 204, 207, 210,
   211, 229, 235–7, 238, 272, 287, 290–1,
   293, 296, 299–300, 316–17, 320, 323
Freud, S. 243, 245, 249n42, 273n122
friendship 220, 232–4, 238, 273–4, 279,
   317, 318
future, the 116, 118, 120, 123, 131, 135,
   233–4, 249, 278–9, 281, 323–4

Gablik, S. 57n4
Gadamer, H.-G. 259, 259n83
Galileo, G. 181
Gardner, W. H. 62, 62 3n20
Gasquet, G. 63–5
gaze 207–9, 313–14
Gelassenheit 187
Genesis, Book of 33–4, 36, 109–13
Gift 97, 186, 255, 272, 292, 307, 308–19, 323
Gilson, É. 8, 11, 12, 19n7, 22n18, 33n50, 38
   n62, 40–50, 50n93, 52–3, 81, 84, 99
Girard, R. 210n29
God
God is at issue throughout the book: the
   following offer only a selection of key
   aspects discussed. See also under Being

as Being-Itself see also as *ipsum esse* 17–22,
   25, 27–9, 36, 37, 108, 318
as *causa sui* 2, 6, 98
as creator 23, 32–6, 43–4, 48, 52, 110, 220,
   302, 308
as *essentia* 19, 21
as eternal/ eternity of 19–20, 108, 294
as *ipsum esse* 21, 22, 45
as knowing 111
as Lord 19–20
as necessary Being 24–5, 281–2
as *ousia* 19–20
as saving 18–19, 21–7
as substance 19, 21, 25
beyond/ without Being 51–3, 107, 185
death of 9n17, 244
essence and existence in 47–8
exigency of 240
existence of 1–2, 15, 28–9, 295
freedom of 236n103
goodness of 34, 35, 52, 319
immutability of 21–7, 105, 110, 260, 288–9
knowledge of 36–7, 41, 45, 53, 54, 98, 184
mind of 43, 44
name of 18–20, 21, 47, 52, 187, 187n114,
   215, 306, 308, 318–20
omnipresence 25
presence of 24
selfsameness of 22, 25, 26, 103, 105
temporality of 107
timelessness of 105
will of 43
Word of 178–9
good, the / goodness 116, 117, 138, 185,
   237, 266
Graham, G. 57
Gregory of Nazianzus 267
Grenz, S. J. 8–9
Grimsley, R. 154
ground 5 , 129, 146, 306
Gunton, C. 107n7

Habermas, J. 78, 201, 318
Hadot, P. 36n58
haecceitas 62–3
Hall, A. L. 226
Hamburger, M. 319n116
Handel, G. 109n12
Hanley, C. 283n11
Hardy, T. 104
Hartshorne, C. 107n7
Hausherr, I. 267n105
hearing 171, 176

Hegel, G. W. F. 1, 4, 8, 12, 13, 47, 81n77, 83, 90–1, 102n139, 103, 113–15, 118, 120, 139, 157, 158–64, 180, 182, 183, 190, 201–6, 207, 210, 213, 216, 217, 221, 223, 224, 229, 236n102, 287, 288, 295

Heidegger, M. 1–16 *passim*, 36, 46n82, 48n86, 57, 63, 63n22, 67–73, 79, 80–90, 93–5, 96, 97n123, 99, 103, 104, 120, 121n42, 122–33, 135, 139, 140, 141n86, 143–8, 149, 151–2, 154, 155, 157, 163, 164–78, 179n87, 180, 181, 183, 188, 217, 218, 219n60, 220, 235, 236n102, 237, 246, 247, 247n32, 248, 250, 261, 265, 268, 270n116, 277–8, 280n7, 283, 289n28, 295–301, 303n74, 308, 309, 312, 314, 323, 324

Heisenberg, W. 143

Henry of Ghent 63n22

Heraclitus 116, 166, 201, 243n21

hermeneutics 12–13, 124n53, 158n23

Hillesum, E. 258n80

Hilton, W. 245n27

history 103–4, 129, 142, 193, 195, 201–6

Hobbes, T. 202

Hofmannsthal, H. von 151n6

Hölderlin, F. 69, 97n123, 128, 129–33, 143–5, 150, 177, 219n60, 301n69, 318–19, 320

Holm, I. W. 261n89

holy, the 129, 264, 301n69, 309

Hook, S. 7

hope 15, 20n12, 35, 127–8, 131, 134, 138, 139, 198, 221, 255, 279, 281, 284, 286

Hopkins, G. M. 61–3, 65, 74, 142, 253

Horner, R. 309n92

hospitality 187–8

Howells, C. 96n116

humour 91n101

Hume, D. 181

Husserl, E. 12–13, 68n41, 72, 82n80, 97n123, 109n13, 116n23, 172, 219, 247, 287, 289n28, 312

Hyman, G. 14n26

hymn 187, 319

I–Thou relation 187n114, 213–17, 220, 225, 240

Idea 5, 42, 71

idealism 83, 241, 245, 248

identity, principle of 175

ideology 156

idle talk 93, 151–2, 155, 158n23, 164, 167, 172, 189, 278

Ignatius of Loyola 267

image 160, 260n85

imagination 78, 160

immortality 24, 31, 106n4, 110, 201n3, 244

impossibility, the impossible 290–4

inauthenticity 167

incarnation 43, 131, 136, 137–8, 139, 294

individual, the/ individuality 30, 48, 92, 119, 122, 123n44, 159, 219–20

infinite, infinity 60, 92, 219, 285

'infinite qualitative difference' 51, 54, 221n66

inscape 63, 65, 74

instress 63, 253

intellect, intellectual 41n71, 48, 59n9

intelligence 151, 162

intelligibility 41n71, 49, 54n110

intention, intentionality 55, 69–73, 81, 84, 86, 112, 113, 190, 191, 195, 230–1, 246, 249–51, 254

intuition *see also* categorial intuition 37, 41 n71, 45, 53, 55, 59, 70, 72, 111, 159–60, 172, 216, 239, 244, 246, 313, 321

Irigaray, L. 211n32

Isaac 18, 19, 218n57, 222, 288

Isaac of Nineveh (Syria) 264, 267, 268, 269

Isaiah (prophet) 77n68

Islam 11, 33n50, 40, 43n76, 187

isness 65–6

Jacob 18, 19

James, W. 57

Janicaud, D. 13, 314n107

Jankélévitch, V. 12, 151, 228–30, 234n92, 236, 256, 291–4, 311, 321, 323

Jaspers, K. 181, 306n84

Jensen, A. S. 69n43

Jeremiah (prophet) 77n68

Jesus (Christ) *see also* Christ 14, 36, 75, 179, 270, 285, 294

Job 77n68, 288, 289

John the Baptist 267

John, Gospel of 179, 197

Johnson, M. 191n122, 254n64, 256–7, 259

Johnson, S. 80

Jones, J. 155–6n20

jouissance 212

'journeying' 145

joy 24, 25, 55, 58, 59, 60, 75, 78, 105, 224, 242, 319–20

Judaism 11, 19–20, 40, 131–2, 141, 187, 220 n62

judgement 169, 248

Julian of Norwich 246n29

Jung, C. G. 243, 247n32

Jüngel, E. 107n7
justice 139, 141, 141n86, 220–2, 223, 228,
    233, 292

Kafka, F. 210
Kant, I. 37n61, 65, 72, 83, 90, 193, 201n3,
    229, 310n94
Kantor, V. 197n139
Kearney, R. 20n12, 284n14
Keller, H. 152n9
Kelly, J. N. D. 319n117
Kenny, A. 37n60, 46n81, 66
Kerr, F. 40n69, 48, 61n19
khôra 186, 188, 255, 302–9, 312, 315
Kierkegaard, S. 1, 8, 12, 13, 47, 51, 74–9, 83,
    90–9, 97n123, 99, 102n139, 104, 105,
    108, 113–22, 123, 124, 125, 128, 132, 135,
    139, 152–5, 157, 164, 189–92, 201n3,
    206, 213, 218, 218n57, 221–7, 259–60,
    261–4, 268, 268n110, 274, 285–91,
    293–4, 295n44, 296, 311–12
King, G. H. 261n89
King James Bible 18
Kingdom of God/ Heaven 232
Kirk, G. S. 175
Kisiel, T. 69n43
Klee, P. 251, 252
kneeling 258
knowing/ knowledge *see also* God, knowledge
    of 41–50, 53–5, 67–73, 83–6, 87, 113–15,
    122, 125, 159, 170, 171–2, 219, 231, 247,
    284, 317, 320
Kojève, A. 206
Kretzmann, N. 39n64
Krishek, S. 227n78

Laclos, C. de 154
Laing, R. D. 212n33, 265
Lakoff, G. 122, 254n64, 256–7, 259
Landkildehus, S. 268n110
Language 9, 78n72, 148–99, 200, 214, 218,
    231–2, 241, 244, 259–62, 265, 278–9, 317
    'as'-structure of 163, 169, 172, 173
    concealing Being 174–9
    crisis in 151–4
leap 71, 176, 263
Lear, J. 287n22
Leftow, B. 106n4
Levering, M. 21n14
Lévi-Strauss, C. 182
Levin, D. 247n32, 270n116
Lévinas, E. 10, 12, 13, 108, 127–8, 187n114,
    214n44, 215, 217–22, 223, 225, 225n73,

228, 229, 239, 247, 247n30, 247n31,
    311n97
life 89n98, 107
Lindbeck, G. 158n23
Lipps, H. 172n72
Loades, A. 258n81
'locality' 143–4
logic 90–1, 114, 162, 172
logocentrism 158, 163, 182
logos 5, 164–74, 180, 182, 307
Lonergan, B. 11, 37–8n61, 49n91, 54n110,
    223
Long, R. 258n78
longing 21, 23, 28, 105, 111, 271–3, 319, 320
loss 77, 138, 149
love 15, 32n47, 35, 78n71, 100, 134, 139, 190,
    194, 195–9, 200, 212, 214, 220, 223–37,
    238, 267, 273, 275, 277, 279, 280, 281,
    284–5, 288–9, 315, 315n112, 319–20
Lubac, H. de 21n15, 25n25, 27n30, 53n109
Luke, Gospel of 227, 285n16
Luther, M. 6, 17n1, 99, 260n84, 274n124
lying 195–6

McLean, G. F. 50n94
McNeill, W. 143
Macquarrie, J. 27n30
McShane, P. 38n61
Maitland, S. 258n79
Malachi, Book of 22n18
Malpas, J. 144
Marcel, G. 101, 212–13, 217, 223, 239, 240,
    253n63, 255–6
Marenbon, J. 7, 9
Marion, J.-L. 12, 13, 82n80, 102n139, 253,
    253n63, 300–1, 309n92, 312–15
Maritain, J. 11, 37n61, 38n62, 41n69, 44, 45,
    49, 49n93, 53n108, 53–4
Marius Victorinus 53
Mark, Gospel of 285
Marx, K. 102n139, 188, 206, 218, 232, 241,
    242n18, 245, 273n122
Mary (mother of Jesus) 137, 285n16
Mascall, E. 41n69, n71
Master-slave dialectic 202–6, 210, 211, 224
materialism 241–2, 245
Mattéi, J.-F. 132n74
Matthew, Gospel of 225–6, 271
matter 44
Mauss, M. 309, 311, 314
memory 51, 77–8, 104, 111, 131, 138, 161–2,
    234–5, 254, 293–4, 323
Mendelssohn, M. 19

Merleau-Ponty, M. 12, 13, 65n27, 149n2, 246–56, 257n72, 258, 258n77, 261, 274–5
Messiah, messianism 188, 221, 229, 233, 319
metaphor 191, 191n121, 214, 254n64, 255, 257, 260n85, 262
metaphysics 3–11, 16, 19, 37–9, 85–6, 99, 124, 164, 180, 182–4, 236–7, 250–3, 257, 280n8, 300, 302
Metz, J.-B. 323n124
Mikkelsen, H. V. 179
Milbank, J. 8, 310n94
Miles, M. R. 257
Mill, J. S. 172
mind 256–7
Mizoguchi, K. 303n74
Moffatt, J. 19n9
Molière 154
Møller Jensen, H. 261n89
Moltmann, J. 107n7
moment, the *see also* the moment of vision 117–18
moment of vision, the 93, 95, 108, 118–20, 121n42, 124, 135, 300
Morgan, D. 57, 142n91
mortality *see also* death 30–1
Moses 18–20, 36, 52, 77n68, 178
motility 249, 250, 254, 257n72, 275–6
motion 114, 116n24, 262, 282, 295
movement *see* motion
Mounier, E. 239–40
Muir, E. 108, 132, 132n77, 133, 136–8, 142–3, 178, 179, 200, 231
Mulhall, S. 131n73
mutability 22, 25, 109–10, 260, 275, 295
mystery 101, 108n11, 120, 214, 251, 255–6, 264
mysticism 8n14, 26n29, 54, 59, 308–9
myth, mythology 60n16, 141–2, 187n114, 236, 307

nature (in epistemological sense) 38, 39, 42, 44, 47, 49, 171
Nature 58–9, 63–4, 181
Nazism 131–2n74, 132, 144n97, 219n60, 292–3
necessity 285–8
negative theology 50–5, 184–5, 284n14, 307–8, 215, 317n114
Neo-Platonism 51, 52–3
New Testament 26, 178, 215n48, 239, 281, 292n37
Newman, J. H. 260
Nietzsche, F. 3, 9n17, 10, 105, 121, 122, 124, 136, 183, 233, 242–4, 245, 273n122, 288, 302

nihilism 105, 184, 242n18, 276, 302, 310n94, 320
nihility, field of 302–9, 312, 315, 316
Nishida, K. 302–4
Nishitani, K. 303n74, 304–6
non-being 29–32, 52n102, 103, 217, 277, 294–309, 310n94
non-violence 221
nothing, nothingness 22, 30, 34, 79, 96–7, 100, 114, 126, 131, 139, 205, 217, 291, 294–309
'Now', the 105, 120–1, 135
Nygren, A. 226

objectivity 5
O'Meara, T. 50n94
One, the 253
ontological argument 24
ontology 115n27, 36, 46, 72, 81, 107, 147–8, 164, 199, 219, 223, 230, 235–6, 253, 272, 320
Onto-theology 3–11, 102
Ortschaft see 'locality'
Orwell, G. 155
Other/ otherness 186, 200–37, 275
   God as other 273
   Human others 193–9, 202–6, 238, 240, 244, 270, 273–4, 317
Otto, R. 108n11, 221n66, 264
ousia 39–40, 170–1, 173, 319
Owens, J. 38n63

paganism 132, 140
painting 63–5, 251–3, 256, 258
Panofsky, E. 109n12
Pareyson, L. 237
Parkes, G. 303n74
Parmenides 104n1, 166, 168, 176
participation 22, 26, 30, 39n64, 98, 193, 234 n94, 253
Pascal, B. 18, 154, 155, 288
passion 115, 116242, 257, 273
Pattison, G. 86n94, 90n100, 119n34, 131n73, 154n15, 189n119, 197n139, 198n142, 227n79, 258n77, 261n87, 261n90, 286 n18, 301n69, 302n71, 310n94, 312n99, 321n121
Paul the apostle 25, 51, 59, 77n68, 112, 119, 124n52, 228, 263
Paulo, C. de 86n94
peace 138, 202
Peirce, C. S. 183n98
Pemberton, C. 64n23

perception 59, 69–72, 165, 169–70, 207, 248–53, 256
Perkins, R. L. 76, 92n106, 127n62
person, personality 49, 238–40
personalism
phenomenology 12, 13, 68, 72–3, 81, 93n110, 147–8, 164–6, 212, 212n33, 219, 245–9, 261–2, 264, 270n116, 289n28, 312–16
Phillips, D. Z. 158n23
Philo of Alexandria 20
philosophy 3, 11–13, 35–6, 50, 54, 71, 83, 84, 95, 115, 122–3, 123n44, 168–9, 173, 176, 248, 283, 287, 307, 310, 314n107
of religion 3, 157–8n23
physis 5
Picard, M. 240, 258n79
Pickstock, C. 319n117
place 142–6, 303–9
Plato 11, 105, 154, 155, 164, 172, 185, 186, 239n5, 244, 287, 306–7
Platonism *see also* Neo-Platonism 42, 236n103
Plotinus 11, 47, 53, 219n60, 236n103, 288
poetry, the poet 58–61, 66–7, 129–40, 150, 155–6, 157, 174, 177, 231, 235, 278, 301 n69
politics 171, 233
Pope, A. 153
possibility (see also potentiality)/
the possible 42, 91–2, 94, 120, 130, 134, 231, 249, 277–324 *passim*
possible existence 48
postmodernity 3
potentiality 42, 44, 45, 122, 279, 280–2, 294
prayer 6, 15, 17, 24, 186–7, 319–20
predicative use of 'to be' 46
presence *see also* Romantic presence *and* self-presence 20, 55, 56–102, 107, 120–1, 122, 135, 154, 156, 173, 174, 184, 188, 201, 207, 214–16, 216, 223–4, 239, 254–5, 265, 275, 308, 312–13, 321, 324
presence-at [*or* to]-hand 86, 87, 171, 172
Pre-Socratics 6, 11, 168, 183
process 114
prophecy 132, 140
Prouvost, G. 41n69, 45n80
Psalms, Book of 23–4, 25, 255n67
Pseudo-Dionysius 51–2, 52n104, 185–7
psychology 159, 172, 249
Pyper, H. 293n41

Quakers 264
quiddity 42, 49

Radical Orthodoxy 38n62, 48n86, 158n23
Rahner, K. 11, 179n87
Raven, S. 175
Rayment-Pickard, H. 104n1
ready/ readiness-to-hand 87
re-enchantment of the world 57, 142n91
recognition 202–12, 224, 227, 230
recollection 161, 201
redemption 136, 139, 200
Reese, W. L. 107n7
relative, the/ relativism 104, 105, 106, 303, 306
relics 56
repetition 93, 108, 116, 121, 123n47, 124, 135, 262, 263
representation (*Vorstellung*) 159–60
resolution, resoluteness 93, 123, 124, 127, 278, 296
responsibility 96, 138, 193, 214, 240, 286, 315, 316n113
restlessness 28, 260, 271
resurrection 244–5
rhetoric 171–2
Ricoeur, P. 109n13, 112n17, 157n22
Rochefoucauld, La 154
Romantic presence 58–67, 77, 142, 238
Rosenzweig, F. 19–20, 141n86, 187n114, 215
Ross, W. D. 168n56
Rousseau, J.-J. 181–2
Rovatti, A. 102n138
Rudd, A. 71n53
Ruskin, J. 181n91
Ryan, C. D. J. 302n70

Saarinen, R. 309n92
Sacred, the 141–2
Sales, F. de 35n56, 228, 229, 260n84, 268
salvation 17–55, 105–6, 215, 289–91
Sartre, J.-P. 1, 11, 12, 13, 79, 82, 90, 95–102, 104, 106n5, 127, 140, 147, 148, 158, 207–12, 213, 216, 216n49, 217, 221, 223, 227, 273, 277–8, 279, 281, 296, 304, 305, 315, 316, 320
satori 66
Saussure, F. 182
Scanlon, M. J. 309n92
Schelling, F. W. J. 30n41, 61n18, 107n7, 236, 305n80
Schleiermacher, F. D. E. 59–61, 69, 74, 77, 78, 223, 224, 257n73
Schmemann, A. 258n75
Schmitt, C. 233

scholasticism 67, 67n41, 81, 85–6, 122, 124, 283n11
Scholem, G. 178
Schopenhauer, A. 35n56
Schrift, A. D. 309
Schrijvers, J. 301n68
science 26, 32–3nn49–50, 71, 183, 195, 206, 243, 245, 283, 316–17, 320, 321–4
secret, secrecy 186, 221, 266–7, 271, 310–11
seeing 258
self 11, 24, 32, 74–7, 93–100, 119, 121, 199, 217, 223, 231, 238, 245, 249, 261, 265, 266, 270n116, 287, 302, 314, 315
self-presence 73–9, 96, 97, 315
self-relation 76–82, 108, 277–8, 299
self-transcendence 240, 304
semblance 164, 172
Sermon on the Mount, the 75, 222n70, 225–6, 311n96, 311n97
sex, sexuality 240, 247, 249n42, 258
Shakers 264
Shakespeare, S. 309n92
Shakespeare, W. 32, 154n16, 231
Sheehan, T. 69n43
Sheldrake, P. 61n19, 142n91
Shestov, L. 93n110, 287–91
Shiff, R. 64
Siger of Brabant 40, 43n76, 49
sign 50n94, 55, 160–1, 163, 180–2, 190
silence 74, 75, 99n130, 110, 153, 174, 177, 182, 231, 258, 274, 278, 318, 319
Simmons, J. A. 218n57
sin 116, 117, 239, 289n28
simplicity of divine Being 45, 47
Smith, R. G. 19n8, 213n38
sobornost' 234–6, 238
Socrates 154, 172, 287
solitude 258, 319
Soloviev, V. 236
Song of Songs, the 264
sophists 155, 173
soul 239n5
space 29, 108, 140–8, 200, 250, 251–5, 275, 302, 317
speech, speaking 170–1, 180, 180–2, 189–99, 320
Spengler, O. 298
Spinoza, B. 287
Spirit (human being as) 76, 190–1, 239, 296–7, 320
Stein, E. 67n41, 81n75, 124n50, 282n9
Steiner, G. 56, 154
Stewart, J. 261n89
Stirner, M. 241

Stoicism 205, 287
Strauss, D. F. 201n3
Studdert-Kennedy, G. 202n4
Stump., E 39n64
Suarez, F. 11, 40, 43n76, 47, 48
subjunctive, the 284, 321
subject/ subjective, the/ subjectivity 5, 11, 67, 74, 79, 82, 83, 99, 101, 119, 124, 159–64, 192, 207, 213, 230, 235–6, 239, 248, 249, 277–8, 304, 315
substance, substantiality 5, 21, 23, 29, 33, 38–49 *passim*, 52, 83, 85, 123, 146, 165, 173, 281, 294, 319
suffering 22, 24, 29, 127, 278
Surin, K. 106n6
Suzuki, D. T. 61, 65–7, 74, 76n63, 77, 100, 305, 308
Svendsen, L. 301n68
symbol / symbolism 50n94, 144, 255

Takeichi, A. 303n74
Talleyrand, C.-M. de 155
tautology 46–7, 217, 282n9
tears 261, 267–71, 272
technology 3–4, 87, 101, 145–6, 151, 153n14, 155, 175, 176, 206, 321–4
Tennyson, A. (Lord) 66–7
Thales 83
thankfulness 309, 315, 318–19
theogony 239
theology 6–16 *passim*, 17, 54, 256, 274n124, 283, 308, 310, 314, 314n107, 323
Theunissen, M. 76n65, 92n106, 93n108, 104n1, 107n9, 126–7, 128n66, 278n4, 285n15
thinking 3–6, 75, 161, 163
thisness 62–3, 65, 71, 308
Thomas (Aquinas)/ Thomism 7, 10–1, 19, 21, 25–30 *passim*, 35–54 *passim*, 80, 81n75, 81n77, 84, 101, 158n3, 184, 186, 239n5, 255, 279–2, 294, 295
Thompson, D. 197n140
thrownness 147, 217
Tillich, P. 2, 27–32, 34n54, 35, 50n94, 108, 120–2, 128, 132, 139, 223, 232n89, 285 n17, 305n80
time 23, 26, 29, 44, 103–48, 156–7, 173, 174, 200, 201, 231, 244, 250, 253, 275, 289, 298–9, 302, 317
Todorov, T. 156n21
Tolstoy, L. 61n18, 122n43, 125–6
topos 303–9
Toumayan, A. 221n64
trace 182–4

tradition 234
tragedy 105, 216n49, 270
transhumanism 322–4
transience 104, 205
trembling 259, 262, 263–7, 270, 272, 318, 319
Trendelenburg, A. 90, 114n20
Trinity, doctrine of 14, 187, 319
Truth 23, 42, 53, 114, 115, 146, 169, 172, 173,
    175, 177, 196–8, 231, 279, 284
  as adequation of *res* and *intellectus*
    (correspondence theory of) 69, 81, 109,
    163, 165, 167, 175, 180, 188, 265
  as *alētheia see* truth as unconcealment
  as judgement 167
  as unconcealment 109, 123, 165–7

Unamuno, M. de 106n5, 216n49
understanding 168
unfinalizability 194, 198, 256, 265
Ungrund 236–7, 305
unity 71
Urmson, J. O. 38
utopia, utopianism 108, 109, 127–8, 130, 131,
    201n3, 219, 219n60, 221, 238, 274, 279, 281

Vattimo, G. 102n138, 108, 237
vertigo 117, 262, 271, 296
violence 138, 139, 203–4, 210, 210n29, 216,
    221, 223, 279
vision 251–2
vision of God 21, 25–6, 28, 45, 48, 54, 55, 56,
    239n5, 273, 311n97
vocativity 20, 187n114, 215
Vulgate 18 and (n3)

Walicki, A. 242n18
walking 258, 262n91
war 31, 201–2, 204, 215, 243n21, 270, 281
Ward, B. 61
Watts, W. 112
Weber, M. 56
weeping *see also* tears 258, 259, 262, 263,
    267–71, 318, 319
Weil, S. 229n86, 230n87, 260n84
Weisser, C. D. 50n94
Westphal, M. 9, 218n57, 320n119
Whitehead, A. N. 107n7, 114
whole, the *see also* being-as-a-whole
    60n16, 89, 114, 115–16, 122,
    127, 302
wholly other 183, 184, 218, 221, 229
Wilkins, J. 181n91
will 5, 75, 124, 229, 240, 243n21
William of St. Thierry 35n56, 228, 261
Wippel, J. F. 38–9n64
Wittgenstein, L. 149, 151n4, 158n23, 172
    n74, 186n106
Wood, D. 218n57
Wordsworth, W. 58–61, 63, 74, 77, 142,
    223, 254
work 127, 129, 205, 247, 286
writing 181–2, 259–62

Young, E. 109n12, 155, 190
Yuasa, Y. 303n74

Zabala, S. 102n138
Zen Buddhism *see* Buddhism
Zizioulas, J. 236n103

Printed and bound by CPI Group (UK) Ltd, Croydon, CR0 4YY